THE KING, THE PRESS AND THE PEOPLE

a study of Edward VII

Kinley Roby

Barrie & Jenkins London

COMMUNICA-EUROPA N.V.

First published in 1975 by
Barrie & Jenkins Limited
24 Highbury Crescent, London N5 1RX

Copyright © Kinley Roby 1975

ISBN 0 214 20098 1

Printed in Great Britain by The Anchor Press Ltd
Tiptree, Essex

For my father and mother

Contents

List of Illustrations

Preface

Albert Edward, Prince of Wales and later King Edward VII, but Bertie to Victoria, who employed the diminutive with withering effect until her death, retains his fascination not only as one of the most colourful English royal personages since Charles II but also because he was a man of such abundant life and energy that, like Tennyson's Ulysses, he became a part of all he met. His biography is a social and political chronicle of the age in which he lived.

Edward's life spanned a period of intense social and political change. He lived to see the deferential society, described by Bagehot in *The English Constitution,* transformed into a democratic society from which nearly all inherited political power had been stripped and in which capital and the organized votes of the working class replaced the ownership of land as the bases on which governments were built and broken. He had a significant part to play in this dramatic movement, welcoming into the highest circles of British social life the new men, the Dilkes and Lloyd Georges as well as the plutocrats, initiating the practice of accepting wealth or political power as a substitute for birth.

The familiar picture of Edward as Prince of Wales is that of a bearded young man, impeccably dressed, with a cigar between his fingers and surrounded by beautiful women, at a gaming table or a race meeting. As king he is usually represented as a stout, commanding figure, draped in his coronation robes, in a pose of impressive dignity. What these partially accurate pictures fail to convey is the man's complexity and the intense drama of his existence accompanying his progress from prince to king. This book explores several of the commonly neglected but absorbing aspects of Edward's life, as well as presenting an explanation of Edward's role in the political and social developments of his age.

Edward was one of the first great public figures to come under the close scrutiny of the popular press and to experience its enormous power to mould public opinion in support or in condemnation of its subject. He suffered a storm of personal abuse from the press almost unprecedented in English history and survived it to impose his personality on the minds of his countrymen to a degree never anticipated during his years as Prince of Wales. But during his long and difficult apprenticeship, he learned to keep before the public an image that corresponded as closely as he could make it to the myth of the ideal prince that the press had been building since his birth. It was a myth which denied him almost all human reality, reducing him to a ceremonial puppet who exemplified middle-class propriety. It had as its fundamental purpose the destruction of popular attachment to Edward and was a subtle extension of the nineteenth-century middle-class drive to reduce the monarchy to an expression of middle- class political and social dominance.

But perhaps the greatest drama in Edward's life was his intensely abrasive and profoundly damaging relationship with his parents. Having blindly made his son's life a misery for eighteen years, Albert died. Victoria, whose dislike for Edward deepened, as he matured, into an emotional response close to hatred, blamed the young man for her husband's premature death and refused to allow him near her for months afterwards. Deprived during his early years of his father's understanding, his mother's love and affection, the companionship of boys his own age, and subjected to a system of education unnecessarily harsh and unimaginative in its content, Edward entered manhood denied a substantive role in the functioning of the monarchy. Forced into an arranged marriage with Alexandra of Denmark, one of the most beautiful women in Europe, Edward found himself matched to a woman with the mind of a child, who was afflicted with congenital deafness that rapidly worsened following their marriage. Edward sought stimulation and companionship in a series of mistresses while he followed a frenetic round of house parties, race meetings, gambling and foreign travel.

Edward's emotional health was so severely undermined by the experiences of his childhood and adolescence that throughout his life he suffered from bouts of recurring depression and an uncontrollable fear of boredom, which made it impossible for him to be alone or unoccupied for even a few minutes. His need to be entertained became proverbial as did his appetite for women, food and cigars. But Edward's life is not the record of a sensualist seeking new delights but a story of his struggle to achieve the dignity of independence and the gratification of having his talents meaningfully employed.

Frequently an object of popular ridicule and condemnation during his years as Prince of Wales, he sought, nevertheless, to carry out his responsibilities with tact and thoroughness. Despite the gambling and divorce scandals in which he became involved and which rocked the throne, he continued to place himself squarely before the public as a man determined to find his place in life and to fill it. When that opportunity came, he proved himself to be a statesman and a diplomat of imposing stature. His belief in himself was vindicated. In the end he won the respect of his people as well as their love. He was a greater man than is generally acknowledged; and had he come to the throne earlier or remained on it longer in good health, the history of this century might have been different.

A Royal Roaring Boy

With such experience all must rejoice, as in a singular blessing, to see, year after year, a succession of scions of the Royal tree springing up round the throne of Queen Victoria.

The Times, November 10 1841

The use of the Queen, in a dignified capacity, is incalculable.

Walter Bagehot

At seven o'clock the Queen, having risen and begun her preparations for the day, suddenly became 'unwell', as the papers were to express it, and was hurried back into bed. Summoned to the Queen's bedside, Dr Locock, obstetrician in attendance, confirmed what Victoria already knew. She had begun labour.

The announcement caused a flurry of activity. Immediately, word was sent to the Duchess of Kent and other members of the family living in or near London. Messengers were also despatched to the Home Office, whose task it was to ensure the presence of the officers of state at the Palace, where they would be called on, if all went well, to confirm the birth of a royal heir to the throne. The normal excitement of the moment was intensified because the Queen had not been thought to be so close to her confinement and final preparations for it had to be made in a rush. The miscalculation was one of the less calamitous medical errors that plagued the Queen's household while Sir James Clark was Court Physician; but it was annoying and, given the poor physicial condition of the Queen in this second pregnancy, might have been dangerous.

In the delivery room with the Queen were Prince Albert, holding his wife's hand and comforting her; Dr Locock, who was to make the delivery; and Mrs Lilly, the monthly nurse. Waiting in adjoining rooms were the consulting physicians – Sir James Clark, Dr Ferguson and Mr Blagden – Victoria's mother, the Duchess of Kent; the Countess of Charlemont, Lady in Waiting on the Queen; various Officers of State, dressed in the Windsor uniform; and Lords of the Privy Council – the Lord Steward, the Lord Chamberlain, Master of the Horse, the Duke of Wellington, the Bishop of London, Sir Robert Peel, the Duke of

Buckingham, the Earl of Aberdeen, Sir James Graham, the Lord Chancellor, the Marquis of Exeter and the Groom of the Stole to Prince Albert.

In the streets outside the Palace, a crowd was rapidly gathering, quiet for the moment but waiting in tense expectation. Still further away from the delivery room were Lords Stanley and Wharncliffe and the Archbishop of Canterbury, all hurrying towards the Palace but destined to arrive too late for the delivery, which occurred at 10.48 am, Tuesday morning, November 9, Lord Mayor's Day, 1841.

No sooner was Edward safely in the world than he was put into Mrs Lilly's arms; and while Dr Locock attended to the Queen, the nurse carried him into the room where the officers were assembled. Having satisfied themselves that it was a live birth, the officials immediately signed a document confirming the birth of a male heir to the British throne. Sir James Clark made the formal announcement of the birth to the waiting functionaries and unofficially to the crowds gathered outside the Palace, who had been awaiting news with the keenest excitement. Earlier in the day when it was learned that the Queen had entered labour, many London shops had closed. Now as the joyful word spread through the city, the church bells began to ring; and crowds surged into the streets, singing and cheering in jubilation.

By degrees news of the birth of a prince spread across the country, and in its wake town after town set its church bells pealing, built bonfires and called special town meetings to express joy and thanksgiving. The source of that joy, exclaimed a writer a few days later in the pages of *John Bull*, was the birth of a prince who would be a Prince of Wales, a title with which 'some of the best and proudest of our national feelings are associated'. Glowing with patriotic pride, he recalled the glories surrounding the Black Prince, one of the first Princes of Wales, 'whom every schoolboy loves'.[1] Darker spirits admitted satisfaction on the grounds that there was now one more legitimate heir between King George V of Hanover and the English throne.

Punch caught the spirit of the moment with 'Punch's Paen to the Princelet', which began:

> Huzzah! we've a little prince at last,
> A roaring royal boy;
> And all day long the booming bells
> Have rung their peals of joy.

The verses close on a note of genuine, if melancholy prescience:

> Our little prince, when he grows a boy,
> Will be taught by men of lore,
> From the 'dusty tome' of the ancient sage,
> As Kings have been taught before....[2]

But that doubtful prospect was in the future; and having been 'exhibited' to the lords of the land, Edward was whisked back to the delivery room and the tender attentions of Mrs Lilly and the wet nurse, his first public appearance having ended.

Honouring both her husband and her father in the naming of her son, Victoria had the boy christened Albert Edward. The choice of the name Albert was in keeping with the Queen's as yet unstated determination that all future kings of England would bear the name Albert. The choice of Edward as a second name was more conventional. Although the Queen had the Duke of Kent in mind when she called her son Edward, the name had been borne by an illustrious line of English kings, dating back to Edward the Confessor, who, having given away the English throne to a foreign upstart, astutely managed to let Harold actually lose it.

It was also an Edward who had been the first English Prince of Wales, a title conferred on Albert Edward on December 4 1841, by the traditional ceremony of placing a ring on his finger, a cap-coronet on his head and a gold verge in his hand, the investiture being made official by the presentation of letters patent under the great seal. He became the twenty-first male heir to the throne to carry the title, which had been held, as well, by two queens, Mary and Elizabeth. Henry VIII had created them both, at different times, Princesses of Wales; but his son, Edward VI, never bore the title. By a statute of the Order of the Garter, issued in 1805, the Prince was declared 'a constituent part of the original institution' and automatically a Knight of the Garter when created Prince of Wales.[3]

Since the time of Edward II, who became heir apparent at the death of his older brother Alphonso, the elder sons of reigning English monarchs have generally borne the title of Prince of Wales, although unlike the dukedom of Cornwall, created in 1337 in favour of Edward the Black Prince, 'Britain's hope and France's fear', it is not hereditary. Title to the dukedom belongs to the eldest son and heir apparent of the sovereign. If the eldest son dies without issue before his parent, the title goes to the next son; but if he dies leaving sons of his own, the title reverts to the Crown, the rule being that only the sovereign's eldest surviving son and heir to the crown can claim the title.

There are other oddities connected with the title. The Duke of Cornwall has no minority. He is of legal age and, at least theoretically, free to claim the revenues of the dukedom from the moment of his birth. (No such freedom was in fact given to Edward or claimed by him. For him to have made the claim would have been impossible, considering the control exercised by his parents over his every action. Until the time of his marriage, he was kept totally dependent on his parents even for spending money.) Another peculiarity associated with the title is that it is high treason for the Duke of Cornwall, as it is with the sovereign, to 'compass or imagine his death' or to violate the chastity of his consort. He is, however, free to 'retain and qualify as many chaplains as he shall please', a privilege Edward never abused.[4]

Three hours after Clark's announcement and with his wife and son well out of danger, Prince Albert, accompanied by the Marquis of Exeter and Colonel Wylde, Equerry in Waiting, left Buckingham Palace in a state carriage, to attend the Privy Council, which had been called into extraordinary session. At his appearance outside the Palace, Albert was cheered enthusiastically by the crowds gathered to hear the medical bulletins read and to be as close as possible to the Queen. Making slow progress through the throngs of people crowding the street, he stepped down from his carriage at the Privy Council office in White-hall just as the Park and Tower guns began a double royal salute of one hundred and one guns, making official the birth of a royal son.

Albert's arrival was followed by that of the seventy-two-year-old Duke of Wellington, who, wearing his Waterloo medal, came strolling through the crowds quite unattended and entered the Council office to tremendous cheering. The purpose of the meeting was to order the form of the thanksgiving prayer to be read for the Queen's safe delivery of a son and to set a date for observing the celebration. Having charged the Archbishop of Canterbury with the task of composing the prayer and settling on Sunday, November 14, as the day of official rejoicing in all of 'the several churches and chapels of England and Wales and the town of Berwick-upon-Tweed' – a separate order had to be composed for Scotland, where the Scottish Kirk could not be commanded – the members of the Council then gave the Prince Consort their hearty congratulations and adjourned.[5]

To Albert's great delight, his reappearance in front of the Council office set the crowds cheering wildly; and he repeatedly bowed, 'bare-headed', as one reporter put it in unconscious comment on the Prince's growing baldness. The Duke of Wellington was also greeted with thunderous cheers. Undaunted by the terrific press of people, he and the Earl of Liverpool, who gave the Duke his arm to lean on, walked out of Downing Street, through the passage under the Treasury and into the Park, followed by an immense crowd. As they passed the Horse Guards, the sound of the guns and the cheering was deafening. The police eventually had to rescue the two men from the rapidly increasing press of people, escorting them past Buckingham Palace and throwing a cordon across Constitution Hill to divide the crowd. Still, a vast and noisy throng followed the Duke to the gates of Apsley House, where, as he entered, he was cheered and cheered again.[6]

Glowing with the double pleasure of seeing his first son safely into the world and experiencing the first warm response given him by the English populace, Prince Albert returned to the Palace amid the cheers of thronging Londoners. Never before had he encountered such enthusiasm; and while there may have been some bitterness in his heart, caused by the knowledge that it was his son as much as himself who was being cheered, the demonstration of popular affection gladdened him. Even the press, which had remained cool towards the Prince Consort, expanded into praise, one writer going so far as to assure Albert that his name would henceforth be remembered with those of the Plantaganets, Tudors and Stuarts.

It was an hour for hyperbole. The *Evening Mail* and *The Times* were so carried away by the event that they found reason to praise the birth because, among other things, it ensured the continuance of the House of Brunswick: 'Never, perhaps, was the British or any other crown worn by a succession of sovereigns who "bare their faculties so meek" as the Princes of the House of Brunswick. In their minds as well as in their conduct, the principles of monarchy and prerogative have been identified with, instead of opposed to liberty and law.'[7] The writer of the article did recover himself sufficiently to admit that there were 'imperfections' in the individual histories of the members of the house.

Taking a high and serious line regarding the birth of the Prince, the *Globe and Traveller* expressed hope that future generations would find reason to celebrate November 9: 'The young Prince will be the possessor of manifest advantages, so far as concerns the mental and moral culture requisite for the due performance of the onerous duties of his rank and station, present and future.'[8] With such a mother as Victoria, the writer continued, the Prince 'can hardly fail to receive the most suitable and valuable lessons in private and public duty'.

As in so many of the articles written about the Prince's future, there is a well buried but still discernible warning. The Prince is received with general rejoicing; the Queen and the Prince Consort are perfect parents and ideal rulers; but it must be remembered that in England a monarch's 'best defence' is the affectionate loyalty of the nation. Therefore, it would be well if those 'lessons in private and public duty' were learned well: '...inculcated with the persuasive eloquence which is inspired by a mother's love...accompanied with the vigilant superintendence of a mother's eye, guided by a mother's heart – watching over his childhood and youth with unceasing anxiety; knowing that it is early in life the character receives the bent for good or evil which it retains.'[9] The message is unmistakeable: the Prince will either grow up 'trained in the knowledge and practice of every excellence' or he will risk losing the sympathy of the people, and place the monarchy in jeopardy.

As for the qualifications possessed by his parents for the task of raising the Prince to perfect manhood, they could scarcely be overstated by the journalists. Continuing the praise heaped on Albert by *The Times*, *John Bull* and others, the *Evening Mail* described him as possessing 'high cultivation of mind, an accomplished taste, an exact sense of the proprieties of his peculiar station, exemplary purity of life, general benevolence', qualities more than matched in the Queen, who was 'more pure and womanly than Queen Elizabeth, more firm of mind and royal of demeanour than Queen Anne'.[10]

With such paragons for parents, such loving people for subjects and a constitution more perfect than any other in the world, Edward was obliged to prosper. It was his patriotic duty to do so, and several writers expressed complete confidence that the thousands of prayers being said for the Prince and for his parents were enjoying a sympathetic reception at the Throne of Grace. It was clear that both God and Prince Edward were being warned to behave well. Respectful as the press was towards the royal family, it assumed the right to warn and to admonish them in a voice of middle-class respectability.

Naturally, in exchange for all these advantages, the Prince would be expected to assume certain responsibilities. He was to become the mainstay of constitutional monarchy in England; and many of the thanksgiving sermons preached on the Sunday following his birth took the constitutional line, pointing out the great advantages of the present form of English government over either despotism on the Russian model or the detested Republicanism of revolutionary France. Thomas Dikes's sermon, preached in St John's Church, Hull, is typical of what congregations heard that Sunday morning. Placing the Prince in the centre of the monarchical system, Dikes, by implication, placed responsibility for its continued vitality squarely with the royal family.[11] The dread of republicanism, still very much alive in the nation, if temporarily quiescent, appears here and in most of the sermons preached on November 14.

Sydney Smith, preaching at St Paul's, was more precise in stating what he felt the nation could expect from the Prince. Framing his expectations in the form of a prayer, he asked God to 'so mould the Prince's heart and fashion his spirit that he may be a blessing and not an evil to the land of his birth.... As he will be the first man in these realms, so may he be the best; disdaining to hide bad actions by high station, and endeavouring always by the example of a strict and moral life to repay those gifts which a loyal people are so willing to spare from their own necessities to a good King.'[12]

The economic note threading its way through the sermon was another echo of press comment. The probable amount of money to be settled on the Prince by grant of Parliament and the extent of his income from such other sources as the Duchy of Cornwall were the subject of lively speculation among journalists. When Smith specified that Englishmen willingly shared out their necessities in order to support a *good* king, the point, clearly made but unstated, that the support might be withdrawn if the sovereign did not measure up to expectations would not have been lost on his congregation. Read closely, many of the sermons and articles dealing with the birth carry the warning implicit in Sydney Smith's sermon.

Led by *The Times,* the press also took up the question of making new peers in honour of the event. *The Times* insisted there was no precedent for doing so. The *Evening Mail* stated that such a move would be ill-advised, pointing out that too many had already been created from 'Irish distillers, joint-stock owners, ironmasters, Edinburgh law agents, Jew bill-brokers, and Highland graziers'. In the writer's view, peerage had become 'a weed-choked field'; and the paper called upon Sir Robert Peel to 'lay it under fallow for a considerable season' before adding to its numbers.[13] By ancient custom, however, and in defiance of the critics, Pirie, the new Lord Mayor, sworn into office only a few hours before Edward's birth, would be elevated to the baronetcy; and by royal favour his predecessor, Alderman Johnson, was also included in the gift of title. The birth of the Prince on Lord Mayor's Day assured their advancement, and only the most churlish resented their good fortune.

On the night of the birth, the spirit of happy rejoicing spread into the theatres, where performances were disrupted or delayed by audiences too full of cheer to sit politely and be entertained. At the Adelphi the audience, loudly demanding *God Save the Queen,* refused to allow the play, *The Maid of Honour,* to begin. Mr Yates, the principal actor, assured the audience that as soon as the vocalists arrived at the theatre, the anthem would be sung by the entire house.

The revelry went on until dawn, only to break out again on following nights. It was left to *Punch* to remind the nation that the arrival of the Prince to such general joy might suggest that Englishmen regretted the presence of a Queen upon the throne or had forgotten the Princess Royal, who had already secured the succession. 'We think there is a positive want of gallantry at this unequivocally shouted preference of a Prince of Wales', the magazine added to its apology. In an outburst of loyal feeling it expressed the hope that the Queen might 'live to see the Prince of Wales wrinkled and white-headed'.[14] The hope was not voiced in vain, for if Victoria did not come to see her son wrinkled and white-headed, she certainly lived to see him grown, like Father William, uncommonly fat and all but bald.

By resurrecting an old story concerning the birth of George IV, *Punch* gained an opportunity to comment further on the future of the Prince, and one must wonder at the almost uncanny success of at least a portion of the prediction. Shortly after the birth of George IV, the treasure of the Spanish galleon *Hermione,* captured by three English

frigates off St Vincent, was brought on wagons through London, escorted by cavalry and infantry with captured Spanish flags waving over the loot, trumpets blowing and a celebrating multitude crowding down St James's Street in company with the wagons. The occurrence was taken to be a good omen for the future reign of the baby because he had been born 'amid a shower of gold'. Experience, *Punch* noted, made it clear, however, that the prophetic sign had been misread. Time would prove that Queen Charlotte's child 'would be a very expensive babe indeed; and that the wealth of a Spanish galleon was all insufficient for the youngling's future wants'.[15]

The mistake of the earlier augurers did not deter *Punch*. Asserting that the coincidence would prove to be a guide to his future, the magazine pointed out that the Prince had been born on Lord Mayor's Day. Even *The Times* had placed 'in genial companionship' the 'chronicle of the birth of the Prince' and 'the luscious history of the Lord Mayor's dinner'.

'What are all these gifts of plenty,' *Punch* asks, having listed the principal items on the menu, 'but a glad promise that in the time of the "sweetest young Prince" that on the birthday of that Prince just vouchsafed to us, all England will be a large Lord Mayor's table! Will it be possible for Englishmen to disassociate in their minds the Prince of Wales and the Prince of Good Fellows? And whereas the reigns of other potentates are signalized by bloodshed and war, the time of the Prince will be glorified by cooking and good cheer. His drum sticks will be the drum sticks of turkeys – his cannon the popping of corks.'[16] Much later Bismarck was to remark that the Prince of Wales was the one Prince whom one would never encounter on the field of battle, and Edward's love of food became proverbial, even notorious.

As for the remainder of the prediction, it could be said with justification that the miscalculation by *Punch* was of the same sort made by the earlier prognosticator. When *Punch* went on to predict that in the Prince's day 'even weavers shall know the taste of geese, and factory children smack their lips at the gravy of the great sirloin', it would have been closer to the truth to say that in his day even a Lord Mayor's feast would have been inadequate to satisfy the appetite of the Prince. As for the weavers and the factory children, they continued to be more familiar with stirabout than sirloin. *Punch* was undoubtedly sincere in its concern with the sufferings of the poor; and even had it not been, as an organ of a certain kind of public expression it could hardly have said of the factory children as Lord Melbourne had done: 'Oh, if you'd only have the goodness to leave them alone!'

During the weeks following the Prince's birth, the spirit of happy augury gradually drew to a close; and *Punch* itself called a halt to the nonsense about diapers and coddlings in the royal nursery which the press was reporting. Noting that a Greenwich pensioner named Weeks, who had unexpectedly inherited a fortune of £120,000, had been confined as a madman for asserting that he intended to marry Queen Victoria and that he and not George III was the father of Queen Charlotte's children, the magazine concluded that he was no more insane than the editor of the *Athenaeum*, who was reporting to his readers that he spent half of every day beside the cradle of the Prince, entranced by the infant's progress. Such folly, *Punch* added, was turning the nation's head and had led to the acceptance and praise of a newly-published book, *Cecil*, by a man named Boone, in which the author, speaking of Victoria's first appearance in the House of Lords, wrote, 'An unaccountable feeling of *trust* rose in my bosom. I speak it not profanely... when I say *that the idea of the yet unknown Saviour*, a child among the Doctors of the Temple, occurred spontaneously to my mind!'[17]

Calling that sort of writing blasphemous, *Punch* pointed out that within the past few weeks Shelley's publisher had been convicted in the court of the Queen's Bench of blasphemy of just the kind Boone was guilty of. Yet the same people who would affect to scream at Shelley 'as at an adder' proudly displayed *Cecil* on their drawing tables. It was time, the editor declared, for the press to stop approaching royalty on its knees. The writer need not have worried. The period of adoration was brief enough when measured against those future intervals in Edward's life when the press rose from its knees, took off its gloves and subjected the Prince to a thorough drubbing.

Despite the blithe tone of the majority of the newspaper articles dealing with the birth and the generally expressed conviction that the Prince had come into a world which, if not the best of all possible worlds, would soon be made perfect through Free Trade, Self Help and the sanctity of contracts, there were shadows lying across England, darkening the brightness around the royal cradle; and they made their presence felt in odd corners and in surprising ways.

In Derby, for instance, the county gentry were anxious to express their patriotic and loyal feelings towards the Queen and called a meeting for that purpose, choosing the County Hall as an appropriate setting for the observance. However, when the sheriff, MPs and assembled gentlemen arrived at the hall, they found the meeting room filled to overflowing with working men and were forced to accommodate themselves on the bench. Mr Bowden, the High Sheriff, took the Chair and accepted a motion to move the address. The motion was seconded; but before it could be submitted to a vote, one of the labourers rose and proposed an amendment.

The address, the man pointed out, congratulated the Queen on her restored health following her confinement. With that sentiment he heartily agreed, but he wished to call Her Majesty's attention to the fact that 'thousands of virtuous women, your Majesty's subjects, are passing through the like natural extremities upon beds of straw, without even a pillow whereon to lay their heads, or sustenance to support them; that starvation and misery are pervading the whole land, and we attribute this state of things to class legislation'. The speaker then appealed to the Queen to 'instruct' her ministers to repeal 'all enactments that have a tendency to rob the millions for the benefit of the few'. He further requested that the vote by ballot be given to every male inhabitant in the election of members to the House of Commons.[18]

At least some of the Derby workers were Chartists, and all belonged to that group of politically active labourers whom in the troubles of 1848 Victoria was to dismiss as those 'wanton & worthless men'.[19] No doubt the readers of *The Times*, where the workers' address of congratulation appeared on the same page with the account of the Prince's baptism ceremony, found it possible to discount the Derby workers as crude boors, wholly lacking in taste, who knew no better than to turn a patriotic occasion into a political squabble. Those same readers must have found it less easy to dismiss Lucy Welch of Sevenoaks, whose pathetic death, resulting from a fatal combination of the working of the New Poor Law and the indifference of those whose responsibility it was in that union to give medical relief to the poor, was reported in *The Times*.

The sixteen-year-old girl had been ill for some time, and her mother had been unable to get any doctor to visit her, all having refused on the grounds that they were too busy or it 'was out of his way'. After several days of anxious hesitation, the mother sent to one of the relieving officers for help; but it was refused again, this time because the girl had not been admitted to the work-house. Lucy's illness grew worse. In desperation the mother put her in a donkey cart and carried her to the dispensary of yet another doctor. That man turned her away because she did not have an 'order' for treatment. By now the girl was in terrible distress, and in trying to get out of the dispensary collapsed on the steps and died. The coroner attempted to return a verdict of 'death by natural causes' but under powerful public pressure was forced to reopen the case. It was then established beyond doubt that the girl had died as a result of medical neglect.

With remarkable courage *The Times* printed the story of Lucy Welch on the same page as its account of the birth of the Prince. As in the case of the Derby meeting, the report's having been placed so conspicuously was in itself an editorial comment. Not trusting to the juxtaposition of the Lucy Welch story and the announcement of the Queen's confinement to make its point, *The Times* unleashed a stinging attack against the Poor Law, the Poor Law Commissioners, Sir Robert Peel and the Union of Sevenoaks. Having given a detailed description of the misery of the work-house poor in Sevenoaks – 86 girls sleeping in 19 beds, 161 boys and girls suffering from swollen glands, itch and semi-starvation – the paper concluded, 'We charge upon the Poor Law Commissioners and their system the entire and unmitigated responsibility for this mass of abomination.'[20]

The Times had seen a portion of the shadow blighting the country and reported its substance. In no sense, however, was the 'Thunderer' covertly encouraging revolutionary doctrines or supporting acts of resistance among the working class. The editorial of January 26, congratulating 'our fellow-Christians' on Edward's christening, stated without qualification that a British prince had never been baptized under 'happier auspices'. Praising the current period of peace as unrivalled in any epoch since the founding of Christianity, the writer expressed pleasure in the prospect of 'our new Edward [taking] upon him the vows of a soldier in what is pre-eminently the kingdom of peace'.

As to the internal stresses to which the British government had been subjected during the preceding ten years, *The Times* expressed confidence in the system. It had been tested and found strong: 'Our system of government has been shaken to its centre...but the balance has proved secure.' And speaking of the less fortunate members of society: 'Even distress serves chiefly to show the admirable patience and moral discipline of the working classes.'[21]

As for the stone quarriers in Dartmoor, who were striking in an effort to force the owners to employ only union workers, *The Times* placed itself squarely against the workers: 'For such a movement at the present, founded on misrepresentation, and forming part of a systematic attempt to establish a dangerous and unconstitutional tyranny, we have no compassion or sympathy, and repeat that it must meet with no compromise, but be put down thoroughly and unflinchingly, even though its progress were only to be checked by a general stoppage of trade throughout the kingdom.'[22]

Although it was generally known that the Prince would be named Albert Edward, *Punch*, having completely recovered from its fit of ecstatic delight over the royal birth, reflected some of the hidden gloom by turning in the issue of January 1 to the question of a name for the Prince. What would be a proper name for the heir to the throne? Having posed the question, *Punch* listed the names of some of England's past monarchs and rejected them all: Henry was discredited on the grounds that had Henry VII been born in humble circumstances, he would certainly have been 'hanged for a coiner and money clipper'. Richard fared no better: 'The second Richard was an imbecile; and the third by no means a respectable potentate.' The name George was declared thoroughly worn out.

The magazine finally settled on the name Lazarus the First as being the most appropriate, 'as indicative of enlarged humanity in palaces'. The country, *Punch* observed in an unusually sober tone, needs a ruler who will 'heal the wounds of wretchedness' and relieve the nation's poverty and suffering.[23] Later in the same issue it ran a parody of the royal christening, called 'The Whitechapel Christening'. The child being baptized is Master Cleaver, 'heir apparent of his father's shambles'. An overseer from Lambeth is one of the child's sponsors; and vagabonds, tramps and baked-potato boys make up the procession.[24]

Although these slurs and others cast aspersions on the perfect social tranquillity into which *The Times* editorial writer pictured the Prince as having been born, the world surrounding Buckingham Palace had at least the appearance of calm. By December the Queen had recovered her strength sufficiently to insist on moving to Windsor. Albert's increasing ascendency in her life was paralleled by her growing distaste for London. Albert loathed living there; and, of course, so did she.

Her decision caused great anxiety among the members of the Court because during her convalescence there was a period of heavy rains which flooded roads and railway lines in the vicinity of Windsor, making travel difficult if not actually dangerous. Dampness had invaded Windsor Castle to the extent that coconut fibre matting had to be laid in the lower corridors and passages to provide a dry and secure walking surface. Although no one was aware of it, those rising waters made more dangerous than usual the typhoid menace haunting Windsor's sluggish and overflowing drains.

The Queen, however, was determined to make the move and equally determined to see Edward christened in St George's Chapel, rather than at Westminster or at the Chapel Royal, St James's, where the Princess Royal had been baptized. Her decision regarding the christening was the first of a long series by which Victoria made clear her determination to set rigid limits on Edward's opportunities to receive popular attention and acclaim. Given the mood of the nation, had the Prince been christened in London, the turn-out for the occasion would have been enormous. But it was not to be; Windsor (lying miles of mud-clogged road from Slough, the nearest rail connection to the capital), and St George's Chapel were chosen for the setting of an event which, judged by the attention given it by every organ of public expression, generated as much interest and enthusiasm as the birth itself.

It had snowed hard on Tuesday night, January 25; and by morning Windsor and the surrounding country were white. At eight o'clock the bells in the churches and chapels began to ring, and the usually quiet town became loud with the rush of people arriving from the station at Slough in omnibuses, carts and vehicles of every description, whose constant passage soon churned the roads and streets into rivers of freezing mud. Sweepers had been working all night, attempting to keep the principal streets of the town clear of snow, but their efforts were not equal to the mud and slush everywhere.

At nine o'clock a battalion of Grenadiers, led by their band, marched through the town on their way to the Castle. At intervals throughout the morning, they were followed by the 72nd Highlanders with their pipers playing, the Royal Horse Guards, and a battery of Flying Artillery. The latter, stationing themselves on the Long Walk, began firing their pieces in a royal salute that continued throughout the morning. In the Castle grounds the military units formed a part of the guard of honour, and the Horse Guards patrolled the approaches to the Castle in pairs. The security arrangements, which were impressive for the time, were designed to control the spectators rather than to prevent any antici- pated attack on the Queen or members of her party.

Admission to the Castle was regulated by tickets, which had been given out very sparingly by the Queen; and wooden barriers were set up at King Henry VII's gateway to check the flow of spectators pouring out from the town. Those invited to attend the ceremonies entered the grounds by St George's gate, which, like the other access points in the Castle precincts, was guarded by heavy concentrations of police. By eleven o'clock the Lord Mayor and Sheriffs of London, with gleaming carriages and liveries, had arrived; along with the rest of the royal party.

The crowds along the roads and at the Castle gates watched the arrival of the nobility in stony silence, which, given the festive nature of the occasion, was unusual, even disturbing. Carriage after carriage, coats of arms blazing, rolled into the grounds past lines of spectators whose silence was broken only by the creaking of the carriages and the jingling of the harness rings. Not even the arrival of the Duke of Wellington provoked a cheer.

At 12.35 pm the procession formed in the quadrangle close to the Queen's apartments and began to move out. The Prince, held by the Duchess of Buccleuch, the Mistress of the Robes, occupied the third carriage; and the Queen and Prince Albert followed in the fifth. In the last carriage, also drawn by a matching pair of cream coloured horses, rode King William IV, the King of Prussia, delighted with his role as godfather. The mood of the crowd improved with the appearance of the royal procession as it emerged slowly from the Norman Gate. The Duchess of Buccleuch held the Prince well up so as to give the people a good look at their new Prince; and the sight of the infant produced a roar of cheering which was renewed for the Queen and Prince Albert and for the beaming King of Prussia.

A very limited number of specially honoured guests were invited to enter either St George's Chapel or the adjoining Wolsey's Hall. Most of the guests were confined to the Hall and were, in consequence, deprived of the pleasure of watching any part of the christening ceremony and had to content themselves with listening to the music. Even those admitted into the Chapel itself were prevented by a barrier from watching the actual ceremony, which took place in the converted choir. The Queen's closet, above the altar, was reserved for the Baroness Lehzen and the Queen's attendants. It was one of the last events in which that remarkable woman was to participate with her beloved Victoria. Within a year she would lose her struggle to retain her power over the Queen and leave for Germany, defeated by Albert and the Baron Stockmar. In the organ loft a few newspaper men were crowded into a narrow space, their presence endured more than welcomed.

Fewer than a thousand ticket holders occupied the Lower Ward of the Castle, an area, as *The Times* observed with subdued criticism, capable of accommodating many, many more people. Arrangements at the Chapel, even granting the limited space available, allowed only a handful of people, most of whom could not be excluded, to view the ceremony. It is reasonable to conclude that the Queen deliberately prevented as many of her subjects as possible from participating in what was surely a public event of great importance. The choice of St George's Chapel, despite its great beauty and its historical associations, was idiosyncratic, considering that Westminster Abbey would have provided a setting more fitting for the christening of the Prince of Wales, providing the nation with an opportunity to celebrate in a fitting manner the royal baptism.

It would be easy to exaggerate the more sinister motives in Victoria's choice of Windsor as the christening place for her son. It must be remembered that she had, at this point in her life, gone far towards surrendering herself to the control of her husband, at least in those matters that did not touch her deeply. Even in those affairs of her private life, such as her relationship with Lehzen, which she had defended against outside influence, Albert increasingly gained a voice. The Prince Consort had no reason to love the English nobility, who viewed him as a foreigner; and with Baron Stockmar's help he had convinced his wife that their family should be sufficient within itself. But whatever reasons are advanced to rationalize Victoria's choice of Windsor, a strong suspicion, strengthened by future events, remains that in her heart she already resented this son, whose arrival in the world had produced a wild outpouring of joy from her subjects and who would one day replace her. Even now, he had begun to be a rival for the affections of her people.

Unlikely as the choice seems, the gold bowl which formed a portion of the baptismal font had been the container of the holy water from which Charles II had been christened. A gold pedestal rose from the bowl, supporting a cherubim holding the elaborate bowl used in the Princess Royal's christening. The water in the font had been brought from the River Jordan by the Reverend Charles Boileau Elliott. It aroused strong interest among those who knew its origins. Following the ceremony there was some unpleasant jostling around the font as people tried to dip their fingers into it.[25]

As the party entered, a march was played; and when it ended, William Howley, the Archbishop of Canterbury, led in a prayer. Completing that, he turned to the royal godfather and asked if the Prince would 'renounce the devil and all his works, the vain pomp and glory of the world, with all covetous desires of the same, and the carnal desires of the flesh, so that thou will not follow or be led by the same?'

Speaking for Edward, the King of Prussia replied in a strong voice, 'I renounce them all.'

The Duchess of Buccleuch then brought Edward forward, and the Archbishop said, 'Name this child.'

'Albert Edward,' replied the King of Prussia in a ringing voice.

Edward was then baptized.

The ceremony concluded, Edward was carried out of the Chapel to the accompaniment of the *Hallelujah Chorus,* sung by the choir, and the booming of cannons in the Long Walk. For the crowds waiting outside the Chapel, the reappearance of the Prince in his carriage marked the high point in the day's observances; and he was cheered and applauded on his return ride even more loudly than he had been earlier.

A state banquet was scheduled for the evening, to be held in St George's Gallery; and at three in the afternoon the public was allowed to enter the Hall to look at the royal plate, valued in that period at between one and a half and two million pounds. That night a thousand candles burned in the room and were multiplied a thousand times again in that sea of gold.[26]

Edward had passed through his first great public function, which in the judgement of many of his subjects, especially those of a serious cast of thought, was his most important. However that may be, it was an occasion that prompted a happy outpouring of warm affection throughout the country. There were illuminations in London and other places, although none of the government buildings or royal establishments were lighted, a fact which brought criticism from the press and puzzled the public. The Queen's refusal to permit a general lighting of state buildings was, however, in keeping with her decision strictly to limit the public aspect of the christening.

The event was, of course, undeniably public in character and provided an occasion for serious reflection as well as celebration. *The Times* crystallized the more sombre responses to the event in its editorial of January 26, giving expression to a point of view typical of the attitude of the middle class. There is a moral earnestness in the writing, alienating to many in the upper classes, and a degree of satisfaction with things as they are that ignored the sufferings of the working class. Only a newspaper so dominated by the values of a mercantile society would have put the issues in the terms chosen by *The Times*.

Having stated with manifest self-satisfaction that the nation had passed through a decade of political and social uncertainty and emerged stronger than ever, the writer pointed to the Established Church and expressed the conviction that it was the strength and unity of the Church which had made the national recovery possible. It was, perhaps, a bit early for such an expression of confidence as Feargus O'Connor and two Chartist conventions were still to come before the ghost of the French Revolution was safely laid in England. Passing from the Church to the christening, *The Times* charged the Prince with the duty of becoming a staunch ally of the national religion: 'If we believe our religion to be true, we must think it of inestimable importance that those who govern us should also believe it, and should act consistently upon its dictates. ... Never was there a time when it was more important that there should be sympathy, upon this essential point, between a Prince and his people.'

In an easy transition the paper moved from religion to social practice, finding its way as clearly marked as when it located a straight path to religious orthodoxy while searching for the cause of England's political stability. The discoveries were equally heartening in this second area: 'There has been a wonderful change for the better within the last century, even in the tastes and surface habits of society: a larger and more wholesome public opinion, and one less liable to be controlled by particular influences, has been brought to bear upon them, and has found the power of making them responsible to its tribunal. The effect of this change cannot but make itself felt, and most beneficially, in the future education and consequent manners of our Princes.'[27]

Dropping back to reflect on the manners and customs of society fifty years ago, the writer excuses the unspecified sins of omission and commission of which society was guilty, forgiving them on the grounds that the public tolerated them. He adds, however, that those same actions would be 'intolerable and therefore inexcusable now'. The reader is not told in what ways society is better behaved, only that it is so. The writer had not, in any case, been laying the groundwork for an essay on social evolution but elaborating a verbal platform from which to issue moral warnings: 'The child of Queen Victoria and Prince Albert ought to be, and we trust will be, a pattern of piety and virtue.'

Victoria and Albert had dutifully seen to the christening of their child and chosen the feast day of the Great Apostle of the Gentiles for the occasion. How the Prince's life is to be conducted from here should have been self-evident to the reader; but in case anyone had missed the point, the writer emphasizes it yet one more time: 'We may well expect the life to be happy which has been spiritually commenced under such auspices; and we may be confident that parents who have so ordered the beginning will not fail in their duty to the end.'[28]

In the arms of the Lady in Waiting, Edward had disappeared into Windsor Castle and was not to emerge publicly in an official role for eight years. He was, in fact, to drop almost entirely from the public gaze. The Princess Royal, his brothers and sisters as they appeared, governesses and tutors and his parents were to surround him and isolate him from the world for the next seventeen years. *The Times* might have spared itself worry over the child's training. Edward's parents had no intention of neglecting their son's education or relaxing from the task of making him into a 'pattern of piety and virtue'. It is worth noting that no writer expressed concern over Edward's chances of enjoying a happy childhood. Such a concern would have been justified, as time was to prove. But then it would have been a concern unlikely to have been expressed at such a time for this, or perhaps any other, child of the period. Victorian hopes for childhood would not have emphasized happiness as a primary concern.

The Long Martyrdom

I do not know how it is that I am ever naughty, for I am much happier when I am good.

The Golden Book of King Edward VII:
Wise and Kindly Words of His Majesty

The object then is, not that he may be taught this or that language, this or that science, or the whole range of accomplishments; but that he may be taught to be a king...

Who Should Educate the Prince of Wales?

Before Edward was out of the nursery, both his parents and his subjects began to plan his education. The most remarkable evidence of the public interest in the child's future training is a small volume, published in London in 1843 when Edward was only two years old, entitled *Who Should Educate the Prince of Wales?* An interesting feature of this curious book is the similarity it bears in its general recommendations to the programme for educating the Prince laid down by Baron Stockmar. The anonymous author appears, as a matter of fact, to have combined the less attractive qualities of Baron Stockmar and Lord Chesterfield, with the result that whereas Lord Chesterfield thought laughter vulgar and Stockmar dismissed it as irrelevant, the author of *Who Should Educate the Prince of Wales?* had apparently never heard of it.

In its views the document is representative of that sober Whiggish element in the population which believed that an English prince was, despite his elevated rank, something in the order of a superior civil servant, thoroughly accountable for his actions to the tribunal of public opinion. 'The education...of a monarch is the affair of his people', the writer insists, laying the basis for meddling in what otherwise might be thought a private affair of the parents. 'Does not the conduct, from boyhood to old age, of George the Fourth,' the writer continues, 'point out the necessity for the most watchful attention to the education of him who is to reign over such a people? Were it only for the sake of moral example, it must be confessed to be of vital importance.'[1] It is instructive that at this time, as later in his life, when some restriction or unpleasant burden was laid on Edward, the skeleton of George IV was whipped out of the cupboard and given a brisk rattle to justify the imposition. Surprisingly, no one ever appears to have argued that because the mother and father of the Prince of Wales were admirable individuals, worry about the child's character could, thankfully, be forgotten.

What did this thinly veiled fear that the 'Old Adam' would rise up in Edward really signify? The anxiety is undeniably present in such statements as 'The Prince's private life must be exemplary.' 'He must be Christian in faith and firm in faith.' The fear is at least partially political in nature as the author of the book reveals when he writes: 'The Prince must be made sensible that our king is a magistrate, honoured greatly, paid most amply; let him therefore be taught that every portion of the wealth he enjoys is the product of the sweat of the brow of his subjects, for the preservation of general order, freedom and security, and is not confided to him as the means of procuring sensual pleasures.'[2] The fear seems to be that Edward might fail to understand that his real role as sovereign would be to protect the position of the middle class against encroachment by the lower class, while, at the same time, assisting the middle class in its continued pirating of what had been hitherto exclusively upper-class privileges.

The political argument, which is really an assertion of middle-class dominance, however, is not entirely convincing. The process of stripping the monarch of real political power had already advanced so far that there was no possibility of its being reversed. At the fall of Lord Melbourne's government in 1839, Victoria had not been able to win more than a two-year reprieve in her struggle to retain her Whig Ladies of the Bedchamber. Despite the insistence of Stockmar and the Prince Consort that the monarch was the permanent prime minister 'who takes rank above the temporary head of the cabinet and in matters of discipline exercises supreme authority' and that the separation of the crown from politics was a 'constitutional fiction', the fiction had become fact. The real administrative power of the government lay with the Prime Minister, and it was a simple fact that no matter how saintly or how debauched he might be, Edward would never possess sufficient power materially to affect the governing of the nation.

If the political answer is inadequate to explain the almost hysterical concern about his future conduct, as expressed in the book, one must look elsewhere. The explanation may lie, in part, in the changing temper of the age. Moral earnestness, that blight of the puritan mind, was spreading in England, particularly among the middle class, who had convinced themselves that their material success was due to their peculiarly sober virtues and saw that the best way of retaining their advantage lay in convincing those below them on the social and economic scale to accept the proposition that the way to prosper in the world was to rise early, work hard, respect authority in all its forms and support the emerging capitalist system by serving it.

The family was the social base of this structure, ruled by a benign male despot who was the earthly exemplar of the divine order. The middle class in particular wished to see in the royal family an idealized portrait of their own domestic arrangements and sought to enshrine in that family their own uncompromising views of moral excellence and sober respectability. The intention is made clear in the author's choice of a teacher for the Prince. The man is to be 'free, known, proved to be free of biases of party or sect, looking upon the pure page upon which he is about to stamp an eternal character with a spirit of devotedness and love, and yet with the highest aspirations that every virtue which might adorn the after-life of his pupil might be proudly traced by himself to himself, looking for no reward beyond the happiness of his future monarch and his future people.'[3] The teacher is as unreal as the prince of the portrait. Neither could be said to exist except as mythical ideal figures.

If the figures are fictional, the anxieties behind the instructions are not. The teacher is to 'throw forth the good in the most attractive colours and to give evil its proper hideousness'. The Prince is to be taught to love poetry, painting and the mechanical arts; but he is never to be set to writing poetry, to painting or to turning a lathe. He is not to 'perform' music. In short, he is not to be allowed to do anything that might give him sensual pleasure. At the same time, he is never to be idle. Sleep is to be strictly rationed: 'Of all the solaces the Creator has bestowed upon mankind, the bed of rest is one of the sweetest; but it must be with him a bed of rest, not of indulgence.'[4] His days are to be spent riding, fencing, hiking and studying. The underlying dread seems to be of sensuality, probably sexuality; and every tendency towards that sort of indulgence is to be destroyed in a constant round of 'wholesome' labour. All that appear to be missing are the cold showers. It is a dreary picture, but it was an ideal of education embraced by the middle class at that time which found its greatest advocate in Dr Arnold, Headmaster of Rugby. That the regime was adopted by Victoria and Albert gives a clear idea of how profoundly the royal family had adopted middle-class values. For the first eighteen years of his life, Edward was to walk that iron road.

The architect of this education was Baron Christian von Stockmar, whom in 1837 King Leopold of Belgium, Victoria's beloved uncle, despatched to England to become her confidential adviser, with the accompanying recommendation that the doctor was 'a living dictionary'. In the course of the twenty years following the death of Leopold's first wife, Charlotte, daughter of George IV and Caroline, Stockmar had ceased to be an obscure physician and had risen to the position of king maker. It was largely through his efforts that Leopold attained the throne of Belgium, and Stockmar had followed that coup with an even more glittering diplomatic accomplishment, actually manoeuvering the Great Powers into guaranteeing Belgian neutrality. The very embodiment of discretion, integrity and high-mindedness, he was respected by Lord Grey, Sir Robert Peel, Lord Palmerston and many other influential statesmen, though none spoke of liking him.[5]

While still a young man, Stockmar had devoted his life to the service of the Coburg family, whose fortunes he advanced assiduously, not least through a remarkably advantageous series of royal marriages, never demanding more for himself than that his protégés succeed. He had done surprisingly well with Leopold, despite that monarch's very deliberate cast of mind, a characteristic which caused George IV to dub him 'le Marquis Pau et Feu'; and when asked to transfer his efforts to Victoria, he did so without a murmur of protest, although the undertaking meant a more or less permanent separation from his family.

With Victoria, however, Stockmar suffered a check. In order to win that intimate and total dependence which his system required, he would have had to replace the Baroness Louise Lehzen in the Queen's affections; and that he could not do. The Baroness had been more than Victoria's governess; she had been the child's comforter and confidante, the young woman's friend and, finally, the commander of her heart and jealous guardian of her own special privileges. Not until Prince Albert, whom his Uncle Leopold (Albert and Victoria were first cousins) placed under Stockmar's direction for his final grooming, had married Victoria did Stockmar discover the means to defeat Lehzen. When at the end of an arduous campaign, fought by letters, memoranda and locked doors, Victoria surrendered in the year following Edward's birth and sent Lehzen to Bükeburg and permanent retirement, not only the Queen but the Prince of Wales fell into Stockmar's hands. By the time Edward was four years old, his parents had committed him to a course of study laid out on the lines suggested by Stockmar and designed to make him 'a model of morality, of piety, of deportment'.[6] He was to be 'truthful, courageous, industrious, intelligent, indifferent alike to popular acclaim and personal interest'.[7]

In fairness it must be added that Stockmar did not expect from his protégés more than he was willing to give himself. The problem, however, was that men of Stockmar's stamp were not and are not common. Frivolity, humour, passion, even a joy of life appear to have been omitted from his temperament. Melancholic and dyspeptic, he served a god of duty whose demands were incessant. He laboured without rest – warning, scolding, drawing up an endless succession of dreary papers on every conceivable subject from the English Constitution to the management of the royal family's grocery budget.

As he grew into childhood, Edward came to fear and detest Stockmar, and with good reason. The Baron was certainly responsible in a large degree for much of Edward's unhappiness in his early years, and Stockmar 'never lost an opportunity to prejudice the Queen and the Prince against their eldest son'.[8] Aside from that, there may have been a natural antipathy, resulting from the grating contact between two totally different personalities, one dour and obsessed with work, the other ebullient and yearning for the joys of human society.

Up to the age of seven and a half, Edward was under the tutelage of Lady Sarah Lyttelton, his governess, and two other women, who taught him French, English and German. He proved to be gifted in languages, speaking German from infancy. In fact he was never able to rid his English of the German influence, an influence that in later years was most noticeable when he became angry and his r's rolled. He became equally proficient in French and formed, a little later, a 'cordial intimacy' with M. Brasseur, his French tutor, which lasted from the time Edward was seven to the end of his life.[9]

There was never any question of sending Edward to school. Neither Stockmar nor the boy's parents would have imagined such a course possible. Could the difficulty occasioned by his rank have been overcome, there remained the insurmountable objection to his fraternizing with boys of his own age, who would be, in the natural course of events, the scions of English noble families. Victoria and Albert viewed the possibility of such a relationship with horror, distrusting and despising as they did the members of England's aristocracy for conducting their lives in a manner the Queen and her Consort considered to be dissolute and hopelessly vicious.

There were also deeply embedded hostilities of a more emotional order. Victoria had not forgotten the degree to which she and her mother had been ostracized by members of George IV's Court and later, largely through the errors of the Duchess of Kent, those who surrounded William IV, although Victoria remained on good terms with the Dowager Queen Adelaide. Neither would she have forgotten the ill will resulting from the Lady Flora Hastings affair in 1839, when, for having failed to realize that Lady Flora was fatally ill and not pregnant out of wedlock, Victoria was publicly hissed at Ascot by the Duchess of Montrose and Lady Sarah Ingestre.[10] For a time she was cast in the role of villainess, not only by a large segment of the nobility but by the popular press as well.

Albert's reasons were different but equally strong. He had never been popular with the English gentry. They regarded him as a foreigner, an interloper, something of an adventurer, who confirmed their suspicions about his character by preferring chess to fox hunting and playing the organ to pursuing pretty women. For his part, Albert detested dancing, drinking and bawdy stories and found the men of the Court lacking in intellectual attainments. He was distressed to find that he could not even persuade Victoria that they should give dinners to which would be invited the most learned men of the day. To these points of contention with the nobility were added a shared anxiety, amounting to a morbid fear, that in some way Edward would become the centre of a faction if he were allowed to mingle with society, even a society of children.

Keeping Edward isolated also meant that he was effectively prevented from sharing in any way his mother's eminence, a position Victoria jealously guarded against all threats of encroachment. It is not unreasonable to suggest again that the deep retirement in which the Prince of Wales was kept as a child was, to some extent, the result of his mother's jealousy. In all the child's suffering during those painful years of his education, Victoria never attempted to intercede on his behalf; and Virginia Cowles is certainly justified in finding the Queen's attitude towards her eldest son 'abnormally egotistical'.[11]

Edward's days in the nursery came to an end; the 'noble experiment' was begun; and never in the years ahead would he have cause to ask, as George IV had done when he was a young man, 'Why doesn't someone tell me what to do?' As much as Stockmar may be credited with being the architect of Edward's plan of education, in its outline the plan bears a remarkable resemblance to the Kensington System, settled on by the Duchess of Kent and Sir John Conroy for retaining in their own hands every vestige of influence over the young Victoria. The similarities of the two systems in their effects suggest that Edward's education may have been modelled to an unspecifiable degree on the education given his mother. As Victoria herself had been, Edward was scrupulously excluded from all contact with the Duke of Kent's relations and the nobility in general. He was denied the companionship of people his own age, as his mother had been. His tutors and mentors were either men from the lower ranks in society or his mother and father. The Kensington System was even refined in one degree. There was no Lehzen to come between Edward and his parents. Remembering her own flight to Lehzen's arms as an escape from the dominance of her mother and Conroy, Victoria had grounds for fearing that Edward's affections might be subverted if opportunity were provided.

In the spring of 1849, Henry Birch, an Eton and Cambridge man, was selected, with much virginal hesitation on the part of Albert and Stockmar, to become Edward's principal tutor.[12] In the beginning he found Edward a difficult student, headstrong and given to temper tantrums. That phase of their relationship passed quickly, however; and Edward developed a strong liking for his tutor. It has been sug-

gested that Birch was dismissed as head tutor because a genuine friendship developed between himself and his pupil.[13] But he seriously
prejudiced his position with Albert and Stockmar in quite another way
by announcing shortly after his appointment that he wished to take
holy orders.[14] Birch was persuaded to postpone that step until his duties
as tutor were at an end. Albert, revealing the depth of his fear that the
Prince might be exposed to influences not entirely his own, insisted
that Birch delay responding to his call, not because he feared the tutor
might become overzealous in religious matters, but that he might find
his loyalty to the royal family divided.[15]

In less than two years Birch was replaced by Frederick Waymouth
Gibbs, a Fellow of Trinity College and 'a firm believer in decorum'.
Although he came to his task highly recommended as being the almost
perfect type of barrister or upper civil servant, from Edward's point of
view he was an unfortunate choice, temperamentally unsuited to the
task of teaching a ten-year-old boy. From the outset, Gibbs recognized
that he had three masters – Albert, Victoria and Stockmar, in that order
of importance – and he made it a principle not to offend any of them.
As for the reports he was to submit daily on Edward's behaviour, he
made the discovery that they were to be critical in nature and not
laudatory. He was supposed to find faults in his charge, and he had no
difficulty in doing that.[16] Typical of the sort of communication he
made to Edward's parents is the following report submitted to Victoria:
'The Prince of Wales' character appears to Mr Gibbs a perpetual
conflict between Impulse and Principle. Speaking generally, his im-
pulses are not kindly. They lead him to speak rudely and unamiably,
to tease his companions...and consequently his playfulness...con-
stantly degenerates into roughness and rudeness. The impulse to oppose
is very strong.... Connected with it, there is in his mind an irritating
feeling that others are irritated against him.... On the other side stands
the Sense of Duty, supported by the wish to gain the approbation of his
Papa and his Mama.'[17]

Was the young Edward such an unpleasant child? The few reports of
him from outside the family suggest the opposite. Archbishop Benson,
who saw him in Scotland in 1848, responded very sympathetically to the
boy, finding him 'of rather slender make with an intelligent expression'.
Lord Macaulay, writing two years earlier, thought him pleasant; and
most observers agreed that he was an attractive child.[18] Some of the
Prince's troubles could undoubtedly be traced to the fact that his older
sister, Victoria, was more amenable to discipline and responded eagerly
to the rigorous schedule of study which went on five hours a day, six
days a week, twelve months of the year, with only an occasional relaxing of the iron round when the royal residence was moved or a
family birthday suspended work.

Another source of dissatisfaction on the Queen's part was that Edward did not sufficiently resemble his father. A month after the Prince's birth, Victoria had written to Leopold expressing the most fervent hope that the child would 'resemble his angelic dearest Father in *every, every* respect, both in body and mind'.[19] Underlying that wish seems to be another, scarcely admitted, that Edward as a separate individual did not exist at all. Since he could not be his father, he was bound to disappoint his parents. Stockmar, of course, could never be satisfied; there would always be some work undone, some virtue imperfectly acquired. It is not to be wondered at that Edward occasionally 'swung a large stick' at Gibbs or pelted him with pebbles. The miracle is that he did not lose his reason.

Gibbs consulted Stockmar daily concerning Edward's progress, and these conversations invariably exposed some new failing on the part of the Prince. 'It is a very difficult Case,' the Baron gloomily agreed, 'and requires the exercise of intellectual labour and thought.'[20] There would be more work, longer assignments until the day inevitably came when Gibbs could do nothing with his young charge, describing the behaviour of the child as that 'of a person half silly'. Driven to the extreme of physical rebellion by his exhausted faculties, Edward sulked, fought with his younger brother, Alfred, and disrupted his instruction with sudden frenzies. Frightened by the violence of these emotional outbursts, Gibbs would suspend studies for the day and urge that Albert take the boy out deer stalking.[21] As a rule Albert remained unbending, and Victoria did not comfort her distraught son with either kind words or embraces. Instead, she pronounced him lazy.

Birch had not ingratiated himself with Albert by suggesting that Edward be provided with boys of his own age as companions, and similar proposals by Gibbs were received coldly. The answer to work neglected was more work; and if the Prince became unruly, he was to be smacked.[22] The Queen was no more lenient. If Edward was disobedient or behaved in a manner which displeased Victoria, she would put him across her knee and, even in the presence of members of the Court, smack his bottom with a slipper.[23]

Discovering that he had no hope of escaping his torture by open rebellion, Edward retreated into a passive indifference, which no amount of browbeating could penetrate; and thus, at an early age, he learned to feign stupidity, a pretence and a symptom of his unhappiness that his parents and the unimaginative Stockmar mistook for reality. Cecil Woodham-Smith has described some of his examination papers, written when he was fifteen, as 'alarmingly backward'.[24] But papers written by a youth struggling under a hated educational tyranny are a poor measure of his intelligence. Their failure is more likely to be, in this case, an outward expression of his rebellion, otherwise repressed.

Albert was soon convinced that his eldest son was dull-witted and made no secret of his anxiety over the fact.[25] In time he came to be so glum over Edward's intellectual limitations that *The Times* took up the subject. As for Victoria's reaction, she seized on the boy's alleged lack of competence to keep him more than ever out of the light falling on the throne.

Through all of his difficulties, Edward retained an affectionate disposition and made lasting friendships with those people who returned his liking. Sir David Welch, his mother's captain of the royal yachts, *Fairy* and the *Alberta*, formed a warm friendship with the seven-year-old Prince that lasted the rest of Edward's life. He established equally enduring friendships with two boys, Charles Carrington, later first Earl Carrington and Marquis of Lincolnshire, and Charles Lindley Wood, second Viscount Halifax, who were introduced as occasional visitors to the royal playgrounds when Edward was six or seven years old. With much misgiving and a flurry of exchanged memoranda between himself and Stockmar, Albert had agreed to the boys' coming; but he was usually present during their visits, filling the youngsters with dread, as was the case some years later when Eton boys were introduced.[26] Despite Edward's starved affections, or, probably, because of them, these relationships were seldom satisfactory, usually culminating in some rude action on the part of Edward or his brother. Their occasional visits to Eton were equally unsatisfactory.[27]

Under Gibbs the hours of study were increased, with predictable results. Edward grew increasingly unmanageable; but no let-up was permitted, despite the attempts of Gerald Wellesley, the chaplain, Dr Voisin, the French master, and Dr Becker, Albert's librarian, to bring the parents to reason.[28] Gibbs, perhaps jealous of his authority and certainly determined to remain in the good graces of the Prince Consort and Baron Stockmar, went on as before. If at the age of twelve Edward behaved badly with the Eton boys or went into fits of trembling rage during his lessons, the system imposed by the parents and executed by the masters was not to be blamed. It was simply that Edward 'had a pleasure in giving pain to others – that it was an ultimate fact in his character borne out by the observation of all around him....'[29] Thrown into constant companionship with an adult so inclined to see the worst in him, Edward came to hate his tutor as heartily as he feared Stockmar, who, from the depths of his perpetual gloom, concluded that the young Prince behaved as he did because he had inherited the madness of George III.[30] In describing the Prince as an exaggerated copy of his mother, the Baron hinted that the Queen was unstable, a view shared by Albert, who dreaded to see his wife's will thwarted and in the matter of the children saw that it did not occur.

Despite his troubles, life held occasional light moments for Edward;

and with these rare releases came glimpses of a brighter, gayer world than he had guessed at in the confines of his parents' homes. In 1846 he was taken to Astley's pantomime and began to perform in family plays. On one of the Queen's wedding anniversaries, as a special 'treat' for the Prince Consort, the children put on Racine's *Athalie,* Edward taking the part of Abner with the Princess Royal in the role of Athalie. He was introduced to the theatre at Windsor and Buckingham Palace, where Charles Kean was a frequent performer, and the opera at Covent Garden in 1852.[31] These experiences awakened in Edward a delight in the theatre that increased with time until theatre-going became one of his chief forms of entertainment. On October 30 1849, he attended his first public function, the opening of the Coal Exchange in the City; and two years later he was presented with a handsome paper cutter by Newcastle Corporation. In expressing his thanks for the gift, he made his first public speech. Later in his life, through incessant practice, Edward became an accomplished public speaker and so thoroughly familiar with the form of the greetings and responses appropriate to his appearances that on one occasion he gave a terrified public official, who had forgotten his lines, a speech of official welcome one line at a time, which the poor man repeated after him in the fashion of one taking an oath.

The first real break in the adamantine walls surrounding Edward occurred in August 1855, when he accompanied his parents on a visit to the Court of Napoleon III and Eugénie in Paris. The visit was a particularly happy one for Victoria, who had become attached to both Napoleon and his Empress and may have surrendered more than she knew to the Emperor's charms.[32] Whatever the causes, the mood of the visit was gay, and the adolescent Edward in his highland costume was an instant success. Despite his mother's opinion concerning his looks, he was attractive to women; and his charm, sociability and warmth won the hearts of the Court ladies, who kissed him, fondled him and treated him with loving yet respectful attention. No wonder the young man's spirits soared. He begged the Empress to allow him and his sister to stay in France.

When he was told that his mother would miss her children, he protested, 'Don't fancy that! They don't want us, and there are six more of us at home!'[33] Whether or not Philippe Jullian is correct in drawing a connection between Edward's enthusiasm for the French Court and the daring décolletage of the women, he certainly discovered a world where gaiety, social intercourse and physical beauty were glorified, where life was unclouded by memoranda, and the carping voice of Gibbs was stilled. He fell in love with France and longed to stay. In his fourteenth year he had discovered a passion that never cooled. Perhaps among all his loves, France stirred his heart most profoundly.

Another effect of the French visit, less easily substantiated, was the budding of Edward's diplomatic gifts and the considerable talents he was later to demonstrate in dealing with events through the medium of people. Definitely not of a 'bookish' turn of mind, he possessed remarkable charm, matched with an enormous interest in individuals. He never forgot a face, and he never forgot a name, and while still a young man he could all but recite the *Almanach de Gotha,* that European social register of last appeal. Albert deplored his son's propensity for 'small talk', gossip and the recitation of what who said to whom; but they were precisely the interests that later enabled him to become so effective as a diplomat. Legge was convinced that Edward had been a 'student of diplomacy' from his earliest manhood and that his training in the art was begun by Napoleon III in 1855 and continued through correspondence and meetings until 1870 and the Emperor's hasty departure from France.[34] Legge also saw Eugénie's hand in the young man's training and held the Empress's diplomatic gifts in the highest regard, referring to her as a 'petticoat Talleyrand'.

This 'child without a youth' was not, however, allowed to stay in the promised land. Hurried back to England, he was plunged once more into his studies, with extra work to make up for wasted time. The routine reasserted itself, and he resumed his mechanical round. In the autumn of the following year, Albert interrupted his son's studies to send him with Gibbs and an older man on a dreary walking tour of Dorset. Plodding along, bored and lonesome, Edward had ample opportunity to contrast the scenes dragging past with the lively memories of Paris. A year later the Prince Consort arranged another walking tour, this time to the Lake District, giving way to Edward's pleadings for companionship by allowing four carefully chosen Eton boys to accompany him and his three tutors. Before setting off, however, Edward was compelled to write a composition on the distinctions between friends and flatterers, presumably to prepare his mind for the dangers posed by his companions.[35] Compared with the Dorset jaunt, the trip was a success; but when Edward submitted for his father's inspection the diary he had been obliged to keep on the tour, Albert was deeply grieved to discover how scanty it was and how lamentably short on philosophical reflections.[36]

Mastering his disappointment, Albert conceded that Gibbs's reports and those of the other masters justified sending Edward and the same Eton boys on a longer trip. On July 26 1857, the Prince of Wales and his companions and attendants left England for Königswinter, near Bonn on the Rhine, where they were to study and take frequent excursions into France and Switzerland. In Germany he visited Albert's brother, Ernest, at Coburg and Prince Metternich at Johannisberg. The ageing Chancellor observed that 'everyone liked the Prince of Wales, but he seemed sad and ill at ease'.[37] Edward's diary entry described the Prince as 'a very nice old gentleman and very like the late Duke of Wellington'.[38] Nothing more disquieting than Edward's kissing a young girl occurred on the trip, and his parents were reduced to criticizing his written accounts of his travels for their shallowness of observation.

His return from Königswinter marked the close, rather belatedly, of his childhood. He was approaching his sixteenth birthday, and as a gesture of recognition of his changed status, his parents gave him an allowance of £100 a year, instructing him to buy his own clothes, although this freedom was given only at the price of a sharply worded letter from the Queen, warning him never to wear anything 'extravagant or slang' because to do so would be an 'offence against decency, leading – as it has often done in others – to an indifference to what is morally wrong'.[39] It is difficult to remember that the woman who wrote this letter was the same person who, as a young queen, glittering with jewels and with her gown sweeping the floor, danced away the night, breakfasted with the sun and loved laughter and gaiety, the same woman, indeed, who had felt her heart going out to Lord Melbourne with a love that was far from filial.

What had happened to that love of life that had once been her greatest charm? At least two writers have blamed Albert for the dulling of her spirits. Maurois has written that Albert 'transformed the light-hearted girl...into a methodical sovereign, deeply conscious of her power'.[40] Edwards was less delicate: 'For two decades [before his death] the gardener of a woman's soul, Albert of Coburg, had trimmed, regulated and toned down the healthy instincts of his wife' and 'drilled out of her' as 'sinful hankerings after worldly pleasures' every expression of *joie de vivre*.[41] It was a change more profound than that to be expected in the natural course of maturing which led Victoria to suggest in all seriousness that wearing a loose coat and slippers was the first step towards moral disintegration.

Following a private confirmation ceremony in St George's Chapel, Windsor Castle, on April 1 1858, Edward, accompanied by Gibbs and Tarver, was sent to live in White Lodge, Richmond Park, presumably to cram for a military examination. The Prince had begged to be allowed to enter the army; but the Queen would not consent to his associating himself in any significant way with that or any other branch of the services. She did, however, give him permission to prepare for a military examination with the purpose in view, at least as he understood it, of qualifying for a commission in the army.[42] He understood that he would not be allowed to become attached to any specific regiment and that his commission would, at least for the foreseeable future, be an unattached appointment. The promise of the examination proved to be nothing more than the carrot on the stick which lured him into more meaningless work.

His move to White Lodge, although presented to him as a move towards greater independence, in no way lessened the rigid supervision under which he had passed his life. In fact, his parents viewed the White Lodge interlude as an opportunity to further isolate the young man from the outside world. Having asserted himself to the extent of asking to be allowed to train for a commission in the army, he was rewarded by being shut up for several months with two of his least liked tutors, Gibbs and Tarver, and limited to the uninspiring companionship of three equerries – Major Christopher Teesdale, Major Lloyd-Lindsay and Lord Valletort – young men in their twenties and of unexceptional character.[43]

In a letter to the equerries outlining their responsibilities, Albert wrote that they were to prepare the Prince to be the 'first gentleman in the country'.[44] In this area, at least, Edward would eventually exceed his father's wishes, for he was to become the first and, perhaps, the last gentleman of Europe, an epithet applied to him with both scorn and praise, depending on the occasion and the speaker. Not content with listing his expectations regarding his son's behaviour, the Prince Consort warned the equerries against 'Lolling, and lounging, slouching, dandyism, practical jokes, frivolities, pleasures which did not instruct, etc., etc'.[45] St Bernard's hand might have trembled in holding such a letter, but Edward was expected to receive similar instructions in a spirit of cheerful thankfulness. At White Lodge one ban was lifted. At long last he was to be allowed to read Scott's novels.

The examination for which he was being prepared proved to be a fiction. On his seventeenth birthday, he was awarded the rank of lieutenant-colonel in the army, unattached, without undergoing any test whatever. Edward was disappointed. He had hoped to begin at a much lower grade and advance through study and practice.[46] Albert and Victoria certainly were aware that there would be no examination awaiting Edward in the fall of 1858. Why then was he incarcerated in White Lodge through the spring and summer? Magnus suggests that the Queen and the Prince Consort were anxious to 'form the character of the Prince of Wales before he came of age'.[47] But if forming his character was what the parents had in mind, it was being done by locking the boy away with older men, denying him access to anyone of his own age and allowing him no contact whatsoever with members of the opposite sex. One of the Queen's favourites, Lady Churchill, wrote Edward some amusing letters while he was at White Lodge; learning of the correspondence, the Queen angrily informed her ladyship that she was not to continue to show an interest in the Prince.[48]

There are at least two other possible reasons why Edward was being given such treatment. Both the Queen and her husband shared the fear, mentioned earlier, that Edward might, like heirs to the English throne in past generations, become the centre of a faction hostile to the authority of his parents. Albert, in particular, felt cut off from the English aristocracy; and just prior to the entry of England into the Crimean War in 1854, there were press reports of his having been arrested as a traitor, and crowds gathered at the Tower to see him brought there in chains. As a product of the Kensington System, the Queen was easily made suspicious; and from the very beginning she had disliked her eldest son. This fear of faction and opposition can be advanced to account for the ban on youthful associates, sports and games that would bring him into contact with individuals not carefully screened by Albert. As he approached that time in his life when he might reasonably have expected to enjoy greater freedom, Edward found himself being increasingly isolated from the outside world as his parents carried out a carefully orchestrated plan, every step of which was designed, in the words of one biographer, 'to lead to the extinction of the Prince's individuality'.[49]

The second fear that obsessed the parents was that Edward would suffer some kind of moral disintegration. This fear finds expression in the Queen's letters to the Princess Royal (who had married Frederick William of Prussia on January 25 1858) and is revealed in the energy with which Victoria cut off the exchange of letters between her son and Lady Churchill. At about the time of Edward's confirmation, the Queen wrote to her daughter, 'May God protect dear Bertie – and work out in him all that is good and pure in his young heart! But a boy and a man after some few years can no longer be protected by his parents. He must fight the battle alone, and himself – and does require constant vigilance not to fall.'[50]

The 'fall' being contemplated with such dread is nothing more nor less than sexual intercourse. Albert appears to have been remarkably indifferent to the charms of women. Even as a young man he preferred the company of men to that of women and at social functions was happy only if he could engage some man in an intellectual discussion. After his marriage he never flirted. Their son's sexual maturing, however, disturbed both mother and father and Victoria began early to hunt for a wife for him. 'We must look for princesses for Bertie,' his mother wrote Victoria in perturbation shortly before his confirmation, 'Oh! if you would find us one!'[51] And a short time later: 'I must repeat again that Bertie's wife must be very near his own age as everyone who has anything to do with him thinks on that depends his whole future life!'[52] Through letter after letter from the Queen runs the implication that Edward is being kept from presumably monstrous acts of debasement only by his father's constant vigilance.

It is probable that Edward was marched off to White Lodge out of jealousy and moral humbug, masquerading as a virtuous and high-minded desire to prepare him for the great task that lay before him. Over and over again during this period, in letters to her daughter, Victoria revealed her true feelings toward Edward: 'Affie [Prince Alfred] is going on admirably; he comes to luncheon today (which is a real, brilliant Osborne day) and oh! when I see him and Arthur and look at...! (you know what I mean!) I am in utter despair! The systematic idleness, laziness – disregard of everything is enough to break one's heart, and fills me with indignation.'[53] On May 24, her birthday, the Queen wrote, again to the Princess Royal, 'The only one of all the children, who neither drew, wrote, played or did anything whatever to show his affection – beyond buying me a table in Ireland – was Bertie. Oh! Bertie alas! alas! That is too sad a subject to enter on.'[54]

As the summer advanced, it became more and more clear that Edward was accepting his imprisonment with increasingly bad grace. He and Gibbs fell out with growing frequency. Observing that Edward was showing mounting resistance to his tutor, Colonel Lindsay, a gentleman-in-waiting at White Lodge, wrote to Albert: 'Nor do I wonder at it, for they are by nature thoroughly unsuited to one another. I confess I quite understand the Prince's feelings toward Mr Gibbs, for tho' I respect his uprightness and devotion, I could not give him sympathy, confidence or friendship.'[55] Years later an old acquaintance of Gibbs', Sir Leslie Stephen, grown deaf and cantankerous, would interrupt a Gibbs' monologue with a profound sigh, followed by the loudly muttered comment, 'Oh, Gibbs, you are so dull.'

On November 10 the parents accepted with relief Gibbs's resignation and by their action headed off a serious explosion. They appointed Robert Bruce as the boy's governor. 'Poor Mr Gibbs,' wrote the Queen in honest dismay, 'certainly failed during the last two years entirely, incredibly – and did Bertie no good.'[56] Entering on his new duties, Bruce discovered that he disliked 'almost everything that Bertie said or did, and composed a number of memoranda to that effect – much to the approval of the Prince Consort, who had commanded him to be frank'.[57]

Spring, summer and early autumn passed with Edward sequestered in White Lodge. He was bored, unhappy and rebellious. Obviously, he could not be kept a prisoner for ever; and his parents took the occasion of his seventeenth birthday to bring to an end the total isolation in which he had lived in recent months. Gibbs was going; Baron Stockmar was to return to Germany permanently. The world was definitely brightening. On November 9, his birthday, Albert presented Edward with his uniform. Although he had been denied the dignity of standing for an examination, which, had he passed it, would have given him some claim to an independent status, the uniform was a sign of his approaching manhood. The stress of the occasion gave the Queen 'a shocking nervous headache', and she was not pleased by Edward's obvious delight in his new regalia. She was more pleased to record that in the afternoon 'Bertie put on his uniform and reported himself to Uncle George [Duke of Cambridge and Commander-in-Chief] who lectured him on obedience'.[58]

Albert took the occasion to write to his brother to say that 'Bertie' would not be allowed in London during the season 'as long as he is neither fish nor flesh, as the old saying is'.[59] To his son he sent a long memorandum on the theme that life consists of duties. Having read it, Edward burst into tears. Recounting the birthday observance to the Princess Royal, Victoria lamented her son's want of seriousness and expressed the hope that he would 'meet with some severe lesson to shame him out of his ignorance and dullness . . .'.[60]

As wretched as the six months leading up to his birthday had been, there was at least temporary relief from the tedium of his days following them. Edward was despatched to Berlin to visit his sister. For the Prince the trip was a great success. He won immediate popularity in the Prussian Court, bearing out an observation made some months before by Sir Frederick Ponsonby, later to be assistant private secretary to Edward, that the Prince was one of the most likeable youngsters he had ever met. Edward was given little opportunity, however, to taste the fruits of his success. His sister and his brother-in-law took their role of guardians so seriously that he was not even allowed to remain alone in the same room with Frederick's uncles, for fear that the boy might be exposed to some crass observation or tainted by overhearing indelicate topics discussed.

Victoria wrote to her mother expressing her delight with Edward and commenting on his immediate success. The Queen received the account very coolly. 'We are glad to hear so good an account of poor Bertie; I have no doubt his visit to you – and the mild but firm influence of Colonel Bruce will do him much good. But we always found that he appeared for the first week – much improved, then (as is always the case with him in everything) he gradually went down hill; not paying attention to what is said or read or what he sees is the real misfortune. His natural turn and taste is very trifling, and I think him a very dull companion. . . . Handsome I cannot think him, with that painfully small and narrow head, those immense features and total want of chin.'[61]

The Princess Royal and her husband received that devastating judgement of Edward without comment and continued their vigilant supervision of his actions. With a single voice they absolutely vetoed a plan put forward by Uncle Charles and Prince Albrecht to take Edward to a hunting lodge in the Harz Mountains. 'You could imagine what company, what a tone and what conversation,' Victoria wrote to her mother. 'You are indeed quite right to stop that shooting excursion for Bertie,' the Queen promptly replied. 'For the future you may always say that we wished him to remain with you and pay no visits'.[62]

Life at Court was made lively, however, with balls and other entertainments. There were, above all, people to talk to who did not wish to examine Edward on academic subjects, lecture him on duty or discover the state of his diary. Aside from his sister, no one was taking mental notes of his behaviour for the purpose of making a report to his father. It was delightful; he danced and talked and made himself thoroughly agreeable. In short, he enjoyed himself.

As might have been expected, his father was disappointed with Edward's activities during his visit. When he returned home, it was discovered that he was much more inclined to speak of people, parties and the theatre than of works of art and architecture. Albert had hoped that he would spend the greater part of his time in Berlin in study and had requested his daughter to take Edward to lectures. The Prince took a rather feeble revenge on his parents for their disapproval by deliberately refusing to mention anything of a cultural nature unless he was specifically asked. With some sourness, Victoria told the Princess Royal she was glad her daughter had found Bertie 'amiable and companionable'. For her part, she found him dull.[63]

On his return from Berlin the plan to keep Edward confined to White Lodge was abandoned; and in January he was sent to Rome, having been told by his father that it was now a settled plan that he would, following his return from Italy, be sent first to Oxford and then to Cambridge and allowed to travel during the vacations. He was also told that he could expect to receive some military training. In arriving at the general plan, the Prince Consort had taken the advice of cabinet ministers, the President of the Royal Academy and the Director of the British Museum, among others, demonstrating a certain thoroughness of approach.[64] The plan itself and Albert's revealing it to his son are two signs that Victoria and the Prince Consort had begun to come to terms with the Prince's approaching manhood.

That was not to imply a lessening of control. In Albert's view the Rome journey was a logical next step in Edward's education. His tutor, Bruce, understood that the young man was not to mix in politics or to associate with people of his own age. Albert further warned Bruce that there would be 'no chance intercourse with strangers' and under no conditions was he to be allowed to talk to journalists. For the first time Edward was travelling incognito, under the totally transparent disguise of a young nobleman, Baron Renfrew. No one was fooled, and King Victor Emmanuel invited Edward to come to Turin as his guest. Victoria, claiming to disapprove of Victor Emmanuel's rough manners, refused to allow the Prince to accept the invitation.[65] Her excuse was as feeble as her son's disguise, but it probably did mask her real motive in keeping Edward away from Turin; which was that she did not wish him to receive the recognition that such a visit would have produced. It must be added in the Queen's defence, however, that given the delicate political situation existing between Victor Emmanuel and the Austrian Empire, she would have been justified in suspecting that Victor Emmanuel wished to gain some political advantage from Edward's visit.

Edward paraded solemnly around the Imperial City in the company of Colonel and Mrs Bruce, an equerry, a chaplain, a doctor, an Italian master, an archaeologist and John Gibson, a painter belonging to the Royal Academy. Bruce followed his instructions very carefully and Edward was spared all 'chance encounters'.[66] He was taken round the Vatican, the Forum, the Coliseum, the Appian Way and St Peter's; but he seems to have shown little interest in those sights. Only in John Gibson's studio in Rome did he brighten up, commenting with considerable enthusiasm on three of Gibson's portraits of a beautiful Italian woman.[67] At a dinner arranged by Bruce, he met Robert Browning; but both the poet and the Prince remained unimpressed. It is doubtful that Edward had ever read a word of Browning's poetry, although the volume *Men and Women*, containing poems that would be among Browning's best known, had been published in 1855.

A more significant meeting occurred between Edward and Pope Pius IX. The interview was a complete success and marks, in one sense of the term, the beginning of Edward's diplomatic career.[68] During the conversation with the pontiff, Edward followed with scrupulous care the instructions he had been given and emerged from the interview without having made a single mistake, perhaps because Bruce insisted on remaining with the Prince, coughing quietly when he thought Edward was moving away from the prearranged topics.[69] The function of the visit to the Vatican may have been, as Jullian suggests, to mollify the Catholic sentiments of Ireland. If such was the case, and it is not an unreasonable suggestion, then Edward conducted himself with tact and grace, displaying genuine diplomatic talents. His position as future head of the Church of England placed him in a delicate position, and he was also in a similar situation in the matter of politics.

Victor Emmanuel was in the process of provoking Austria to attack Piedmont, and Emperor Napoleon III was waiting eagerly to go to Victor Emmanuel's aid. The Pope expressed fears that there would be violence in Rome. Edward preserved the Pope's good will by being sympathetic but said nothing to embarrass the British Government, which was willing to hazard an occasional cast into those waters but had no intention of wading in them. In April the climax came; war erupted between Italy and Austria, with France entering on the side of the Italians. Edward's proposed tour of North Italy and Switzerland was cancelled, and he sailed for Gibraltar and Spain on May 2. His very cordial interview with the Pope probably laid the groundwork for the thoroughly speculative rumours, which were to follow Edward the rest of his life, hinting that he entertained a secret sympathy for Catholicism and died having received the last rites of the Roman Church.

Returning from Spain at the end of June, Edward was sent at once to Holyrood House in Edinburgh, where he was to cram for his entrance to Oxford. The Prince was less reluctant than usual to accept incarceration, probably because he could see Oxford at the end of it. He settled down to work, and pleased his teachers with his industry, although his mother expressed the opinion that he would make a better impression on his guests – middle-aged scholars were his only dinner companions – if he learned to part his hair a different way.[70] His mother's advice went unheeded; but for perhaps the first time in his life, his studies did not. In September, as this period of serious work was drawing to a close, Albert summoned a group of distinguished men to an educational conference to discuss his son's future training, but this conference was overshadowed by the Prince Consort's election to the presidency of the British Association for the Advancement of Science, which met in September in Aberdeen.

The appointment attracted national attention, not only because it was a signal honour for Albert but because it provided the press with an opportunity to review the Prince Consort's position. The *Morning Post* took the occasion to congratulate the Prince on his appointment and to express pleasure that yet another instance was offered of the desirability of Edward's following in his father's footsteps. The highest praise came from the *Daily News*, which praised Albert's increasing Englishness; and the *Daily Telegraph* was delighted to report that Edward had taken up composing quadrilles and smoking cigars.[71] Improvement all around. In fact, however, Albert was no more English than he had ever been, which is to say, not at all. He was rapidly slipping into that burdened role of the man whose work is never done; his natural seriousness of mind was turning into a brooding gloom; and he was ageing at an alarming rate.

Given this growing darkness of spirit and his capacity for influencing the Queen's line of thought, the parents viewed Edward's entrance into Oxford, not with joy and pride, but with profound anxiety. Fears were increased because the Prince Consort had failed completely to convince the Vice-Chancellor of the University that the ancient practice of associating men with particular colleges should be set aside in Edward's case. Neither royal authority nor German logic – the Prince of Wales belonged to the entire nation, not to any section thereof; therefore, he belonged to the entire University, not to a specific college – could sway the ancient rule; and Edward was attached to Christ Church by a very reluctant Prince Consort.

The press gave some slight notice of Edward's entrance into Oxford, but, in general, refrained from making any critical comment about the training he had received. *Punch,* displeased with the life Edward had been forced to lead, took the occasion of the educational conference held in September to print a mild remonstrance:

A Prince At High Pressure

Thou dear little Wales – sure the saddest of tales,
Is the tale of the studies with which they are cramming thee.
In thy tuckers and bibs handed over to Gibbs,
Who for eight years with solid instruction was ramming thee.

Then to fill any nook Gibbs had chanced to o'erlook,
In those poor little brains, sick of learned palaver,
When thou'dst fain rolled in clover, they handed thee over,
To the prim pedagogic protection of Tarver.

In Edinburgh next, thy poor noddle perplext,
The gauntlet must run of each science and study;
Till the mixed streams of knowledge, turned on by the College,
Through the field of thy boy-brain run shallow and muddy.

To the South from the North – from the shores of the Forth,
Where at hands Presbyterian pure science is quaffed –
The Prince in a trice, is whipped off to the Isis,
Where Oxford keeps springs medieval on draught.

'Gainst indulging the passion for this high pressure fashion
Of Prince-training, *Punch* would uplift loyal warning;
Locomotives we see, over-stoked soon may be,
Till the supersteamed boiler blows up some fine morning.[72]

Edward was disappointed to learn that he was to live apart from his contemporaries, but Albert was in no mood to compromise on this issue. The Prince might belong to Christ Church, in the manner of other mortals; but the choice of his companions would rest with Albert, exercising control through his agent, Bruce. That was absolute, and Frewin Hall, a specially fitted house off Cornmarket Street, became the royal residence. Lecturers came to the house, and Edward, in the company of a few specially chosen undergraduates, listened politely. Albert made numerous trips to Oxford to check on his son's progress, chiefly because he could not rid himself of the dread that Edward would waste time in frivolous activities. Of course, the Prince was not allowed to play cricket. George IV, as a young man, it was recalled, had been fond of cricket, making that game wholly unsatisfactory. Football was forbidden, likewise billiards, which suggested cigars. Tennis was allowed, but because Edward was allowed to play it only with his equerries, who always beat him, he soon grew weary of the game.[73] Albert's view of sports was as bizarre as his view of Oxford, which he thought was only justified as a place of study.[74]

Despite the burdensome restrictions placed on his activity, Edward had managed to gain a measure of freedom. Fortunately for Edward, Bruce, himself no anchorite, grew desperate at the enforced confinement at Frewin Hall, and on his own initiative allowed Edward to ride to hounds, in order to give himself some diversion. The Prince Consort's worst fears were realized. Edward made the acquaintance of two members of the Oxford Bullingdon Club, Henry Chaplin and Frederick Johnstone, who were to remain lifelong friends. They introduced him to fox hunting and cigars, at least.[75] His life at college, lacking though it was in that intimate contact with other young men, was not entirely isolated. For example, during his first week he attended lectures outside Frewin Hall, reported at Chapel every morning at eight o'clock, thus avoiding fines; and on Monday and Tuesday evenings went to the Town Hall to hear Charles Dickens read from *A Christmas Carol* and *The Pickwick Papers*.[76]

Slight though his freedoms were, Victoria and Albert's scheme for denying their son access to the world of his contemporaries was wrecked. Albert would never regain that perfect ascendancy over his son's will that he had maintained before the Oxford venture. Horses and tobacco were to prove stronger than the Prince Consort's influence. He still had the power, however, to make his son's life uncomfortable. An example of his gift for inventing misery are the 'convivial meetings at dinner', which he insisted his son hold three times a week at Frewin Hall. Eminent scholars and 'two unhappy undergraduates' were invited for the purpose of discussing literature and other academic subjects. The wine flowed as though wrung from a stone and no one was allowed to smoke.[77] But Edward was still close enough to his childhood habits of endurance to be satisfied with the crumbs of pleasure that had begun to fall into Frewin Hall from the table of the greater and more exciting world outside the range of his father's authority. He worked hard at Oxford and won the commendation of the Dean of Christ Church for the quality of his written work, an achievement that startled his parents but won him scant praise.

The Queen and the Prince Consort found it difficult to come to terms with their son's achievement. Victoria, writing to the Princess Royal, acknowledged that Edward had passed his examinations well, but she gave him no praise for his efforts and remarked that he had grown no handsomer.[78] This concern with Edward's looks had been growing in the Queen's mind for the better part of a year and dates from the time of his Italian trip in the spring of 1859. In a typically exaggerated attack on her son's shortcomings, Victoria expressed her terror at the thought that were she to die Edward would come to the throne. This anxiety follows and is closely related to another fear, expressed in the same letter, that she and Albert had only three years and a half remaining in which to exert their authority over Edward. Then 'he will be of age and we can't hold him except by moral power! I shut my eyes to that terrible moment!'[79]

What did the Queen wish to hold Edward from? What did the parents imagine was going to happen at 'that terrible moment' when age freed Edward from their control? Immediately after her startled and emotional outburst, Victoria's references to the Prince of Wales's physical appearance increase to the point of becoming obsessive. On his return from Spain, Victoria notes with grim satisfaction that 'they' mean to make 'Bertie' work very hard at Holyrood House. 'He is a little grown...but his nose and mouth are much grown also; the nose is becoming the true Coburg nose and begins to hang a little, but there remains unfortunately the want of chin which with that large nose and very large lips is not so well in profile.'[80]

The references to his appearance multiply as the year advances, with the Queen denying that Edward has any attractiveness or that he is at all good looking, a claim contradicted by photographs of the Prince taken at this time and by the response of others to him during this period. Victoria, however, was determined not to be pleased: 'He is grown and spread,' she wrote in September, 'but not improved in looks; the mouth is becoming so very large and he will cut his hair away behind and divide it nearly in the middle in front, so that it appears to make him have no head and all face.'[81]

The culmination of these outbursts occurred in April 1860 when Edward was once again visiting his sister in Germany. 'He is not at all in good looks,' the Queen wrote, 'his nose and mouth are too enormous and he pastes his hair down to his head, and wears his clothes frightfully – he is really anything but good looking. That coiffure is really too hideous with his small head and enormous features.'[82] The Princess Royal found herself with nothing to say on the subject, and the Queen instantly became nettled with her daughter's restraint and wrote that she thought her silence strange. No doubt the young woman found it quite impossible to respond to the flood of letters focusing on the enormous size of Edward's nose and the knob-like appearance of his head. She must have felt relief when the Queen dropped the subject, which she did just before Edward's departure for America.

Victoria appears to have feared and hated Edward's increasing sexual maturity as much as she hated the thought that he would one day fill her position as monarch. She was both fascinated and revolted by her son's appearance, and her discussion of his features appears to have been a way of discussing his sexual maturation. As a young woman, Victoria had not been a prude. Despite her remarkably sheltered life, she was not backward in frankly appraising Albert's physical attractiveness. She once told Lord Melbourne that she would not marry Albert unless she was satisfied that she could 'like' him. She did, in fact, find him sexually appealing; and she praised his beauty frankly and without false modesty. But the appearance of sexual attractiveness in her son, with its promise of sexual activity, she found appalling.

It is difficult not to conclude that this part at least of the aversion to her son was acquired following her marriage, a result of Albert's influence. Cecil Woodham-Smith does not exaggerate the degree of Albert's antipathy to sex when she writes that he was 'unbalanced' on the subject. Some of his horror seems to have rubbed off on the Queen. The 'terrible moment' when Edward would be out of his parents' control and they could no longer 'hold him' was, in the minds of Albert and Victoria, the time when he would be free to have sexual intercourse, which is certainly why the Queen and her husband began their search for a wife for Edward before he was seventeen years of age.

While he was at Oxford, Edward reached his eighteenth birthday. The event was without fanfare either inside or outside the family. Aside from the letter the Queen wrote to her daughter in April of the same year, shudderingly expressing her dread lest she should die 'next winter', she makes no mention of the fact that on his eighteenth birthday Edward became constitutionally of age to rule without a regent, hence Victoria's anxiety and her insistence that Edward must agree to rely utterly 'in every thing, on dearest Papa, that perfection of human beings'.[83] She probably knew very well that Edward would, were he to become king, dispose of his father as she had disposed of her mother, and for much the same reasons. It is not likely that the thought gave her any pleasure.

The Times noted the Prince's birthday with an editorial, expressing relief that the possibility of a regency was now passed, no 'disparagement' being intended of the 'abilities and virtues' of the Prince Consort. Having expressed the hope, by now a formula, that the Queen would rule in health indefinitely, the paper drew attention to the remarkable growth in knowledge, manufacture, material wealth and the arts in the years since Edward's birth and observed that the monarchy was now as popular as it had been in the time of Elizabeth I. Condemning every monarch from Charles II, who 'degraded the Crown', to William IV, guilty of 'extravagances' and 'inconsistencies', the writer pointed out that only the present sovereign combined the proper private virtues with 'strict adherence to constitutional maxims'.[84]

When it came to the subject of Edward as a potential ruler, the paper had nothing to say. Edward was a cipher in the nation and had been so little in the public eye that interest in him was almost completely academic. Appearing at intervals in the Court Circular, his name evoked no excitement. He could have walked the streets of London without being recognized. As a consequence the paper was forced into generalities: The Prince could look forward to a felicitous reign if he followed 'in the footsteps' of his parents. 'It is the happiness of a King of England that we require from him no brilliant military achievement, no extraordinary diplomatic legerdemain, no startling effects, no scenic pomp, no histrionic dexterity. He may be great without the possession of extraordinary talents, and famous without dazzling exploits. Let him set his people an example of domestic life.'[85]

Had he read the editorial, Edward might have looked back over his life and wondered at the discrepancy between *The Times* view of what would be expected of him as king and his father's view of his responsibilities in that role. He might have concluded that Albert's insistence on study, moral purity, spiritual dedication were misplaced. If what *The Times* said was true, his years of drudgery were largely wasted, at least irrelevant. Edward had been trained as if he were preparing to undertake a knightly quest that would last all his life, as if he were embarking on a spiritual errand of universal significance. *The Times*, in striking contrast, defined his role chiefly in negatives. When the list was ended, what scope remained for the future king? To set an example of domestic tranquillity. No white chargers, no campaigns, no adjusting of diplomatic balances, not even a special dash. Just domestic virtue. It was difficult to decide which view, *The Times*' or Albert's, was the more inhibiting. Albert's efforts to extend the power of the Crown were futile, but *The Times* was wrong in asserting that Edward's influence would be exclusively moral. Even forty years later, despite the general decline of hereditary power in England, an English monarch of strong determination could still influence both domestic and foreign policies. But it was the continuing intention of the press throughout the remainder of the century to play down the political power of the throne.

His birthday passed; the Oxford year drew to a close. He made one more visit to Berlin in the spring; then on July 10 1860, Edward, with a large suite in attendance, sailed from Plymouth for Canada and the United States. For better or worse, the journey was to be the birth of the man. It was his deliverance from the thraldom of childhood and his awakening to the world and to his power in it. Here was a lesson worth learning; Edward learned it; it did not have to be repeated.

3

A Glimpse of Empire

We like the old Shakespearean way of denominating kings by the name of their kingdoms – this youth should be announced among us as *Young England;* and every heart should devise welcomes, in which enthusiasm should know no bounds but those of delicacy and propriety.

Harriet Beecher Stowe

As the *Illustrated London News* pompously observed at the time of Edward's departure for North America, 'the journeyings of potentates are seldom without purpose'. The Prince's trip was not an exception. But why the journey was being undertaken at that particular moment was not generally understood, nor did the nation suspect how profoundly family concerns had mingled with considerations of state to bring about the Prince's departure. Typical of the failure to grasp essentials of the situation was the *Illustrated London News's* assertion that Edward's journey was a logical next step in the 'careful and judicious education which the son of the Queen has received'.[1]

On both sides of the Atlantic journalists turned into romancers to account for the Queen's decision to allow Edward to represent her in the Canadian adventure and then to continue his visit as a private citizen in the United States. *The Times* satisfied itself by saying that Edward went at the invitation of the Canadian Government and that its first thoughts on learning of the voyage were of 'the mighty destiny of the Empire which has founded these communities'.[2] The London *Saturday Review* assumed that the Prince was making his official entrance into public life and that his education was to be put to the test by this assignment. The *New York Times* saw the visit as an event in the 'romance' of history, which derived 'poetic interest' from the fact that one of the oldest monarchies had chosen a youth of eighteen as its representative. Spurning reasons, the *Spectator* exclaimed rapturously that the trip would contribute toward 'enlarging opportunities', add to the wealth of the nations involved, increase the pursuit of knowledge, and widen and elevate 'every form of social happiness'.[3] In this diversity of views the papers come together in one important respect: they assume the existence of a pattern in Edward's life conforming to their own concepts of what a royal life ought to be. The myth of Edward as prince and future king had begun to take shape at the expense of the reality of Edward the person.

Given the history of Edward's role in his family, the decision to allow him to step forward at this time as the Queen's representative is astonishing. Not only did it contradict his parents' policy of keeping him out of the public eye, it reversed Victoria's practice of jealously reserving for herself all the plaudits directed towards the throne. Perhaps sensing the radical nature of the decision to send Edward abroad and fearing that he was too young for his task, the *Saturday Review* warned Edward to remember that 'the Sovereign whom he represents is the principal object of the enthusiasm which will attend his progress', and that he must not allow his head to be turned by the 'incense' of loyalty which will rise round his progress. The key to understanding Edward's sudden emergence from obscurity is that his parents were in disagreement about whether or not he should be allowed to travel in an official capacity as representative of the Crown. Victoria was thoroughly opposed to giving Edward any significant position to fill, while Albert thought the Prince old enough to carry out satisfactorily a representative function such as the Canadian trip offered. But the Queen would never have given her consent, determined as she was to suppress her son, had she not been growing daily more hostile to Edward and finding his presence more and more intolerable. In the end her desire to be rid of him overwhelmed her wish to keep him cloistered. She allowed the plans for the journey to go forward.

To begin with the tip of the iceberg, the official 'occasion' for the Canadian visit was the opening of the Victoria Bridge, built by the Grand Trunk Railroad across the St Lawrence River at Montreal, and the laying of the cornerstone of the Parliament buildings at Ottawa, an action that would symbolize the uneasy union of Upper and Lower Canada in a confederation of provinces. The Victoria Bridge, universally acknowledged to be one of the engineering marvels of the age, was sufficiently great an achievement to justify the Prince's being called on to dignify with his presence the completion of the work. Also, it was fitting that the son of the man who was credited with having brought the Great Exhibition into being nine years before should take up a hammer in the cause of commerce and drive home, along with the silver rivet, the lesson that progress and technology were marching shoulder to shoulder in the New World.

Of course, the reasons behind Edward's peregrinations were considerably more complex than those suggested by the laying of a foundation stone and the opening of a bridge. The Crown was in an awkward situation. During the Crimean War Canada had raised, outfitted and sent across the sea a regiment of infantry, called, initially, the 100th

Regiment or the Royal Canadians and subsequently the 1st Battalion of the Leicester Regiment. Their arrival in England created a stir of interest in Canada and things colonial and placed the government under an obligation, which Canada immediately exploited by requesting that once the war was brought to a successful conclusion the Queen should visit her North American colony, as her father had done.

This suggestion held no appeal for Victoria, who let it be known that she had no intention of setting out on an ocean voyage to the west. The Queen did not see herself as Ulysses, despite the fact that *The Times* had dubbed Edward the English Telemachus. The government supported the Queen, pointing out that such a strenuous journey would expose Her Majesty to unreasonable risks and would, in any case, require too long an absence from England. Canada responded by requesting that Victoria appoint one of her sons Governor-General of the dominion. Victoria found that proposal equally odious. The boys were too young, the suggestion was untimely, and so on. Later, her prime ministers – Gladstone was one – attempted to involve Edward in colonial administration, but Victoria invariably fought all such proposals. Given the royal parents' dread that their children, especially Edward, should find themselves in an advocate position on any political issue or separated from the immediate dominance of the parents, it was impossible to agree to the Canadian request. Something, however, had to be done; and the Queen agreed that when the Prince of Wales attained sufficient maturity, he would make a state visit to Canada.

It is unlikely that Victoria had any intention of honouring that promise. Had it not been for the strong urging of the Prince Consort, who saw in the Crown the logical link between England and her colonies, and Henry Pelham Clinton, fifth Duke of Newcastle and Secretary for the Colonies, both of whom pressured the Queen to allow Edward to make an appearance in Canada, the historic journey would never have been undertaken. At the time Victoria herself was rather anti-American and shared the indifference of Palmerston, her Prime Minister, towards the dependencies.[4] It had, after all, been less than a hundred years since the country allowed her American colonies to slip away.

In 1860 that indifference was felt by the majority of both of the great parties, who assumed that as the colonies grew more populous and prosperous, they would in the nature of things become independent. The idea of 'Empire', that 'somewhat anomalous whole', as the *Standard* described the phenomenon of England and her dependencies, was in its embryonic stage; and among the Cabinet Ministers only the Duke of Newcastle actively supported the Prince Consort's position that it was the duty of England to strengthen imperial bonds existing between England and her outlying colonies.[5]

The Prince Consort's difficulties in attempting to persuade the Queen to allow Edward to visit Canada were nothing compared with the hostility with which she met the suggestion that he should visit the United States. But Albert, eager to advance the power of the Crown and anxious to improve relations with the United States, persevered; and with the assistance of Lord Lyons, British Minister in Washington, Lord John Russell, Foreign Secretary, and the Duke of Newcastle, he won his point, Victoria gave in, with the face-saving act of recalling that her father had been well received there.[6]

Neither husband nor cabinet could ever have convinced the Queen of the necessity of letting Edward step forward into the royal glow had not deep personal feelings welling up in the Queen made her son's presence all but intolerable to her. The exact nature of those feelings must remain vague; but they found expression in the letters sent to the Princess Royal, which over and over again refer to the shortcomings of 'poor Bertie' and his wretched showing in contrast with handsome, lively, adoring 'Affie', who looked so much like his father and who would never inherit the throne.

Victoria was rapidly approaching that stage in her relations with Edward when she could no longer abide having him near her. Her hostility towards her first-born had grown as he had grown, and the closer his approach to maturity, the more virulent became her feelings. He was a walking reminder of her mortality, a limit to her power, a denial of Albert's pre-eminence, the worm in the apple of her perfection. Nevertheless, to act on these feelings was another matter and likely to arouse equally powerful, equally painful counter-emotions. To send Edward to Canada was to admit what she had been at great pains to deny, that he was old enough and competent enough to claim that share of responsibility that was his by right of birth. But in compensation for that defeat, the trip would take him away for four months, and on his return he would be sent at once to Cambridge. The balance was tipped. She let him go, stipulating that in the United States he must go incognito, assuming the identity of Lord Renfrew, and sleep only in hotels.

The arrangements for the journey were, of course, made with the most scrupulous care. Albert placed the Duke of Newcastle, who within four years was to die of a brain disease, in charge of the Prince and the entourage. The Duke was a predictable choice. A tall, reserved man, severe of countenance and with a huge light red beard, his solemnity of bearing and demeanour were such as to startle one writer into remarking that in comparison with the Duke, Robert Bruce was a frivolous man. Bruce, who was to accompany Edward, had been promoted from the rank of Colonel to that of Major-General the preceding December, a mark of the parents' satisfaction with his services. The other members of the suite were the Earl of St Germans, Lord Steward of the Royal Household, who was the special representative of the Queen; Major Teesdale and Captain Grey, Edward's equerries; Dr Henry Acland of Oxford, the Prince's physician; and two men of the press, Nicholas Arthur Woods, a journalist representing *The Times,* and G. H. Andrews, R.W.S., an artist and journalist representing the *Illustrated London News.*

The disagreements within the royal family concerning the journey were matched by a division of opinion in the country as to the wisdom of the trip. At that time it was widely believed in England that the United States intended to annex Canada, and the anti-American feeling was aggravated by a deep division of opinion over the slavery issue in the States. Finally, the immigration of thousands of Irish into the United States made it appear to many Englishmen that allowing the Prince to enter the young uncouth nation was tantamount to thrusting him into a lions' den. And as has already been mentioned, the government, especially Palmerston, who had become Prime Minister in 1859, saw no advantage in England's attempting to retain her colonies and saw only useless expense in Edward's projected tour. But the Prince Consort's persistence overcame all obstacles; and not only did he get the necessary support for Edward's journey, he also won approval for Prince Alfred to sail for the Cape of Good Hope to lay the foundation stone of the new Cape Town harbour breakwater.[7] The Queen raised no objections to Alfred's trip.

By June all arrangements for Edward's journey had been made, but the arrival of a letter made it necessary to modify these plans. President Buchanan, who had been waiting for the certainty that Edward would be allowed to visit the United States, having been assured on that point by Lord Lyons, wrote on June 4 to the Queen, inviting the Prince of Wales to Washington: 'You may be well assured that everywhere in this country he will be greeted by the American people in such a manner as cannot fail to prove gratifying to your Majesty. In this they will manifest their deep sense of your domestic virtues, as well as their convictions of your merits as a wise, patriotic and constitutional sovereign. Your Majesty's Most Obedient Servant, James Buchanan.'[8]

The tone of this letter may have expressed more warmth of feeling than Buchanan actually felt for Victoria, although his contacts with England had been close. Immediately prior to his being elected to the Presidency in 1856, he was American Minister to Great Britain for three years and helped to smooth over the troubles in British Honduras when the Monroe Doctrine appeared to be in danger of being infringed. He had also visited the Queen at Windsor, where, in his own estimation, he was received with a cold and barren civility.[9]

However, the Queen's response, written from Buckingham Palace on June 22, was even more friendly in tone than Buchanan's and suggested a degree of shared affection quite out of keeping with the evidence. Whether or not one sees Albert's influence at work, the President could not on this occasion protest about coldness: 'My Good Friend: I have been much gratified by the feelings which prompted you to write to me, inviting the Prince of Wales to come to Washington. He intends to return to Canada through the United States and it will give him great pleasure to have an opportunity of testifying to you in person that these feelings are fully reciprocated by him. He will thus be able, at the same time, to mark the respect which he entertains for the Chief Magistrate of a great and powerful State and kindred nation.

'The Prince of Wales will drop all royal state on leaving my dominions, and travel under the name of Lord Renfrew, as he has done when travelling on the continent of Europe.

'The Prince Consort wishes to be kindly remembered to you. I remain ever, your friend, Victoria R.'[10]

The edict on staying in hotels could not withstand the force of a personal invitation from the Chief Executive, and arrangements were made for Edward to remain at the White House during his Washington visit as a very special guest of President Buchanan and his niece, Harriet Lane, who served as his housekeeper. The city of New York extended a similar invitation to the Prince through the agency of Mr Dallas, American Minister in London, who then passed it on to the Queen by way of Lord John Russell. That invitation was also accepted, although concern was expressed about Irish Americans and, oddly in this context, about the safety of American railroads.[11] In March the *New York Times,* expressing its satisfaction over the projected visit of the Prince, hoped that Edward would come to New York but begged that he be spared 'the hospitalities' of the city, which 'consist of a series of annoyances, tortures, and indignities, to which no man ought to be subjected except by due process of law'.[12] Apparently, the Prince had more to dread than violent and hostile Irishmen.

The long process of preparing for the journey ended on the morning of July 9. Edward left Osborne with his mother and father, Princesses Alice and Louise and Princes Arthur and Leopold, Alfred having already sailed for Africa. The family drove together to Trinity Pier at East Cowes, where Edward said goodbye to everyone except his father and boarded the royal yacht, *Victoria and Albert,* for the sail to Plymouth and the waiting *Hero.*[13] Because there was a fair wind and clear weather, the Queen went aboard the *Faery* and accompanied the *Victoria and Albert* for a short distance before turning back to Osborne and blessed peace, the ugly duckling consigned, if not to perdition, at least to the North Atlantic.

At about 7.10 pm, the *Victoria and Albert* entered Plymouth harbour, the arrival being announced by a royal salute from the cannons of the *Ariadne* and the citadel. The yacht was welcomed by the cheers of the crews of the men-of-war and the assembled spectators. Never before had Edward drunk such a sparkling draught; but the journey had only just begun, a triumphal journey during which the roar of adoring crowds filled him with astonished delight.

As soon as the yacht came to anchor, she was boarded by Rear-Admiral Sir T. S. Pasley, acting Commander of the port, and other military men, accompanied by the Corporation of the Borough of Devonport, led by the Mayor, Mr N. Wilson, and the Recorder, Mr C. Saunders. Having received and accepted with thanks the addresses of the Corporation, Edward, delivering a reply of his father's composition, said, 'It shall not be my fault if I fail to convey to our brethren across the Atlantic the feelings entertained by the Queen and the people of England for the descendants of those men and for the countries which they have founded.' Having made a few more comments about the 'great possessions of the Queen', he stepped back and the Corporation withdrew.[14]

Edward said goodbye to his father and went aboard the *Hero*, where his suite was waiting to receive him. Dinner was served in the specially fitted rooms which had been set aside as the royal apartments. At the head of the table sat the eighteen-year-old Prince, while on either side of him were ranged the middle-aged and even older men who were the visible sign of his importance, his protection against the shock and menace of the world and a reminder of his parents' control. The Duke of Newcastle's papers were swollen with memoranda prepared by the Prince Consort on how Edward was to conduct himself, what he should say on various occasions, how the theme of Empire and its link with the Crown should be handled and what his lessons were to be on the voyage out.

Another young man, finding himself so hedged in by age and worthiness, might have sunk into depression. Not so Edward. His experience with worthy men was already extensive. He was neither overawed nor depressed. In fact his spirits soared. He was embarking on an adventure, banishing boredom. He had escaped from White Lodge; and he would soon discover something he had never guessed, nor been allowed to discover – that he possessed the ability to win people's affection and attachment. He would also learn that he had moved to the centre of the stage, that the shouts of greeting which he heard and the cheering were for him and not for his mother – despite some of the editorials to the contrary. People revered the Queen, but they were delighted with the son and frank in their demonstration of that enthusiasm. Edward was cheered not because of his mother's supposed domestic virtue; he was cheered because he was the legendary Prince of Wales, heir apparent to a throne. He was the embodiment of privilege, wealth and power, all that remained in the English speaking world of romance and chivalry; and how deeply that world hungered after the novelty was evident every step of the Prince's way from St John's, Nova Scotia to Portland, Maine.

At seven o'clock the next morning, the *Hero* was ready to leave the Sound. Her officers and crew had been up since four o'clock, readying the ship for sea. Edward rose somewhat later but was on deck to watch the departure. As they passed the royal yacht, the Prince Consort and his suite, standing on the paddle box, waved a farewell to Edward, who went aft to the taffrail to wave in return.[15] For both it was a significant parting. The Prince Consort, waving to his son, might for nearly the last time in his life have felt a mild rush of pride and satisfaction in his son, emotions that, unfortunately, would scarcely survive the year. Four miles off the port, southwest of the Eddystone, the Channel Fleet was waiting for the arrival of the *Hero*. As she and the *Ariadne* approached, the fleet opened into two lines with sails trimmed, allowing the *Hero* to pass between them and take the lead down the Channel.[16]

For two days Edward was seasick; then he recovered and began to take an interest in what was going on around him. One of the first things he asked to see was a ship under full sail at close quarters. Captain Seymour, pleased to indulge his young passenger's fancy and undoubtedly happy to see him recovered, signalled the *Ariadne* to come within speaking distance and checked the speed of the *Hero* by trimming sail. The result was one of those beautiful sights that have all but vanished from the sea. A young midshipman, very close to Edward in age, has left his recollections of the scene from aboard the *Hero*: 'It was a superb thing to show the Prince. As the beautiful frigate came ranging up she lifted to the sea. Her copper shone like burnished gold; above the long line of guns; aloft her taut mast and rigging; her cloud of white canvas as steady as if carved; while above all her long blue pendant soared and flickered upward like a tongue of blue flame.'[17] From the bridge of the *Ariadne*, Captain E. W. Vansittart received the megaphoned compliments of the Prince with a bow and returned them to the Prince and Captain Seymour. The *Hero* resumed full sail, the *Ariadne* swept away to resume her position, and the Prince returned to his lessons.

One of the charges which the Duke of Newcastle bore was to personally instruct the Prince in the geography and political history of Canada, particularly the hostility existing between Catholics and Protestants.[18] Newcastle took his responsibility in this matter seriously; and as soon as Edward was well enough to attend, the maps came out and the studies commenced. General Bruce was astonished to discover

that Edward was taking an interest in the lessons and showing no resentment toward his mentor, prompting Bruce to write 'quite hopefully'
to the Prince Consort.[19]

At this distance, Edward's compliant attitude does not appear to be
remarkable. These lessons had a purpose. Canada lay to the west, and
he was bound there as his mother's official representative. He might
have accounted for his presence aboard the *Hero* by saying, as he had
done years earlier to the Empress Eugénie, that he was not wanted at
home; but no such thought is likely to have troubled him. He saw himself engaged on a serious enterprise. As he would demonstrate over and
over again in those long and frustrating years that lay between him and
the throne, whenever he had a meaningful responsibility to carry out,
he met the challenge with courage and perseverance, cheerfully accepting the rigours attendant on carrying it through.

Whether fantasy or fact, it was regularly said that Queen Victoria
enjoyed fair weather whenever she made a public appearance, and the
'Queen's weather' became a byword for beautiful days. Edward did not
share his mother's good fortune in weather. When he arrived at St
John's, Newfoundland, on the evening of July 23, it was raining in
torrents; and his landing was postponed until noon of the following day.
Coming ashore dressed in his colonel's uniform and wearing the Ribbon
of the Garter, he was greeted by Sir Alexander Bannerman, Governor
of Newfoundland, and escorted to Government House, where a reception was held in his honour and fourteen speeches delivered. In responding, Edward said, in part, 'I am charged by the Queen to convey to
you the assurance of the deep concern she has ever felt in this interesting
portion of her dominions.'[20]

Whatever excitement Edward felt at landing in North America, it
was not conveyed to his parents, to whom he wrote that first day ashore,
'The Governor, who is rather an odd man and about 75, received me
very kindly, and the Government House is very comfortable. St John's
is a very picturesque seaport town, and its cod fisheries are its staple
produce.'[21] It must have been a very disappointing letter, and there is
a distinct possibility it was intended to be so. The Duke of Newcastle
sent a note to the Queen that same day expressing pleasure with
Edward's conduct; and Bruce with practised nastiness wrote, 'H.R.H.
acquitted himself admirably, and seems pleased with everything,
himself included.'[22]

The procedures followed at St John's for receiving and entertaining
the Prince became the form followed throughout his Canadian journey.
Beginning with an informal welcome at quayside or station, the Prince
would then attend a formal reception, at which he would be introduced
to all the local government officials and as many other guests as could
reasonably be greeted. He would then have a ride around the city or

1. 'The Royal Road to Learning': from *Punch*, October 1859
By permission of the British Museum

2. Edward in the Uniform of a Colonel: from *Harper's Weekly*, July 1860:
from *Harper's Monthly Magazine*, April 1885.
By permission of *Harper's Magazine*

countryside, dine privately and in the evening attend a ball. It is an interesting fact that Edward was not allowed to attend any formal dinners during the trip. The reason for the ban is not clear, but it is possible that either he was thought to be too inexperienced to be able to carry out the task of making after-dinner speeches or that the drinking after dinner would be dangerous. The thinking was probably tortuous and of the same order that made it a rule that while in the United States he stayed only in hotels, a stipulation the Queen frequently placed on Edward's travels throughout her life.

It is unlikely that Edward was disturbed by the ban on dinners. After all, he had suffered through his share of those at Oxford. What was allowed and what gave him immense delight were the balls. He attended his first one at St John's, and he threw himself into the affair with all the charm and liveliness that he possessed in such abundance. His enthusiasm was irresistible, and he won the hearts of those present by mixing freely with the company and dancing not only with the wives and daughters of the officials but with the wives and daughters of the fishermen as well.[23]

The *Illustrated London News* wrote of the ball that the Prince made a very favourable impression with his 'unpretending and genial disposition', adding without comment that 'the noblemen who attended his Royal Highness did not mingle in the festivities of the dance'.[24]

Edward never was nor did he ever profess to be a democrat; but he did like people, and their class was no bar to his pleasure. Although he would, later in life, be unyielding in his expectations that his person be held in proper respect, he had the country gentleman's confidence and casualness, being as ready to dance with one of his tenant's daughters as with a duchess. When he was able to do so in later life, he chose his men friends from widely differing backgrounds. He was an aristocrat, but he was not a snob. Aboard the *Hero* he immediately let it be known that he wished to be addressed Sir, rather than your Royal Highness. He was discovering his gift for putting people at their ease without losing his dignity. It was a valuable talent, and he set about to perfect it.

Practically the entire population of Newfoundland had come to St John's to see the Prince, and he pleased everyone by making himself conspicuous. The wife of the Archdeacon of St John's wrote to relatives in England that Edward had captured the hearts of the inhabitants: 'His appearance is very much in his favour, and his youth and royal dignified manners and bearing seem to have touched all hearts, for there is scarcely a man or a woman who can speak of him without tears. The rough fishermen and their wives are quite wild about him, and we hear of nothing but their admiration. Their most frequent exclamation is, "God bless his pretty face and send him a good wife!" '[25] Another comment made frequently about his appearance was that he bore a remarkable resemblance to the likeness of Victoria stamped on coins.

On July 30, Edward landed at Halifax, Nova Scotia, having paused briefly at Charlottetown, Prince Edward Island, for a wet and dismal day of sightseeing. On Prince Edward Island he began to trace his grandfather's footsteps. The island, originally named St John's, was in 1799 renamed Prince Edward Island in honour of Prince Edward, as the Duke of Kent was then styled. A huge crowd awaited the Prince of Wales in Halifax, and the streets were decorated with colourful arches. Before he was out of Canada, he and his suite would be thoroughly weary of arches. He was greeted by the usual officials with speeches to present; but in addition to them, 3,500 school children, dressed in white and blue, sang 'God Save the Queen'.

Even today Newfoundland is *terra incognita* to most Canadians, and it was not until he arrived in Nova Scotia that Edward was thought to have truly arrived in America. Here he encountered for the first time American newsmen, who had been assigned by the major newspapers to report his activities; and it was during Edward's Canadian visit that press telegrams first came to be used to any extent. One New York reporter, determined to have instant access to his home office, transmitted to his paper long chapters from the Gospel According to St Matthew and the Book of Revelations in order to monopolize the wires while he was gathering material for his daily report on the royal journey![26]

The Prince of Wales mania, which, soon after, infected the United States, had seized Canada. The whole country, 'from Halifax to Lake Huron, and almost from Labrador to Lake Erie resounds only with preparations for the Prince's visit', one journalist wrote, describing the obsession. Newspapers were filled with acrostics on his name, anecdotes of his childhood or promises of his glorious future. His picture turned up in pork and bean advertisements and as an advertising attraction for cider. You could not even sit down to a meal in a restaurant, the writer insisted, without having his portrait loom dimly from beneath the gravy. There were Prince's boots, Prince's coats and Prince's umbrellas. The whole nation was bedecked with coronets and feathers.[27]

Edward loved it all. He had no lessons, no worries; and he had found a country wholly lacking in archaeological treasures. The only 'ruin' he was compelled to view was the Duke of Kent's Lodge near Halifax. His grandfather had lived there for a time when he was Commander-in-Chief of the British forces in Canada. Nothing remained of the buildings except the rotunda beneath which the royal band played for that most music loving of princes. Edward broke a piece of sweetbriar from the ground where the lodge had stood and sent it to his mother.[28]

In Halifax for the first time, Edward encountered some public resentment. The stated cause of the irritation was financial, but a sense of class feeling still lingers on the pages recording the squabble. The *Halifax Arcadian Recorder* voiced the complaint, choosing the preparations for the Prince's ball as the target of its attack, angrily stigmatizing them as 'something which will stick in the crop of the people for a long time'. The paper went on to accuse the wealthy men of the community of wishing to display themselves and their 'fair Friends' before the Prince. That being the case, the paper insisted, those same men should have paid for the affair. Instead, they had turned it into a 'pay ball' and persuaded the government to take £1,000 'of the people's money' out of the provincial treasury to cover expenses.[29] There is no direct attack on the Prince, but the implication is made that the common people have little share in the festivities attending the reception of royal persons and should not be expected to pay for their entertainment. Nevertheless, the ball at Halifax went off without any unpleasantness; and nowhere in the city was Edward exposed to critical comment.

Having spent a month in the maritime provinces, Edward sailed for Quebec, entering one of the most politically sensitive regions of Canada, where the French-speaking population gave more allegiance to France than to England and little enough to either. Fiercely independent in political matters and militantly aggressive in their Catholicism, the city was and remains the embodiment of French-American culture and the heart of Lower Canada. In no other North American city, with the possible exception of New Orleans, is the European atmosphere so powerfully present. When Quebec fell to the British, it was a purely military defeat. Culturally and spiritually the city remained defiantly itself, its people building a subtle and complex society, shaped by two great forces, their inherited civilization and the immense wilderness stretching north from their very walls.

Disembarking under the towering cliffs, Edward, with the Duke of Newcastle at his side, braced for trouble, met the official delegation and was driven into the city, where Newcastle immediately noted the French Tricolor flying side by side with the Union Jack on the towers of the Roman Catholic Cathedral. The Duke asked the Roman Catholic Archbishop of Quebec to replace the Tricolor with St George's Cross, a request that was cheerfully granted, the French Catholics having made their point.[30]

By one of those ironies of fate, Edward's efforts to show every consideration to the Catholic sensibilities in Quebec laid the groundwork for severe trouble later in the trip. In order to placate religious feeling, Edward visited all the major Catholic churches in Quebec, balancing those visits with an equal number of visits to Protestant churches. Rumours, however, were hastily despatched west out of Quebec with the story that Edward had gone only to Catholic churches, that he had participated in ceremonies in which he had been attended by 100 priests, that the Host had been carried before him in processions, and other misrepresentations of a similar order, likely to offend the Protestant population of Upper Canada, especially the Irish Protestants. Although nothing definite can be stated, the rumours may have been deliberately circulated by the enemies of the Cartier-Macdonald government, who were anxious to discredit the government and sow dissension.

It is interesting that once again, and relatively soon after his visit with the Pope, Edward was being accused of pro-Catholic leanings. What is equally ironic about the efforts of the Prince to placate Catholic feeling is that they were all scuttled by Newcastle's refusal to allow Edward to address the Roman Catholic hierarchy of the province as 'My Lords' in his formal speech to them. By that single omission he offended the entire Roman Catholic community of Quebec.[31] It was the kind of error that Edward, later in life, would not have allowed to occur. He was listening, watching and learning; and he was rapidly forming an understanding of the importance in human relations of preserving the dignity of those with whom one hopes to reach a mutual understanding. The 'My Lords' would have been a small price to pay for the good wishes of the Catholic clergy of Quebec.

On August 24, Edward reached Montreal by train. The pace of his activities was quickening, as evidenced by the array of duties he had to perform in Montreal, the first, and most important of which, was the opening of the Victoria Bridge. At Montreal his suite was enlarged again by the arrival of two young men of his own age, Lord Hinchingbroke, one of the boys who had been an Eton playmate at Windsor ten years earlier, and Charles George Eliot, youngest son of the Earl of St Germans. Their arrival provided Edward with welcome relief from the unvaried companionship of men so much his senior.

Fortunately August 25 broke fair; and arrangements were hastened for the dedication of the bridge, a two-part ceremony involving laying a foundation stone on the Canadian side of the span and then going to the middle of the bridge to drive the final rivets. In a sedate ceremony lacking in surprises, the cornerstone was put down under Edward's supervision; then the dedicating party boarded a train, drawn by a wood-burning engine, for the ride to the centre of the bridge.

A work crew was waiting for the Prince; and as soon as the official party reached the exact centre of the bridge, the workmen began hammering in the final rivets. At last the men stepped away from their work; and in a thickening pall of smoke from the train, Edward advanced, gripped his hammer and energetically drove in the silver rivet that completed the bridge. As soon as the rivet was in, Edward dropped the hammer and joined the stumbling rush back to the train to escape the smoke. It was a ragged conclusion to what had been intended as solemn ceremonies.[32]

In Montreal Edward stayed in the home of Sir John Rose, Governor; and spent his few free hours in happy conversation with the family, with whom he had formed an immediate friendship.[33] In company with his entire entourage, he witnessed an Indian lacrosse game between sixty Algonquins and the same number of Iroquois, as well as war dances and other Indian entertainments.[34] The high point of the visit was, of course, the ball. Of the twenty-one dances, Edward danced twenty with the greatest energy, singing along with the orchestra when it played his favourite tunes.[35] The supper tables were fitted with fountains of champagne and jets of eau de cologne. To the great delight of Montreal society, Edward danced until 4 am. One imagines that Newcastle, Bruce, Lyons and company were less entertained.

By the time Edward reached Montreal, the New World had begun to know him a little and to like what it saw. One of the striking aspects of the Prince's relationship with his subjects prior to his journey and with the men of the press, who in the ensuing years would do so much to mould his public image, was how little was known about him. Writers found it impossible to refer to his favourite sports, pastimes, friends or even interests. It might be said that he had none; and that assertion would, to a disturbing degree, have been true. But the writers lacked the knowledge to say even that much. Before he left England, a story had circulated alleging that he was of a grave demeanour and physically delicate, making it unlikely that he would shine at social functions.[36] The rumour preceded him to Canada; but his obvious delight in jokes and banter and his easy success in social situations thoroughly dispelled those misconceptions before he had reached Montreal. As for the other rumour that he was not interested in women, it was evaporated by the warmth of his frank attentiveness to every pretty woman whom he met.

He was not, of course, allowed to speak with reporters; neither was he able, despite stories circulated later about midnight escapades in New York shorehouses, to break the close watch of his guardians, whose diligent attention kept him away from the world as effectively as they kept the world away from him. But he could not be kept entirely isolated. He was observed chatting amiably with those people allowed inside the magic circle. It was noted that he was relaxed and easy in his manner and that his general bearing was pleasing. The reporter for the *Illustrated London News* wrote that Edward's journey as far as Montreal was marked with very favourable signs and that his personal life had come to please him: 'Emancipating himself from the trammels and paraphernalia of Royalty, the Prince of Wales has thrown himself into the innocent gaiety of social life, with the fullest intention of making things agreeable to himself and pleasant to those who surround him.' The writer was very serious in his conviction that the trip was of the greatest political importance and equally convinced that it would have a profound influence on Edward. 'It would be strange, indeed, if his Royal Highness returned home without having made a rapid and gainful stride toward that manhood on the verge of which he stands.'[37]

At the same time, the *New York Times* printed an editorial discussing the Prince which was so pronounced in its tone as to be almost eccentric. Praising Edward for the 'gentleness of his demeanour and the cultivated yet kind refinement of his manners', the article attributes these qualities, which have won the Prince so many admirers in such a short time, to the 'inspiring influence' his mother has exerted on his character. 'The purity and elevation of thought and feeling', the writer continued, 'which the Queen has engrafted on the mind of the Prince it is which gives that charm to his presence which is the result of such highly cultivated moral beauty.'[38]

On September 1, Edward laid the foundation stone of the Parliament buildings in Ottawa. Fifty-six years later, in 1916, the building burned and the Duke of Connaught, Edward's brother, then Governor-General of Canada, used the same stone to lay the foundation of the new buildings.[39] On the following day, the Prince and his companions had the bizarre and dramatic experience of riding a timber shoot on the Ottawa River. The purpose of the shoot was to move logs past a stretch of falls where the force of water driving onto the rocks would have smashed them into kindling. In the midst of a dozen companions, all dressed in frock coats and top hats, Edward clambered onto the raft and sat down, taking a firm grip on the narrow seat. 'I wish,' Edward lamented, stepping ashore when the dramatic ride was over, soaked and beaming with pleasure and excitement, 'that it had been a mile longer.'[40]

On September 3, Edward left Ottawa for Chats Portage where navigation of the Ottawa is broken by another set of beautiful falls. Edward had a brief sampling of the rigours of river travel, and was marched around another falls; then westward to Arnprior, where they boarded carriages for the short ride to Almonte, to the south of the river, where a train was waiting to carry them to Kingston and the Orangemen troubles.[41]

There is a variety of explanations on record as to what provoked the trouble between the Irish Protestants and the Prince of Wales's party; but, basically, the answer is religious bigotry and political opportunism. Kingston and Toronto were centres of the Orangemen factions, and the membership of the lodges had bitterly resented the enthusiastic reception given Edward by the Catholics of Lower

Canada.[42] The stories which had preceded Edward from Quebec concerning his attendance at Catholic ceremonials and riding under
Catholic arches were all believed at Kingston.[43] As a consequence, the
Orangemen in Kingston were determined that Edward should stand
as the heir of William of Orange, their hero. To make the final approach to town, Edward had boarded the steamer *Kingston*. The
reception and celebrations had been planned well in advance; a private
house had been reserved for Edward, and everything appeared to be
in order. However, as the *Kingston* steamed toward the landing, Newcastle saw that he was taking his royal charge into a hornets' nest.

The Orangemen were out in force. The Mayor of Kingston, a Mr
Strange, had given his support to the Orange lodges and was prepared
to demand that the Prince take part in a parade in which the lodge
men would march in their full regalia. In addition, two Orange arches
had been raised in the main street of the town, with the intention of
making Edward pass under them. One of the arches, covered with
orange paper, was decorated with portraits of the Prince of Wales and
of Garibaldi. Under Edward's portrait was printed the motto, 'The
faith of my forefathers and mine'.

The Duke took a brief look at the situation and sent a note ashore,
datelined 'Off Kingston, Sept. 5', refusing to allow the Prince to take
part in such a partisan affair. The Mayor countered by refusing to
board the steamer to give the address of welcome. The ludicrous proceedings were made more so by the fact that a stiff wind was buffeting
the steamer so badly that the captain was obliged to take his boat away
from the landing and steam in behind a small island in front of the
town while negotiations went forward. The effect was to give the appearance that the Prince was hiding. The town band retaliated by
playing 'Boyne Water' and 'Croppies Lie Down' as further provocation.

No compromise could be reached; and the Duke ordered the captain
to go on to Belleville, creating a breach between Newcastle and
the Canadian Minister J. A. Macdonald, whose constituency was
Kingston. Sharp words were exchanged, but the Duke was not moved.
Meanwhile, two firebrands from Kingston, Flannigan and Robinson,
hurried their bands, men and banners aboard a train and rode ahead to
Belleville, arriving ahead of the Prince and forming another procession.
This time the Duke took one look at the shape of things and ordered the
boat on to Coburg. Flannigan and Robinson, zealous to the end, took
to the train again, determined to force a procession on the Prince. This
time, however, the railway officials delayed the train so long at various
stops that Edward had reached Coburg, enjoyed his reception and was
on his way to Toronto before the Kingston men could reach him.[44]
At first it appeared that there was going to be serious trouble at Toronto

with the Orange faction there, but a compromise was struck and serious unpleasantness avoided.

Official visits out of the way, Edward went at once to the Niagara Falls and was enormously impressed by them. For the first time the Falls were illuminated with Bengal lights, a kind of firework that burned with an intense flame. As was everyone who saw it, Edward was astounded by the sight.[45] Edward could not see enough of the Falls; and on September 17 he crossed to the American side to look at them from there, marking the only time he was on United States soil officially as the Prince of Wales. His greatest treat, however, was watching Blondin cross the Falls on a tightrope. Thirty-six years old, slight of build, five feet six inches tall, Blondin was probably the finest tightrope performer the world had ever seen. He walked over the thundering cataracts of Niagara Falls and back again on stilts, carrying a man on his back, as casually as his audience strolled their pavements.[46]

At Hamilton Edward brought his official duties to an end with a speech in which he said that he was about to visit 'that remarkable land which claims with us a common ancestry, and in whose extraordinary progress every Englishman feels a common interest'.[47] He was tired, and the speech reflects the general weariness of the party, especially Newcastle, who generally avoided such banalities in framing the Prince's public statements. The *New York Daily Tribune* correspondent, who had been with the suite since Halifax, wrote just prior to Edward's entry into the United States that Edward would not have cause to regret the end of the seven-week ordeal. Although it was seldom reported and more seldom noted in the official accounts, Edward had been, as the writer put it, 'the target of a species of coarse ribaldry and stale, untidy rhetoric'. On September 19, his last full day in Canada, he inaugurated a waterworks in Hamilton, gave a speech and attended a ball.

Edward crossed from Canada to the United States on September 20, on the Detroit and Milwaukee Ferry steamer *Windsor* in company with the Governor of Michigan, Mayor Bull of Detroit and fifty other dignitaries. The river was crowded with brightly lighted boats, festooned with lanterns. A crowd of 30,000 met Edward at the landing, many of whom surged aboard the steamer, creating a crush so intense that several of the official party were literally squeezed off the side of the boat into the river, from which they were fished out with much rough good humour. One observer remarked rather sardonically that the interest could not have been greater had George Washington come back to life.[48]

The following morning, Edward got into an open baroche drawn by four white horses to ride through the town, but the crowds were so immense that for a considerable period of time he could not move.

Preserving his good humour, he stood up at intervals and bowed to the crowd, which cheered him again and again. One journalist, wearied and harried, observed testily that 'nobody expects an American crowd to preserve composure and serenity when the least provocation to excitement offers itself.'[49] Eventually, the Prince's carriage broke free, and he was able to look at a few streets before boarding the train for Chicago.

At the time Edward entered the United States, the country was a confusing mixture of gentility and barbarism. To travel from Boston, Massachusetts, to St Louis, Missouri, was to pass from a world of lighted cobbled streets, theatres, libraries and civilized grace to a city that had grown from a wilderness fur trading post into a metropolis in a matter of thirty years. Sprawling and shanty built, its streets lost in mud or dust, according to the season, populated by a constantly changing conglomeration of businessmen, tradesmen, buffalo and Indian hunters, eastern farmers on the move west, river gamblers, slave-owning plantation owners and deerskin-clad mountain men enjoying a drunken spree, St Louis typified the violent, tumultuous life of the western United States.

Chicago, although it had a population of 100,000, was raw and unfinished with its shanties, mud streets and frontier roughness. In Cincinnati Edward's suite was appalled to find pigs wallowing in the streets. More important, perhaps, than the surface crudities of national life was the background of the approaching elections which would take Abraham Lincoln into the White House and plunge the nation into the 'Irrepressible Conflict', the American Civil War.

The coming storm was not unheralded. A newspaper editorial, written in late July, anticipated with remarkable accuracy what was approaching: 'Many observers of tolerable accuracy and who are under no special imputation of lunacy, believe that Mr Lincoln will be the next President of the United States. Unconscious of the wreck and ruin which his election must inevitably occasion, the Republican Party, with suicidal energy and with frightful cheerfulness, is pressing forward to a triumph which must bring along with it anarchy, revolution, disintegration, oceans of blood, and a mortality mocking the achievements of the palmiest pestilence.'[50]

The chief issue in the nation was that 'peculiar institution' of the South, slavery. Sectional differences over tariffs and trade may be raised to explain the growing hostility between North and South, but they are of minor consequence. What was tearing the United States in half was slavery. States, cities, towns and families were being fragmented by the conflict. It had entered the question of where the transcontinental railroad should be laid, which territories should become states and whether they should come in slave or free. Among the

Abolitionists of the North, the Fugitive Slave Act of 1850, which allowed slave owners to pursue runaway slaves into free states, was a hot iron on the conscience. Wherever one looked in the United States the threat of Southern secession loomed and the injustice of slavery was a shadow on the land.

As recently as October 1859, the anguish and mounting hysteria had found expression in John Brown's raid on the federal arsenal in the town of Harper's Ferry, Virginia. Brown, accompanied by thirteen whites and five blacks, set in motion his scheme to found an abolitionist territory in the Appalachian mountains and conduct a guerrilla war against the slave-holding states, with the final end in mind of raising a slave revolt across the South. He failed in that audacious plan; but brought to his trial lying wounded on a cot, Brown conducted himself with such courage and dignity that the state of Virginia, in hanging him, gave the anti-slavery forces a hero and martyr.

In a widely circulated letter to his children, Brown wrote of his approaching execution that he was as content 'to die for God's eternal truth on the scaffold as in any other way'. He was hanged on December 2 1859. Despite the widespread repudiation of Brown's action by the northern press and politicians, Ralph Waldo Emerson struck the deeper note when he wrote of the dead man, 'That new saint...will make the gallows glorious like the cross'. Brown was dead; but as the Civil War marching song said of him, his soul went marching on. It was marching while Edward travelled east across the country, marvelling at the vastness and the emptiness of the land. It was marching a country to war. Speaking in defence of Brown in the Concord Lyceum, Henry David Thoreau caught the spirit informing the nation when he said, 'I do not wish to kill nor to be killed, but I can foresee circumstances in which both these things would be by me unavoidable.' And so they proved to be, if not for Thoreau personally, then for many thousands of other American men from both North and South.

In the meantime, Edward was headed for Chicago where a crowd of 50,000 turned out to greet him, marched along with him in growing numbers to his hotel and cheered him loudly as he entered. Edward was met at the station by the Mayor, 'Long John' Wentworth, whose size was such that Edward's five feet four inch frame came about half way up Wentworth's waistcoat, a contrast highly pleasing to the newsmen. One wrote, 'It is believed the Prince shook some of his [Wentworth's] hand and addressed a few complimentary remarks to his lower waistcoat button', adding that when the Mayor stepped out of the railway car, 'he looked pleased all over, which is saying a great deal in a few words'.[51] Wentworth accompanied Edward to the Richmond House and had almost as much trouble as Mayor Bull had experienced in getting his guest safely housed. At about one o'clock Edward responded to the continued presence of the throng outside his hotel by coming outside on the balcony to exhibit himself by marching up and down, one writer noted in disgust, 'like a dwarf at a county fair'.[52]

In Chicago there was a great deal of trouble, probably unnecessary, over how Edward was to be addressed, Lord Lyons and Newcastle holding out for a strict observance of the incognito and everybody else cheerfully ignoring it and addressing Edward as the Prince of Wales. Some of the stress of the situation may have descended on Edward, who began to react sharply to the pressure of the journey. He suddenly developed a severe headache and other symptoms of exhaustion, which were not reduced by the singing that went on under his windows for the greater part of the night. It was immediately determined that his itinerary should be interrupted long enough to provide the Prince with some rest from the constant strain of public engagements.

Arrangements were made for Edward to spend a few days hunting on the prairie at the hamlet of Dwight's Crossing, where the game was reported to be abundant. Dwight had not existed six years before and had mushroomed into existence with the arrival of the railroad. The cost of land had climbed from ninety cents to twenty-five dollars an acre. The settlement had a saloon and a Temperance League and every encouragement for a bright future. As soon as Edward had settled into the modest house where he was to stay and which had been rented from a Mr Spencer, he hurried out to the stubble fields with his shotgun, but all he managed to shoot was an owl. Fortunately, the next day was livelier, and fourteen brace of quail and four rabbits were killed.[53]

An incident occurred the second day that must have amused, puzzled and embarrassed Edward and his party. The Prince approached a farmhouse at about noon, and one of the group suggested stopping for a rest and a look at the prairie home. Edward agreed, and as they were advancing up the path towards the house, the front door was suddenly flung open and the farmer, with a welcoming wave of his arm and a loud voice, invited everyone in – with one exception: 'Not you, Newcastle,' he shouted. 'I have been a tenant of yours, and have sworn that you shall never set foot on my land.'[54] Following a hasty and confused consultation, the entire group turned and walked away.

The country through which Edward was moving was still primitive and its people explosive. St Louis, at that time the very heart of the Middle West and its centre of culture and urban life, retained many of the qualities of a frontier town. Whether moved by the approaching visit of the Prince of Wales or exhorted to action by one of its spiritual leaders is uncertain, but a few weeks before Edward's arrival, a group of St Louis citizens decided to 'clean out' a section of the city. The area was rich in saloons, gambling halls, houses of prostitution and decrepit tenements occupied by 'a number of degraded men and women, who have been a constant pest to the whole community, providing prisoners for the calaboose and workhouse, and furnishing countless examples of immorality and vice'.[55]

A mob of six or seven thousand gathered and attacked the quarter, smashing windows, driving out the inhabitants, throwing everything from inside the buildings into the streets and burning it. Once the rooms of the prostitutes were reached, sheets from their beds and underwear from their closets were carried into the street, nailed to clothesline poles and borne triumphantly as banners in the forefront of the advancing army. Foolishly, the police attempted to intervene but quickly repented and drew back, confining themselves to the fringes of the mêlée. With bonfires burning brightly, with corruption purged, the crowds cheered the defeat of Sin and went home. While Garibaldi marched on tyranny, St Louis marched on vice. The next morning the inhabitants of the district went briskly to work carrying off the wrecked and charred furniture, replacing the smashed glass.

A newsman wrote of Edward's experience there: 'It was the freest and best enjoyed visit of all that he has made, and I am sure that the blandishment of cities, however sumptuous and artificially regal they may be, will give him no such real and unaffected delight as that which he found in the quiet seclusion of the little prairie village.'[56] Edward may have enjoyed hunting, but he loved dancing, and beyond everything else he needed to be surrounded by people. The journalistic distortion is, however, typical of much American writing in that period as well as later on the supposed attractions of frontier or near-frontier life, a life which was, in point of fact, characterized by deprivation, loneliness, boredom and wretchedness. Dwight's Crossing had nothing to offer Edward that an afternoon's shooting did not exhaust.

The writing is of a piece with the *New York Times* editorial lavishing praise on Victoria. Edward, like his mother, was being fitted to a set of pre-cut conventions, designed to show them possessing characters and styles of living that had little to do with the real people. It was a dangerous tendency that the press was determined to cultivate. In the coming years it would work to Edward's grave disadvantage. The Prince delighted in people, activity, social involvement and dreaded above all other things being alone. A less contemplative and solitary man could hardly have lived. It is astonishing that those who wrote of him could not bring themselves to say as much. Unable to come very close to Edward, the press satisfied itself with treating him in general as a ceremonial figure, concentrating on peripheral events and persons for colour.

In comparison with Chicago, his reception in St Louis was subdued. Only the very poor of the city met him at the station, quietly curious, poking their heads into his carriage as he set out for Barnum's Hotel. The next morning the Mayor came to escort the Prince to the Great Fair. Edward was whirled away to join in celebrating the region's hundred-year-old struggle to tame the wilderness.[57] The American novelist Winston Churchill recorded the Prince's visit to the fair in his novel *The Crisis* in the chapter 'How the Prince Came'.

The fact that an enterprising Yankee had followed closely behind the Mayor's carriage with a wagon advertising his clothing store was only one of the things that offended Newcastle and others in the Prince's suite. While Edward liked Americans for their bonhomie, their frankness and geniality, his staff were often repelled by the informality they encountered.

They were also upset by the poverty in places like St Louis and the roughness of American manners.[58] When they were served lunch at the fair, they were taken into a wooden shed where trestle tables had been put together and heaped with joints of beef, mutton and piles of buffalo tongue, surrounded by huge jugs of beer. The Americans attacked the meat with pocket knives, shocking the Duke, who called them 'ravenous animals'. The Prince was not in the least troubled and certainly not disgusted. He had already begun to develop an appetite of considerable size and he understood that eating was a serious business. He entered into the spirit of the lunch with gusto.[59]

Boredom threatened Edward on the journey from Cincinnati to Washington; and he described the trip to Pittsburg as 'a long and fatiguing railway journey devoid of any interest'.[60] These attacks of boredom were not the vapours of a spoiled and over-indulged youngster. Characterized by depression and anxiety, they were to menace him throughout his life and may, in part, be traced to his early and still-to-be-resumed experiences of being cut off from intercourse with people his own age or allowed any meaningful activity that was not a form of drudgery. Locked up in the train with his suite, the old sense of imprisonment returned, and he spent some unhappy hours struggling with his own depression.

On October 3, Edward arrived in Washington, having visited Pittsburgh and Harrisburg, and was greeted by a crowd of 1,000 people. Conveyed to the White House, Edward was introduced to President Buchanan and his niece, Harriet Lane, and immediately made welcome. The formal reception began about noon and passed off very smoothly and comfortably, except that the Englishmen, including the Prince, were startled and offended to see men spitting. Killing flies with a squirt of tobacco juice was at that time something of a national pastime.

Edward was disappointed to discover that the President's scruples would not allow him to permit dancing in the White House, not even on the rugs. But there was so much to do and to see that Edward was far from being desolate. There was a succession of receptions and levées and similar diversions. He made an extensive tour of the government buildings and was especially impressed with the Capitol and the Federal Office Buildings. He wrote to his mother that the government offices were very efficiently arranged: 'All the Public Offices are in the same building, and we might easily take some hints for our own buildings which are so very bad.'[61]

On October 5 Edward accompanied the President and Miss Lane on an excursion down the Potomac to Mount Vernon. It was an historic occasion, producing a flood of emotion in both the United States and England. Buchanan wrote to Victoria that the visit 'to the tomb of Washington, and the simple but solemn ceremonies at this consecrated spot will become an historical event and cannot fail to exert a happy influence on the kindred people of the two countries'.[62] Victoria replied with equal warmth. Much of the anti-American feeling in England was dissipated by the visit and the continuous evidence of affection in America's treatment of the Prince.

The following year Cambridge University set 'The Prince of Wales At the Tomb of Washington' as the subject of the English poem competition, which was won by Frederick W. H. Myers: it begins

> Behold he reared a race and ruled them not,
> And he shall rule a race he did not rear:
> Warrior and Prince, their former feud forgot,
> Have found a meeting here.[63]

Edward's own written response to the event took the form of a letter to his mother, in which he said only that the house itself was falling rapidly and unfortunately into decay and that they had seen all the rooms, including the one in which Washington had died. It was yet another of his opaque communications in which the writer carefully did not give himself away, 'unfortunately' being the only word that gave any clue to his personal feelings about the event. His reticence in his letters to his parents was both defensive and retaliatory. By never writing the kind of letter they wished him to write, he took subtle revenge on them for past offences; and by hiding his feelings from their gaze, he preserved his privacy and denied them grounds on which to attack him.

The pressures being generated in American politics could not be entirely diverted away from the Prince; and those that reached him came in the form of strong Southern demands that, as a representative of the British Government, formal or informal, he should visit the slave-holding states. By the visit the Southern faction hoped to make a favourable impression on public opinion in England. After much uneasy consultation, Lord Lyons and Newcastle unwisely accepted the invitation of some Southern representatives to visit Richmond. It was far less than the Southerners wanted, and generated resentment among them. They had hoped to take Edward on an extensive tour of 'show place' plantations to demonstrate how humane and paternalistic the system of slavery was.

A great slave sale had been scheduled to take place in Richmond; but when news reached the city of Edward's approaching visit, it was immediately cancelled. Edward arrived in Richmond on a Saturday evening and went directly to the Ballard House. There were large crowds in the streets, and the atmosphere was sufficiently hostile to prevent Edward from emerging from his rooms until the following morning, when he left Ballard House to attend church. No police protection was offered him, with the result that he and his party were badly jostled. The mood of the crowd became increasingly sullen as he emerged from church and went to view the capitol. He and his companions were cursed constantly, and there was a threatened incursion into his apartments.[64] Following his visit to the government buildings, his guides made a final effort to involve him with the slavery issue by suggesting he visit the slave quarters at Haxhall's plantation. Edward, however, had made up his mind that he had gone as far as he was going in the business of placating Southern feeling and flatly refused to get out of his carriage, leaving Newcastle and Lyons to pacify his hosts as best they could and insisting on a quick return to Washington, showing by his decision more sense than his advisers.[65]

From Washington, Edward went to Baltimore and then to Philadelphia in a train decked out in American and British flags and drawn by a locomotive called the *George Washington*. On his first night in Philadelphia, Edward walked unrecognized through the streets, enjoying the celebrations of an election night in an American city. Many of the people in the streets were looking for him, but he passed unnoticed. With the election of a Republican Governor in Pennsylvania, ensuring Lincoln's entry into the White House by providing the deciding vote in the electoral college, something else passed unremarked on that night. The spirits of Daniel Webster and Henry Clay, both of whom had died in 1852 and who had been the embodiment of all the forces, North and South, for compromise and peaceful solutions, drifted quietly out of American national life, relinquishing the land to the keeping of John Brown's more martial ghost.

After Edward had left Washington, Buchanan wrote to Queen Victoria, 'In our domestic circle he has won all hearts. His free and ingenuous intercourse with myself evinced both a kind heart and a good understanding.'[66] The affection expressed appears to be genuine and, with the exception of the Richmond experience, increased among the general population the longer the visit continued. An indication of the state of popular feeling was the reception given Edward in New York. Probably nothing more tumultuous would happen to him again. He received the tribute of the Indian nation and passed through the grandeur of his coronation; but for size, noise, enthusiasm and sustained celebration, Edward's reception in New York was unique.

It began when he stepped off the *Harriet Lane* at South Amboy on the afternoon of October 11. Lines of soldiers and troops of horse were drawn up at the plaza of immigration; and as he stepped ashore, the Twelfth Regiment band struck up the English national anthem. Mayor Wood strode forward to welcome Edward to the city and to conduct him to the waiting carriage. The reception he received was astounding. There was an enthusiasm and a sense of anticipation in the city that was all but a madness. The Duke attributed the mood of the people to their love for the Queen and then later to the growing affection of Americans for England.[67] Both explanations were wildly off the mark. The reception was for Edward – for that day, that week, he was New York's darling.

From the Garden to the Park, the streets, windows and roofs were jammed with people. Banners flew over the streets carrying mottoes which read, 'Welcome Albert Edward', 'Welcome Lord Renfrew', 'Welcome Victoria's Royal Son', and 'God Save the Queen'. At the City Hall Edward and his suite mounted a raised platform, accompanied by Mayor Wood and Alderman Boole. All the troops then passed in review with colours flying and bands playing. Behind every company tramped a pathetic black man, dressed in tattered clothes, carrying a water pail and a dipper, a mute reminder in the midst of celebration of the nation's shame.

Once the marching was over, Edward re-entered his carriage and was driven to the Fifth Avenue Hotel through enormous throngs of people, who deluged him with flowers. Edward entered his hotel by a private door on Twenty-third Street and barely reached his rooms before collapsing from exhaustion. As had occurred in Chicago, he developed a violent headache and had to take to his bed. Hopes for rest were dashed, however, by the throngs of people who gathered in the streets outside the hotel and kept up a constant roar of cheering and singing and calling for the Prince to come out. Edward was obliged to make an appearance at the window and receive the cheers of the crowd. It was nearly morning before it grew quiet enough for him to sleep.[68]

The high point of his visit to the city was a ball; but from the beginning the arrangements for the gala were completed under the greatest difficulties, not because there was opposition to the Corporation's sponsoring the dance, but because the demand to meet the Prince on a social occasion was so overwhelming that it could not possibly be gratified. After much hesitation the committee in charge of the preparations settled on the Old Academy of Music as being the most suitable building for the ball. The ballroom could have held six thousand people; but in the interests of 'crinolines and comfort' only three thousand tickets were issued, provoking a howl of rage and indignation from those who found themselves consigned to limbo.[69] On October 12, the Prince, with very little idea of the problem he was creating, arrived at the Academy to discover to his astonishment that two thousand eager New Yorkers had crashed the gates.

Undismayed, Edward took his assigned place in the hall, and the dance began. He had scarcely taken a partner and led her onto the floor when with a terrific sound of splintering wood, the overburdened floor suddenly collapsed, falling three feet before jamming. No one was hurt, and carpenters were immediately summoned to repair the damage, a piece of work that was carried out in two hours. No sooner, however, had the orchestra begun to play again when an outbreak of thunderous hammering announced the fact that one of the carpenters had been sealed under the new floor. It was proposed that he should stay there until the dance was over, but he made such effective use of his hammer beating on the floor that another pause ensued while he was freed.[70]

As varied an experience as the dance had been, New York had a treat in store for Edward that totally eclipsed the ball. The Corporation arranged that the Volunteer Fire Department should put on a parade in his honour. Carrying torches, the six thousand man brigade marched through Madison Square and past the delighted Prince with all their equipment, while Edward watched with growing excitement, exclaiming at intervals with unchecked glee, 'This is for me, this is all for me!'[71] And it was with genuine regret that he watched the end of the parade pass through the square and into the darkness.

After New York, Edward stopped briefly at Albany and then went on by train to Boston, where he met with a more restrained welcome than he had received in New York but one which was fully as warm. The New York Daily Tribune carried an editorial on the day of Edward's departure from New York regretting that George IV had not visited the United States and expressing the belief that had he done so the War of 1812 would never have been fought. The writer added that, although Edward was suffering from considerable stress in having to travel as he was doing, he could comfort himself with the knowledge that 'he is doing much to strengthen the feelings of amity and mutual kindness between the two great Anglo-Saxon peoples who have heretofore shed each other's blood'.[72]

Boston provided Edward with the usual round of entertainments. There was a ball. He met Longfellow, Oliver Wendell Holmes, Emerson and other notables. He visited Harvard and Mount Auburn, where he planted two trees, a Virginia and a purple beech.[73] One Boston editor wrote of him, 'He is fully qualified to shine even in Republican America, and his geniality of disposition sometimes strongly contrasts with the hauteur deemed necessary to maintain his "state" by some of his attendants.' Harriet Beecher Stowe, reflecting on Edward's visit and remarking with dubious taste that 'at the feet of this Young England, American citizens have laid that deep and chivalrous homage with which they have always regarded womanhood enthroned in the form of his noble mother', praised Edward's behaviour and his demeanour.[74]

Having been granted a day's holiday in honour of the Prince's visit, the school children of Boston welcomed Edward with genuine enthusiasm. A music festival was held at Music Hall, and Edward attended. The programme opened with an 'International Ode', 'Our Father's Land', written especially for the occasion by Oliver Wendell Holmes and sung by 1,200 public school children to the tune of 'God Save the Queen'.

On October 20, he left Boston for Portland, Maine, in a special train of three carefully fitted out cars. As Edward was rolling north, the manager of the Revere Hotel opened the royal apartments for public inspection, and throngs of the curious walked through the rooms to look at the place where the Prince had spent his private hours. In Quebec arrangements were in progress for the sale of the fittings of Parliament House, which had been done up for the Prince.

Edward spent about two hours riding around Portland; then he went down to the harbour where he was greeted by the spectacle of five British men-of-war fully decked out with flags and streamers flying and their yards thickly studded with sailors standing erect upon them. Carrying with him a number of limbs from American trees to be made into canes, and two grey squirrels and a mud turtle as presents for his mother, Edward boarded the *Hero*. Immediately, the royal ensign was hauled aloft and all the other flags, with the exception of the Stars and Stripes, were lowered. As the royal ensign unfurled at the masthead and Edward reached the *Hero*'s deck, every gun in the fleet and all the shore batteries from Fort Preble and Munjoi Hill fired a salute. The band on the *Hero* struck up 'God Save the Queen', and the sailors and marines in the fleet sang in accompaniment with the band.[75]

The *Hero* sailed from Portland for England on October 22, but it was November 15 before Edward reached Plymouth, the voyage having been protracted by severe storms and constant adverse winds. On November 9 he celebrated his nineteenth birthday. The *Hero*'s midshipmen insisted on giving Edward a special birthday gift and settled on an afternoon dinner to be held in the gun-room, from which place the ship's marines had to be turned out to provide room for the tables. The Prince attended, accompanied by General Bruce; and everyone was talking and laughing and looking forward to a very convivial dinner with no idea that anything was amiss. The company thoroughly enjoyed the meal, had listened with pleasure to the ship's band play 'The Roast Beef of Old England' and was sharing jokes and laughter provoked by the stories of China, India and the Crimea being told by the older officers when suddenly a tremendous sea rushed in the stern port, which had been opened to counter the strong atmosphere of marines pervading the gun-room, and swamped everyone, leaving three feet of the icy North Atlantic ocean sloshing around the room, the scuppers having been plugged. The Prince was drenched, but he struggled out with everyone else, laughing with delight.[76] It was one of his last unrestrained moments before resuming the boy's life which awaited him on shore.

In the wake of his visit, Edward left an impression of solid worth. A Boston editor wrote that he struck all who made his acquaintance 'as possessing remarkable decision for his years, of great intelligence, a person recognizing the respect due his station and prompt to award it, unpretentious, a gentleman without a tittle of abatement; and such an individual as, in this country, would make a successful man'.[77] That was high praise, coming from a New Englander. The increased poise and self-confidence which Edward had gained did not, however, please Bruce, who regretted having to report to the parents that Edward was becoming increasingly impatient of restraint and more self-important.[78]

Although Lord John Russell dismissed the Prince of Wales's trip with the remark that 'the tours of great personages seldom have more than a transient effect', it seems fair to say that the American visit had a very real influence on British policy in the ensuing struggle between the Union and the Confederacy. War broke out five months after Edward's return home, and a year later the *Trent* affair was to bring Great Britain and the Federal Government of the United States to the very edge of war; but the sympathies of Victoria and Albert remained squarely with the North.

On November 8 1861 the British mail steamer, *Trent*, carrying two Confederate diplomatic agents, J. M. Mason and John Slidell, was stopped off the New England coast and boarded by marines from the U.S.S. *San Jacinto*, under the command of Captain Charles Wilkes. Mason and Slidell were removed from the British ship and taken to Boston. Wilkes had made a serious error in not sending the *Trent* into port for the purpose of determining whether or not she was in violation of existing neutrality agreements. Removing her passengers offered the British Government a gross insult. The American Congress, however, immediately voted Captain Wilkes a commendation for his action, while the English press demanded that war be declared against the North. Public feelings on both sides of the Atlantic were soon so irritated that neither government felt able to back down from the challenge. For a brief period Lincoln refused to take any steps to calm England's anger, and Palmerston was inclined to give way to public opinion and declare war. English troops were sent to Canada and other preparations for armed conflict undertaken.

Fortunately for both countries, the Atlantic cable was temporarily out of commission, preventing the governments from exchanging insults or in other ways intensifying the crisis. Of equal importance was Victoria's, and Albert's, determination to prevent any irreparable damage from occurring to the friendly relations which had existed between the two countries. The Queen immediately invited the American diplomat, J. L. Motley, who was in London for discussions with Lord Russell, to Balmoral to extend to the Federal Government her appreciation for the warmth of Edward's reception in the United States and her assurances of personal support of the North in its struggle to preserve the Union.[79] Meanwhile, the Prince Consort had altered the wording of Lord Russell's harsh note to Washington regarding the *Trent* affair, making an equally moderate response from Lincoln possible. Under the pressure of his cabinet, exerted mainly by the powerful Charles Sumner, Lincoln released Mason and Slidell, sent Lord Lyons a note acceptable to the British Government; and the tension subsided.

Apart from this rather dramatic aspect of the Prince's visit, it is probably true that the spirit of Empire was increased by his journey. For several months the British people had daily reminders of the fact that they possessed close ties with distant lands. North America, India, China and Africa were in the news in a very prominent way during the summer of 1860, and not a single day passed without the major newspapers reporting the activities of Edward in Canada and the United States. Although the progress of Garibaldi's military ventures received more news coverage than did the travels of the Prince of Wales, the press responded very enthusiastically to items of news involving Edward; and that interest generated as well as reflected a desire on the part of the public to read about events occurring in the United States as well as western Europe.

On December 3 1860, President Buchanan, in his message to Congress, said, 'The recent visit of the Prince of Wales in a private character to the people of this country, has proved to be a most auspicious event. In its consequences it cannot fail to increase the kindred and kindly feelings which, I trust, may ever actuate the government and people of both countries in their political and social intercourse with each other.'[80]

Opening Parliament on February 5 1861, the Queen replied in the same spirit: 'The interest which I take in the well-being of the people of the United States cannot but be increased by the kind and cordial reception given by them to the Prince of Wales during his recent visit to the continent of North America.'[81] Victoria even went so far as to scold the Princess Royal for making an anti-American remark in one of her letters to her mother. 'We are somewhat shocked at your speaking of "those horrid Yankees",' the Queen wrote, scolding her daughter, 'when Bertie was received in the United States as no one has ever been anywhere, principally from the (to me incredible) liking they have for my unworthy self....'[82] That Victoria accepted without hesitation Newcastle's explanation of the enthusiasm with which Edward was received in the United States may account for her readiness to defend the Americans, but it is beside the point. Whatever the cause, she was at least temporarily converted to a pro-American feeling at a time when her goodwill was of enormous importance; and Edward had produced that effect.

As for the influence of the trip on the Prince himself, enough has already been said to show that he had gained in poise, confidence and maturity. They were not qualities which would make life easier when he returned to the restricted existence the Prince Consort and the Queen had mapped out for him. Even as his ship made its way towards England, Victoria complained that the delay in his return wasted time that he should have been spending at his studies. There was bound to be trouble. Edward had tasted independence and freedom, and he had learned his capacities.

Perhaps *Punch* best summarized the potential threat to the parental authority in a cartoon showing the Prince, just returned home, sitting with his feet up on the mantelpiece, a cigar in his mouth, a half-emptied glass of whisky beside him and a top hat on his head. Edward is saying to his shocked father, who is attempting to wave away his son's cigar smoke and screwing up his face in an expression of extreme distaste, 'Now Sir-ree, if you'll sit down and liquor up, I'll tell you about my travels.'

4

Fallen from Grace

The atrocious crime of being a young man, which the honourable gentleman has with such spirit and decency charged upon me, I shall neither attempt to palliate nor deny. . . .

Pitt's reply to Walpole

Edward slipped quietly into England and into the confines of his family, vanishing beneath the surface of national life with scarcely a ripple. His swift disappearance was puzzling and disappointing to those who had hoped to welcome their Prince home with celebration and ceremony befitting the return of the heir apparent. The *Illustrated London News* observed with just a hint of truculence that the country was very proud of young Edward but was sorry that no opportunity had been given for expressing that pride. 'As yet no occasion has arisen for giving him a personal welcome; but he may be sure that the very first time he makes a public appearance he will learn unmistakably from the reception that will be given him that England is glad to see her Marcellus safe at home again.'[1]

Edward's parents had no intention of putting him on parade for the nation. Victoria was irritated by the slowness of his return, lamenting the time lost from study. When he finally arrived, she was sufficiently pleased to write to the Princess Royal that he was well, grown and 'decidedly improved', adding, 'he tells us a great deal of what he has seen'. The praise, however, comes grudgingly and is rounded off with the observation that he looked 'a little yellow and sallow – and his hair so fair near Affie. Affie is very dark and handsome I must say.'[2] Three days after reaching Windsor, he was packed off to Oxford to resume his studies.[3] Immediately following his return to England, he enjoyed a brief summer season of praise from his mother and father for the way he had conducted himself in America and on his 'improvements'. It was soon winter again, however, with notes and memoranda falling around Bruce like snow and nearly all of them concerned with 'Bertie's' shortcomings – smoking too much, expressing his opinion, showing poor judgement (not agreeing with Bruce or his parents) and liking excitement.

It was all the same again, Edward lying out on the plain in a shallow trench, Bruce flying over and reporting his movements to the parents, who kept busy laying down a barrage on the Prince's position. Nothing had changed. The American trip might as well not have taken place. Or had it? In fact, everything appeared to be the same; but in reality nothing was the same. Edward had not only matured physically and emotionally during his travels to America, he had freed himself to some degree from his parents' domination. Their psychological control of him had weakened. He would go up to Oxford and resume the role of subject son, but the role was no longer assumed without reflection or critical evaluation. Bruce was to have trouble with this new prince, and the trouble was not remedied but intensified by efforts to take disciplinary action. Edward's insubordination was the pressure exerted by a maturing and independent spirit on the galling and stultifying rules of childhood. The bonds could not long hold.

The Prince's stay at Oxford was brief. He came home for the winter vacation; and then on January 18 he was sent to Cambridge to take up residence at Madingley Hall, a large country house, located some four miles outside the town and designed as a residence for Edward that would effectively separate him from undergraduate life. By his own demands, however, Edward forced his father and Bruce to allow him the freedom of entertaining friends of his own choosing and to bring to an end those dreary dinners through which he had suffered at Oxford. As a further breach in the fortress wall of his isolation, Dr Whewell, Master of Trinity College, where Edward was enrolled, set aside in the college private rooms for Edward's use. The action was a gesture of sympathy and a protest against Edward's exclusion from normal undergraduate life. Whewell acted without Albert's consent, and the Prince Consort was not pleased.[4]

It is another mark of Edward's increasing maturity that he could respond warmly to his new teachers without associating them in his mind with the onerous aspects of his life. His tutor, Joseph Barber Lightfoot, later Bishop of Durham, won Edward's lifelong friendship and esteem. But his most vivid relationship at Cambridge, discounting the rollicking companionship of Charles Carrington with whom he hunted the 'Drag', was with Charles Kingsley, Regius Professor of Modern History. Edward read history under Kingsley, attending lectures at the professor's house with five or six other 'carefully selected' undergraduates. The course of study covered English history up to the reign of George IV. The initial mutual liking between teacher and pupil grew swiftly into an affection and regard that did much to alleviate the loneliness of the Prince's life.[5]

Things did not, however, go smoothly at Madingley Hall. Unwilling or unable to tolerate patiently the cramped character of his life, Edward began to have outbursts of bad temper reminiscent of his tantrums in the nursery; but these new explosions could not be quelled by thrashings and the deprival of sweets. There were sharp exchanges between Edward and Bruce and between Edward and his father, who on several occasions was summoned to Cambridge to deal with the rebellious young man.[6] On one occasion Edward fled the house altogether and took a train to London, only to find a carriage waiting for him when he arrived. An equerry had telegraphed ahead. There were the usual head shakings in the royal household over the 'Bertie' problem.[7]

During this often tense period, the Queen was less concerned with her son's behaviour than she might have been, chiefly because she was diverting herself with the task of finding Edward a wife and actively enlisting her eldest daughter's help in the search. Two years earlier *The Times* had printed a list of the princesses it thought potential royal marriage material, whose basic requirements consisted of being Protestant, of royal blood and of suitable age.[8]

The list was surprisingly short. Only seven girls out of the flourishing brood of Europe's blue-blooded families were deemed eligible; and, of course, given Victoria's bias against the English cousins, the candidates were all from over the Channel. The names have the chiming of ancient glory in them, although it was a glory already on the wane: Princess Alexandrina, daughter of Prince Albert of Prussia; Princess Anne of Hesse-Darmstadt, niece of the Grand Duke of Hesse and of the Empress of Russia; Princess Augusta of Holstein-Glucksburg; Duchess Wilhelmina of Würtemberg; Princess Alexandra, daughter of Prince Christian of Denmark; Princess Mary of Saxe-Altenburg; and Princess Catherine of Oldenburg, sister of the Grand Duchess Nicholas of Russia. *The Times* chose Alexandra as the most likely candidate, for the reason that Prince Christian was heir presumptive to the throne of Denmark.

The guess proved to be a good one, but certainly late in 1860 the Queen was opposed to any alliance between Edward and the Danish family. Writing to her daughter on December 18, she expressed lively interest in Princess Elizabeth of Wied (missed by *The Times*) and Anne of Hesse-Darmstadt, having half settled in her own mind that 'the future choice of Bertie must lie between them'.[9] The Princess Royal had called her mother's attention to Alexandra, who at seventeen was already a remarkable beauty and causing a stir of admiration throughout the court circles of Europe, despite the fact that she had scarcely appeared outside her nursery and continued to play with the younger children of her family as though she were still a child.

Victoria was not impressed. 'You know, dearest,' she wrote to her daughter, 'we must feel very anxious about this choice [of wife] and the beauty of Denmark is much against our wishes. I do wish somebody would go and marry her off – at once. If Bertie could see and like one of the others first then I am sure we should be safe.'[10] The anxieties were both personal and political. The Queen was perfectly aware that the German Government would view a marriage between Edward and Alexandra with suspicion and alarm. The complex troubles connected with the provinces of Schleswig and Holstein had commenced to exercise European governments, and Germany had no desire to see Denmark gain a powerful ally in England by the device of joining the two royal families through matrimony. Prussia need not have worried. Victoria was sufficiently Germanized through her own background and the influence of Albert, and was herself so eager to prevent her daughter-in-law's family having the slightest shadow of Danish influence that she sided with Prussia in the controversy as though by instinct.

The personal side of her antipathy for the Danish royal family is less easy to define. She considered the mother's family 'bad' and the father's 'foolish'.[11] By 'bad' she meant immoral, especially Alexandra's grandmother and great-aunts, who, with their numerous relatives gathered at Rumpenheim, the family castle on the Main near Frankfurt, continued to enjoy themselves in much the same way that Victoria used to do before being laundered by Albert's moral soap. Through the mother's family there was also a connection with the Cambridges, descendants of Adolphus, First Duke of Cambridge and son of George III. Both Victoria and Albert were against the Cambridges, root and branch, considering the women (who had won their particular dislike) vulgar and indiscreet.

Edward was not included in the planning at these early stages of wife hunting, and he could not have been particularly interested in the proceedings since he had no desire to marry. What he did want was to become associated with the Guards and was eagerly pressing General Bruce to aid him in that effort. Bruce, however, proved difficult. The older man knew that the moral 'tone' of the Guards left something to be desired, that the young officers kept mistresses; and being aware of the Prince Consort's peculiar ideas on 'purity' as far as his son was concerned, Bruce was understandably reluctant to urge Edward's case. The matter was taken out of his hands, however, when in March Albert decided to allow Edward to take a ten-week course in infantry training with the 1st Battalion, Grenadier Guards, at the Curragh Camp in Ireland.[12] Albert, determined that the course should be made as rigorous as possible to dispel any thoughts in Edward's mind that pleasure might be associated with the summer, ordered that in the ten weeks Edward would become competent to command a battalion. It was an impossible task, and by setting it he ensured his son's failure. Albert drew up a memorandum detailing his plans and had it initialled by Edward.[13]

But for Edward there was only delight as he looked forward to the accomplishment of his dream of becoming associated with the Guards. He had scarcely had time to savour that pleasure, however, before his family life was shaken by the death of the Duchess of Kent, the Queen's mother, an event which plunged Victoria into a degree of grief out of all proportion to the loss. On March 16 the Duchess, seventy-five years old, died after an illness that had begun nearly two years before. At the time of her death, she was in constant pain; and death was a release. But Victoria saw it otherwise, falling into an ecstasy of suffering that seemed almost to threaten her sanity.

Even allowing for every possible exaggeration, there can be no doubt of the terrible nature of Victoria's grief. Cecil Woodham-Smith points out that the Queen had no previous experience of death, and watching her mother's dissolution overwhelmed her.[14] But even that explanation does not account for the incredible flood of tears that poured forth and would not stop, the refusal to be comforted, the unwillingness to leave Frogmore and the room where her mother had died. There is something ominous, almost frightening, in the way Victoria flung herself into mourning. Her grief seemed to take on the aspect of a consuming rage against that which she could not command.

The Duchess of Kent's death created new tensions within the family, tensions with the potential for becoming public issues; and the Princess Royal, arriving in England for the funeral, was shaken by what she saw was taking place between Edward and Victoria. From Germany on April 4 she wrote to Victoria about her concern: 'Only one thing pains me – when I think of it and that is the relation between you and Bertie! In the railway carriage going to Dover I thought so much about it, and wished I could have told you how kindly, nicely, properly and even sensibly he spoke. . . .' She went on to say that she was sure he had a kind heart and a warmth of feeling that her mother would, in time, come to recognize. After praising her father's treatment of Edward, she got to the point of the letter: 'I can only hope and pray that there may never be an estrangement between him and you – as it would be the source of endless misery to both.'[15]

What had shocked the Princess Royal was the extreme tension existing between the Queen and her eldest son. The latest difficulty had been produced by Edward's conduct at Frogmore during those trying scenes which marked the end of the Duchess of Kent's life and the obsequies following. Victoria had been furious because the Prince had not, in her opinion, shown sufficient grief, and she condemned him for causing her additional pain. So deep was her resentment that by the following October she fully recalled his calm manner at Frogmore and pointed to it as an indication that he lacked the brains to feel emotion. But even in referring to this lack, the Queen was more concerned with the fact that he had aroused her fury than that he was too little moved by the Duchess's death.[16]

Victoria responded to her daughter's critical letter with a brisk counter-attack in which she catalogued the variations and depth of her sorrow, her inability to face life and her desire to remain grief-stricken. Then, with a sudden shift in tactics, she turned on the Princess Royal and wrote, 'As regards Bertie – I quite agree with you, dear child – that he must be a little more tender and affectionate in his manner – if he is to expect it from me [Vicky had not made such a suggestion] – and take a little more interest in what interests us if he is to be at all pleasant in the house.' She then accused her daughter of heaping coals on her head by telling her everything 'stupid and silly' that Bertie had said, thus making her more angry and more wretched than she already was. This last was probably a reference to Edward's ill-timed remark that he thought his mother's grief excessive. Victoria's closing comment indicated that the situation between mother and son had not improved: 'He left on Monday. His voice made me so nervous I could hardly bear it.'[17]

Responding to the general uneasiness about the state of her mother's mind, the Princess Royal chided her for not trying to overcome her sorrow. Victoria replied that she wept every day and did not want to feel better. 'The more distant the dreadful event becomes, and the more others recover their spirits – the more trying it becomes to me! The slightest approach to ordinary habits is so painful to me.' Two days later she wrote that she 'loved to dwell on her [mother]' and did not wish to be 'roused out of my grief', adding that Vicky could not understand 'the sort of quiet, serious state of mind which I am in and wish to remain in'.[18]

Fortunately for Edward, he had escaped to Cambridge and did not have to participate in the long lamentation over the Duchess of Kent. The Prince of Wales's life continued in its dull routine of studies, lightened by occasionally riding to hounds and an over-indulgence in food and cigars. But the summer vacation brought the long-awaited flight to Ireland and military life. Edward was not dismayed by the rigour of the training schedule planned for him and seems not to have realized that he could not possibly complete the course of study the Prince Consort had outlined. He went off to Ireland with a light heart, having won for himself a respite from the boredom of his life.

Colonel Percy, Edward's commanding officer, closely supervised the young man's training and soon saw, if indeed he had not known from the very beginning, that Edward was not mastering the steps in the programme in the time set out. He was not satisfied with Edward's progress; and when the Queen and the Prince Consort came to the Curragh in August to watch Edward perform, Percy refused to allow the Prince of Wales to command a company, informing the disappointed young man that he was 'imperfect' in his drill and gave his orders indistinctly. Edward, togged out in a colonel's uniform, had the humiliation of performing the duties of a subaltern during the dress parade before the Queen. After the ceremonies, Victoria called Percy to her and commended him for treating Edward 'just as any other officer'.[19] She may not have distinguished between the duties being performed by Edward and those of the other men of colonel's rank on the field, although she would certainly have read Percy's reports on Edward's progress. Writing of the review of the troops, she noted that 'Bertie' had 'marched past with his company and did not look at all so very small'.[20]

The greatest event of the summer for Edward was not, however, the review of the troops but rather the advent of Nellie Clifden, a pretty young 'actress' whom Edward's fellow guardsmen smuggled into his rooms one night and, from the evidence, a good many nights thereafter. At this distance in time, it is difficult to credit the trouble those frolics caused when three months later news of Edward's indiscretions at the Curragh reached Albert. But during the late summer only Edward and those officers conniving with him knew; and from what was later said, General Bruce slept peacefully through it all, secure in the belief that his charge was doing likewise. It was too good a story to be kept quiet, however, and by early autumn was providing the London clubs with material for cheerful speculations on the doings of the young prince, who might, it appeared, make a man after all, and in spite of his father.

The Duchess of Kent's death temporarily disrupted the Queen's search for a suitable wife for Edward; but by the middle of April she was pressing her search once more and had, surprisingly, ceased to dislike the Danish princess as a prospective daughter-in-law. The reasons for the change are chiefly the enthusiasm of the Princess Royal for Alexandra and the Queen's response to the young woman's beauty, which she characterized on examining the girl's photographs as 'outrageous'. Earlier, in February, the Princess Royal had argued persuasively that 'Bertie' was going to require more than cleverness in his bride. 'I think of our English ladies,' she wrote, 'their manners and appearance and of how much Bertie admires them and of what use would cleverness be – without some attractions to captivate him....'[21]

The Queen had apparently reached the same conclusion. She had also learned that Alexandra was mild-mannered, lacking in opinions, passive and still remarkably childlike. In February she had stated firmly to the Princess Royal that the woman who married 'Bertie' would require 'superiority of mind' and 'a certain determination', as well as 'great cleverness' if she were not to be tyrannized, since, in Victoria's opinion, those who allowed Edward to gain the upper hand over them were 'invariably' taken advantage of and treated with rudeness. Only those who 'never knock under, but hold their own, are always most liked, and who get on best with the nameless individual'.[22] The 'nameless individual' is, of course, Edward, although it is difficult to find the thoroughly dominated Prince in the description given by his mother, who is more interested in attacking him than in describing the qualities she wishes to see in his bride.

Actually, the last characteristic Victoria wished in Edward's wife was independence of spirit, and the true state of her feelings on the matter are exposed in a letter written to her daughter in early September. Victoria had written to Alexandra's mother and, to the Queen's delight, Princess Christian had replied with 'great discretion and prudence'. What Victoria had insisted on with the Princess Christian was the total separation that Alexandra must be prepared to effect between herself and her relatives; further, that she must expect to submit completely to the Queen and not attempt to exert any political or family pressure on Edward. 'I have been thinking a great deal about it,' the Queen wrote to her daughter, 'and it is the Cambridges we must take precautions against – if matters are not to take a very disagreeable turn for me. Bertie and his wife must be one and the same with us – or else my peace will be at an end.'[23]

Pared to its essentials, Victoria's letter says, in effect, that before any marriage contract is entered into, it must be clearly understood by Alexandra's parents that nothing must threaten the Queen's control over her son and that she wants no interference from outside with either him or herself. In expressing the fear that her peace might be at an end if 'precautions' were not taken against the Cambridges, she really meant that any loss of control over Edward would bring an end to her peace of mind. Her dread of the Cambridges was little more than distaste seized on and magnified as an excuse for rigour in dealing with Alexandra's family and continuing her domination of Edward and, by extension, his wife-to-be.

That is not to say that the Queen was indifferent to the moral calibre of the people connected with her family. She had, if anything, an over-developed sense of what constituted moral fitness in those around or near her. Writing to Vicky to thank her for helping to bring Alexandra and Edward together, she said that while 'Bertie' must have benefited from meeting the Danish princess, she feared that he was not capable of loving anyone or showing 'enthusiasm about anything in the world'. This observation led her to remark that she had no intention of allowing that 'odious Prince of Orange' to marry Lenchen [Princess Alice], that she and Albert would 'never give one of our girls to a man who has led a life like that young man has done! You and I know what it is to have a spotless husband. . . . I for one could not give one of my sweet, innocent loving girls to an immoral man!'[24]

Victoria's outburst began as a discussion of Edward's proposed marriage and seems, in some tortuous way, to have been turned into an attack against him, the 'nameless' one, who is forever in her bad graces. In another letter she expressed great pleasure at the way in which one of Edward's meetings with Alexandra had been conducted, but added, 'Poor child, I pity him much.' There were no grounds for pitying him in that situation and what she was doing was setting him up for more criticism. The letters of this period reflect an undeviating intention to dominate every aspect of her son's life, and the cumulative effect of them is extremely unpleasant. Edward gains limited approval when he behaves in exact accordance with her ideas and ideals and the equally unrobust interests of Albert. Edward and all other men are judged by the same emasculating standard. It seems an unavoidable conclusion that Victoria's hostility towards her son was a hostility towards the more aggressive and forceful aspects of his maleness, especially his positive attitudes toward sex, which she feared and resented and which presented themselves as a threat to her.

For his part, Edward was walking meekly enough through the elaborate rites of royal courtship. Having insisted that he would marry only for love, he immediately fell in with his parents' intentions regarding Alexandra, whose existence had been carefully kept from him at the beginning. After their initial meeting, Edward told his mother and father that he was pleased with their choice, and gave them the impression that he had fallen in love. Several weeks later, sensing a veiled resistance in his son's sudden coolness towards Alexandra, Albert drew up a memorandum and presented it to Edward. The document points out that the meeting with Alexandra had been arranged under the most difficult circumstances, that Edward had asked to meet the young lady before proposing and had now met her, that everyone had risked a great deal in bringing the two together, especially his sister Vicky, and that Edward had better settle for Alexandra at once.[25]

Albert also put into the memorandum some solemn nonsense about Edward's needing to make up his mind as to whether or not he were truly in love and about the necessity of not causing embarrassment to the families by continuing the negotiations unless he was prepared to commit himself. Edward had no difficulty in penetrating the true meaning of this message and told his father that he was ready to go ahead with the proposal if Alexandra were willing. Throughout the negotiations there had been some slight pretence maintained by both families that the two young people's feelings were being consulted; but in reality they were simply told to respond in certain ways, and they did so.

But in early October, Edward began to show alarming signs of rebelling. Although in September he had been willing to assure his mother that he loved Alix, as she was coming to be called, he was now unwilling to make such protestations, causing the Queen to become angry with him and accuse him of being incapable of feeling. Even the Princess Royal, who had been his staunch ally despite the fact that she was hurrying him towards marriage, became indignant, pointing out that it was inconceivable that Edward should remain so unmoved by Alexandra's beauty when she felt her own heart race in the presence of it.[26] The Queen grew despondent and wrote to her daughter that the marriage might not occur. Edward suddenly expressed a dread of having children and feared that marriage would cut him off from his friends.[27]

At this point, Albert produced the memorandum that brought Edward to heel. The rebellion was over. Edward was once again able to tell his mother that he loved Alix. It had been a feeble resistance at best, and Sir Sidney Lee, describing the Prince at this period in his life, wrote that the strict discipline to which his father had subjected him 'had restrained in him every sense of independence and had fostered a sentiment of filial awe'.[28] What Lee meant was that Edward was terrified of his father, and so he was. That he had put up any resistance at all to the marriage suggests how seriously he was opposed to it, at least at that time.

To discover what was creating Edward's anxiety, it is necessary to recall the events at the Curragh Camp involving Nellie Clifden. During his stay in Ireland, he had become more than ever impatient with the restraints placed on his life. Determined to fight free of them as far as possible, he arranged to continue seeing Nellie in Cambridge. His expressed fear of having children, which he told his parents was standing between him and his marriage, may have been very real; but it was probably Nellie and not Alexandra whom he feared would bear them. As for his being cut off from his friends, it is reasonable to suppose that Nellie was the chief 'friend' he had in mind.

This knowledge he hoped to keep from his mother and father, and he reached his twentieth birthday in safety. His mother curtailed the celebrations as far as possible. 'We could do nothing,' she recorded and refused to allow him to have the traditional *feu de joie,* presumably because she was still too stricken by her mother's death to permit such an official expression of happiness. How frequently in her dealings with her son a meanness masqueraded as something else and how frequently she indulged her selfishness while pretending to be under the sway of a more noble emotion.

A week later she had something substantial to feel aggrieved over. Albert found out about Nellie. According to Sir Philip Magnus,

Edward was given away by Lord Torrington, who had come into waiting and had brought the story of Edward's frolics with him from London.[29] Having confirmed the tale, Albert wrote immediately to Edward, charging him with the crime and claiming that his heart was broken by what he had learned and that while he could not face his son, he wished a full confession to be submitted through Bruce.[30] Heavily burdened by an exaggerated sense of having done wrong which was deliberately fostered by his father's hysterical letter, Edward made a full confession and swore that the liaison was at an end. Having stripped away Edward's pretences to the dignity of personal privacy and having exacted the abjectness of spirit he had demanded from his son, Albert was ready to be conciliatory and to forgive the penitent for 'the terrible pain' he had caused his mother and father.[31] As a perfectly orchestrated coda to the proceedings, Albert travelled to Cambridge for a long talk with his son, which he concluded by fully forgiving Edward but expressing doubt as to whether God would be as merciful.

A partial explanation of Albert's completely unbalanced reaction to what in a young man was only to be expected, is the fact that by the autumn of 1861 the Prince Consort was ill. He had aged in advance of his forty-two years; he was stooped, weary with incessant work and growing increasingly discouraged by what he believed to be the herculean tasks facing him. Albert's conviction that the nation would flounder if he did not perpetually struggle to keep it moving forward was as absurd as the certainty that terrors and calamities were sure to follow in the wake of his son's affair. Albert's tendency to imagine that the sky was falling increased as he grew older. This anxious state of mind, which appears to have become chronic, was undoubtedly intensified by the physical malaise into which he was sinking and which was, although undetected at this and for some future time, the first stages of typhoid infection. The Prince Consort was in serious need of rest and competent medical attention. He got neither until it was too late.

Just prior to going down to Cambridge on November 25, Albert had written in his diary that he was not well and had scarcely slept for two weeks.[32] He was in the hands of Sir James Clarke, whose services the Queen had perversely retained since the unfortunate Lady Flora Hastings affair, when his gross mishandling of that case had destroyed his private practice. Two days following his return from Cambridge, Albert's symptoms were worse, and Dr Jenner was called in. Jenner examined the Prince Consort and remained the night at Windsor, having given, it must be supposed, his opinion to Dr Clarke. Rumour of the Prince's condition had by this time reached Lord Palmerston, who, as Prime Minister, felt compelled to request that yet another doctor be summoned to make an examination. On December 3, in a remarkable letter, the Queen replied to Palmerston that the Prince Consort had

WHERE IS BRITANNIA?

(See "The Petition.")

3. 'Where is Britannia?': from the *Tomahawk*, June 1867
By permission of the British Museum

AT LAST!

(DEDICATED TO H.R.H. THE PRINCE OF WALES)

4. 'At Last!' from the *Tomahawk*, March 1868
   By permission of the British Museum

THE P••••E OF W•••S *to* K••G G••••E IV.

(LOQ.) "I'LL FOLLOW THEE!"

5. 'The P . . . . e of W . . . s to K . . g G . . . . e IV': from the *Tomahawk*, June 1867
   By permission of the British Museum

nothing but a feverish cold. In her journal that day she wrote that 'good kind old Sir James' had assured both her and Jenner that there was no need for alarm 'either present or future'.[33]

Sir James had made another crucial mistake. His diagnosis was again quite wrong. Finally, on December 7, faced with overwhelming evidence, Clarke was forced to admit that Albert had typhoid and convey the true state of her husband's condition to the Queen, who was on the point of collapse from fear and worry about Albert. What Jenner's original diagnosis was is not known. If he recognized typhoid symptoms, he thought himself obliged to defer to Clarke and keep the diagnosis to himself since his views were not those of the senior physician.

Eventually, two other physicians were called to the Castle, but by then it was too late to reverse the progress of the illness. On the morning of December 14 Albert died with his family around him. Sequestered in Cambridge and in deep disgrace, Edward had not been told of the seriousness of his father's condition and was not summoned to Windsor until the night of December 13. Had the Queen prevailed, he would not even then have been called; but Princess Alice and Lady Augusta Bruce, who was then attending the Queen, had their way and dispatched a telegraph to the Prince of Wales. Victoria did not want Edward at Windsor because she had become unshakeably convinced that his 'fall' had brought on Albert's illness, and she would come to believe that he occasioned her beloved husband's death.

That there was anything more seriously wrong with the Prince Consort than was being reported in the press from December 9 onwards was not known at Cambridge, where, had there been any suspicion of the extent of Albert's decline, General Bruce would have been writing to either Sir Charles Phipps, Victoria's Keeper of the Privy Purse, or Lady Augusta Bruce, the General's sister and Victoria's close friend. In part this failure of communication can be charged to those around the Queen who were determined that she should not be more alarmed than necessary. Phipps feared that if word of Albert's condition were reported in the press, Victoria would read exaggerated accounts of it in the papers and become convinced that she was not being told the truth. This mistaken concern even extended to the question of seeking additional medical advice; and the Queen, who became furious when Dr Watson and Dr Holland were brought in at the Prime Minister's insistence, tried her best to keep Watson (who, with the exception of Jenner, was the only man among the four with real medical competence) from remaining at Windsor, and was supported in this folly by Phipps.[34]

The telegram warning Edward of his father's critical condition reached Madingley Hall about nine o'clock on Friday evening. Accompanied by General Bruce and Major Teesdale, Edward left at

D

once for Cambridge, where a special train was summoned; and the Prince started for London shortly before twelve. At Charing Cross Station they were met by a private carriage and driven directly to Waterloo Station, where they boarded another special train for Windsor, arriving at the Castle at about 3.00 am, at the same time as the Queen received from the doctors, for the third time that night, news that the Prince Consort was holding his own and that the crisis was passing. By 6.00 am Brown, the Windsor apothecary, told Victoria that there was reason to hope that the crisis had already passed safely. At nine-thirty Albert was dead.

Edward was shaken by his father's death, coming as it did almost without warning. The position in which he suddenly found himself placed was about as difficult as could be imagined, for his mother was absolutely sincere when she wrote to her Uncle Leopold shortly after Albert's death: 'England, my unhappy country, has lost *all* in losing him.'[35] It was fortunate for Edward that he was not able to look forward and see what the next forty years had in store for him as his father's heir and his mother's successor, obliged to perform the most dreary of official tasks, denied any real authority, 'a deputy King, it may be said, minus all the pride and *kudos* of kingship'.[36] But that was in the future, and in the present he was called upon to play the role of chief mourner. His problems in this regard were somewhat lessened by the fact that the Queen decreed that the funeral would be completely private.

The Queen's companions were far too concerned with her welfare to suggest that something was owed the nation, even in death; and it was left to the *Daily Telegraph* to express sorrow that the public would be totally excluded from the funeral ceremonies. The paper noted that royal funerals during the reigns of the first two Georges were 'little better than a masquerade, half ghastly and half ludicrous'. Held at night, they were 'perfectly scandalous exhibitions of impropriety', the torchlight processions being the occasions for drunkenness, scuffles and robbery.[37] Whatever the implication of its having called forth the ghosts of the Georges, the paper pointed out that Albert belonged, at least in part, to the nation. After all, he was, up to his death, the second most important man in it. There is a gentle reminder here of the constitutional relationship between the importance of a Prince Consort and that of a Prince of Wales. On this crucial point the views of the nation and those of the Queen were wildly divergent.

The funeral was held in St George's Chapel at Windsor with Edward representing his mother in a ceremony she felt unequal to attending. The body was interred at Frogmore, near that of the Duchess of Kent; and for Victoria, the mausoleum became a holy shrine. Shortly after the burial services, the Queen made a public announcement that subscriptions would soon be taken to raise some permanent memorial to the memory of Albert. She dragooned Edward into writing a letter in which he publicly associated himself with her 'overwhelming anxiety to pay her husband's memory all public honour'.[38] In the course of the ensuing months the Albert Memorial Fund became a source of public controversy, basically because the memorial sponsored by the Queen was not to be a library or a hospital or a museum or a public building but simply a memorial. The subscriptions dribbled in.

It is not easy to comprehend fully the desperate position in which Edward found himself with respect to his mother. It was absolutely essential that he appear to be participating fully in the mourning and to be carrying his full weight as the man of the family; but the role was not easy nor, strictly speaking, possible. That is not to say he was treating his father's death with indifference. There is no evidence for such a conclusion. But he could not, given his mother's state of mind, offer her any useful emotional support or derive any relief for his own pent up feelings by sharing his grief with her. Nor were the rest of the family of much help to him, all except Alice being too young; and Alice was so completely at the disposal of Victoria that there could not have been much time left over for Edward. Isolated from his mother by her irrational belief that he had killed her husband, Edward was left to deal with his grief largely on his own and to cope with the anguish inflicted by Victoria's accusation as best he might.

The British press were unanimous in their praise of Albert, setting aside, at least temporarily, their deep antagonisms toward this foreign prince who had, in Strachey's view, ruled the woman who ruled England. Some of the response was conventional in character, expressing regret for the passing of a good man, whose presence would be missed, etc. Beyond that formal recognition of the death, however, lay a deeper concern. 'His death,' the *Daily Telegraph* reported, 'cannot be regarded but in the light of a great and national calamity.' The precise nature of the calamity was the effect upon the Queen of his unexpected passing. To a greater degree than might have been guessed, the press was aware of the extent of Victoria's grief over her mother's death, expected though this death was; and the *Daily Telegraph* writer, reminding his readers that she was still in mourning for the Duchess of Kent, that her health had been endangered, and that a long gloom had been cast over the Court, expressed the fear that the Queen might not be able to stand up to this latest loss.[39]

Demonstrating the same failure of understanding that had marked its reporting of the background to Edward's departure for Canada and the United States, the press stated that the Prince of Wales would immediately begin to fulfil those duties and to accept those responsibilities for which his father had 'so nobly tutored' him. The long apprenticeship which he had undergone, the rigorous study, and the travels would now be converted into the use for which they were intended. So confident were the writers of their ground that the *Evening Mail,* wildly off the mark, reported on the Wednesday following Albert's death that Edward had 'already taken his place by his mother's side, as her stay and support in her distress', and that she had 'within a few hours of his father's death endeavoured to associate him with her in the arduous work of the British monarchy'.[40] The specific reference was probably to the letter Edward had written concerning the Albert Memorial Fund; but the general reference was towards the broad range of constitutional functions in which Edward would be expected to share. Unfortunately, this was far from the truth. Edward was given nothing to do.

The *Evening Mail*'s error was repeated over and over again by editorial writers in the week following the Prince Consort's death, and the conviction that Edward would step into his father's role was accompanied by a series of observations less encouraging. There was in the writing a note of warning, of thinly veiled hostility. After mulling over the behaviour of past princes, the *Daily Express* of Dublin noted that many of them had the excuse of vicious parents to mitigate their responsibility for having lived worthless lives, but the sons of Victoria and Albert lacked that excuse. 'They have received many and precious talents, and fearful will be their responsibility if they do not use them well!'

The writer continued in much the same vein throughout an account of Edward's return to Windsor Castle after he had left the Queen at Gosport, when 'he "trod alone its banquet hall deserted" and stood by the coffin of his illustrious father – he must have sadly and prayerfully pondered these things in his heart; if not, it will be more tolerable in the day of judgement for Philip of Spain than for him.'[41]

This kind of writing was typical of the press response during the week. The *Evening Mail,* in what might be interpreted as a similar warning to Edward, reminded its readers that Albert had 'kept the faith he had pledged with simple and unswerving fidelity, and in the heyday of youth ruled his passions and left no duty unperformed'.[42] There was a whiff of Nellie Clifden in the wind. In another article on December 18, the *Evening Mail* gave an extended description of Edward's qualifications to serve as the Queen's right hand. He was, the paper pointed out, two years older than his mother when she assumed the throne. He had been specially educated for the position. 'The Prince ought now to show the faculties which will make a good King. . . .' He should assume the role of head of the family, become his mother's mainstay and helpmeet, and so on.

The mildness of the tone is misleading, however, and within a few lines disappears entirely. 'The Prince must make up his mind, if he wishes to gain the affection and esteem of the country. The national good will is not to be obtained without some sacrifices, and the Prince has before him...two paths, those of duty and pleasure. Exposed to many temptations, his Royal Highness must resolve to earn public applause by resisting all that will draw him from the side of a mother and a Queen who requires his help.'[43] It is remarkable that it was the *Evening Mail* and other conservative papers, rather than *Lloyd's Weekly London Newspaper* or *Reynolds's Newspaper* and the more liberal journals, that lectured Edward on this occasion.

Granted that young people, including princes, were, in the mid-nineteenth century, thought to be improved by receiving moral lectures, press reaction to Edward was, even by the standards of the time, exaggerated. By the simple act of being born, he had awakened a fervour of rejoicing; and before he was known to the country as anything more than a face and a name, he became a public hero by sailing to America. The public took an intense interest in him; and because they felt so strongly about him and about his role, reaction to him tended to fluctuate wildly. Those fluctuations were faithfully recorded in the press, where the process of myth-making over Edward went on steadily and where condemnation of him came when his actions did not fit the pattern created for him.

It is not difficult to discover in the warnings and descriptions being printed at this difficult period in Edward's life a strange duality or ambiguity in the writers. There is, on the one hand, a strongly expressed hope that this young Prince of Wales will now come to the fore as an English, as opposed to a German, prince and that he should show vigour and spirit. At the same time – almost in reaction to that wish – he was warned against displaying those traits that would reveal his manhood in any but the most unexceptionable ways. He was to be simultaneously a true, strong-blooded English gentleman, sharply contrasting with his father in style and interests, and precisely like his father in everything pertaining to duty, restraint and purity of body and mind. The expectation was, of course, absurd; but it is worth looking at the sources of it.

At the political level, the expectation is readily understood. Throughout Victoria's reign the political power of the throne waned, while it became popular in the same period to speak solemnly about the great influence for moral good the Queen and the Consort exerted on public and private life. The middle class, into whose hands the power of governance had fallen, were not in the least anxious to have the political leverage of the throne regenerated. Their great power lay in the Commons, and it was the influence of that body they wished to see increased at the expense of both the Lords and the Crown. For this reason they desired that Edward should follow in his mother's wake as a strictly constitutional sovereign.

But that was only one aspect of the problem. A second is the terrible dread of, and consequent fascination with, sexuality. The press of the day devoted a large proportion of its crime reporting to crimes resulting from sexual passion, and the nation reserved its greatest frenzies of moral outrage for those crimson cases (such as the Valentine Baker affair, to be discussed later) in which a gentleman was caught behaving like a 'sexual animal'.

It could be argued that this sexual prudery was in part a result of an attitude to woman at the period – seeing her as both goddess and whore. 'Good' women were pure, devoted, undemanding sexually. 'Bad' women were sexually voracious and thus socially threatening. And these two 'types' had to be seen as totally separate. The glorification of women was represented in those imagined virtues of the Queen – purity, goodness and duty, which were seen circling the throne like attendant Graces, providing an edifying example to the world of virtue. How deeply this principle of female nobility had been implanted in the minds of the middle class of that day may be guessed at by the following extract from *The Women of England,* written in 1839 by Mrs Ellis specifically for the women of the middle class. The paragraph is a long one, but no paraphrase could convey the almost religious zeal with which Mrs Ellis makes her case:

> How often has man returned to his home with a mind confused by the many voices, which in the mart, the exchange, or the public assembly, have addressed themselves to his inborn selfishness, or his worldly pride; and while his integrity was shaken, and his resolution gave way beneath the pressure of apparent necessity, or the insidious pretences of expediency, he has stood corrected before the clear eye of woman, as it looked directly to the naked truth, and detected the lurking evil of the specious act he was about to commit. Nay, so potent may have become this secret influence, that he may have borne it about with him like a kind of second conscience, for mental reference, and spiritual counsel, in moments of trial; and when the snares of the world were around him, and temptations from within and without have bribed over the witness in his own bosom, he has thought of the humble monitress who sat alone, guarding the fireside comforts of his distant home; and the remembrance of her character, clothed in moral beauty, has sent him back to that beloved home, a wiser and a better man.[44]

Such attitudes towards women, peculiar to the middle class, led inevitably to the double standard, widespread sexual guilt and all its attendant psychological horrors. From the eighteenth century and perhaps earlier, the politically ambitious middle class had been condemning the sexual laxity of the upper classes and claiming that their own domestic arrangements were proof certain that they were better suited to rule than their dissipated social betters. By the middle of the nineteenth century that claim had come home to roost in the form of a Queen more akin to the middle classes than any previous royalty, dedicated to death, whose mourning weeds wrapped themselves for forty years around her son's life; and the English middle class glorified that black and bitter figure as their ideal of woman. In 1859 Tennyson had dedicated *The Idylls of the King* to Prince Albert. It is worth noting that in Tennyson's version of the legends, Camelot comes to grief because Arthur will not see that men cannot live by duty alone.

Perhaps no greater irony existed for Edward in the period immediately following his father's death than the popularly held belief that he was his mother's chief support in her grief. Years later, at the time of his coronation, a child's life of the King, dealing with Albert's death, solemnly records that 'the Queen and all the nation were plunged into grief. . . . The Prince's grief was so great at the loss of his father, that it was feared he might become ill, so he was sent on a tour in Egypt.'[45] It is at once shocking and somehow genuinely comic that such a falsehood should still exist forty years after the event. Victoria could not bear to have Edward near her. Everything about him irritated her, even the sound of his voice; and it was finally decided that the best temporary solution was to send him to the Near East on the journey that had been planned while his father was still alive.

The decision was not reached lightly, and Edward was not completely abandoned during those weeks before his departure. His sister Vicky had written repeatedly to her mother, attempting to alter the Queen's attitude; but Victoria would not be moved. 'If you had seen Fritz [Albert], day by day get worse and finally die, I doubt if you could bear the sight of one who was the cause. . . .'[46] With that reply the Queen laid bare the colour and the depth of her conviction; and in making it she gave final shape, the most monstrous shape her troubled mind could devise, to that profound aversion which she had so long felt toward her son. Fate had placed in her hands the ultimate justification for all the hostility and dislike she felt towards Edward.

In one part of her mind she must have known that Albert had died of typhoid and not of a broken heart over his son's loss of virginity, but she *felt* that Edward had killed him. Perhaps she felt he had in the sense that he would one day be King of England, supplanting not only his mother but his father as well. On February 6 he left England; and the Queen, to cheer him on his journey, sent a message by way of Bruce. She instructed Bruce to see to it that Edward passed his time concentrating on serious thoughts and to keep the possibility before the Prince's mind that before he returned to England his mother might be dead of sorrow.[47] She provided him with a memorandum setting forth what he was to do in the event of her death. Edward had much to bear. A month before his departure he remarked to friends that he had lost a father who had always been 'kindness itself' to him, and he feared he had often given his father pain by his conduct.[48] The Prince of Wales had a forgiving heart. Saddled with unearned guilt, he was driven out of his home like a leper with his mother's unspoken curse for company.

Given the circumstances, however, his going was probably the healthiest thing that could have happened to him, although the initial separation was painful. The Queen noted that after he had said good-bye to her and walked away, he came back again and 'was low and upset, poor Boy. So was I.'[49] His long atonement had begun and would last for forty years. He travelled from Osborne to Dover with his Governor, General Bruce; Major Teesdale, Colonel Keppel and Arthur Meade as equerries; and Dr Minter as physician. Canon Arthur Penrhyn Stanley, Regius Professor of Ecclesiastical History at Oxford and later Dean of Westminster, was prevailed upon by the Queen to travel separately to Alexandria and join the Prince's party there as spiritual adviser, a task which the Dean sought unsuccessfully to avoid. Stanley went with the greatest reluctance and in his first days with Edward was confirmed in his dread. But though initially shocked by what he considered to be the Prince's frivolity, he was greatly surprised to find himself coming very quickly to like the young man. 'It is impossible not to like him,' he would write later, reflecting on his remarkable change of attitude towards the Prince of Wales.[50] But this meeting was in the future when Edward arrived at Dover, after his trying separation from his mother.

The Prince was not booked for a direct passage to Egypt but went by way of Vienna, Venice and Trieste, where he was met by the Emperor Francis Joseph's brother, the Archduke Maximilian, later Emperor of Mexico, who was, as a writer once observed, 'executed by his revolting subjects'. Victoria had insisted on Edward's observing an incognito on the journey, and the press reported at the time of his departure that 'under the present mournful circumstances' the Prince would decline to receive on his travels 'all honours and hospitalities'.[51] The point was certainly made in Vienna, where, despite the Emperor's personal invitation to make use of the Hofburg, the Prince stayed at a hotel. It was rumoured that Edward stopped on the way to Vienna for a meeting with Alexandra, leading *Reynolds's Newspaper* to predict that the marriage, which had been discussed as a possibility, was 'certainly in store for the future'.[52]

If it seemed early days after the Prince Consort's death for Edward to be resuming his courtship, it must be kept in mind that the decision to meet Alexandra would not have been his but his mother's. Before his trip the Queen, in her first meeting with Palmerston following Albert's funeral, discussed her son with the Prime Minister, who expressed concern that there was something amiss between Victoria and the Prince of Wales.[53] The Queen dismissed the doubt, saying that it was her wish that Edward travel and then marry as soon as possible, that having been the Prince Consort's intention regarding the boy. Palmerston, having in all probability a shrewd idea of the true state of Victoria's feelings, agreed that such a plan was a good one.

In this as in things which followed, there was a clear indication of what the Queen's mind had suffered in the shock of the Prince Consort's death. It had become her unswerving determination that everything that Albert had intended or which she imagined that he had intended would be carried through. 'No human power,' she wrote to King Leopold, 'will make me swerve from what *he* decided or wished. ...I apply this particularly as regards our children – Bertie etc – for whose future he had traced everything so carefully.'[54] She would, of course, always know what Albert's wishes had been or would be. By taking that line, she placed all her decisions beyond challenge or appeal and had only to say that '*he* would have wished it so' to close any argument. Had he known his mother's mind, Edward would have had reason to be anxious. She had given Leopold the technique she would employ to cut Edward off from every vital function of the Crown as long as she lived. From the moment of his father's death, Edward performed only those tasks which his mother thought inconsequential or else ones he had worked out behind her back with the government of the day.

It should not be thought that the Queen was simply using Albert's ghost to crush the opposition. As far as was humanly possible, she denied the fact of his death. None of his equerries was dismissed nor his grooms. His rooms were maintained as he had left them, and every evening hot water was taken to his chambers and fresh clothes laid out on his bed, as though he would return shortly, shave and dress for dinner. It was part of Victoria's plan to follow through with Albert's intentions to complete the purchase of Sandringham before Edward left England.

The Sandringham estate, located in Norfolk near Hunstanton and Castle Rising, was the property of Lord Palmerston's nephew, Spencer Cowper. At the time that Palmerston suggested it to Albert as a likely property for the Prince of Wales, the Hall itself was small and delapidated; and over the 8,000 acres comprising the estate the shooting was run out. Rents from the property totalled about £7,000 a year. The Prince Consort had considered buying the Somerleyton estate near Lowestoft, the property of S. Morton Peto, MP; but, deciding against Somerleyton, he began negotiations for Sandringham. The property was purchased for £200,000, and over the next ten years the old Hall was torn down and a new one built from Humbert's designs. Edward had nothing to do with these negotiations for the purchase of a country property. It would not have occurred to either his father or his mother to consult his wishes in the matter.

But the choice proved to be a happy one. Sandringham provided Edward with many happy years of country living, a mode of life to which he proved admirably suited; and it was here that the sophisticated boulevardier astonished his guests both great and small by insisting that they admire his pigs, which he bred to prize-winning specifications. It was at Sandringham that Edward became an English gentleman and, in the process, lodged himself firmly in the hearts of the vast majority of his English subjects, who, in spite of George Meredith and the abominable Sir Willoughby Patterne in *The Egotist,* still considered the English country gentleman the apogee in human attainment. Edward came to be associated with those ancient pursuits – shooting, farming, racing and hunting – which marked the wealthy country man as one fixed in a ruling-class tradition.

Even in the third quarter of the nineteenth century it was a nostalgic image. Old England, whatever it had been, was swiftly disappearing; and many writers, chief among them Thomas Hardy in his Wessex novels, later chronicled its passing. Edward would be the last King of the Greenwood, to use E. M. Forster's romantic designation of that age before the Great War, a period which has itself become in recent years the object of a growing nostalgia. The picture of space around figures on a sunlit lawn; the sounds of bird song and soft voices and women's laughter may be a false one, but the nostalgia is real enough; and it is nostalgia for a golden age that Englishmen sensed had passed even by the middle of the last century. It is for this reason that Edward's association with the country and its pursuits was so important in forming his national image.

Having crossed the Channel, Edward's progress through Europe was leisurely. He stopped at Darmstadt to meet the Grand Duke, whose second son, Louis, was engaged to Princess Alice and with whom Victoria had contrasted Edward to the latter's grave disadvantage. In Vienna he met the Emperor Francis Joseph, making a good impression on that durable old monarch. While in Vienna he also met Laurence Oliphant, an astonishing Scotsman whose adventures had spun him around the world. He was Lord Elgin's private secretary in China, *The Times* correspondent during the Franco-Prussian War, novelist, spiritualist and much more. He was joining Edward's party as official guide to the Adriatic coast. Oliphant found the Prince to be neither studious nor highly intellectual 'but up to the average and beyond it in so far as quickness of observation and general intelligence go'.[55]

The royal group reached Alexandria on February 24 and immediately encountered trouble because Said Pasha, Viceroy of Egypt, could not be prevented from welcoming the Prince with a 21-gun salute, having with difficulty been restrained from ordering a *feu de jois*. Bruce was furious with the Viceroy for having broken the pretence of the Prince's incognito, but one's sympathies are with Said Pasha, who smiled, bowed and expressed his regrets, saying that his subjects would not allow him to do less by way of welcome for the exalted son of the great Queen.[56] Even a Viceroy does not have an opportunity every day to fire his cannons.

Edward travelled by train from Alexandria to Kasr-el-Nil, where, on the steps of the palace, the Viceroy welcomed his guest. Said Pasha's hospitality had become notorious for its liberality, and for Edward he outdid himself. A palace was placed at Edward's service, and for four days he and his suite explored Cairo and the surrounding country before setting out on the journey up the Nile.[57] From the outset of the Egyptian venture, Edward kept rifle and shotgun close at hand in order to take advantage of the shooting; and Stanley, who did not at first have a very high opinion of his spiritual charge, immediately set about persuading Edward to give up Sunday hunting. Much to Stanley's satisfaction as well as to his surprise, Edward consented to the restriction without complaint. In his first encounter with the Prince, Stanley had been put out by Edward's remark that it was far more amusing to shoot crocodiles than it was to poke about ruins.

On March 4 Edward went aboard his Nile steamer, furnished by the Viceroy, and moved up the river to the Palace of Djizeh. Edward and his party continued their journey by camel from Djizeh to the site of the Pyramids, where they arrived late in the afternoon. After camping overnight in the sumptuous tents erected by the Viceroy, everyone in the group struggled out of bed in the chill dawn to watch the sun rise. Edward was the first up, and he climbed the Great Pyramid by himself to witness the sun's return, much to the astonishment of some passing Bedouins who could not understand why Edward did not have himself carried to the summit.[58] After spending most of the day wandering around the Pyramids the party returned to Djizeh, and on the following afternoon set out for the Upper Nile.

Edward was scarcely out of England before reverberations from his mother's attempts to force the nation to join her in honouring Albert's memory were echoing across the country. Throughout February and March a great deal of newspaper space was given to accounts of costly memorial projects, but the space was not given so much to record the establishment of the memorials as to draw attention to their existence in the hope that they would be funded. As the weeks passed, it became embarrassingly clear that people were not particularly anxious to spend their money on any sort of memorial for the late Prince Consort. The matter rapidly became a class as well as a political issue.

In February, less than a week after Edward's departure, Lord Derby, leader of the Conservative opposition, foolishly proposed that the government abstain from all important legislation because of the death of the Prince Consort. *Reynolds's Newspaper*, which in this period had the largest circulation of any newspaper in the world, immediately attacked Derby for 'folly' and 'flunkeyism', pointing out that if the death of Albert were the national calamity it was reported to be, then all the more reason to work hard to overcome the loss. If not, then the suggestion was hypocritical and disgusting. 'Is Royalty more sacred than humanity,' the paper demanded, 'and is a dead German of greater importance than the whole British nation?'[59]

Five weeks later *Reynolds's*, still reporting regularly on the question of the memorials and the official attitudes towards national mourning, attacked *The Times* and Lady Hardwick for their appeals to the working class for money for the Albert Memorial, which the Queen was anxious to have brought to completion – and at the nation's expense. *Reynolds's* had already expressed its view that if the memorial had been designed as a school or hospital and not just as a monument the money would have flowed in, but as it was people were not ready to give their money. As to this new appeal to the workers, the paper was thoroughly disgusted by it, showing its scorn of the manoeuvre by printing a verse of doggerel:

> But grief they say is always dumb,
> But that with which the Prince you follow,
> Reminds us of a muffled drum,
> It is so dismal and so *hollow*.[60]

It cannot be argued that *Reynolds's Newspaper* represented a fringe element of radical opinion. Although the paper grew increasingly radical in sentiment during the next three decades, at this time, as well as later, it spoke for a very substantial section of the middle class, whose views were well represented by the paper. Of particular interest in the attack on Derby is the reference to a 'dead German', an epithet which brought to the surface once again the old hostility felt toward Albert during the Crimean War in the 'fifties, when it was speculated that the Prince Consort was guilty of treason. Fortunately for Edward, while the subject of his father's memorials was being argued in print, he was physically separated from the dissensions and intent on other things.

The journey up the Nile to the First Cataract was uneventful, except for the frequent stops along the river which allowed the Prince to go ashore to hunt and view the local attractions. During this trip Edward's interest in shooting developed into an obsession. The tempo of his hunting increased as the journey continued.

He was not, however, constantly at his guns, and in the course of the seven days he spent steaming up the Nile, he found that he liked Stanley, towards whom he had, initially, maintained a polite and slightly ironic reserve. His resistance to the Dean was based on his conviction that the Queen had set Stanley on him, not so much to minister to his soul as to torment it. He found, however, that the churchman wished him well and wanted to be as much a friend to the young man as the difference in their ages permitted. Once Edward became aware of Stanley's real intentions, the reserve was quickly discarded.

At the First Cataract, the party visited Assuan and the island of Philae to view the ancient ruins, which at that time were thought to have been the centre of ancient Egyptian worship. Two days later he was in Luxor. Coming ashore at midnight, he was met by a huge crowd bearing flaring torches, which cast a dark and smoky light over the scene. The Duke of Coburg had arrived from Cairo slightly ahead of the Prince's party, making possible a dramatic meeting between Edward and his Uncle Ernest in a place as exotic as any Edward had as yet visited.[61]

The morning after reaching Luxor, Edward, surrounded by a large mounted guard and followed by his suite, rode to Karnak, remaining there the entire day. At two o'clock a magnificent lunch was ferried up the river from Luxor, where it had been cooked, and served in the Temple to the entire party. Edward's love of food was becoming well known; and Fadel Pasha, the Governor of Upper Egypt, into whose hands Habib Effendi had delivered the task of meeting the Prince's needs, had the meal prepared with Edward's fondness for eating in mind. After the meal was over, Edward spent the short time remaining until sunset exploring the Temple and the other ruins.

The following two days were taken up with wandering about on the opposite side of the river from Karnak, visiting the Tomb of the Kings, Koorna Palace, the Memnonium, the Colossi and Medinet Hàboo, and, of course, shooting. On Wednesday Edward dropped down river to Keneh, where he got in some more shooting. Braced by that tonic, he visited the Temple of Dendera. Bishop Stanley, surrendering to a romantic desire to meditate alone in the Temple by candlelight, remained behind. After the daylight had faded, he sat alone in the silence of the Temple, but religious thoughts eluded him, and he found his mind turning on the sculptured face of Cleopatra and marvelling how much her features resembled those of the Bishop of Oxford.[62]

It was not Stanley's only lapse. He and Bruce were to have prescribed and supervised a rigid programme of serious reading for Edward, but the only book Edward actually read on the trip was Mrs Henry

Wood's sensational best-seller, *East Lynne*, in which Lady Isabel Vane runs away from home but returns disguised as a nurse to care for her children and, after long service, to regain the love of her husband. Edward thought the book delightful.[63]

On March 27 the Prince dispatched the first telegram sent from Alexandria to London. He went aboard the *Osborne* at Alexandria and reached Jaffa on March 29. Two days later he was in the Holy Land, where no English prince had set foot since Edward I, 600 years earlier.[64] After leaving the *Osborne*, the royal party with fifty servants and a contingent of 100 Turkish cavalry set out on horseback for Jerusalem. The shooting was excellent; and Edward thoroughly enjoyed himself.

After five days of sightseeing in the Holy City, they set out for Bethlehem. As Edward's party was approaching Bethany, Stanley saw two flocks, one made up of white sheep and the other of black goats, grazing on a hillside. The Dean spurred ahead and, reaching the Prince's side, pointed them out to him. Stanley wrote later that having done that much, he 'fell to the rear, feeling that I had at least done my best'.[65] Edward left no record of his feelings as he gazed on the symbolic flocks, grazing on that storied hillside. When confronted with either the ancient or the edifying, he usually said, 'Very interesting', and passed on.

Having grown a luxuriant beard during his journey through Palestine and having substantially thinned out the wildlife in the Holy Land – Magnus records that Edward shot lizards when nothing else was in sight – he entered, as the climax of his tour, the Mosque of Hebron, which had not been penetrated by a Christian since 1187.[66] Dean Stanley had tried some years earlier to enter the Mosque only to be turned away. On this second occasion the Governor of Hebron had asked that the wishes of the Moslems be honoured and no entrance made; but Stanley wrote to Suraya Pasha, Governor-General of Palestine, expressing the Prince of Wales's displeasure at being denied entrance to the shrine. Suraya, accompanied by a regiment of cavalry, arrived in Hebron on April 7 and personally escorted Edward and his party into the church.[67]

By May 20, with visits to Beyrouth, the Cedars of Lebanon, Tyre, Sidon, Rhodes, Patmos and Smyrna behind him, Edward had reached Constantinople, where Sultan Abdul Aziz, despite the difficulty raised by the official incognito, honoured Edward with a state breakfast. The British Ambassador at the Sublime Porte, Sir Henry Bulwer, was astonished by the skill the Prince displayed in dealing with the Sultan. Writing to Lord John Russell, he praised the way in which Edward had brought up for discussion with Aziz all the subjects with which Bulwer had primed him, expressing his conviction that a trained diplomat could not have improved on the performance.[68] Bulwer added, as a further observation, that in his opinion Edward would not learn much from either study or books, but he would learn all that he needed to know through observation and would use that knowledge effectively. It was an astute judgement and accurately anticipated Edward's method of dealing with problems.

Even with Constantinople, Edward's wandering was not at an end. He was now off to Greece, where the itinerary called for an extended exploration of ancient monuments. He reached Athens on May 29. While still in Constantinople he received a letter from the Queen, which General Bruce read to him and to which Edward listened with great pleasure. Bruce wrote to his sister to say that the Prince had felt that the praise given by his mother had been earned. He added that he thought it 'a hopeful feature' in the Prince's character that he had 'a strong love of approbation'. Victoria had temporarily substituted the carrot for the stick.

Cheered by what he believed to be his return to his mother's good grace, Edward arrived in Athens in high spirits; but his lightness of mood was seriously checked by the sudden and dangerous illness of Bruce, who collapsed with a fever from which he never recovered, although he managed to fight off death until June 27, when he finally succumbed.

Leaving Bruce in Athens for what was expected to be a slow but certain recovery, Edward sailed for France, having been obliged to cut short his stay because of political disturbances which culminated in King Otho's being deposed. In France Edward visited the Emperor Louis Napoleon and the Empress Eugénie; and because his incognito made it necessary that he be treated as Lord Renfrew rather than the Prince of Wales, he was able to have a splendid time. Seven years before, he had been captivated by life at the French Court. Now that he was twenty, its attractions proved even more delightful than he had anticipated. As E. F. Benson has put it, the short time Edward spent in the French Court 'produced a more intimate subjective impression than all the temples of Luxor and Dendera, and the Mosque of Hebron, and the Acropolis at Athens, and even the crocodiles on the Nile'.[69] This brief visit to France was very important to Edward's future career and to the history of Europe, for it was with this visit that Edward's attachment to France took firm root and grew with time into his determination that England and France should form close ties of friendship.

Edward returned to Windsor on June 17 1862, after an absence of four months, during which he had been an exile in all but name. The Queen found him 'improved', as she always did after one of his long absences; but when Bruce died, she appointed in his place, with the new title of Comptroller and Treasurer, General Sir William Knollys, a man of sixty-five and old enough to have been Edward's grandfather. Everyone with any claim to influence attempted to persuade her to appoint a younger man; but she refused to listen, closing every discussion on the subject with the statement that the Prince Consort would have wished it. These discussions proved, if any proof were needed, that Victoria intended to take no advice on how she would handle her son. For his part, Edward accepted Knollys without complaint. He wrote to his mother. 'As you feel sure that dear Papa would have approved of the appointment, that will make it doubly my duty to like and get on well with him.'[70] Was he writing in bitterness? Perhaps, but his mother had thoroughly frightened him. He was willing to go a considerable distance, and that over very rough ground, to placate her. Accepting Knollys was one of his shorter journeys.

Looking back to Edward's Near East travels, one comes almost inevitably to the conclusion that except for giving him the opportunity to visit interesting portions of the Mediterranean world, the journey was a waste of time. The heir to the throne should have been doing more important things with those four months. He ought to have been receiving practical experience in the routine business of administering the monarchy. There were those in the government who thought so and urged on Victoria, as a suitable beginning, the proposal that Edward should open the International Exhibition, which had been scheduled for May. It was thought that since Albert's name was so closely associated with the Great Exhibition of 1850, the task was especially appropriate.

Victoria violently rejected the proposal. Insisting that the entire family would observe the strictest mourning for a full year, she forbade anyone to propose such a scheme to the Prince. Those in Palmerston's government who had made the suggestion quickly withdrew it. Thus it began, and so it would continue. Edward was to do nothing, take part in nothing, learn nothing that had to do with the practice of statecraft. In particular, and more especially, he was not to be connected with, serve with or give his name to any organization with which the Prince Consort had been associated. The Queen's ban was absolute. In short, Edward was to be kept from his proper and constitutional role by a mother whose bitterness and resentment paraded as grief and whose tormented selfishness wore the garment of duty.

5

The Danish Connection

Oh, for a voice of song,
Whose love-begushing accents should outwoo
The woodland cushat's fondest, softest coo,
A voice of Song, to sing as should be sung,
With tenderest inspiration's melting tongue,
So lovesome Royal Bridalty's delight!
Epithalamium in Honour of The Marriage of Their Royal
Highnesses The Prince and Princess of Wales

When Edward returned to England on June 14, he found that the
Queen had placed restrictions on his future actions more circumscribing
than those his father had so rigorously maintained. Following the death
of General Bruce in late June, Victoria further limited the Prince's
freedom by putting him in the hands of the ageing Knollys, whose
charge was to prevent the young man from doing anything 'hurtful' to
himself or 'unfit for his position'. To emphasize her point, the Queen
made the comptroller answerable to herself alone for the Prince's
behaviour. A major clash between mother and son seemed inevitable
and from Edward's point of view would have been entirely justified.
The confrontation did not occur. Edward accepted his situation calmly
and continued to treat his mother with the utmost tenderness and
solicitude. Considering her feelings before his own, he did nothing and
said nothing to offend her and seemed determined utterly to efface
himself. He had, or so it appeared, lost the will to resist. Delighted with
his behaviour, she wrote that 'Bertie' was 'most affectionate, dutiful
and amiable' and in her journal she thanked God 'for the blessed
change' in her son. He was 'serious, wishing to do right, anxious to
marry in March or April'.[1] Victoria had settled on an early spring
marriage. Edward had nothing to do with choosing the date and merely
acquiesced, thereby gaining her approval.

Why was Edward being so compliant, so willing to surrender his
pathetically limited independence, which he had won with such
difficulty? There is no single answer to the question, but a fundamental
consideration is that his training had solidly grounded him in obedience.

Further, his mother's openly expressed disgust over the Nellie Clifden affair and her terrible accusations at the time of Albert's death had burdened him with guilt and temporarily destroyed his ability to fight her. In addition, his mother as grieving widow was a figure compelling his pity and indulgence; he would have found it unthinkably cruel to give her additional cause for sorrow, which defiance on his part would certainly have done. Finally, and perhaps of greatest importance, he could see an avenue of escape opening out in front of him. He would marry. His mother's mind was set on it, and he was past opposing the match. Once he was married and living in Marlborough House and Sandringham, he would be free, or so he must have hoped, to go his own way. So for the time being he did as he was told, meekly, as a dutiful son, accepting in silence the humiliation of being ordered about like a child, trying to expiate his guilt.

A troubling aspect of his life during the summer of 1862 was that he had nothing to do except wander around Osborne, Windsor or Balmoral, following his mother in her moves from place to place, or make occasional visits to Sandringham to watch the progress of the renovations being carried out there – a short, plump, but smartly dressed young man with a cigar and a cane sauntering in rather bored fashion among the piles of stone and timber. Naturally, no social activities were allowed because of the deep mourning; and he was not permitted to undertake any official duties. The International Exhibition had brought, and was continuing to bring, many foreign statesmen and heads of government to London, and the Queen was again approached in an attempt to persuade her to allow Edward to receive the most important of these visitors and to extend to them an official welcome. The Queen was absolutely adamant in her refusal to allow Edward any such role. Further appeal, she made clear, would be useless and impertinent, running contrary to the wishes of Albert, 'Our Beloved Prince and Master and Guide and Counseller'.

The summer dragged slowly to a close. Edward's boredom was relieved only slightly by the increasing tempo of the marriage negotiations being conducted by Victoria and Princess Louise and the marriage of his sister Alice to Louis of Hesse-Darmstadt on July 1, another family match which had been sanctified by Albert's approval. With Alice's future settled, the Queen completed her plans for making an emotionally charged journey to Coburg, to renew her acquaintance with those places which had been the settings of Albert's childhood and youth. With Edward safely housed at Osborne, his travelling orders in hand, she left England in late August and on September 2 reached King Leopold's palace at Laeken, near Brussels. Stopping at Laeken had more purpose than simply that of visiting Leopold, whose position of influence and importance with the Queen had long since faded.[2]

She was to meet Prince Christian and Princess Louise, who were at Laeken with two of their daughters, Alexandra and Dagmar; the latter would later marry the Czarevitch Alexander of Russia following a brief engagement to his older brother Nicholas, terminated by the latter's premature death.

Edward was still in England while his mother was meeting Alexandra's parents and suffering intense mental anguish because she was forced to carry through the interview without Albert to support her. She had been unwilling to meet them all at lunch and took her meal apart from the rest of the guests, leaving her three young daughters to represent her. While the Prince and Princess might have understood the Queen's reluctance to break her mourning by socializing over lunch, Prince Christian and his wife, not to mention Alexandra, must have been puzzled by Edward's absence. After the meal, however, Victoria was obliged to meet the Prince and to tell him that she approved the match. This meeting was followed by a more pleasant one for the Queen. Dressed in a plain black dress, Alexandra entered the Queen's room alone in order to have a few moments of private conversation with her future mother-in-law. Victoria was enchanted by the girl and gave her the sprig of white heather Edward had picked in Scotland, expressing the hope it might bring her luck.[3]

On July 4, the Queen left for Coburg. Her departure was the signal for Edward to emerge from hiding. He had slipped quietly into Brussels and registered at a hotel there; and as soon as his mother had left Belgium, he jumped into a carriage and drove off to Laeken to see Alexandra. Before leaving England he had made a journey to Windsor to lay a wreath on his father's coffin, and it was his mother's belief that he stopped to pray for his father's blessing.[4] Once near one another, Alix (as she was called by those close to her) and Edward met every day. They went sightseeing together and began to learn something about each other. Although they could hardly have been in love, there was a mutual liking that soon enabled them to feel a certain amount of affection for each other. On July 8 Prince Christian moved his family back to Brussels and into the hotel where Edward was staying, thereby bringing the courtship one tentative step nearer its conclusion.

The following day Edward, Alix and her family, in response to Leopold's invitation, returned to Laeken to walk in the royal gardens. Before setting out Edward sent his mother a telegram: 'Now I will take a walk with Princess Alexandra in the garden and in three-quarters of an hour I will take her into the grotto, and there I will propose, and I hope it will be to everyone's satisfaction.'[5] The previous day Edward had spoken to Prince Christian, telling him that he loved Alexandra and wished to marry her. In describing the effect of his declaration on the girl's father, Edward wrote, 'I don't think I ever saw anybody so

much pleased as he was.' Some writers have regarded this comment
as naive, but it may not have been so ingenuous as has been suggested.
There may have been a barb in it, as there may also have been in the
final clause of the telegram to his mother, notifying her that he was
about to propose.

At Laeken the Prince and the rest of the party were welcomed by
King Leopold, who, to no one's surprise, suggested a stroll in the garden. Supervision of the physical process of getting Edward and Alix
engaged had been placed in Leopold's hands, and he carried out his
duties with the humourless thoroughness that had marked his entire life.
Everyone went into the garden, and after a suitable interval Alix and
Edward lagged behind the others. Edward proposed and was accepted.
He took her hand, and she kissed him. The following day the newly
engaged pair toured the battlefield of Waterloo, the trip being another
of Leopold's suggestions. From the garden to the battlefield: one wonders if Leopold had a liking for symbols. Returning from Waterloo, the
young couple were treated to a state banquet in their honour; and on
July 11 they travelled together to Cologne where they parted, Edward
going to join his mother at Coburg and Alix returning to Denmark.[6]

The Queen had been told by telegram and letter of Alexandra's
acceptance, and on July 16 official notification of the engagement was
released to the British press, the communiqué having been drawn up
by Victoria in her own hand. It was a marriage, she wrote, 'based
entirely upon mutual affection and the personal merits of the princess',
and was 'in no way connected with political considerations'. And she
added, 'The revered Prince Consort, whose sole object was the education and welfare of his children, had long been convinced this was a
most desirable marriage'. With the first part of the telegram, the
Queen hoped to soothe Prussian nerves, recently jangled by the closer
ties between England and Denmark, and to convince the world that
this was an affair of the heart. She also had an obsessive dread that
Alexandra's family would gain some influence over Edward or her
court by the connection, and was determined to prevent that from
happening.

The English people received the news with delight. Lord Granville
sent Edward a letter of congratulation and appears to have spoken for
the country when he wrote, 'It is impossible to exaggerate how pleased
everyone in all classes here is with the good news.'[7] Princess Alice had
been married in a privacy that was almost surreptitious; and for ten
months the nation had been sunk in official gloom, neither levée nor
royal appearance relieving the grim mourning of the Court. The announcement of Edward's engagement appeared to break this pattern
and seemed to promise a partial return to cheerfulness. The nation
applauded the news.

Unfortunately, Edward was not present to receive the good wishes of his countrymen. He was sequestered with his mother in Coburg, where he alternately bore the grumblings of his Uncle Ernest, who considered the Danish alliance an insult to Germany, and the tears of his mother, who had immersed herself in yet deeper grief by going through all of Albert's youthful belongings and visiting every place in and near Coburg that had associations with the Prince Consort.

Naturally, she met Baron Stockmar, grown old and feeble, who on greeting her burst into tears, as did she, when he lamented in a quavering voice, 'that I should endure this cruel blow, drives me at times half mad. An edifice which, for a great and noble purpose had been reared, with a devout sense of duty, by twenty-three years of laborious toil, has been shattered to its very foundations.'[8] Well might Victoria weep; and if it seems unlikely that a man shaken by grief would have expressed himself in such measured phrases, it is necessary to remember that Baron Stockmar would not have admitted that strong emotion justified weak syntax.

At the end of September Victoria returned to England, but Edward did not accompany her. Instead, she directed him to join his sister Vicky and her husband for an extended tour of the Mediterranean; and she placed in his hands a memorandum outlining his activities between October 1 and his wedding in March.[9] Her directive ensured that Edward would be kept away from Alexandra during this long period, a remarkable injunction to place on a young man who had just become engaged. Her justification to those who questioned her on the subject was that she thought it unwise for engaged people to see much of one another before the wedding. There would be too much opportunity for disagreements and dislikes to arise.

This was the stated reason. The real reason was something else. Before leaving Coburg, Victoria had invited Alexandra to come to England to visit her during the month of November, making a particular point that she was to come alone. Since Edward had not yet proposed when Victoria extended the invitation, her acceptance must have been a foregone conclusion and the proposal in the garden a mere ritual. Prince Christian agreed somewhat reluctantly to the Queen's request, apparently aware that Edward would be out of the country. Alix had no choice but to accept the Queen's strange invitation, although she felt that she was being placed on trial – which was not the case at all. Prince Christian, who was to deliver his daughter into the Queen's charge at Osborne, was informed that he would be welcome for two days and was then to return home. What his feelings were about such orders is not recorded, but he certainly made no protest.

It is in her handling of Alix's father that Victoria's reason for keeping Edward away from his fiancée's family emerges most strongly. She had, as mentioned earlier, an almost pathological dislike of the Danish royal family, and she was very nervous that Edward might be influenced by them. The point can be made that Victoria was justified in not allowing Edward to visit Denmark because such a visit would have been interpreted on the Continent (and in Prussia especially) as a gesture of political support of the Danes in their struggle with Prussia over control of Schleswig and Holstein.

Plausible as the argument is, it had little to do with the Queen's decision. When he learned at Laeken of the Queen's plan to keep Edward and Alix apart, King Leopold, whom no one could accuse of libertarianism, took Victoria aside and attempted to persuade her that she was acting unreasonably. The Queen refused to listen to him on the subject; and Leopold concluded, rightly, that the purpose behind the Queen's ordering Edward to stay out of England during Alexandra's visit to Osborne was to gain personal control over the girl.[10] If she could dominate Alexandra's mind, she would accomplish two things: she would nullify as far as possible any influence her family might have on her, and through her she would secure another means of controlling her son.

Edward had quietly sided with Leopold on this issue, but when no progress was made, he gave up the enterprise and went off with his sister and her husband on the royal yacht for a long cruise. When one remembers that he had spent the entire spring on an extended tour, had been more or less totally unoccupied throughout the summer, only to be sent away in the autumn on the ridiculous grounds that if he were to see much of Alix they might come to dislike one another, it is curious and little short of a miracle that he did not revolt against the treatment he was receiving. He endured this as he had endured the rest, that is, as best he might. Alix wrote him long letters, giving him at least some contact with the person he was going to marry.

They met briefly in Calais as she was returning home from England in the last week of November, but they had only two days together before Alexandra left to be with her family for her eighteenth birthday on December 1. Her mother had insisted that she be allowed to return home in time to celebrate that birthday with her family, a request that enraged Victoria, who had intended to keep the girl with her until that date. Nor was the Queen any happier with her son once he was back home with her again. She fell back into her old complaints against him, finding him generally unpleasant to have around the house, and thinking the sooner he married the better. She also wrote to Leopold that she feared Alexandra was much mistaken about Edward, and that she was in for disappointments.

It seems reasonable to ask why the wedding was taking place at all. There was no political reason for an English alliance with Denmark.

In fact such an alliance could only foment trouble between England and Germany, but that difficulty had been shunted aside. If political considerations were not at the base of the marriage contract, neither was love. Edward and Alexandra hardly knew one another, and the important arrangements connecting them had been made before they had more than met. What then was the reason? It was not a pleasant one, although not, of course, an uncommon one for such arrangements at this period. Albert and Victoria had decided that to prevent Edward from throwing himself away in loose living he required a wife, a woman to meet his physical needs and, if possible, anchor him to a home. They looked around and found one in Alexandra, whose impoverished family were delighted to attach her to the most sought-after bachelor in Europe.

March 10 was set for the day of the wedding, and by any standard the ceremony should have been conducted in Westminster Abbey as one of the great national events of the age. The nation was in a mood to celebrate this wedding. Their sense of romance, however falsely stirred, had been wakened by the unfolding story of the Prince of Wales's courtship of the beautiful Alexandra. Beyond this, the people were happy that Edward was not marrying a German, at least not a Prussian; and the English felt no hostility toward the Danes. Victoria was not, however, willing to satisfy her people in the matter. To the immense chagrin of everyone, she decreed that the wedding would be held in St George's Chapel at Windsor, where no royal wedding had taken place since 1122. She said that she felt incapable of facing the crowds; what actually stopped her was that, if the wedding were held at Westminster, she would have been required to appear in state, which would have meant abandoning her mourning for a day. This she absolutely refused to do.[11]

There was a brief flurry of protest in the press, which subsided quickly and was buried in the outpourings of praise and welcome for Alexandra. There appears to have been a general determination to make the best of what was clearly an unfortunate decision. At this point there was almost no criticism of Edward to be found in the press, or any of the solemn moralizing over the duties of the heir to the throne. This was to come in the spring.

As March approached and the anticipated arrival of Alexandra drew near, the publishing houses released a flood of poetry, led, suitably enough, by Tennyson's 'The Poet Laureate's Welcome to The Princess'. It was in this period that Tennyson was becoming acquainted with Victoria; and he visited the Queen for the first time at Osborne in May 1863, beginning a friendship which ended only with Tennyson's death in 1892. On that first visit he talked to Victoria about immortality of the soul, insisting, she recorded in her diary, that scientific discoveries had not interfered with this. He added that without immortality there was no reason why there should be a God.[12]

Tennyson's poem was a celebration of Alexandra and her arrival in England. The verses seem strained and even comic in part; but while such oddities as Tennyson's arrow-storm of exclamation marks are largely attributable to custom and, therefore, taste, the martial element in the poem is not. In its tendency to run to war imagery, the poem anticipates a welter of blood-drenched poems dedicated to Alexandra. There is also the unfortunate sense of a subject being painfully developed:

> Sea-King's daughter from over the sea, Alexandra!
> Saxon and Norman and Dane are we,
> But all of us Danes in our welcome of thee, Alexandra!
> Welcome her, thunders of fort and of fleet!
> Welcome her, thundering cheer of the street!
> Welcome her, all things youthful and sweet,
> Scatter the blossoms under her feet!

The Sea-King's daughter is a reference, of course, to the viking past of the Danes and is intended as flattery. The sea-king image, however, is unequivocally that of a warrior devoted to murder, robbery with violence, rape and arson, with a sideline in slave trading. There is a continuation of the spirit of brutal aggressiveness in the 'thunders of fort and of fleet' and 'thundering cheer of the street'. The poet speaks of blaring trumpets, flames flaring along the headlands, the clash of bells and of cities running with fire. The concluding lines move from excitement to incoherence.

> Blissful bride of a blissful heir,
> Bride of the heir of the kings of the sea,
> O joy to the people and joy to the throne,
> Come to us, love us and make us your own!
> For Saxon or Dane or Norman we,
> Teuton or Celt or whatever we be,
> We are all Danes in our welcome of thee, Alexandra!

This is clearly not one of Tennyson's best poems.

Lesser poets than Tennyson made no effort to conceal the violence of the passion stirred by Alexandra's approach. One writer, whose poem was recited by Miss Avonia Jones at the Theatre Royal, New Adelphi, to a packed house on the night of Tuesday March 10, devoted one verse to the might of the Danish vikings. The stanza contains the line, 'Thy battle-raven's gore-beaked hideousness'.[13] In another poem, the lines,

> 'Out of the strong came sweetness': so of old
> The Hebrew riddle ran: and now we see

The riddle set and solved again. Behold
The lion's mouth with honey filled for thee.

In yet another poem:

In their Valhalla, lo! the Viking Dead,
Drain the deep mead-horns to the Danish Maid,
Thinking how those sea-dragons o'er the wave
Bore them to song and shield and dance of glaive.

In 'A Talk With Thames' the same poet gives the following lines to the river:

I have glassed the gleam of pageants; blood has mingled with my tide;
Celt and Roman, Sax and Norseman, have fought along my side.[14]

The examples quoted by no means exhaust the supply. Over and over again, Alexandra's beauty and virginity are placed in conjunction with reference to fighting and blood. Perhaps it was only the nation's jingoism surfacing at an inappropriate moment; but there is another kind of excitement present in these poems, something close to sexual excitement that is not released in the conventional lines praising Alexandra's beauty, but does find expression in the lines devoted to descriptions of violence and blood.

Many of the poems also display a preoccupation with death, in particular Albert's death and the Queen's grief. A. C. Rathbone's 'An Ode to The Marriage of H.R.H. The Prince of Wales with Alexandra of Denmark' deals conventionally with the coming marriage and then reverts to Albert and the Queen:

His soul is gone
To Heaven's rest –
He leans upon
His Maker's breast,
Albert the Good, whose virtues, half divine,
Find in the British Heart a sacred shrine.

The poem closes with an appeal to God to protect Victoria and extend her reign 'to life's remotest stage'.[15] W. Aytoun simply forgot in the middle of his poem that he was writing a marriage ode and fell into melancholy over the Queen's suffering:

Oh, Royal Lady! honoured and most dear,
Whose bitter woe no human tongue can tell, –
For whom, while bending o'er that piteous bier,
From eyes unused to weep, the tear-drops fell![16]

Digressions such as these give an idea of Victoria's hold on the popular imagination, her power to keep a sense of guilt alive among a portion of her people on a subject over which they were inclined to feel guilty anyway, and the way in which she cast a gloom over the approaching festivities. The melancholy preoccupation with change pervading literature of the Romantic period took in Victorian middle-class culture the debased form of a morbid interest in death and mourning. Victoria's eternal sorrowing was, in part, an exemplar of this obsession and aroused in her subjects a sense of awe that gave her great psychological power.

As might be expected, sermons on the marriage abounded and followed the predictable lines, asking for divine protection for the young couple and comfort for the Queen. Edward was not criticized in the sermons, although there were many solemn warnings about the heaviness of his duties to come. Of all the sermons preached, none attempted to penetrate more deeply into the spirit of the occasion than the one by the Rev. John Hunt of Christ Church, Haxton, on the topic, 'The Marriage in Heaven'. 'There are many grounds,' the Rev. Hunt suggested, 'on which marriage might claim our thoughts. In this life, where we are surrounded by mystery, where we pass from mystery to mystery, this is the greatest of all mysteries. By it the existence of man is continued on earth.... Strange wonders are these earthly connections.'[17]

The Queen may have made up her mind to marry off her eldest son in a 'quiet little Berkshire borough', but London chose to go ahead with its celebration as though the marriage were being held at Westminster. To give point to the preparations, Edward and Alexandra would pass through London on their way to Windsor, following Alix's arrival at Gravesend, scheduled to occur on March 7.

The day dawned bleak and wretchedly cold. There was no sun, and intermittent, freezing showers of rain fell throughout the day but failed to keep the population from turning out in hordes to welcome the Danish princess. Having paused off the coast at Margate to allow the Mayor of that town to come aboard and present Alexandra with an address of welcome, the royal yacht made its way slowly up the Thames through hundreds of private boats, crammed with well-wishers, who had come to cheer Alexandra, while the shore batteries at Tilbury and Nore boomed a welcome.[18]

The yacht tied up at Gravesend, surrounded by cheering, shouting crowds. Edward was supposed to have been waiting for Alix at the pier, but he had been delayed and did not arrive for another half hour. It was one of the few times in his career that he was late for an important occasion, punctuality being one of his virtues. On the other hand, it must have been one of the few times Alexandra was on time. She would delay her husband often in the future while she played at readying herself, and he paced the floors below, muttering a litany of mixed English and German curses. When at last Edward's carriage did draw up at the dock, he leaped down and ran up the gangway in his eagerness and with a complete disregard for decorum, he threw his arms around Alexandra, who was hurrying towards him, and kissed her, to the wild cheering of the crowds.[19] Bestowing that kiss was surely one of the most popular public acts Edward ever performed, and it went far towards creating the public image of him as a man of warmth and passion.

Edward, Alix, her family and staff and Edward's extensive staff left Gravesend by train for the short run to the Bricklayer's Arms Station in Southwark where they were met by the Lord Mayor, sheriffs and other officials in full regalia. Leaving the train, the party formed a carriage procession and set out for the long ride to Paddington Station. At London Bridge (lavishly decorated and sporting a triumphal arch at its north end) the reception committee members, aldermen and councillors in their carriages joined the procession.[20] Everywhere along their route the crowds were dangerously thick, but in the City the crush became so intense that a way had to be cleared for the carriages by the Life Guards, who at one point actually made a charge with drawn sabres,[21] leading *Reynolds's Newspaper* to observe after the wedding that 'a portion of the people has been trampled and a portion has grovelled in the dirt'.[22] The paper was referring not only to the procession but to other instances as well in which severe harm was done to people by police and cavalry mounts. Lord Malmesbury complained that at times between May 7 and 10, and particularly on the seventh, numbers of streets in the City were completely blocked by the crowds, and 'if it had not been for the good temper of the people, some dreadful catastrophe must have occurred'.[23]

All along the route the streets were draped with flags and bunting and the windows crowded with spectators. Along Piccadilly the houses of the wealthy were crowded with spectators, including Alexandra's Cambridge relatives at Gloucester House. None of Edward's family was among the watchers, the Queen having prevented the Princess Royal from travelling to London to observe the procession.[24] In the Park Lord Ranelagh had mustered his 17,000 citizen soldiers of the Volunteer Army, and everywhere in the area of the procession the streets surged with thousands of people.

A striking aspect of the procession was the seediness of the royal carriages. Lord Malmesbury, a former foreign secretary, recorded his impressions of Alexandra's welcome and wrote that he 'was never more surprised and disappointed' than he was at the appearance of the Queen's equipages. 'The carriages looked old and shabby, the horses very poor, with no trappings, not even rosettes and no outriders. In short the shabbiness of the whole cortége was beyond anything one could imagine, everybody asking, "Who is the Master of the Horse." '[25] The *Evening Mail* stated flatly that the turnout was inadequate for the

occasion. 'There may have been reasons with which we are unac-
quainted for the exceptional plainness and simplicity, not to use a
harsher term, of the royal equipages....The jewel [Alexandra] was
there, but assuredly it owed nothing to the setting.'[26]

Victoria would have given instructions covering so important an
aspect of the Princess's reception, and the conclusion is inescapable
that she specified the kind of impression her carriages were to make.
The previous year she had entered empty carriages in the International
Exhibition parade to remind the world of her loss. But if her intention,
in this instance, was to give a reminder of grief, she failed, giving instead
an impression of niggardliness and meanness. Indeed, the showing of
the carriages may have been an early indication of the miserliness that
became one of the Queen's striking characteristics in the following
years. Alexandra might have been hurt by the lack of royal display on
her behalf, but fortunately she was apparently first too excited and then
too tired to notice. Her father, however, might have remembered that
Victoria had declined to invite him to stay in the palace when he had
come to fetch his daughter home in late November of the previous year,
forcing him to stay overnight in a hotel. No doubt he was more prepared
than his daughter for her rather mean eccentricities.

It was generally held by the press that Alexandra's reception was the
greatest outpouring of loyalty that century. Many contemporary
journalists believed that the gathering of people on the occasions of the
reception and celebration of the wedding was greater than the numbers
who came out for the opening of the Great Exhibition.

Having escaped the situation encountered in the City and avoided
being pitched headlong out of their carriage at Slough, Edward and
Alexandra drove in pouring rain through Eton and on to Windsor,
where the royal princes and princesses rushed to the door to meet Alix
and give her a belated but extremely warm reception. The Queen did
not come forward at once but waited for Edward to bring the girl to
her, which he did after the first of the greetings were over. Victoria
embraced Alix and kissed her but apparently found the scene disturbing
because almost at once she withdrew to her room to weep. A few
minutes later Alexandra slipped into her room to comfort her and, as
Victoria described the event, 'knelt before me with the sweet loving
expression that spoke volumes'.[27]

The young woman had taken the measure of her future mother-in-
law. Dressed in lilac and white, the semi-mourning which the Queen
had prescribed for the women of the family and the Court, but which
would not have been demanded from Alexandra, the Princess made her
gesture of adoration and submission and won Victoria's approval.
Alexandra was not very intelligent, her childlike qualities having been
recorded by many observers; but on this occasion at least, she acted

with a shrewdness and accuracy of psychological perception that charmed and disarmed the grieving widow, whose grief was a weapon as well as a shield.

There was neither time nor opportunity between Alexandra's arrival and the wedding for either her or Edward to reflect at any length on their approaching marriage. Events carried them forward with a rush. There was turmoil, brief but upsetting, over what wedding dress the bride would wear. Leopold had sent a magnificent dress of Brussels lace, but it was finally decided that one of English manufacture would have to be substituted.[28] More disturbing moments came when Victoria insisted on taking Edward and Alexandra into the mausoleum, where Albert was buried, to tell them that they had his blessing. Alexandra burst into tears and Edward appeared 'moved'. The wedding portrait was taken on the morning of the tenth with Alexandra in her gown, Edward in a morning suit and the Queen, profoundly swathed in black, seated in profile, staring up at a white marble bust of Albert. It is no wonder that when Alexandra appeared shortly afterwards in the Chapel she looked disturbed.

On the night before the wedding London was brightly lighted with thousands of gas jets, and one reporter wrote that all the people of the city appeared to be out walking. In Cork and Dublin and other Irish cities there were displays put up by newspapers and the corporations, but in Cork a mob attacked a chemist's shop that was decorated in honour of the marriage and broke the windows. The mob then marched on the Hibernia Hotel and smashed all the illuminating devices there and on the other hotels. Repeatedly, mounted police charged into the crowd but without effect. Quiet did not return to the streets until the city was once more restored to darkness.

Dublin experienced nothing worse than hostile letters in the nationalist press, and only the Catholic University turned off its illuminations in response to the threats. On the day of the wedding huge crowds poured into Dublin to watch the review and marching of 6,000 troops in the park. At Kingstown an estimated 10,000 people gathered to watch the naval display. At the hour of the wedding H.M.S. *Ajax* fired a twenty-one-gun salute while the people cheered. It is a sad truth that during Victoria's reign, through indifference, insensitivity and carelessness, successive governments and the Crown allowed much good feeling and loyalty in Ireland to drain away unrecognized, unvalued and, at last, irredeemable.

At Windsor the wedding morning broke cold and cloudy. A white frost stiffened the ground, and the hundreds of spectators who came crowding into the town were soon hugging themselves and stamping their feet to drive out the cold. The town itself was trimmed with flags, banners and streamers strung over the streets, which gave a cheerful touch to the scene once the sun managed to struggle through and shine palely on the chilled crowds. Overzealous, the police turned away some two hundred ticket holders on the mistaken conviction that all the assigned places in the open sheds erected to house the ticket holders were taken. They were not.[29] Confusion resulted from the fact that it was so cold in the stands that the people kept coming down from them to walk around, and the police misjudged the numbers that had been admitted.

The Bishop of Oxford preached the wedding sermon on a topic of his own choosing, only slightly amended by the Queen. He had proposed to speak on the theme, 'Rejoice with them that do rejoice'. Victoria approved, instructing him, however, to add the words, 'And weep with them that weep'.[30] As Edward waited for Alix, he frequently glanced up at his mother, seated in Catherine of Aragon's closet, a tiny recessed box above and to the left of the altar, either in concern for her or in search of further signs of her approval.[31] Dressed in black and wearing her blue Garter ribbon, she was a powerful and sombre presence.

C. T. Longley, Archbishop of Canterbury, conducted the service, assisted by four bishops and the Dean of Windsor; and Jenny Lind accompanied the choir in singing the chorale which the Queen had chosen for the occasion.[32] The piece was one of Albert's compositions. While the chorale was being sung, the Queen was temporarily overcome and had to be led out to recover herself.

Following the service there was a wedding breakfast, which the Queen did not attend. After the ceremonial meal Edward and Alix came to bid her goodbye, then left by train for Southampton, where they boarded one of the royal yachts to be conveyed to Osborne for their honeymoon, free at last, presumably, to find out the best and worst about each other. Their departure from Windsor was uneventful except for a spirited approach to the royal coach at Slough by a group of Eton boys, with Randolph Churchill in the fore, who broke through police lines, chains and wooden barriers to rush the carriage and cheer the pair.[33]

'Ah, dear brother, what a sad and dismal ceremony it was!' wrote Victoria to the King of Prussia, describing Edward and Alix's wedding. The press did not pass such a grim judgement on the event itself; but in a swift change in tone from that which dominated the writing up to Alexandra's arrival, they looked into the Prince of Wales's future with the darkest misgivings. *The Times* stated gloomily that 'the heirdom of a great empire was incompatible with goodness and common sense, with loyalty, filial feeling and truth'.[34] On the day of the wedding the *Daily Telegraph*, determined to be cheerful, insisted that on such a morning, 'philosophy would be out of place'. With the next stroke of the pen, the editor was warning the Prince to listen carefully during the marriage ceremony and catch 'all the solemn notes which sound for HIM in the music of the Wedding March'. He is especially to be aware that 'never yet in its ample scope did graver fears and graver hopes cluster about the Heir of the Empire', and to remember that while 'Victoria has made it *queenly* to be good, and pure and faithful', it would be his task to make it 'princely'.[35]

The *Evening Mail*, ruminating on the marriage, recalled that 'there had been only four marriages of the Prince of Wales in this country', and that bad omens, vindicated by the results, surrounded them all. The writer hoped that Edward's marriage would be an exception. The editorial went on to inform the Prince that 'whatever the case in former times, the country had become strict in demanding from its Princes, in addition to their public virtues, a high standard of morality'.[36] The *Globe and Traveller* began gently enough by expressing pleasure over the Prince's accepting the huge, wrought iron Norwich Gates from the International Exhibition, which the people of Norfolk had bought by public subscription for Sandringham.[37] But a few days later the paper was preoccupied with making a comparison between Edward's marriage and that of George IV, 'not in the spirit of coarse censure of the past', the paper observed, and 'still less in vain and overweening confidence in an unchequered future – never yet vouchsafed to man – but in the spirit of sober comparison of the two epochs'.[38]

The most strongly worded commentaries in the public press appeared in *Lloyd's Weekly London Newspaper* and *Reynolds's Newspaper,* which Edward read regularly. *Lloyd's* editor, Blanchard Jerrold, reminded his readers that the characters of Alexandra and Edward were unknown to the public, that the Prince had been given little opportunity 'of showing the stuff of which he is made', and that intellectually he was a stranger to his people. The only justification for the enormous out-pouring of loyalty and sympathy which the Prince had so far com-manded was that 'the white flower of a blameless life' which his father had lived demanded it in his name. And it was to his father and his mother that he must look for the answer as to why he was being cheered. He must expect to be judged by the 'lofty example' given by his parents; and he must commit himself to proving 'worthy of his illus-trious mother and distinguished sire', live a life which was 'blameless and cloudless', as had his parents, and maintain a court 'pure in all its domestic relations'.[39] As if that were not enough, Jerrold added that it would have been disgraceful had the English, 'a great and free people', been carrying this frenzied loyalty 'to the feet of a boy'. That, of course, was exactly what the crowds were doing; and in doing so they were not giving a moment's thought to the blameless flower of Albert's moral life, nor to the Queen's spotless domestic arrangements.

Reynolds's Newspaper did not even pretend to believe that the people were cheering Albert and Victoria. Its line was that the entire undertaking from start to finish was a national disgrace. The first point made in the attack was that whole segments of the nation were in dire poverty and enduring suffering from hunger, cold and sickness. It pointed to the Lancashire spinners, in particular, and noted that while an entire fleet was sent to accompany Alexandra to England, not a single ship would the government press into the service of carrying the starving labourers of Lancashire and their families to the colonies where there were jobs waiting for them.

The second theme of the editorial was political in character, calling into question the entire principle of monarchy and reverting, as so many papers did, to the personality of George IV. Questioning the character of Edward and observing that nothing was known of it, the writer complained that the 'last Prince of Wales was as grossly belauded, and his wedding, if not as expensively, yet as slavishly celebrated as the present Prince and his marriage. Then, as now, the theatres were opened freely to the public, mobs shouted, bonfires blazed, corporations crouched, bishops blessed, and the people's gold poured forth in floods to glorify a royal swine.'

The final element in the excoriation of the royal show was essentially moral. 'Something is rotten in the state of England,' the editorial said, pointing out that the nation seemed to be totally indifferent not only to human suffering and injustice within England but abroad as well, pointing to the Polish suffering at the hand of Russia and other international issues which were going unremarked. There would be ghosts at the wedding feast, the paper predicted; and they would be the spirits of starving Lancashire spinners and their children. 'Is not the present time a crisis of national agony? Coventry ribbon makers! and Spitalfield weavers! funeral shrouds, not wedding favours, would, at this moment, be the appropriate produce of your attenuated hands and idle looms. Men and women, emasculated operatives of Lancashire, what would be your gifts and prayers, pearls or tears, blessings or curses, could you but proclaim your wrongs and assert your rights?'[40]

Two long, dense columns of print carried *Reynolds's* thundering indictment; and it closed with the bitter conclusion that, in the last analysis, perhaps the display was proper. It had been exploited by the shopkeepers of the nation to advertise 'pills and pants, sloe leaves and slops, tallow and treacle'. And that is what ought to be done: 'What, in the name of all that is reasonable, is the use of a Prince of Wales – or, for that matter, of a constitutional monarch – but to conjure the money of simpletons from their own into the pockets of publicans, courtiers, prostitutes, place men, and other political vermin who batten and thrive on the follies and calamities of the human race?'

SHE STOOPS TO CONQUER.

'She Stoops to Conquer': from the *Tomahawk*. July 1867
By permission of the British Museum

BEWARE!

FORTY CENTURIES LOOKING DOWN UPON HIM.

(DEDICATED TO THE ROYAL TRAVELLER IN EGYPT

7. 'Beware!': from the *Tomahawk*, February 1869
   By permission of the British Museum

In the next forty years of the newspaper's history, nothing, not even the paroxysms produced by the Mordaunt scandal and the Baccarat affair, would match the bitterness of *Reynolds's* attack on royalty carried on that wintry March Sunday in 1863. It called the Queen a miser and a thief. It accused the government of being vicious and corrupt and such royal appointees as Phipps fawning dogs, and it characterized Edward and Alexandra as useless nonentities. It damned the philistinism of the business community and the stupidity of the populace. It was a magnificent jeremiad and a ringing denunciation of a system gone wrong.

In almost any other nation of the world it might have been the opening gun of revolutionary, or at least republican, intentions, but Englishmen read it that Sunday morning and simply nodded or fumed according to their political colouring. No tramp of approaching armies disturbed Alix and Edward honeymooning on the Isle of Wight.

What the press was doing was attempting to prevent the public from forming an emotional attachment to Edward as a person. If he was to be loved (and no section of the press saw any reason for loving him), it was not as a man but as a set of values and as a symbol of selfless service. His public embrace of Alexandra was acceptable because it fitted neatly into the scheme the press had shaped for him: young men should love the women they are to marry. But in almost every section of the press from *The Times* to *Reynolds's* the underlying and recurring theme in the editorials was that these royal personages were expensive to the nation and not much of value could be expected from them in terms of their contribution to the common good. These attacks, more often implied than stated, despite *Reynolds's* forthrightness, went beyond Edward to the whole concept of monarchy. Looking back in time, the writers saw with dread the figure of George IV; and looking forward, expected the worst of princes to come. The political message is unmistakable: we pay too high a price for our royalty. We would be better off without them. Such an attitude, strengthened by time and repetition, must almost inevitably have had its influence on Edward and made him see that his best defence against attack was to keep his personal life as private as possible and to be seen as often as possible fulfilling a ceremonial role.

6

Birth of a Gentleman

Royalty is a government in which the attention of the nation is concentrated on one person doing interesting actions.... Most people when they read that the Queen walked on the slopes at Windsor – that the Prince of Wales went to the Derby – have imagined that too much thought and prominence were given to little things. But they have been in error; and it is nice to trace how the actions of a retired widow and an unemployed youth become of such importance.

Walter Bagehot, *The English Constitution*

One of the first ways, perhaps prophetic, in which the Prince of Wales, as a newly emerged element in national life, caught the attention of his countrymen was through the Parliamentary debate over his allowance. As a result of his father's careful management, the funds of the Duchy of Cornwall had increased to about half a million pounds. The amount had been substantially reduced, however, shortly before Edward's marriage by the purchase of Sandringham and by his large contribution to the Albert Memorial Fund, made immediately following the Prince Consort's death. After some symbolic skirmishing between the government and members of the opposition, Parliament voted Edward an income of £50,000 a year, £10,000 of which was to go to Alexandra for her own use. Her father, learning the size of grant, remarked to an acquaintance that the sum was £8,000 more than his yearly income. The £50,000, added to the interest from capital investment and the Sandringham rents, brought Edward's income up to £115,000 a year.[1]

Under ordinary circumstances, such an income ought to have sufficed; but what few members of the government appeared willing to understand was that Edward would be expected to assume the social responsibilities properly belonging to the Crown, and which in the ordinary course of events would be paid for out of the Crown incomes. Further, Edward would be taking his place among members of an aristocracy who, in many individual cases, had incomes far in excess of his. Following his marriage, the Court, to the degree that it can he said to have existed as a centre of national social life, was maintained by the Prince of Wales and paid for out of his private revenues, with the result that year after year he overran his rents and interest and had to draw on his capital to make up the difference. It was not a healthy situation. Reports that he was spending more than his annual income led to speculation that he must be in debt, a persistent rumour that caused him much embarrassment and which by the 1890s became a serious problem to him, contributing to his other difficulties with the press and the dissenting element in the nation.

Within a year of his marriage, grumblings over his mother's withdrawal from national life began to find echoes in the press. Edward and Alexandra had been holding a semi-formal Court at Marlborough House and occasional levées at Buckingham Palace, but they were not the Queen. Aside from the quite genuine feelings of loss which people in all classes experienced at Victoria's continued withdrawal, there were some feelings about the fact that she was paid enormous sums of money to maintain a public position, and to support trade. Responding tartly to these muted requests for her return, she announced that she would never again be seen at levées, drawing rooms, State concerts and balls. She had, she said 'higher duties' to perform. An editorial in *The Times,* pointing out that the 'living have their claim as well as the dead', had no effect.

Punch portrayed her as the statue of Hermione in *The Winter's Tale,* with Britannia, figuring as Paulina, appealing to her, saying, ''Tis time, descend; be stone no more.'[2] The *Pall Mall Gazette,* on the other hand, in its first issue, defended her withdrawal. A member of Parliament, Mr Ayrton, attacked her for neglecting her duty; but John Bright, the well-known radical orator, seizing a political advantage, praised her for harbouring her grief, insisting that it showed great feeling. When Ayrton attempted to reply, he was howled down.[3] But in all these discussions, no one appeared to take thought of what the Queen's continued absence in Osborne and Balmoral meant in economic terms to Edward. Victoria never contributed a penny towards his expenses, and the government was unwilling to risk her anger by diverting any part of her income into her son's pocket. Thoroughly aware of what these costs were doing to his capital, Edward accepted the burden without taking any steps to attempt to secure from Parliament an additional grant of money. Indeed, such an effort would probably have resulted in public embarrassment for the Prince. His appeal would have been rejected and, as the decade advanced, with increasing hostility.

Despite his gloomy economic prospects, Edward and his bride's return from Osborne had about it the quality of a triumph. From the moment of their entrance into Marlborough House, they inaugurated a period of splendour and gaiety in social life that London had not known since the days of George IV. It became clear at the very beginning of his social career that the Prince of Wales took his pleasure seriously; and any hostess who hoped to enter the favoured inner circle reserved for Edward's friends had to cater to his tastes. Amusing Edward became something of a vocation for those who took their roles as the intimates of royalty seriously. It was an expensive and a burdensome task, but the young Prince possessed a personal charm unequalled by any monarch or royal heir since Charles II. He had the gift of making any effort seem worthwhile. Also, the social prestige accruing to those whom Edward favoured was enormous. For the members of that group rapidly coming to be distinguished as the Marlborough Set, no greater reward was desired.

Of course, the Queen kept a watchful eye on the behaviour of her son and daughter-in-law and did not like the style of life into which she saw them entering. In her opinion the guests flocking to Marlborough House on weekday evenings and to Sandringham for long weekends were too mixed, too fast and too frivolous to make suitable companions for the Prince and Princess. Soon after the marriage she wrote to Lord Granville, telling him that she thought the young couple should accept dinner invitations from only 'Lord Granville, Lord Palmerston and possibly Lord Derby and three or four other great houses [*sic*] in London, Westminster House, Spencer House, Apsley House...and not to *all these* in the same year'.[4]

Edward ignored his mother's scheme for keeping himself remote from the social scene. In addition, he launched a totally new plan for royal dinners. In place of the appallingly long meals, eaten off the gold dinner service and punctuated by brittle conversation, Edward introduced an abbreviated dinner with fewer courses and shortened the time spent over wine before joining the women. The tone of these new evenings was to be gay and relaxed; this latter goal he achieved by completely altering the guest list, banishing learning and welcoming beauty. In that first London season, which became a glittering succession of galas, dinners, receptions, dances and theatre parties, Edward and his bride surrounded themselves with the most attractive and spirited young people society could provide. Anyone Edward found diverting was invited; and this group soon came to include beautiful women, Americans, wealthy Jews and, later, several trusted journalists. The stiffness, the formality, the awful ponderousness of the Queen and Consort's dinners were swept away, along with the gold plate and serious discussions concerning literature and science. In their place came laughter, witty conversation and practical jokes. For the last Edward had a lifelong weakness (it was the type of joke his father had singled out for condemnation in the White Lodge year). Under this assault the tone of society underwent a swift change, acquiring in its metamorphosis a dash and brilliance long absent.

Despite the surface appearance, it would be a mistake to conclude that Edward had no proper sense of his own dignity, as his mother feared, or that he was inviting his guests to behave as though they were not in the presence of royalty. No one was more punctilious than the Prince in his insistence on proper form. But he did alter the forms; and his adjustments in the system of protocol hedging him, such as insisting on being called 'Sir' as opposed to 'Your Royal Highness', were designed to put his friends and acquaintances at their ease without endangering his dignity. Occasionally, individuals presumed on the relaxed etiquette; but they did not make the mistake a second time. Edward could be brutally direct in dealing with a breach of manners. During a billiard game at Marlborough House, he ordered a guest's carriage because the man had said to him, following a particularly bad shot, 'I say, Wales, get hold of yourself'. From such a dismissal there was no appeal.

The conservative aristocrats were shaken to learn that at Marlborough House and at Sandringham they were expected to deal in an evenhanded way with other guests who included men who had been grocers' clerks in their youth, women whose connection with nobility was extremely delicate, Catholics, Anglicans of High Church persuasion and rakes such as Lord Hastings and Charles Beresford. At the same time, those withdrawing in shock and haste from such a scene of jollity were likely to bump into William Gladstone. The Queen turned her eyes toward heaven, and the Granvilles sniffed; but Edward was right. He had taken the measure of his age. And if a weathervane is not precisely a repository of principles, it is a source of accurate information concerning the direction of the wind. Edward trimmed Marlborough House and Sandringham to run before the prevailing winds of his age.

By the 1860s the traditional aristocracy, the landed interest, had already lost much of its grip on the future. By the time Edward reached his majority, their decline had begun. Ironically, devotion to the land was their undoing. While they clung to agriculture, the ancient source of their wealth and power, and remained at much the same economic level that had prevailed since the Napoleonic Wars, the wealth of the rising bourgeoisie surged ahead. The wealth of the manufacturers soon outstripped that of the landowners; the plutocracy of capital began to replace the aristocracy of birth and land and to crowd in larger and larger numbers into the halls of power.[5]

Some of the great families had the foresight to diversify, but many landed families – the Sykes of Sledmere, the Derbys, Boultons, Peels, Arkwrights, Fieldens, Cuthberts, Whitbreads, along with a gallery of companion clans – had only within the past half century made the transformation from Hull merchants, iron production, engineering and brewing into landowners and must have viewed a return to trade 'as bloody as the going o'er' and simply clung to their new found respectability. It was a fatal mistake, at least in the long run.[6] In addition to the threat to their power from the new money, there was also the danger to their political hegemony posed by the swiftly increasing franchise that government after government voted into existence. Edward, in a coincidence no fiction writer would dare employ, died just in time to avoid the agony of being forced to break the power of the House of Lords in its last stronghold by packing it with appointees ready to carry out the will of the Commons.

It would be absurd to suggest that Edward had anticipated all these developments in 1863 and begun shaping his social life in accordance with profound insights into the nature of English society. He was certainly no scholar, guest books, stud books and the *Almanach de Gotha* being the only volumes he ever glanced at; but he had an almost uncanny sense about people. And being a snob only about order and precedent, he was able to select his friends from among those who were most interesting and most useful to him. If they were women, they must be beautiful and intelligent, at least sufficiently intelligent not to bore him; and he was bored very easily. If they were men, they must be wealthy, entertaining or useful, for it was from people that Edward learned. Therefore, it became increasingly natural that he should draw into his circle those men who moved in the very centre of the nation's political and economic life, who possessed power and understood its uses. For these reasons, over a period of fifty years, the group around Edward was a shifting mirror of the emergent political and capitalist world.

Four years after Edward's arrival as the leader of society, Walter Bagehot published his book on the English constitution, in which he asserted that England was essentially a 'deferential community' with 'the rude classes at the bottom' deferring 'to what we may call the theatrical show of society'. In Bagehot's opinion, this deference was translated into an acquiescence in and welcome of the rule of the aristocratic classes.[7] Marx's view of the same social phenomenon, which would come later, was that this acquiescence was not natural to the 'rude classes at the bottom' but was the result of an intense, harsh schooling in humility begun and continued by their relation to the ruling class. But there is no denying that the English held simultaneously and without apparent discomfort quite contradictory social attitudes.

A story illustrating this strange duality of mind was once widely repeated and, true or not, illuminates the ambiguity. A Hyde Park speaker was attacking the royal family and drawing some applause along the way when suddenly his audience turned and began running towards the street. 'What is it?' he called. A straggler shouted back, 'They say the Prince of Wales is driving past.'

In some very fundamental way, Edward came to represent in the popular imagination all that tradition to which Bagehot refers, while at the same time standing for the newly emerging world of capital. Later on, writers would pick up these divergent traits in Edward's public character and make them serve a function in their work. In *Esther Waters* by George Moore, Arthur Barfield says that he wished his old home, Woodview, to remain 'County' as long as the walls held together. 'He wasn't a bit ashamed of all this ruin. You could receive the Prince of Wales in a ruin, but he wouldn't care to ask him into a dissenting chapel.'[8] This is the traditional, deferential aspect of the public image. In *Lady Chatterley's Lover* D. H. Lawrence exploits a contrasting element in that image. Clifford Chatterley's godfather, Leslie Winter, owned a home called Shipley, where, in the story, Edward was once a guest. Winter is showing Edward around the estate and remarks, 'The miners are perhaps not so ornamental as deer, but they are far more profitable.' Edward responds, 'You are quite right. If there were coal under Sandringham, I would open up a mine on the lawns, and think it was first rate landscape gardening. . . .'[9]

Edward came to stand for the entire tradition of the landed gentry, while at the same time making respectable through his recognition those most prominent representatives of the growing commercial world. But the sphere of life into which he introduced such men as Sir Thomas Lipton was dominated by the customs of the landed aristocracy, whose values were its salient features. Hunting, cards, shooting, racing, house parties, observing the London season were the diversions of that society of which Edward was the pinnacle. For forty years he worked steadily to break down the barriers between the classes and smooth, in ways not responsive to measurement, the passage of some of his countrymen into the new world. By the latter part of the nineteenth century, this voyage had become an anxious one, taken with many nostalgic glances back towards a rapidly receding land across the wake of a swiftly moving ship whose destination was obscure and whose officers, to say the least, were no longer gentlemen.

With important qualifications, Victoria was generally satisfied with Edward during those first months following the marriage. When she saw her son immediately after the honeymoon, she did not think him improved and was soon complaining that Alix was too thin and living too hectic a life. Further, although she still loved the Princess dearly, she had come to the conclusion that the girl was stupid and was forced to admit that the girl's deafness was increasing. The affliction that had come to Princess Louise had fallen on her daughter. It was a sad burden that Alexandra would bear throughout the remainder of her life, a handicap that often made her seem more dull of mind than she really was and which reduced her conversation to smiles, punctuated by sudden and loud laughs. There was also the matter of Prince Alfred's infatuation with his sister-in-law to worry Victoria. The young man was spending all his spare time in Alexandra's company and thoroughly agitated his mother by doing so. Victoria was convinced that he would cause trouble between husband and wife, but the three appear to have got on without strife.[10]

In July Alexandra became pregnant, but she did not alter the pattern of her life. She continued to follow a strenuous social regimen, and the Prince urged her on. Victoria lamented it. As the autumn passed into winter with no indication that the Princess was suffering from the pace, the social life increased in tempo. She and Edward were moving in an increasingly sophisticated circle of acquaintances and giving shape to the new society which was growing around them. But as Alexandra's pregnancy developed, another condition was advancing with equally certain results and causing Alexandra acute anguish. The hostility between Denmark, Austria and Prussia, provoked by conflicting claims to the tiny agricultural provinces of Schleswig, Holstein and Lauenburg, had reached a dangerous stage.

These tiny duchies, which had been awarded to the King of Denmark as partial compensation for his surrender of the Norwegian crown in 1815, held since the days of Sweyn Forkbeard, were German in speech and social affiliation. Only Schleswig had a strong Danish element; and when Holstein became a part of the German Bund, Schleswig remained outside with its German element clamorously demanding affiliation with the Bund, while the Danish party sought permanent links with Denmark. The issue of the duchies was further complicated by the fact that they were the possession, not of Denmark, but of the Danish King.

In 1848 the Germans in Schleswig revolted against their ruler and were aided by friends and relatives in Holstein, but the assistance expected from the Frankfurt Parliament was late and feeble. William I made a half-hearted effort to assist the rebels, but the Danes fought back stoutly and Prussian interest subsided. With the German element overwhelmed, the 1852 European Treaty of London confirmed the relationship between Denmark and the duchies as it had existed before 1848. Frederick VII had been King of Denmark for more than a decade when the latest troubles erupted, but by 1863 he was forced, much against his will, to grant Denmark a new constitution, under the provision of which Prince Christian and not his son, Duke Frederick of Augustenburg, was chosen as his successor. Frederick VII died shortly after granting the constitution and opened the way for the growing turmoil by annexing Schleswig to Denmark.

The German Bund had no objection to Christian's assuming the

Danish throne; but by the rules of succession the thrones of Schleswig, Holstein and Lauenburg could forcibly be argued to belong to Duke Frederick of Augustenburg, son and legal heir of King Frederick VII and cousin to Alexandra. In 1852 King Frederick had accepted money from the Danish Government to relinquish his personal claims to the provinces; but his son argued that his father had no authority to separate his heirs from their rightful inheritance. To bolster his claims, a legitimate plebiscite conducted in the duchies showed that all of Holstein and Lauenburg and half of Schleswig wanted Duke Frederick as their ruler. The German states responded. Acting through their Bund, they ordered Saxon and Hanoverian troops into Holstein in December 1863 to eject the Danes and to declare Duke Frederick VIII the ruler of the duchies.

Beginning in early January the English newspapers nervously traced the development of the conflict, which became increasingly complicated as initiatives by various governments were put forward to reconvene the London Conference of 1852. Austria, France and England appeared to favour the Conference, although England's position was made difficult by the Queen's sympathetic support of the German position, an attitude not reported in the English press. Then Austria's support of the Conference became increasingly doubtful as, under the influence of Bismarck's disingenuous argument that the two major German powers must take control before the situation got out of hand, her government came into line with Prussia. Bismarck was planning a daylight robbery under the guise of a peace-keeping mission. Had it not been so outrageous, it would have been laughable.

In any event Hapsburg and Hohenzollern acted in concert to usurp the initiative taken by the minor states. Bismarck set aside the Augustenburg claims and told King Christian that pretences on Denmark's part that she controlled the duchies were insolent. It was clear that the contested provinces belonged to Prussia and Austria. Foolishly believing that England and Russia would come to his defence, Christian defied the combined might of the two great German states marshalled against him and vowed to go to war. Adding the final bizarre touch to the incredible proceedings, Russia warned everyone that if the Treaty of 1852 were abrogated, she would renew her own claims in the area.

With these exciting events as background, Alexandra struggled to come to terms with her own feelings of loyalty to Denmark, and to her father in particular. Although she had been told before her marriage that she was to give up her family allegiances, she made it very plain where her sympathies lay; and in this matter she took Edward with her. Naturally, Victoria was furious over her son and daughter-in-law's abandonment of the pro-Prussian line; and their defection became one more piece of evidence in Victoria's continuing case against her son.

The Danish sympathies of the Prince and Princess of Wales were much closer to the popular bias of the country than Victoria's German bent, which had become so pronounced recently that at the time of the marriage she attempted to force Edward and Alexandra to adopt German in place of English as the language of their common discourse. *Lloyd's,* without referring to the Queen's pro-Germanism, wrote that whatever popularity the royal family enjoyed, it derived none of it from its German connections and was loved *despite* its German origins.[11] As Prussia and Austria became increasingly direct in their moves to swallow the duchies, popular feeling in England swung toward support of Denmark; and although it would be difficult to give hard evidence in support of the contention, it is nonetheless true that Alexandra's Danish background was an important element in that support.

Interest in the progress of the Danish-Prussian troubles was temporarily abated by the sudden and extremely premature arrival of Edward and Alix's first child on January 8, a full two months ahead of schedule. Cynics have observed that first babies can come at any time, the rest require nine months. But no such doubt need surround this birth. The child was genuinely born prematurely. Victoria's warnings suddenly seemed less silly than they had a few months earlier; and Alexandra's insistence on keeping up her social life, less dashing. On the day labour began, she accompanied Edward to Virginia Water to watch him play ice hockey. Throughout the day the Royal Horse Guards band sat around a charcoal fire on the bank and played almost continuously. Alexandra remained in her sled, bundled in heavy robes, watching the hockey until four, when she gave in and allowed herself to be taken back to Frogmore House. She had suddenly become very tired, and no sooner had she gone indoors than the contractions began.[12]

Much has been written about the inadequate preparations for the baby's arrival and the anxiety occasioned by the event for the mother's as well as the child's welfare. Edward and Alexandra, despite their earlier lack of concern for Alix's health, were certainly upset by the birth and undoubtedly felt that they were in some way responsible, whether medical evidence led to that conclusion or not (and it seems not to have done so). Lady Macclesfield recorded that following the delivery and the giving of official witness to the birth, carried out by Lord Granville, who chanced to be present, Edward, having remained with Alix during the delivery, lay down on the bed beside his wife. The two then put their arms around one another and burst into tears.[13]

At the Queen's insistence, the child was christened Albert Victor, the parents managing with some difficulty to get Edward Christian tacked on the end. The Prince of Wales was angry at his mother's meddling in such a brazen way with a matter which might reasonably be thought to concern himself and Alix; but he did not quarrel with his mother over the matter, satisfying himself by calling the boy Eddy, a circumvention followed by everyone except Victoria. She wrote to Leopold at that time insisting it was her right to concern herself with the child's upbringing and that she expected all major decisions involving the child to be cleared with her.[14] Such an attitude on her part seemed certain to provoke resistance from her daughter-in-law, if not her son; but the Princess kept her temper well in hand and simply arranged the child's management to suit herself.

The people received the news of the birth with quiet pleasure. On January 11, the *Evening Mail* printed a remarkably warm account of the affection felt by the nation for Edward, Alexandra and the child and spoke of the 'universal good will which the Prince and Princess of Wales have won'. The paper then urged Victoria to attempt to throw off her grief, expressing the hope that 'the charm of new life may wean the Queen from the sadness of the past, and dissipate the sorrows of the last two years'.[15] *John Bull* was equally pleased with Edward and the Princess but almost sharp in its expressed wish that 'the Royal Mourner' would find solace in the child's birth and once again take her proper place at the head of her people. The paper acknowledged that nothing could wholly dispel her gloom, which for two years her people had sadly shared with her, 'but in the affection of her children, and in the dutiful loyalty of her people, we trust that she will willingly recognize that her lot is not without many alleviations'.[16]

Unfortunately, there was not much opportunity for the nation to celebrate Albert Victor's birth. News from Denmark and the duchies crowded reports of the baby's progress off the leader pages. On the day following *John Bull*'s appeal to the Queen to come out of seclusion, *Lloyd's Weekly London Newspaper* expressed the fear that England was drifting towards war with Germany and that in Germany it was believed that England intended to come in on behalf of Denmark. The editor pointed out that if the Germans relied on any national sentiment in their favour in England to keep the country out of the fighting, they were woefully mistaken. 'Public feeling has been led of late against the German influences that have been at work among us.'[17]

Reports of heightened tension along the Schleswig–Holstein border increasingly upset Alexandra. Her recovery, which had begun rapidly, slowed. She remained too thin, wept frequently and brought Edward to an intense pitch of antagonism toward Prussia, from whence his sister was writing self-righteous letters about Prussia's right to intervene. In an effort to make himself effective as a peace keeper between Denmark and Prussia, he proposed that he be allowed to act as an official channel of communication between England and Denmark; but Victoria instantly counter-attacked with notes to her ministers, warning them that the Prince was not 'discreet' and in other ways undermining

Edward's chances of serving a useful role in the unfortunate affair. Once again his mother had defeated his attempts to come forward and assume a responsible role. With remarkable perception she had implied to the men who would have to work with him that he was incompetent and untrustworthy, 'the Poor Boy'. It would have required a much stronger-willed man than Edward was in 1864 to carry through and successfully combat his mother's iron determination to suppress him.

On February 1 the combined forces of Germany and Austria crossed into Schleswig and swiftly demolished the Danish defences, forcing Christian to acknowledge a total military defeat. He had guessed his danger at least a week before the invasion, and on January 24 *Lloyd's* reported the beleagured King's message to the nation: 'In the event of a war for the protection of the independence of Denmark, if all forsake me, I hope for the support of the Danish people.' It is fortunate that he had prepared himself for that eventuality, because the Danes were left to their fate. Sweden, France, Russia and England watched the invasion and did nothing more serious than criticize the invaders. On February 4 the Queen's message on the war was so mild in tone that it provoked anger and amazement in the country. The *Evening Mail* described it as 'the ideal of negative perfection'. The *Daily News* reported the speech and observed that the nation was without a policy, had failed in its treaty obligations and had lost its honour.

On the fourteenth, *Lloyd's*, breaking a two-week editorial silence on the war, lashed out against the government: 'Again we have befriended the weak until they were attacked, only to leave them in the hands of their enemies – and to lay ourselves open to the gibes and sarcasms of the entire press of continental Europe.' *Punch* printed a cartoon in which John Bull was placed between the Princess of Wales and the Princess of Prussia. Edward's disgust with his mother's German sympathies and the government's feeble policies drove him to make a brief effort at opening lines of communication with the Tory opposition and genuinely frightening the Queen; but that aberration passed swiftly, and he subsided into his customary passivity.[18]

Smarting under the rebuff his mother had given him over the Danish troubles, Edward looked around for some means of asserting his independence and found it in April with Garibaldi's visit to England. The Italian patriot, who in 1860 had made possible the unification of Italy, was received in England with widespread and tumultuous enthusiasm as a hero and a liberator. Edward, responding to the excitement, made up his mind to pay Garibaldi a visit. The Queen was horrified by this latest act of defiance. Her dislike of Garibaldi, aside from whatever objections she may have had to the Italian's republicanism, was solidly rooted in the antipathy Albert had felt for the hero of Palermo. Four years earlier Victoria had sent Vicky a photograph of Thérèsa, the

Queen of Naples, dressed in her hunting costume. Victoria noted that the Queen Dowager was 'a great sportswoman and an excellent shot. Pity she didn't shoot Garibaldi – Papa says.'[19] That was all the encouragement Edward needed to persuade him to visit Garibaldi.

In paying Garibaldi the compliment of a call, Edward was quite properly reflecting the almost universal approval shown by the English people of all classes. As in the Prusso-Danish conflict, Victoria was quite out of touch with her subjects' feelings. Having arrived in England on April 3 and London eight days later, in golden weather, Garibaldi travelled as the guest of the Duke of Sutherland and was immediately lionized by London society. The Duchess of Sutherland gave a dinner in his honour at Chiswick House; and there is a certain irony in the fact that he was entertained in the suite of rooms which the Duke of Devonshire had originally redecorated at enormous cost for the late Emperor Nicholas of Russia's visit. The guest list for the dinner was not studiously republican, including among a great many other notables the Duke and Duchess of Argyll, Earl Granville, the Duchess of Norfolk, and the Earl and Countess Russell of Clarendon.

Throughout his stay, which lasted nearly three weeks, Garibaldi was kept constantly before the public in social and official functions. He attended Her Majesty's Theatre and sat in the Duke of Sutherland's box, went to the opera, the House of Commons, the Crystal Palace twice and was presented the freedom of the London Fishmonger's Company. On April 20 Gladstone gave a dinner in his honour. Among the guests were the Archbishop of Canterbury, the Archbishop of York and the Bishop of London. The English Church was well represented in Garibaldi's welcome. It was the venerable Dr Milman, Dean of St Paul's, who gave the speech of welcome to the liberator when he reached London. Visibly moved by the event, the Dean thanked Garibaldi in Italian for having achieved a dream of the Dean's youth, to see Italy unified.

On April 17 Garibaldi visited Tennyson and planted a memorial tree in the poet's garden. Tennyson's gardener watched the tree until dark and then, thinking it safe, left it unattended. As soon as he had left, souvenir hunters forced their way into the garden and stripped the tree of its branches, leaving a forlorn wand sticking out of the ground to cheer Tennyson on his morning walk. The intrusion was not unusual; Tennyson was much troubled by admirers who wanted something unique as a remembrance of their visit to the great man's house.[20]

Garibaldi's stay in England was marred by the ill-founded belief which developed among his staff that his continued presence in England was likely to precipitate an 'incident' of some sort. Nothing seemed farther from the truth. A rumour also spread among the common people that the Queen objected to Garibaldi's making a progress through the country, as he had originally intended to do. To add to his troubles, he was not well, and it was that fact as well as the uneasiness among his staff that led to his decision to leave England on the twenty-second. In London and elsewhere mass meetings were held to protest against the Queen's hostility to the patriot. On the twentieth the *Standard* printed an editorial suggesting that Garibaldi was being forced out of the country as the consequence of an intrigue between the Queen's ministers and Louis Napoleon of France, who was particularly displeased by his presence in England.[21]

Edward visited Garibaldi privately on the twenty-second. The following day he wrote an account of his visit to his mother, and it is impossible not to believe that behind the bland and cheerful tone is a fine acid spray playing over the words. Remarking that business had taken him to London, Edward added, almost as a by-the-way, that he had improved the occasion by stopping in for a private visit with Garibaldi, noting that he had, of course, despite heavy pressure from several sources, refused to receive the Italian at Sandringham, as had been several times suggested. He had refused, he noted, because he had not wished to embarrass either her or the government. Edward proceeded to give a glowing account of Garibaldi's character, saying he was sure the Queen would have liked him. He concluded by saying that Garibaldi had spoken of the Danish war and how much he felt for the poor Danish soldiers who had died.[22] The Queen was angry and let her son know her feelings. He responded that he did not accept the charge that he had done wrong in making the visit, that he had been of age for some time and was thoroughly responsible for his own actions.

Had Edward been able to sustain that kind of spirited response to Victoria's bullying, the history of his life up to 1901 would have been quite different; but he had been damaged by his childhood training to the degree that in important ways he was incapable of resisting his mother's dominance. Guilt and a lurking sense of inadequacy, coupled with a desire for approval, undermined his strength to resist. In other ways, in such matters as his social life, for example, he was able to exert a genuine independence. In the matter of allowing him a suitable role to fill commensurate with his position, he found himself unmanned, unable to bear up under her constant appeal to his dead father. Edward had been told too many times that he was incompetent. Perhaps he was weakened by the fear that the responsibilities he sought would turn him into the drudge Albert had become. No final explanation seems possible. Unhappily, in reaction to his difficulties, he came increasingly to work out his frustrations by increased self-indulgence rather than by a sustained struggle to make a place for himself in the nation's ruling structure.

As soon as the hostilities between the German and Austrian states and

Denmark were at an end, Alexandra began agitating for permission to travel to Denmark to visit her family. Throughout the summer Edward put pressure on the government and on the Queen to allow the visit to take place. The Queen opposed it. Her private reason was that she did not want Edward in the company of Alix's family, whom she continued to despise; but she spoke about diplomatic problems, the likelihood of their encountering hostility from the Danes, Albert Victor's uncertain health and so on. Nothing, however, turned Alexandra's mind away from her family, and the Queen was forced to give way when the Prime Minister refused to say that the visit would in any way compromise England. In compensation for her defeat, Victoria forced Edward to sign a paper agreeing not to say anything on the trip to which his mother might object, and to visit his sister in Prussia.[23]

After a very stormy two-day crossing from the Scottish port of Dundee, during which Alix, Edward and even the stewards and stewardesses were violently ill, the *Osborne* encountered more moderate seas just off Elsinore, making it possible for the Prince and Princess to be on deck for the arrival. King Christian and Alix's mother were on the jetty and were rowed out to the yacht; as soon as they were aboard, Alix embraced her father twice, according to custom, and then her mother. Breaking away from her mother's embrace, she suddenly turned and threw her arms around Edward's neck in a burst of joy at being home. On shore the waiting throng cheered; the band played 'God Save the Queen'; and when the royal party reached the dock, the burgomaster read the Prince and Princess a speech of welcome in Danish. Edward smiled, nodded and chatted with his father-in-law, completely ignorant of what the burgomaster was saying.[24]

Despite the fears that he would be accorded, at best, a cold reception, Edward had a great success in Denmark. Initially Danish public opinion about his visit was very much divided. There was little actual hostility but a general feeling that England had let them down and a determination not to make much of a fuss over Edward. The liberal press in Copenhagen had advised its readers not to support any demonstrations of affection for the visitors. But with his characteristic ability to win the affection of people, the reports of him that began to appear in the press were full of praise, and he was soon winning hearts everywhere.

The hunting notwithstanding, Edward's stay with his wife's family at the Castle of Fredensborg was not a pleasant one for him. The fault was neither his wife's nor her family's. It was, rather, the Prince's extreme susceptibility to boredom that made the visit difficult. Even by the most conservative standards, the Danish court was slow and uneventful; and Edward suffered agonies of deprivation, caught between the atrocious cooking that no one in the Danish royal family seemed to notice and the dreary and interminable games of loo that constituted the evening entertainment.[25] Alexandra was blissfully happy. As long as she was in the midst of her family, all was well; and so it remained with her all her life. The same could not be said for her husband.

The dreariness ended, however, on September 23, when the Prince left Copenhagen for Stockholm, having laid to rest almost all the feelings of resentment that the Danes had harboured. As a parting shot Victoria had told Edward that he was not to stay at the palace in Stockholm but to register in a hotel there; but Edward had no intention of refusing the King's invitation to be his guest at the palace. He and Alexandra took advantage of every opportunity for entertainment; and on the twenty-eighth they attended a magnificent ball given by the Queen Mother at her palace of Drottningholm on one of the large islands of Lake Malar. There were many dances, and the King led off at a furious pace which continued throughout the evening. A great supper was served at eleven, followed by more entertainment and an exhilarating gallop back to Stockholm, some seven miles distant from Lake Malar. The two carriages were drawn by four horses each and lighted by blazing flambeau, borne by galloping outriders.

Edward wrote to his mother that he was sorry to have acted contrary to her instructions and stayed in the palace, explaining that accommodation in the city was inadequate and that he intended to see Alix housed satisfactorily. Victoria, deeply distressed by the great success of the Stockholm visit and the warm attention Edward's journey was attracting in the press – by September 21 he and Alix were front-page copy – as well as the Prince's refusal to send Albert Victor home as she was demanding, ordered Edward and Alix to cancel their plans to visit Paris, to return to England by way of Belgium and to go at once to visit Vicky in Prussia.[26] There were no State reasons for making such a change in the arrangements; Victoria ordered them in revenge for Edward's having flouted her instructions about the hotel, and because of her jealousy over the success of the two visits. Having to go to Prussia was a bitter experience for Alexandra, who still felt deeply about the suffering imposed on Denmark by the Germans. She went, but the encounter with the Prussian Crown Prince and Princess was not a success, and Edward was angered by his brother-in-law's behaviour. The Queen's insistence on the meeting might have led to a serious breach, but both sides of the family kept their heads and the unpleasantness passed.

Missing Paris was, of course, a real disappointment for Edward. By the middle of the 1860s, his connections with France were well established. He liked the French and prided himself on his ability to speak the language like a Parisian. But the friends he made there were, for the most part, members of the old French aristocracy who had little sympathy with the growing republicanism of the age or, later, with the group of men who ousted Napoleon III. Nevertheless, Edward was able to make his own contacts with the emerging French governments and to keep in touch with the realities of French political life. French social life was certainly not foreign to him; and he was an active member of numerous Paris clubs, among them the Cercle des Champs-Elysées, the Jockey, the New, the Rue Royale and the Yacht Club de France.[27]

On his return to England Edward resumed his unending pursuit of diversion. There were rumours of his having been attentive to some Swedish women, but they were quickly dissipated in the rush of more exciting gossip. After all, Sweden was far away, and the Prince was home. In the year following his father's death he was seated in the House of Lords; but at this stage of his life the Lords saw little of him. He divided his time among the race events, the shooting, house parties, and his clubs, going regularly to the Turf Club for political discussions and to the Cosmopolitan Club, where he met a cross section of the nation's most talented men from all the professions, being exposed to personalities and intellects he would not otherwise have encountered. Since he did not read books, these contacts were of the greatest value in broadening his range of ideas.[28]

No lack of intelligence kept Edward from reading but rather an inability to pursue any solitary occupation. He tried to interest himself in salmon fishing; but that lone pursuit, conducted in the company of wind and water and an only slightly more communicative ghilly, plunged him into depression and acute anxiety. He needed people around him, diversion, excitement and, preferably, the spice of sexual titillation. Edward was emotionally scarred by those long years of imprisonment during which he was driven through studies like an animal being whipped through a hoop. It is a miracle that his behaviour was not more bizarre.

The two years following the Prince and Princess's return from their Danish journey were a period of relative calm. In June 1865, George, their second son, was born. There were no complications, and Alix was soon accompanying her husband again. Thus far, whatever gossip there was concerning Edward's attentions to other women had been very discreet and did not become truly public property until 1867. Georgina Battiscombe takes the position concerning Edward's infidelities that, had Alexandra loved him as much as he loved her, he might have had a less roving eye, observing that the Princess's beauty may have chilled her heart.

All conclusions as to why Edward emerged as such an obsessive womanizer must be tentative. It is true that he had married an exceedingly beautiful woman, towards whom he showed the most tender concern; but to balance the asset of her beauty was her increasing deaf-ness. As a further handicap, despite her widened experience of the world, she remained something of a child, almost an innocent. Edward delighted in witty people, gay conversation and the excitement of stimulating social intercourse. Alexandra had neither wit nor con-versation. In addition, there was that pervasive restlessness of mood and appetite that led Edward to devour gargantuan meals, smoke quantities of cigars and cigarettes during his waking hours and to be constantly engaged in something interesting. It would have been surprising if such insatiability had not been as characteristic of his sexual needs as it was of his other appetites. Finally, in having affairs, Edward was living out the myth of lusty prince and lecherous squire. Only the strictest element in English society was honestly chagrined and shocked by his whoring. For the most part, he was admired for it.

This is not to imply that he received public encouragement for such behaviour. On the contrary, the press continued to demand a spartan style of life from the Prince of Wales and were outraged when he fell short of expectations. This intolerance on the part of the press made it increasingly difficult for the organs of middle-class opinion to come to reasonable terms with Edward the man. It was not enough for *The Times* to lament that man is frail and prone to folly. By attempting to reduce the Prince to a purely ceremonial figure and thus rob him and his position of real power in the affairs of the state, the press succeeded in making it all but impossible for Edward to exist as a man. That, of course, was the intention. If he was to exist at all, it was to be as an image of middle-class respectability.

1867 brought an end to the quiet. In October of 1866 Edward persuad-ed his mother to allow him to go to Russia to participate in the marriage of Alexandra's sister, Dagmar, to the Grand Duke Alexander. Before leaving he expressed a desire to serve in some way the cause of Russian and English friendship; and although he was given no announced diplomatic assignment to carry out in Moscow, Disraeli felt his presence in Russia justified the government's granting Edward a thousand pounds towards expenses. In the first stage of their acquaintance, Dis-raeli had thought Edward a buffoon; but within a few years he was seeking Edward's advice and listening with the utmost seriousness to what his Prince was saying. It has been the habit since Sir Sydney Lee's biography to cast Edward in the shape of an intellectual lightweight. One biographer wrote that Edward's views were never consistent enough to allow him to exert real influence on either domestic or foreign policies, as though consistency has ever characterized the behaviour of governments. As Fielding observed, principles among politicians are very much a matter of hats. But as to consistency, Edward was consistent in one principle and that was his conviction that the nations of Europe should exist together in peace and amity. He worked towards that goal for forty years.

Pregnant again, Alix did not accompany her husband to Russia. The Queen would not have allowed her to take the two boys with her, and she did not enjoy travelling without her family. She had in that period a need to have her children near her at all times. On his return, which was heralded by a spate of gossip concerning his frolics with Russian beauties, Edward found that his wife was not well. Her health swiftly collapsed, and in February she was declared dangerously ill with rheumatic fever. The *Daily Telegraph* published a guarded report on the Monday following the announcement: 'His Royal Highness the Prince of Wales was recalled suddenly from Windsor on Saturday, in consequence of what was represented to be the serious illness of the Princess.'[29] This sombre announcement was followed by a more general statement concerning the Princess's illness and an assurance that there was no need for alarm or anxiety. Press response remained very restrained, and there was a general sense of doubtful hope in the reports of the progress of the disease.

To complicate the situation, Alexandra was in the final stage of her third pregnancy. On February 20, five days following the onset of her illness, she entered labour and gave birth to a daughter, christened Louise Victoria. The confinement was not affected by the fever, and the child was perfectly healthy. The *Lancet* observed that 'it was very rare to see such a complication as parturition during the course of rheumatic fever'.[30] Not until the twenty-fifth were the doctors able to report that the patient was beginning to enjoy some restful sleep; and with the publication of the first genuinely hopeful news, public relief found instant expression. The newspapers expressed the nation's thankfulness. The *News of the World* carried a long article praising Alix as a woman and concluded by saying that she deserved the description of 'Wife and Mother, the two greatest titles given to woman'. By the twenty-eighth she was well enough to allow Edward to leave her side, where he had remained through the most critical period, and attend Court at Buckingham Palace, arriving there with an escort of Life Guards and accompanied by Knollys and other members of his staff.[31] It was a joyous occasion for the Prince. Alix was out of danger.

July came before the Princess had regained her strength enough to be wheeled into the open air; and in August she and Edward left for a two-month stay in Wiesbaden, a German resort in the Taunus hills near the Rhine, which had been a popular health spa since the days of the Romans. What problems Edward faced there can be deduced from a report published in September concerning his activities. He was said to be bathing and breakfasting every second day at the Hotel de la Rose, risking a few gold pieces at the tables, walking about alone in the crowds and taking coffee under the trees in the Kursaal. 'He looks well,' the account concluded, 'full of health and enjoyment, and has a pleasant, restless way of getting through the day.' Alexandra occasionally rode out in a carriage, but spent the greater portion of her time on the balconies, playing with the children.[32]

Edward had to occupy himself in this fashion for two months; and, of course, he found agreeable companions with whom to pass the lazy hours. Reports of his gambling and womanizing began to flood into England, creating a flurry of gossip in society and providing the journalists with a perfect topic to brood on. Dissatisfaction with the Queen's withdrawal had not abated and began to be expressed again as news of the Prince of Wales's gambling became news copy. *Reynolds's Newspaper* printed a very stiff editorial asking why the Queen did not visit Ireland, and took the opportunity to excoriate Edward. 'Even the Prince, though that young person, whose whole life is consecrated to fashionable recreation, might find something to amuse him in Ireland, refuses to go there even for a single week.'

The writer became increasingly bitter as he developed his theme: 'Though the Queen were to take up her permanent abode at Balmoral, or some other favoured locality even farther north; and the Prince of Wales were to devote himself for the remainder of his days to the beauties of Wiesbaden and the delights of its "hells", neither England nor Ireland would be one farthing the worse.'[33] The Prince's personal life was now a subject for adverse comment, as it had not been before this time; and the Wiesbaden holiday marks the beginning of that public scolding of the Prince of Wales, which, as André Maurois has observed, 'became a recognized hobby of all the Pharisees in the land'.[34]

But it was not only the Pharisees who had skewered the Prince, and it was not only Edward who was being roasted. Royalty itself was feeling the fire, and the fault was largely the Queen's. It was her seclusion rather than her son's fast living that genuinely rankled. It was, however, much easier for the middle-class journals to attack Edward for gambling and chasing women than it was for them to attack the Queen for miserliness and a selfish disregard for the rights of her subjects. To give added colour and drama to the expression of the country's increasingly resentful feelings, the summer of 1867 saw the birth of the *Tomahawk*, one of the most remarkable comic periodicals of the day. It combined wit, lively commentary, irreverence and a strong social conscience with a vitality that made *Punch* appear staid. The country was ready for the *Tomahawk*.

In one of the earliest issues, the magazine gave a bogus report of a speech by H.R.H. The Prince of Wales, purported to have been delivered at London University on the general subject of education. The magazine informed its readers that the Prince intended to speak at a later date on the past history of philosophers 'and of this date he has almost mastered the pronunciation of the more difficult names and gotten the general headings memorized'.[35] This attack was followed a week later by an assault on the Queen, who was reported to be preparing to attend a Grand Military Review in Hyde Park. 'Nothing, we are assured, will be suffered to prevent or interfere with this grand military spectacle, save the death of some foreign potentate who is in no way related to the royal family.' Refreshments were to be provided for the crowds: 'half-a-dozen sandwiches and a few bottles of lemonade.'[36]

Carrying its attack into the holy of holies, the journal condemned the Queen's efforts to enshrine Albert's memory. With scathing sarcasm *Tomahawk* suggested that the interior of the new Albert Hall be decorated with murals based on themes in Albert's life and on his various virtues. It suggested that one mural be titled 'Disinterested Sacrifice – Albert the Good in the act of sacrificing his future prospects in life by accepting £30,000 a year and the hand of the Sovereign in marriage'.[37] Later in August it printed a cartoon showing the Queen with Brown beside her, her head cloaked. The inscription read 'The Mystery of the Season'. In the same year Walter Bagehot published *The English Constitution,* in which he warned, with a stylistic sign and inclination of the head towards Edward, 'Grave and careful men may have domestic virtues on a constitutional throne, but even these fail sometimes, and to imagine that men of more eager temperaments will commonly produce them, is to expect grapes from thorns and figs from thistles.'[38]

Determined not to be intimidated by his critics, and to set the tone for the new year, Edward accepted an invitation from the Duke of Beaufort to come to Badminton and participate in 'a great meet'. *Bell's Life in London and Sporting Chronicle* reported that Edward arrived at Badminton on February 25, and stayed over the twenty-seventh, enjoying some fine hunting and killing a fox in Charlton Park after a run of three-quarters of an hour. It should have been a routine hunt with the added excitement of a specially large field. Unfortunately for both Edward and the Duke, the meet was held on Ash Wednesday, arousing, as one writer put it, 'no small amount of indignation'. Excitement became so general that the papers fell out among themselves and began quarrelling over the affair.

The *Pall Mall Gazette* condemned the *Morning Post* for printing information about the meet, and thus contributing to the offence. The *Post,* in turn, accused *John Bull* of printing false information in its February 29 issue in which it announced that 300 persons turned out to ride with Edward. *John Bull* then attacked the Duke of Beaufort for having planned the meet: 'The Duke will not be in a hurry to give a party to royalty on such a day again; and we are sure that the Prince of

Wales only needs to have his attention called to the sorrow he had unwittingly caused some of the Queen's most loyal subjects, to prevent him again lending the weight of his august presence to so untimely a festival.'[39]

In the midst of the hubbub created by the Ash Wednesday meet, Edward attracted still more criticism by organizing a stag hunt with Her Majesty's stag hounds, to be run over the course known as the 'Melton of the Metropolis' or the 'Harrow Country'. The run was 'all grass with plenty of fencing, bullfinches, wattles, dykes, posts and rail and an occasional style with a drop into a lane'. Five hundred horsemen were present for the event, and a stag from the Queen's herd, called 'The Doctor', was released at Bate's Farm at the start of the hunt. It was a run of twenty-four miles to Paddington and was done in two hours and twenty minutes. Some reports had it that the stag hounds pulled down and killed the cornered beast; but it is far more likely, considering that he had a reputation as a superb runner, that he was boxed and taken back to his herd to run another day.

In addition to the Prince of Wales, the field included Lord Colville, Colonel Kingcote, Colonel Teesdale, Lord Hillsborough and many more, some of whom belonged to a different aristocracy from the one embracing Edward and his friends. Among that colourful fraternity, whose fingers were as light as their hearts and purses, were such notables as 'The King', 'Tom Wakely' and 'Dr Douglass', whose names were on police lists if not in *Debrett*.

Out of the original five hundred, only about thirty, the Prince among them, rode into the narrow court at the back of the Great Western Coal Depot where the stag had been trapped. To the great astonishment of those travellers in the station, the Prince suddenly appeared with his companions, got aboard a train and rode back to Windsor in the best of spirits. *The Times* confined itself to noting that the hunt had been held and the deer had a reputation as a good runner. Other papers were less objective, heaping criticism on Edward's head for participating in such folly. For the most part, the comments were stiff and solemn and rather boring, but the *Pall Mall Gazette* brought a gently malicious wit to bear on the event.

The paper began by noting that the Prince had taken part in the stag hunt, but turned at once to a story emanating from the town of Salford, where a group of men, inspired by Edward's ride, decided to have a pig hunt. After buying a boar from a farmer, they let the animal out into a field and began peppering it with bird shot to make it run. The tormented creature, 'its skin riddled like a collander with pellets', fled into a farm pond, where it was finally shot to death by a man named Midgely. The writer confessed that while he was fully aware that running a tame deer for two hours until its feet were worn down and allowing it to be pulled down by hounds was not cruelty, he was rather surprised that the magistrate, Mr Trafford, found it was not cruelty to pursue and riddle a pig. The writer was happy to report, however, that those looking for some sign that justice had not fled the land should be cheered by the magistrate's warning that if it could be proved that the publican, on whose premises the plan was made, had allowed the subscription for such a sport to be got up in his place of business, his licence was in grave danger.[40] It was a wonderfully effective way of exposing the wretchedness of the stag hunt (as well as the pig hunt) and made far more lively reading than the solemn cantings of other editors.

In part to counter the effects of the bad public image he was acquiring and in part to quiet Irish discontent, Edward consented to make a formal visit to Ireland. The government agreed to pay all his expenses, thereby encouraging the Irish to believe that they were not totally forgotten. Gladstone had proposed a permanent appointment in Ireland for the Prince of Wales, but Victoria was infuriated by the suggestion; and before giving her permission for the visit, she forced Disraeli to withdraw his suggestion that Edward should hunt one of the Irish counties on a regular basis.

Edward's attitude toward the plan is less easy to ascertain; and while there is little reason to believe that he would have welcomed being permanently billeted in Ireland as Viceroy, he might personally have been more interested in establishing closer ties with Ireland than the records suggest, his negative formal response being chiefly an echo of the Queen's refusal to allow the plan to mature. It must be added, however, that his continued exclusion from useful activity and his fervid pursuit of diversions to ward off the terrors of boredom were compounding into something close to a personal tragedy. He was becoming increasingly that unemployed youth in Bagehot's phrase, whose mind was a skein of frivolities wound on an irrelevance.

As for the Queen, she sensed exactly the degree of danger present in allowing Edward the freedom to establish a counter-court in Dublin; and, in fairness, she saw how dangerous such a development would be for Edward himself. How could any foreigner survive the furnace of Irish nationalism? And the Queen had other reasons for opposing the Irish connection. Lady Augusta Stanley, writing to her husband from Balmoral shortly before Edward's Irish visit, reported that the Queen would not 'hear of anything but flying visits there for herself or any of the family. I believe she is so afraid lest any of them should be taken up by, or take up the Irish as to throw Balmoral into the shade, now or later.'[41] She added that General Grey was very angry with the Queen for her attitude.

As an occupied country, Ireland was constantly in a state of unrest.

In 1868 the principal superficial irritant was the Fenian movement, six of whose members were being tried for murder in connection with the gunpowder explosion at the Clerkenwell House of Detention. Those charged with a crime were William Desmond, Nicholas English, John O'Keefe, Michael Barrett and Ann Justice. Out of the six only Michael Barrett was convicted. The trial, known as the Fenian Trial, was being conducted while Edward was in Ireland, and its echoes touched the royal family in disturbing ways. Alfred, the Duke of Edinburgh, was in Sydney, Australia, and a Fenian there attempted to shoot him. On the second night of Edward's presence in Ireland, in the county of West-meath, one of the landed gentry, a magistrate and Deputy Lieutenant, was shot to death while driving home, presumably by Fenians. No attacks were made on either Edward or the Princess; but as he rode through Dublin on Wednesday morning, his detachment of the 12th Lancers were loudly hissed for the part they had taken in the Water-ford election disturbances of that year in which an Irishman, Colonel Keily, had been lanced and killed without cause by one of the troop. It was an uneasy truce that Edward enjoyed throughout the visit.

The *Victoria and Albert* brought Edward and Alexandra into Kings-town harbour at about 8.30 am on Wednesday April 15. The men-of-war accompanying the yacht steamed into the harbour and fired a twenty-one gun salute as the smaller vessel sailed between the large ones and tied up at the Victoria Pier at noon. Huge crowds had gathered to welcome them; and appearing on deck, they were greeted by tremendous shouts and repeated salvos of artillery. Going directly into carriages, they drove to the Castle through throngs of people. Press reports differ markedly on the degree of enthusiasm shown the Prince, the *Nation* reporting that what scattered cheering there was had resulted from the planning of the police and the Castle authorities and the popularity of Alexandra.[42]

But other Irish papers, including the *Daily Express,* the *Cork Reporter* and the *Galway* insisted that the crowds between Kingstown and the Castle were huge and tumultuous. And there is no doubt that Alexandra won Irish hearts before she had been ten minutes in the country. Edward's charm took a little longer to make itself felt; but with con-siderable canniness, he asked the authorities of Trinity College to grant the student request to be given credit for the examinations of the term as a compliment to the Prince and Princess of Wales. The request was granted.

If the first day of his arrival was marred by doubts as to the authen-ticity of the crowd's response, no doubts troubled the reports of the following day, when Edward and Alix drove out from the Castle to the Punchestown Racecourse to receive the acclamation of 50,000 specta-tors gathered there to greet them. All along the route to the racecourse, the roads and railway lines were jammed with people who cheered and shouted their welcome. Edward shook thousands of hands; and the *Evening Mail* asserted, 'There has never been so great a gathering of the peers and gentry in Ireland since George IV came over as there is in Dublin today.'[43] The Irish press put aside its nationalism to sing the praises of Alexandra, whose 'peculiar charm' captured the hearts of the people. The *Daily Express* pointed out that the people of Ireland were loyal and were only wanting an opportunity to express that loyalty.[44] The *Derry Journal,* in company with other Irish papers, pleaded with the Prince to stay among them for a month or six weeks each year and to build a Balmoral in Ireland. The *Cork Reporter,* speaking out of one of the most radical sections of the country, admitted that Ireland was not disloyal and that the Prince and Princess could make a 'real conquest of this unconquered portion of the United Kingdom' and that it hoped they would try.

How much of this outpouring of affection and enthusiasm was merely the spindrift blowing from the most easily stirred portion of the Irish nation is difficult to judge. Certainly the more truculent among Irish journals did not cheer Edward's arrival. They expressed no personal animosity toward the Prince of Wales, but, as the *Nation* put it, 'The Prince of Wales does not come to our shores as a Messiah of mercy. Did the government intend anything of the sort, there was no need for all the vain display and grotesque tomfoolery that have characterized the proceedings of the past few days.' As for the results of the visits, the paper was equally negative: 'The Prince of Wales, perhaps, has amused himself, the Government have got up such a display in Dublin as every wealthy and strong Government, having money to spend and plenty of soldiers, police and detectives, can get up in every large city within their dominions; but for the rest, all things remain as they were....'[45] Some idea of the state of domestic affairs in Ireland is given in a letter written in 1856 by Frederick Engels to Karl Marx. 'The landowners [of Ireland],' Engels wrote, 'who everywhere else have taken on bourgeois qualities, are here completely demoralized. Their country seats are surrounded by enormous, wonderfully beautiful parks, but all around is waste land, and where the money is supposed to come from is impossible to see. These fellows ought to be shot.'[46]

It was widely hoped in Ireland that the Prince had brought with him amnesty for some, if not all, of the political prisoners currently under arrest or undergoing trial. No such thing was done. Edward had not been entrusted with any substantive function beyond showing himself and his wife to the populace. Perhaps nothing in the way of amnesties was justified, but it does seem that the government allowed an opportunity to ease the bitterness corroding Irish sensibilities to slip. But that nothing was done is not to be wondered at. Throughout

Victoria's reign the Irish were alternately threatened and ignored. There was the cry of the wounded heart in the Irish editorial on amnesty which pointed out that even some English papers had expressed hope that the Prince might be given the power to extend amnesty and that the Irish themselves had half believed that something might be done. As one Irish journalist put it, that hope was ruthlessly crushed: 'not one jot has been abated by the pressure of the English rule upon the lives of Irishmen; not by a single turn of the screw has the iron which has pierced the people's hearts been withdrawn. . . .'

Would Edward have urged a different policy towards Ireland had he possessed the power? At the very least there would have been a change in emphasis. Although he may have combined those qualities of the early kings of Britain, natural autocracy with a genuine desire for the improvement of conditions and welfare of the poor and a total absence of snobbishness, he was not a democrat. But he did despise violence, and worked all his life to deny it a role in international affairs. He loathed Bismarck's policy of blood and iron. On the other hand, his political conservatism did not extend as a bias against even the most politically radical politicians. For example, Sir Charles Dilke, and Joseph Chamberlain, the red mayor of Birmingham, were on good terms with the Prince. Throughout his career Edward opposed Home Rule, but he would have made every effort to sustain England's presence in Ireland without the use of force.

His sojourn in Ireland at an end, Edward was thrown back on his conventional amusements. Once again he visited his clubs, played cards, smoked, drank, entertained his friends and fulfilled his boring duties as the Queen's representative at the opening of exhibitions, bridges, public buildings and charity drives. In the course of his life Edward heard and responded to thousands of speeches from mayors, corporations, chairmen of boards and presidents of benevolent associations. Fortunately for Edward, he did not dislike these duties and gave generously of his time, asking only that the ceremonies be conducted on time. When they were not, he was direct in his criticism.

Alix was expecting yet another child in the spring of 1868; but as with the earlier pregnancies, she did nothing to curb her activities. There is not an easy explanation for the way in which the Princess flung herself headlong into her social life or why she refused to slow down her pace as her pregnancies advanced. Perhaps it was that she felt compelled to keep going in order to lessen Edward's opportunities for involving himself with other women. The preceding year, one of their Marlborough neighbours, Countess Frances Waldegrave, had remarked that Edward was neglecting Alix: 'The Prince is the most selfish of brutes. He only thinks of amusing himself and pays not the slightest attention to her.'[47] But in fairness, despite the evidence of his increasing philandering, it should also be said that Alexandra was passionately fond of parties and dancing; and despite her limp, she would dance the night away, pregnant or not.

The life Edward was living had effects other than simply influencing his public image and keeping a small but steady wind of rumour about his private life blowing through society, occasionally slamming doors and rattling windows in the national press. Edward was becoming hard, set in his ways and less and less tolerant of interference with what he considered to be his personal affairs. In May, Victoria asked Edward to take Alix out of London for a few weeks and give her a chance to recoup her strength before facing the ordeal of the confinement. Edward's response was very sharp and less than honest. He told his mother that her absence from the city made it necessary for him and the Princess to 'do all we can for society, trade and public matters'.[48] The truth of his claim could not be denied, but he was not staying in London for the sake of trade. Desperately needing a sense of his own value and denied a proper role in the craft for which he had, presumably, been trained, he increasingly compensated by becoming more autocratic in that sphere given to him to rule.

An example of how the course of his life was being directed is the quarrel that he precipitated with the governing body of White's Club, to which he had been elected as an honorary member in 1866. Club rules prohibited smoking in certain areas, but Edward and his friends wished to have the rules set aside. An extraordinary general meeting was called to confront the challenge, and the vote went against smoking. It was a painful snub to Edward and one he was not prepared to endure. 'Very well,' he is reported to have said, 'I will found a club of my own in which I can smoke when and where it pleases me.'[49]

The premises opposite Marlborough House on Pall Mall having fallen vacant, the Prince took them and opened the Marlborough Club with an initial list of four hundred members. Edward personally looked over all names submitted for election, and he strongly disapproved of anyone's resigning. He worked hard for the club; and, with the exception of the Turf and the Cosmopolitan, paid few further visits to his other clubs. He and his companions were likely to arrive late at the Marlborough and to play very noisy games of bowls behind the house. In fact they created such an uproar that the neighbours lodged complaints. In retrospect the entire White's episode seems trivial, even silly; but it does illustrate Edward's insistence on having minor matters his own way; and there was more of the spoiled child than the commanding man in his behaviour toward White's governing body.

From the time of its formation following his marriage, Edward's 'set' had been considered frivolous, self indulgent and morally unstable by the more conservative sections of society; but no one had suggested that it was actually vicious. All that was changed by the Lord Hastings scandal, which broke in the late spring of 1868, following Edward's return from Ireland, blackening the reputation of the Prince's circle. Through intemperate gambling on horses, Hastings, one of the Prince's close friends and racing companions, had been driven deeply into debt. In a desperate effort to extricate himself, Hastings foolishly determined to risk everything by attending the Derby and betting on one of the favourites, *Lady Elizabeth*. The horse lost and Hastings was unable to meet his debts. Saved from criminal proceedings by a group of men who came forward to deal with his creditors, Hastings became the focus of a violent reaction in the country against gambling. Within a short time, however, the attack broadened into a republican assault on the privileged classes and was directed not against individuals but against the class structure itself.

In an attempt to blunt the drive, *The Times*, the *Morning Post* and other journals joined in deploring Hastings's folly and warning other members of the aristocracy what they could expect if they acted with a similar lack of responsibility. 'And if other young men of his rank,' 'Argus' wrote in the *Morning Post*, 'followed in his wake, they must not expect to be let off without being exposed to an amount of odium which they will feel difficult to bear.'[50] Hastings's ridiculous and absurd squandering of a fortune, with its overtones of arrogance and in-difference to what was demanded of a man in his position, touched a public nerve. It was immediately remembered that the Prince was an inveterate race attender, a gambler, a womanizer and the centre of a society of wealthy hedonists who had nothing better to do with their time than throw away money that had come from the grinding labour of those beneath them. The Marlborough House set was no longer indulged by a complaisant public. The Prince and his set were now the centre of critical attention, and Edward's reputation suffered further erosion.

In July Alexandra bore her fourth child, Victoria, and in November she and Edward left England for a six-month tour of Europe and the Near East. They stopped in Sweden for a brief visit with the King to renew their acquaintance, begun so auspiciously in 1864; and Edward appalled his mother by allowing the King to initiate him into the order of Freemasons.[51] Following a six-week stay in Copenhagen, the Prince and Princess made their way to Egypt by way of Austria and Prussia, where Edward was invested with the Order of the Black Eagle. Sir Samuel Baker and the Duke of Sutherland met the royal pair in Egypt and accompanied them up the Nile. The travel arrangements, even more elaborate than those made for the Prince six years earlier, were the work of Baker and the Khedive, who spent vast sums of money on the boats and furnishings to ensure that Edward and the Princess travelled in the utmost luxury.

The trip was a repetition of the Prince's earlier visit with Edward shooting at crocodiles, hyenas, lizards and waterfowl. Somehow, the slaughter went forward without the zest of his earlier experience. Alexandra went ashore from time to time and rode around on a milk-white donkey, a gift of the Khedive. The rest of the party visited temples and ruins along the way but not with much show of interest. The boats were the centre of life; and after Karnak no one showed more than a polite interest in archaeology. The most bizarre event of the trip occurred at Wadi Halfa, where a ten-year-old Nubian boy captured Edward and Alexandra's attention. In jest someone suggested taking him back to England, and he announced his readiness to go. When asked if he did not want to tell someone he was leaving the place, he replied that he had no one he cared to see. In a lapse of judgement Edward decided to send the unfortunate child back to Sandringham as his pipe cleaner, a joke that may have seemed better then than it does now.

On the banks of the Nile, dressed in a silver earring, Hakim was an interesting and appealing personality. At Sandringham he was less attractive. In the first months he was a pet of the family and guests, who were delighted with his shining smile and amusing Eastern costume. The servants found him less satisfying. During his years along the Nile, he had kept alive by stealing. In his new home, surrounded by such opulence as he had never dreamed existed, Hakim continued to steal, first from his fellow servants and then wherever his eyes led him. In an effort to check the habit, Edward placed him in the hands of Mr Onslow, the vicar, who gave him Christian instruction but failed to teach the boy to distinguish between what was his and what belonged to others. Offences grew more serious. He took one of the Prince's guns and returned it broken. Then he ordered a vast number of neckties in a London shop and charged them to Edward. The climax of his criminal career was the lifting of Prince Alfred's 'very particular' umbrella. Edward sent the boy away to be brought up by a clergyman, having despaired of his pipe cleaner.[52]

A Mrs William Grey accompanied the Prince and Princess on their Nile journey and left an account of the trip which gives a remarkably clear picture of the days and weeks spent on the river. It is extraordinarily dull reading. No one seems to have done anything except ride on the boats and occasionally go ashore to paint, ride a donkey or watch a funeral. She and some of the other women in the suite found some diversion in looking over the women's quarters in the Viceroy's palace. Of the five hundred female slaves in the harem she writes, 'They are dressed in the most ridiculous and tasteless manner, in the European fashion, but no two alike....I think it is a great pity that they do not have a regular costume, as their present way of dressing very much spoils the otherwise so very Eastern effect and look of the Harem.'[53]

The attitude of the travellers towards the people among whom they were moving is well caught in her account of an episode which occurred at the First Cataract, where a group of native men were set to swim down the rapids while the Prince and his party watched from the shore. The swimmers all went down among the rocks with great skill and, climbing from the river, ran back calling out for 'baksheesh'. 'However,' she wrote, 'they had to do it over again, and then they got a handful of silver to divide amongst themselves. This was the moment to see the savage type display itself in full force. The shouting and the screaming that the sight of those wretched coins in one of the men's hands produced, cannot be described. Still, there was no fighting, they only seemed to be using very bad language in very high voices, and a single motion of a stick was enough to cow and quiet these poor, good-humoured Arabs.'[54]

After Egypt Edward and Alix visited Constantinople, the Crimea, Greece and France, returning home on May 12 1869. The trip, if it served no other purpose, met the Queen's requirements. It had kept Edward occupied for six months and out of trouble, allowing the scandalous rumours about him, which had become a permanent element in society, to dissipate. He did not of course come home in any way chastened. He simply took up where he had left off and immediately plunged into his dispute with White's.

He had been married six years. He was an accomplished traveller and a practised womanizer. He had established himself as the leader of fashionable English society. Having formed the pattern of his life, he was still without a significant role to play in the government of his country. Disraeli laughed about 'Prince Hal', and gloomier observers recalled George IV. But he was neither Hal nor George. His was a very complex character in which seriousness was almost inseparably mingled with frivolity, true earnestness with superficiality. He was rapidly approaching that watershed of his life, after which he could no longer be called a youth, unemployed or otherwise. His life had begun to harden in its mould. The next decade might well be decisive in determining the ultimate shape of that life; and at the close of 1869, the prospects were hardly encouraging.

7

Letters and Lampoons

And there's a lust in man no charm can tame
Of loudly publishing our neighbour's shame.

Juvenal, *Satire* IX

By 1870 the average educated Briton was fully aware that the secure
world of his ancestors, with its finite space and time, fixed creation
and religious certainties, was lost to him. All systems were suspect, all
received tradition doubtful, all hierarchies shaken by the work of
Darwin and Lyell, and later, for some, Marx; Lyell's geological studies
revolutionized man's view of the earth as thoroughly as Darwin's
observations modified his concept of origination. Textual scholars such
as Eichorn were about to attack the belief in the divine inspiration of
the Old Testament writers. Twenty years earlier, in *In Memoriam*,
Tennyson had published his record of a man, tormented by religious
doubt, winning through to a shaky affirmation of faith retained. By
1867 Matthew Arnold, scanning that same world, fell back from Tennyson's position, exclaiming:

Ah, love, let us be true
To one another! For the world which seems
To lie before us like a land of dreams,
So various, so beautiful, so new,
Hath really neither joy, nor love, nor light,
Nor certitude, nor peace, nor help for pain;
And we are here as on a darkling plain
Swept with confused alarms of struggle and flight,
Where ignorant armies clash by night.

Dover Beach might have been an anticipation of the Franco-Prussian
War but was more convincingly an expression of the generalized
anxiety about man's relationship with his universe which had gripped
the western world.

The stress ought to have driven men together for mutual support,
but it appears to have had the opposite result. The republicanism and
secularism, which had gained a hold on the minds of many Englishmen

a generation earlier, were given impetus by the intellectual climate. Classes drew further apart in wealth and sympathy, working men began to recall their Chartist heritage; the newly christened bourgeoisie, particularly its dissenting element, grew increasingly shrill in pointing out the moral shortcomings of their countrymen. The upper class, alarmed by the hostility it increasingly encountered, withdrew into the West End, leaving the East End to starvation, disease and the rack-renters. Having already published the notorious *Poems and Ballads*, Charles Algernon Swinburne, that 'unclean, fiery imp from the pit', as John Morley of the *Saturday Review* labelled him, was at work on *Songs Before Sunrise* and would write of Jehovah, 'Thou art smitten, thou God, thou art smitten; thy death is upon thee, O Lord.' With that line and other extravagances, he prepared the world for change.

Altogether, the mood of the nation was hostile to privilege, and it was a time for those with wealth and social position to lie low, but all unwillingly and with little blame, Edward was suddenly catapulted into the centre of a scandal that brought the nation into the streets, shaking its fists, hissing and groaning, while the popular press predicted terrible consequences for the English monarchy.

The cause of the uproar was a beautiful, dark-haired young woman named Harriett Sarah Mordaunt, the twenty-one-year-old wife of Sir Charles Mordaunt. The young couple moved into the Prince's circle, and by 1868 Harriett had become sufficiently intimate with the Prince of Wales to cause her husband anxiety. He forbade her to exchange any more letters with Edward or to indulge in any more flirtation with him. But as events were to reveal, Sir Charles's instructions went unheeded.

Harriett and her husband had been married in 1866. Since that time they had lived the casual, gay, unproductive lives common to people of their class and social station. For two years there were no children; and then on February 29 1869 Harriett was prematurely delivered of a boy at Walton Hall, Warwickshire, Charles's country estate. Within two days it became clear that the child was suffering from an eye infection that appeared to threaten him with blindness but which, in fact, was completely cured in twenty-one days. Discovery of the ailment, added to the trauma occasioned by the premature labour, appears to have unhinged Harriett's mind. She brooded over the supposed calamity until March 8; then, calling her husband to her bedside, she told him that in the past she had been guilty of repeated adulteries, that Lord Cole was the father of the child and that she had been intimate with Sir Frederick Johnstone and the Prince of Wales. Following that painful interview, she confessed to the maid her certainty that Sir Frederick was carrying a disease, presumably venereal, and that she had transmitted the infection to her child and caused its blindness.

Her confessions to her husband and to the maid were the out-

WASHING DIRTY LINEN!

[SEE THE SCANDAL OF THE DAY

8. 'Washing Dirty Linen!': from the *Tomahawk*, March 1870
   By permission of the British Museum

9. Cartoons from *Fun*, the *Sydney Bulletin*, the *St Stephen's Review* and *Ariel*, May and June 1891
By permission of the British Museum

pourings of a disoriented mind, tormented by grief and driven to self-accusation. Whether or not she had in fact been sexually unfaithful to her husband is impossible to say and, at least at this distance, appears to be of minor importance. She was obviously in an acutely disturbed emotional state. Given her condition, whatever she said at this stage should have been treated cautiously or disregarded. Unfortunately, Charles Mordaunt took his wife's confession at its face value. Six days later, on March 14, he forced open her desk and discovered a valentine and a handkerchief from the Prince of Wales, as well as letters from him and other men.[1] Some of these letters, but not those from the Prince, were later characterized in court as damning. On the fifteenth, Mordaunt left the Hall without having had any further conversation with his wife following their final bedside meeting on the thirteenth. The parting was final. Although Mordaunt returned briefly to Walton Hall while Harriett was still there, he never saw her again.

On the sixteenth her mother, Lady Moncrieff, came to stay with her daughter. Four days later her father arrived. On April 30 Mordaunt's agents served her with a divorce citation. Her state of mind worsened, and on May 6 her family brought in four doctors to examine her. A few days later her mother-in-law called and formed the opinion that the young woman was shamming. Harriett Sarah Mordaunt had ceased to exist as an individual. In the view of her relatives, she was mad and unaccountable for her actions. Her husband and his agents, on the other hand, saw her as an adulteress seeking to escape the consequences of her actions, a woman no longer fit to be the wife of Sir Charles Mordaunt and beyond the claim of sympathy or human compassion.

Shamming or not, by the end of May it had become necessary to provide Harriett with a professional attendant. Dorothy Frances Caruthers was brought in to look after her until August, when she was replaced by Sarah Barker. Later, both women were called into the witness box to make public statements concerning their charge's behaviour. Sir Thomas Moncrieff watched his daughter until the end of July and then, making up his mind to act on her behalf in the divorce citation, entered a plea of insanity, which, if proved, would prevent her husband from securing a divorce.

The Mordaunt faction immediately contested the plea, accused the plaintiff of shamming and demanded that the suit for divorce on grounds of multiple adulteries be granted. It is worth noting that a single instance of adultery would have been sufficient to win the case; but the petition charged her with adultery with Viscount Cole in May, June, July 1868, at Chesham Place and in July 1868, and January 1869, at Walton Hall; adultery with Sir Frederick Johnstone in November and December 1868, at Walton Hall and December 1868, at the Alexandria

F

Hotel in London; and adultery with 'some persons' between July 15 1868, and February 28 1869.[2] Among the 'some persons' was, presumably, the Prince of Wales and a Captain Farquhar, whose name surfaced at the trial.

How did Mordaunt gain such detailed knowledge of his wife's past actions? The answer is that he took her almanac-diary, along with the letters, from her locked desk. The diary contained compromising entries of meetings, dinners and teas with the men named. It did not, however, give any indication of what, if anything, had occurred at those meetings. That she was having sexual intercourse with the men was deduced by her husband and his solicitors from the facts of the meetings. Not surprisingly, given the prevailing attitude towards women at that time, no one ever expressed the slightest doubt that it was Mordaunt's right to break into that desk or suggested that he had, in any way, deprived his wife of her rights by that action. The question of whether or not Harriett would answer the petition was fought in the courts through the early summer; and on July 10, four physicians – Orford, Jones, Reynolds and Burrowes – were sent down on Mordaunt's behalf to examine her. Affidavits were filed and answered; and on July 27 Lord Penzance, Judge Ordinary of the Court of Probate and Divorce, decided that the question of Harriett Sarah Mordaunt's sanity would have to be settled in open court. The 'great Warwickshire scandal' was launched.

The case eventually came to trial on February 16 1870, in what the *Daily Telegraph* described as 'one of the most inconveniently arranged courts in Westminster Hall'. The interest in the case, which had been building since the previous summer, was intense. The trial promised to have something to delight everyone who took pleasure in public humiliations. Additional police were assigned to the court and the streets approaching the court to control the crowds struggling to gain entrance. At one point in the trial, the gallery became so crowded that Lord Penzance warned the spectators against over-burdening the structure; but his warning was ignored. The risk of being pitched into the well of the court was as nothing compared with the thrill of watching the case unfold. And it must be admitted that revelations of the most astonishing sort were made on every one of the trial's ten days. It was the twenty-fifth before Lord Penzance gave his charge to the jury.

It is not certain when, exactly, Edward learned that he was to become involved in the scandal. The original divorce petition had been served nearly a year before the trial actually took place, but Lady Mordaunt's counsel, Dr Deane, Q.C., may not have served the Prince with a summons until very shortly before the case came to trial. In any event it must have been a nasty shock, the severity of which may be recorded in a letter which he wrote to the Queen to tell her that he would be appearing at the trial as a witness, noting that he had been subpoenaed by Sir Charles Mordaunt's counsel.[3] Perhaps the stress had muddled him, as well it might have done. He suddenly found himself in trouble with his wife, his mother and the British public. There was some discussion among the Prince's advisers – Earl Granville and the Lord Chancellor were among those consulted – about whether or not he should respond to the summons. Fortunately, it was decided that he should testify in order to clear his name of any charge of serious wrongdoing. To have refused would have created a crisis of confidence, not only in Edward but in the English judicial system as well. The decision was made easier by the fact that Alix also felt that he should testify.[4] His appearance was set for the twenty-third.

The purpose of the trial was to determine the sanity or insanity of Harriett Mordaunt at the time of her being served the writ of divorce, but from the beginning it was clear that Harriett herself was on trial. After the case had been concluded, *John Bull* and several other journals found serious fault with the manner in which Lord Penzance had conducted the trial, more specifically for having allowed the impression to be gained by jury and spectators alike that Lady Mordaunt's morals were the object of the court's interest.[5] But it is difficult to see how the Judge Ordinary could have prevented the testimony from emerging as it did. Once he decided to try the case in open court, rather than insisting that the parties reach an agreement in private, the complainant's evidence was bound to include what Harriett herself had confessed. Both sides would use that testimony in attempting to establish their cases, one claiming it to be true, the other, delusory.

The testimony given by Elizabeth Hancox, the nurse attending Harriett during her confinement, provided the ground on which Mordaunt's lawyers were establishing their position. In brief, the nurse testified that one of the first questions Harriett asked of her was whether or not the child was diseased. The nurse asked if she meant deformed and the mother replied, 'No, you know what I mean. Is it born with the complaint?' Hancox replied that there was nothing wrong with the child, and Harriett went to sleep, apparently satisfied. But when she awoke, she demanded again if there were any sign of disease upon the child.[6] This obsession increased over the following days, intensified by the fact the child developed eye trouble. Finally, she told the nurse that the child was not her husband's but Lord Cole's and that 'from the child's eyes being bad I must do something'. What she did was to tell Hancox that Sir Frederick Johnstone was a 'fearfully diseased man'. She refused to nurse the child except in front of her husband, and then only pretended to do it. Subsequently she told Hancox that no one must see the baby since it was not fit to be seen.

'I am sorry I have brought such a poor, miserable, horrid little thing into the house,' she said.

Harriett was now beginning to suffer from fits of 'excitement', during which she repeatedly told the nurse that she must talk to Sir Charles. Between the eighth and the thirteenth she repeatedly told Mordaunt that she had 'been very wicked and done wrong with more than one person'. Sometimes these confessions occurred with the nurse present and sometimes not. Sir Charles testified that she had said to him that she had had intercourse with the Prince of Wales, Sir Frederick Johnstone and Lord Cole in 'open day'.[7] By the fourteenth he had made up his mind to believe her stories, despite the evidence he had from the nurse and from his own observation that she was in a very strange state, given to sudden fits of weeping and that when she saw anyone other than the nurse, she became extremely nervous and excited. When asked by Lord Penzance if he knew what the word hysterical meant, he answered, 'I believe that when men cry it is not called hysterics, but when women cry it is.' There was general and sustained laughter in response to that sally and Lord Penzance did not suppress it.

Space will not permit a full account of the astonishingly contradictory testimony given by the doctors who were called during the trial. Nearly a dozen men had examined Harriett since the preceding year; and although they could all agree that she was now mad, they could not agree on the nature of her illness (the majority held out for puerperal psychosis), or whether or not she had been mad at the time the writ was served. The state of medical knowledge concerning mental or emotional ailments is indicated by the testimony of Dr James Anderson, who told the court, without eliciting laughter, that he thought he could recognize an insane person by his smell. Dr Reynolds said only that he was forced to conclude that her state was caused by either 'extreme disease or extreme shamming, and after all I have seen I think it is the former'.[8]

The details of Harriett's behaviour from March of the previous year until the time of the trial would appear to remove all doubts about her mental state. She wandered about the house at night, dressed only in stockings and a cloak, attempting to break into the servants' rooms. Bird, the butler, was visited frequently; and when she could not force his door, as she invariably attempted to do, she would call loudly for a hammer so that she might smash it in. What Bird's reactions were to these midnight thunderings is not recorded. She smeared herself with excrement and 'performed the offices of nature without a utensil' wherever she might be. When taken driving, she regularly attempted to throw herself from the carriage while it was moving. She repeatedly threatened to kill her child. There was a period in June when she seemed to grow quieter and the baby was brought to her in the hope that he might rouse her from her silences and lethargy. For a few moments she walked about the room, cradling the infant in her arms; but tiring of it, she put the child on the floor, gave him a book and told him to amuse himself.

The list of her extraordinary actions could be extended without exhausting the record. To add to her troubles throughout these months, she was forcibly subjected to physical examinations by groups of doctors, sent by her husband, apparently to determine whether or not she had contracted syphilis. No trace of a venereal disease was ever discovered. Her physical degeneration following her confinement, however, was startling. Her beauty faded and she grew extremely fat. The beautiful young woman who had received a valentine from the Prince of Wales was no more. One of the last people to visit her before the trial testified that in the middle of their talk she suddenly threw herself full length upon the floor with her face buried in the carpet. Asked if she found it comfortable to lie in such a position, she replied in a muffled voice, 'Sometimes.'[9]

Whether founded in reality or built out of the febrile fancies of a troubled mind, Harriett Mordaunt's confession pulled Edward forward into unwanted notoriety. He found himself cast in the role of seducer, corrupter of youthful wives and disrupter of marriages. Three days before his appearance in court, he was attacked by *Reynolds's Newspaper* in astonishingly harsh language: 'If the Prince of Wales is an accomplice in bringing dishonour to the homestead of an English gentleman; if he has assisted in rendering an honourable man miserable for life; if unbridled sensuality and lust have led him to violate the laws of honour and hospitality – then such a man, placed in the position he is, should not only be expelled from decent society, but is utterly unfit and unworthy to rule over this country, or even sit in its legislature.'[10]

And, of course, there were the letters, those dangerous messengers, once dispatched by Edward in the lightest of moods and which now came flying back at his head like brickbats. Eleven were put into the record on Monday February 21, but were not read in court. The mystery surrounding their contents had, however, been dispelled a week earlier when a Birmingham newspaper printed them, a breach of judicial confidence which actually helped Edward since the letters were almost painfully harmless in content. 'My dear Lady Mordaunt,' one reads, 'I am quite shocked never to have answered your kind letter, written some time ago, and for the very pretty muffetees, which are very useful this cold weather . . .'.[11] Another expresses regret that she is 'unwell' and unable to receive him. Her illness proved to be measles. None of the letters mentions their having met, and the final one in the set tells her that he and Alix are off to Egypt. He suggests several times that they arrange to meet; and on that basis it could be argued that he was acting improperly towards a married woman, since at no time does he suggest that Sir Charles be present. But the letters are undeviatingly innocent of innuendo as well as interest, so much so that quoting them is pointless. Their existence, however, had been known for months before they were published, and had excited endless speculation. It is no wonder that a few years later when another scandal swept the Prince into its burning centre, it was with dread he recorded in his diary, 'Letters!'

Having announced in court that he had heard that the Prince of Wales was to appear as a witness, Lord Penzance exposed himself to ridicule and censure by stating his willingness to place his private rooms at the Prince's disposal and his readiness to consult Edward's convenience in setting the time of his arrival. *Tomahawk,* in particular, attacked his lordship for allowing himself to appear in the role of a toady. But since it was necessary to go back to the reign of Henry IV for a precedent for a Prince of Wales's appearance in a court of law as a witness, the Judge Ordinary's extravagance of expression regarding his preparedness to make straight the royal path may be dealt with generously. The case had become a lawyers' muddle, and the *Solicitor's Journal* carried an article dealing with precedents.

In addition the situation was dangerous. Edward had been accused in court of having had sexual intercourse with Harriett Mordaunt, not once but several times since her marriage. Furthermore, he had been reported by reliable witnesses to have been seen visiting Lady Mordaunt when she was alone and having arrived at these trysts in a hansom cab, presumably in order to avoid detection. The situation was bristling with opportunities to explode a political bomb under the Prince, and Lord Penzance was anxious to see that nothing of the sort occurred. In fact, the Queen, by way of her private secretary, General Sir Henry Ponsonby, and other august personages, had made it very clear to Lord Penzance that she did not want to hear so much as the detonation of a political firecracker in the Prince's vicinity.

On the twenty-third Dr Deane closed his case for the petitioner by telling Lord Penzance that the names of the Prince of Wales and Sir Frederick Johnstone had come up repeatedly and that Johnstone's name 'has been mixed up with one of the most hideous stories ever introduced into any case'. Deane added that he intended to begin with these two men by calling his royal highness. At that point Edward entered the court and, having been sworn, went into the witness box. Dr Deane came forward to begin the questioning; but before he could put his first question, Lord Penzance leaned forward and said to Edward that under the law, 'no witness in any proceeding, whether the party to a suit or not, shall be liable to be asked or bound to answer, any question tending to show that he or she has been guilty of adultery'.

With the warning delivered, the Judge Ordinary motioned to Dr Deane to begin. The counsel spoke into a tense silence which gripped the densely packed courtroom: 'I believe your Highness has for some time been acquainted with the Moncrieff family?' Edward's answer was a clear, 'I have.' The tension was broken; the spectators breathed normally again as the questioning went rapidly forward. 'Were you acquainted with Lady Mordaunt before her marriage?' 'I was.' Had he provided a wedding present? He had. The next few questions brought out that while Edward continued to see Lady Mordaunt after her marriage, he saw her in the company of the Princess or, sometimes, Sir Charles. It was established that Edward and Charles Mordaunt knew one another, and on one occasion served as opposing captains at a pigeon shoot at which Lady Mordaunt kept score for both sides. Then, without preparing the ground, Dr Deane said, 'We have heard in the course of this case that your Royal Highness uses hansom cabs occasionally. I do not know whether or not it is so.' 'It is so' was the Prince's immediate answer; and it might have ushered in gales of laughter (given Edward's persistent use of hansom cabs as a screen for reaching his places of assignation), but there is no record that the spectators made the slightest stir. The next question was the final one and marked a peak in the rising action of the drama: 'Has there ever been any improper familiarity or criminal act between yourself and Lady Mordaunt?' In a firm and carrying tone of voice Edward replied, 'There has not.' The defending counsel, Mr Sergeant Ballantine, immediately rose and said, 'I have no questions to ask his Royal Highness.' The threat of cross-examination evaporated like a summer mist. Edward turned to Lord Penzance, bowed somewhat stiffly and left the court.[12]

The general public was incensed at seeing the heir to the throne testifying in a divorce court proceeding, and they let Edward know their feeling by hissing him in the street and in the theatre. At a public dinner held in the City on Wednesday night, the guests responded to the toast, 'To the Prince of Wales' by shouting back at the toastmaster, 'To the Princess.' In defiance of public dissatisfaction, Edward and Alix went skating several times during the week of the trial in Regent's Park, drawing huge but respectful crowds. The weather that winter was exceptionally severe, and at the time of the trial the Thames was jammed with blocks of ice two feet thick. At Blackfriar's Bridge the blocks formed a solid mass from shore to shore and were covered with snow.[13]

In the midst of all the excitement of Edward's appearance in court, only the *Standard* had the objectivity to look beyond the Prince and the scandal to consider the plight of the woman whose name was being made into a synonym for a slut. 'An adverse decree,' the paper observed, 'would send her forth into a perpetual ostracism from everything that makes life worth having and would condemn her at two and twenty to a living death for all her remaining days.'[14]

Fortunately for Harriett Mordaunt the jury, after being out for only ten minutes, returned a verdict finding that she was 'utterly unfit' to 'answer the particulars, and to instruct her attorney for her defence'. Technically she had been saved, but as she was broken in mind, had lost her physical beauty and her marriage was ended, the victory seems to have been bought at a ruinous price. A writer for the *Pall Mall Gazette* asked how so much misery could have heaped itself on two such young and favoured persons. Unable to discover an answer, the journalist noted that in a similar situation a Spaniard or an Italian would have murdered his wife, a Frenchman would have quietly left her, but only an Englishman would have dragged her through the mud of a divorce court, condemning the entire families on both sides to ridicule, humiliation and exposure.[15]

By any standard of judgement acceptable to humane persons, the Mordaunt trial should never have been held, and it is impossible to agree with Lord Penzance that the open forum of a public court was the proper place to judge Harriett Mordaunt sane or insane. The trial was a national disgrace. Nothing in its proceedings redeemed its vulgarity, cruelty and lasciviousness. Why, then, had it been allowed to occur? The answer was, apparently, through a paralysis of horror brought on by the demented confession and accusations of a pathetic young woman in the grip of severe emotional disorientation. So shocking and debilitating to those in positions of power was the confession of this young wife and mother of the privileged class to multiple adulteries that reason and charity departed from all those, ranging from her husband to the Judge Ordinary, who were forced to confront that confession. In this era it was the first duty of an upper middle-class woman to maintain an unsullied reputation. The behaviour expected of her varied from social group to social group, the women of the Marlborough Set, for example, being allowed greater freedom of action than were those in the Court circle. But all had to be blameless, virtuous and above reproach in the eyes of the world. The inviolability of marriage and the purity of the wife were publicly beyond appeal. To a confession of the sort Harriett Mordaunt had made, the system had only one response.

The law moved behind the offended husband and was summoned on behalf of society to perform an act of ritual purification. But the act could not be carried out because the accused was palpably mad. Therefore, the process was abortive and the damage worse at the end of the ritual than at its beginning. But an emotional catharsis was needed in the community and scapegoats were sought and easily found. The journals raged against the folly and corruption of the upper classes. Edward and his friends were excoriated. Royalty was charged to be pure in mind and heart. But it was really Harriett the mob wanted; and, denied their victim, they turned on those women of the upper class who had attended the trial. 'They have no right to intrude their loathsome presence upon the Hall of Justice,' *Tomahawk* thundered. 'Let them keep their be-rouged cheeks and dyed hair from the Courts of Law....It is an intolerable nuisance to discover their brazen painted faces leering and gloating in Westminster Hall! Hide your sin, Jezebel!'[16]

Edward did not hide his sin and went out nearly every day after the close of the trial to skate in Regent's Park, drive along Rotten Row and attend the theatres in the evening. Gallantly, Alexandra accompanied him. Sir Philip Magnus has written that the Mordaunt exposé caused a deep rift between the Princess and her husband, but it may have produced nothing more serious than the temporary anguish of embarrassment and hurt pride.[17] In a letter to Princess Louise, congratulating her on her forthcoming marriage to Lord Lorne, the Princess referred to Edward as 'my naughty little man', an epithet that probably adequately characterizes Alexandra's view of the affair. The Princess was not constituted for serious reflection and dark musings. A cloud of worry might temporarily darken the quiet azure of her mind, but it was soon gone, puffed away by some new delight.

Although he was hissed at Ascot, Edward managed to avoid any serious confrontations with his subjects, perhaps because his wife was so popular. Wherever she appeared there was unstinted cheering and expressions of affection. Some of that goodwill necessarily spilled over to grace Edward; but, nevertheless, he remained unpopular during the spring and summer of 1870. The irritation with him and his mother might have been worse had it not been for the diversion created by the Franco-Prussian War, which France, diabolically manipulated by Bismarck, precipitated by declaring war on Prussia on July 15. Within a month the forces of the Second Empire had sustained over 120,000 killed, wounded or captured, among the latter, as the Germans triumphantly reported, one Emperor. The disastrous war brought to an end Napoleon III's empire; and with its collapse the fading away of one of the most vibrant, most sophisticated, most superficially delightful eras of French national life. Napoleon's surrender at Sedan destroyed the dream of empire. France was once again declared a republic; and Empress Eugénie and her son, the Prince Imperial, fled to England.

Early that summer Alexandra had gone to Denmark to visit her parents. Edward was to follow; but the sudden outbreak of fighting between France and Prussia obliged Alix to hasten back to England, much to her disgust. Edward was, of course, strongly pro-French in his sympathies, his opinion, as usual, running counter to that of his mother, who sided with the Germans. She remembered Albert's having predicted that the vain and immoral French would have to be put down.[18] Edward followed the progress of the war with increasing alarm, and on August 21 wrote to his mother, 'I cannot bear sitting here and doing nothing whilst all this blood letting is going on.' He asked to be allowed to take letters to the Emperor and to the King of Prussia but was refused permission to act in so formal a way.[19]

Perhaps the most galling of his burdens that summer were the public accusations that he was pro-German. Almost it would seem out of deliberate wrongheadedness, the press simply included him with his mother in this respect. But he did not allow either unfairness in the press releases or hostility from the Queen to interfere with his efforts to help the French. Throwing himself into war-relief work, he gave his name and his time to the effort until he thoroughly alarmed the Foreign Office, which was anxious to maintain England's neutrality in the affray. In his enthusiasm Edward had participated in a scheme to send flour to the ravaged provinces of France. This kind of overt action by the Prince of Wales was bound to be taken up by Prussia as a breach of neutrality and the government sent him a sharp note telling him to desist. Immediately he took a new direction.

In October he wrote to the deposed Empress Eugénie, placing Chiswick House at her disposal. The Queen was angry, claiming that he was playing into Bismarck's hands by giving the new republican government of France reason to distrust England.[20] The argument was empty of virtue. Edward's act was entirely characteristic, the gesture of a gentleman. He acted from the finest motives, those of love, compassion and fidelity to an old friend. The French understood this, and there was no criticism. Edward's sister, Victoria, on the other hand, wrote to find fault with Edward's pro-French feelings, accusing him of holding them out of jealousy of her husband's accomplishments as a soldier. Well might the Prince have felt betrayed.

Although the Franco-Prussian War may have somewhat relieved the hostile public pressure exerted on Edward following the Mordaunt trial, it did nothing to improve the position of the Crown. The collapse of Napoleon III and the immediate success of the bloodless revolution that created the republican Government of National Defence under the enthusiastic leadership of Leon Gambetta only served to excite republican sympathies in England. The leaders of this radical element were Joseph Chamberlain; Sir Charles Dilke, a liberal politician who spoke fearlessly on behalf of a republic; Sir Henry Hoare, M.P.; Charles Bradlaugh, orator, agitator and professed atheist, who regularly attacked Edward for not living a life of Christian morality; and George Odger, orator and disciple of Karl Marx. At the turn of the decade all these men were prophesying the death of monarchy in

England. In the summer of 1871 Odger predicted that were the Queen to die, royalty would die with her; and Bradlaugh demanded to know why Englishmen should choose her successor from a family whose sympathies had never been with England.[21]

Gladstone had attempted to come to Edward's defence in the matter of the French war relief effort but without much success; and over the period of the next two years, his efforts to secure employment for the Prince caused Gladstone much personal grief and further alienated Victoria, who already loathed her Prime Minister. The Prime Minister's proposal was to send Edward to Ireland to replace the Viceroy and give him a full-time job carrying out the formal, public duties of that official. Gladstone proposed to pay the Prince of Wales the same salary paid the Viceroy, conveniently forgetting that the salary fell short by several thousands of pounds of meeting the Viceroy's expenses. The Queen was furious with Gladstone for having made such a suggestion. The argument that Edward would receive invaluable training in government had no influence on her. On no account would she consider it, and she let him know in the clearest terms that she considered the suggestion a meddling with her private family affairs.

In order not to offend his mother, Edward was obliged to appear to oppose the plan to send him to Ireland, and he wrote to Gladstone to that effect. At the same time, he was anxious to keep his options open; and informally he let Gladstone know that his mind was not closed to any proposal. As a further indication of his interest, he invited the Prime Minister to Sandringham to discuss the Irish plan; but Gladstone, falling into one of his dark moods of despair, let the opportunity slip and the visit passed without his ever raising the Irish proposal. Edward was still talking about it years later, after he had become king and his son was in need of employment. Aside from the Queen's opposition, there was also the opposition of all those around her who saw any division of her power as a diminishing of their own importance. Those individuals closest to the Queen, such as her daughters, Louise and Beatrice, her son, Leopold, and her private secretary, Sir Henry Ponsonby, as well as the rest of her senior administrative staff, kept a sharp watch on the Queen's position to ensure that her power was not eroded. This group had no way of checking the vast constitutional drift of influence away from the throne; but the bureaucracy surrounding her resisted any division of her powers because of the threat to their own status. Edward's sisters, either out of jealousy of their brother or from a genuine conviction that he was incompetent, encouraged the Queen to deny him any meaningful share in her official activities.

As Edward continued to remain jobless, the tide of public scorn mounted; it now began to take the form, in addition to the platform orators' attacks on royalty, of publications of various kinds ridiculing the monarchy. Charles Bradlaugh led off in 1870 with a scurrilous publication called *George, The Prince of Wales, With Recent Contrasts and Coincidences*. The little book operated on a simple strategy: by denying any grounds existed for comparing the notorious career of George IV as Prince of Wales with that of Edward, Bradlaugh made precisely that comparison and moved cheerfully along the edge of a slander with an abundance of quoted attacks on Edward taken from such journals as *Reynolds's Newspaper*, the *Royal Leamington Chronicle*, the *Tomahawk* and the *Belfast News Letter*.

Not content with lambasting Edward, Bradlaugh suggested that Queen Victoria had no right to occupy the throne. George II, Bradlaugh insisted, 'was thrice married, once privately in 1759, at Curzon Street Chapel, Mayfair, to Hannah Lightfoot, a Quakeress, and afterwards on September 18 1761, publicly to the Princess Sophia Charlotte of Mecklenburg-Strelitz. As Hannah Lightfoot was living at the time of the second marriage, the offspring of that bigamous union would have been illegitimate if George III had not been King of England.' He added that, of course, the Lightfoot marriage was denied; and as everyone knows, the weight of a royal denial, such as was made in the Mordaunt case, 'is of greater value than any evidence'.[22]

The attack was moderate in its language, but that it was made at all boded ill for the Prince. Parading Edward's failings was rapidly becoming a warming-up exercise for editors who saw themselves as spokesmen of the social conscience; and in place of the image of a young hero, the writers were creating the picture of a vain, irresponsible incompetent. And it must be admitted that there were occasions when Edward seemed to be playing into the hands of his detractors. In 1870 and 1871 he participated in the Army War Games as Commander of a company of Hussars, which on one occasion was declared by the umpires to have been wiped out by cannon fire after Edward led them in a charge against a battery of militia men. When told that he and his men were either dead or prisoners, he wheeled his company and ran away. Undoubtedly done as a joke, the action was deliberately misunderstood and used against Edward.

A pseudonymous Captain Pipeclay published *The Battle of Foxhill, The Prince of Wales in a Mess, or, The Mill, the Muff and the Muddle*. The book describes Edward's capture in the War Games and opens with three stories about a tailor, a monkey and a mouse. The tailor goes soldiering to parade and makes a fool of himself; the monkey tries to become a soldier and after loading a cannon looks down the muzzle and blows its head off. The mouse, saved from drowning in a brewer's vat by a cat who agreed to save him if he could eat the mouse, runs down a hole and escapes the cat, saying that he would not let the cat eat him because he was 'in liquor' when he made the pledge. Having told these

unedifying stories, Pipeclay launches into an attack on Edward for not
assisting in the support of the poor in Windsor. The writer then returns
to the War Games and gives a mocking account of Edward's failure in
them. His spleen exhausted, he closes with a summary of the cost to the
nation of supporting this strutting tailor, stupid monkey and mouse
'in liquor'.[23]

As the summer of 1871 faded, Edward left England for the Continent,
where he visited the battlefields of Sedan and Metz, going on from them
to stay with the Hesse-Cassel family at Jugenheim.[24] Although he
attempted to maintain an incognito, the effort was unsuccessful and the
press knew his movements. Consequently, in September, when he left
for a flying visit to Hamburg and some quiet gambling, he was quickly
tracked down. His presence at the tables was reported in the English
papers, with *Reynolds's* setting the tone for the critics of Edward's pastimes. The week before, in an effort to drum up sympathy for the royal
family, *The Times* pretended to be seriously concerned about the Queen's
health – she had a sore throat and a boil under one arm. The paper also
expressed regret that it had ever criticized the Queen.

Reynolds's refused to be diverted by *The Times*'s tactics: 'The Queen,
it is said, is just recovering from a serious illness, and it is felt that she
may die any day. So, for that matter, may we all.'[25] Sentiment dismissed, the paper continued, 'But the question of what will follow the
reigning sovereign's demise is upon everyone's tongue. . . . Even the
staunchest supporters of monarchy shake their heads and express
anxiety as to whether the Queen's successor will have the tact and
talent to keep royalty upon its legs and out of the gutter. . . . When,
therefore, the people of England read one year in their journals of the
future king appearing prominently in the Divorce Court, and in another of his being the centre of attraction at a German gaming-table,
or public hell, it is not at all surprising that rumours concerning the
Queen's health have occasioned in many quarters much anxiety and
apprehension.'[26]

It was his gambling that served as the excuse on this occasion for
attacking Edward. He was staking gold, the writer raged, 'upon the
chance of a card or the roll of a ball – gold, be it remembered, that he
obtains from the toil and sweat of English working men, without himself
producing the value of a halfpenny'. The paper was almost equally
incensed by the fact that foreigners and Englishmen stood six deep
around the table to watch the Prince place his bets. As to the argument
that the Prince was obliged to gamble because nearly everyone else did
at spas and watering places, it was demolished by the writer's asking
whether, if Edward went to Salt Lake City, he would be expected to
take 'a score or two of wives'. Those who took up *Reynolds's* complaints
and defended Edward against them were unable to do better than ask,

'Would you have the Representative Man of the Richest Country in the world a sordid and penurious niggard?'[27]

Victoria was damned for not spending her money, and Edward for squandering his. Was it simply that the middle class in England had grown weary of royalty and were listening to the siren song of the republican agitators? Undoubtedly, the oratory of the great radicals had some effect; but one must go beyond the Odgers, Chamberlains and Bradlaughs for an answer. This much is clear from what subsequently happened. The hold these men had on the average Englishman was tenuous in the extreme and, when the time came, it was shrugged off without a tremor. The real complaint of the middle classes against the Crown was that it was not doing its job, a job for which it was very highly paid. The irritation with Edward was a reflection of a deeper irritation with the Queen. She had ceased to fulfil her role. There were ugly rumours about her relationship with John Brown, her indispensable Scots attendant, about her drinking and about her miserliness. Edward was drifting around England and Europe like a restless ghost whose materializing was in the company of fast women and cards or in Paris as the Duke of Lancaster, his incognito there, where he was titled by the French press as a *'Boulevardier'*. The appellation might have pleased Edward; but it did not please the majority of his English subjects, who viewed all things French as morally tainted.

For several years Edward's popularity had been sinking. Not even the death of his son, John, the sixth child, born prematurely at Sandringham on April 6 1871 (who lived only twenty-four hours, having hastily been christened Alexander John Charles Albert), not even that loss to him and the still-popular Princess restored him to favour with his subjects. In fact the child's death occasioned a particularly crude magazine attack in *Figaro,* which, although published in a French journal, was promptly reprinted by English papers, under the title of 'Mummery at Sandringham'. The unidentified journalist wrote concerning the burial service: 'The miserable mockery of interring with a royal funeral ceremony a piece of skin and bone, grandiloquently called "Prince", not twenty-four hours old, took place at Sandringham on Monday....And to augment the folly of the entire proceeding, the Court goes into mourning for the wretched abortion, which, as our readers will observe, was carried to the grave by four stout men!'[28] When one recalls the praise heaped on Edward and Alexandra at the time of their wedding, it is difficult to believe that such a shift in public feeling could have occurred in so short a time. Oddly enough, throughout this period Edward could walk along the London streets without attracting attention, for the reason that a number of men in London bore a striking resemblance to the Prince and chose to dress like him and imitate his gestures. As a consequence he could move about with little chance of being taken for himself.

The carping and sniping at Edward in the press did not have any real effect on his movements. He continued to travel, fulfil his public functions, attend race meetings and, in general, make himself available to the country. Alexandra, having recovered her health and spirits which had been somewhat cast down by the loss of her child, accompanied her husband; and Queen Victoria's admonition to her son to take better care of Alix by leading a quieter life was received from Dean Wellesley, who had been its unwilling bearer, and gently dismissed. 'I am sure a sedentary life would not suit her,' Edward told the Dean, thus disposing of the matter.[29]

In early November 1871, he went to Scarborough to visit Lord Londesborough. On the nineteenth, two weeks after his return from Scarborough, he began to complain of dizziness, chills, headache and depression. His personal physician, Dr Lowe, was concerned, but Edward insisted on going up to London for a theatre party. Returning to Sandringham feeling more ill than when he had left, Edward submitted to another examination. This time Lowe discovered fever symptoms. Dr Gull, standing in for Dr Jenner, who was in Scotland with the Queen, was summoned from London; and he confirmed the diagnosis of typhoid infection.[30] The two physicians judged Edward's condition to be grave.

To increase the worry, Lord Chesterfield, who had occupied Edward's rooms at Londesborough Lodge following the Prince's visit, was reported to be dangerously ill. The *Lancet* and the *British Medical Journal* identified the source of the fever as the sewers at Londesborough Lodge, the latter publication adding that typhoid of a particularly violent sort was prevalent in London.[31] Then, on Friday December 1, Lord Chesterfield died at Bretby Hall, Burton-on-Trent. By this time Edward was critically ill. Warned to be prepared for the worst, the Queen and other members of the royal family began to arrive at Sandringham.

Unlike his father's attack ten years earlier, Edward's fever was diagnosed early. Nevertheless, there was cause for worry. On at least one occasion the Queen was told that there was no hope, but Edward clung to life. On Sunday night, December 10, a crowd of nearly one thousand Londoners gathered in Fleet Street to wait for news. Just after eleven o'clock, a bulletin was released which read, 'Not so desponding: Prince now sleeps.' The crowd broke into cheers of heartfelt relief. But it was the eighteenth before Jenner and Gull considered it safe to report Edward out of danger.

The effect of Edward's illness on the English people was remarkable. The anti-royalist feeling in the country evaporated; and Sir Charles

Dilke, who was making a speaking tour of the country, found his audiences suddenly hostile. Addressing a crowd estimated at two thousand at Bolton on November 31, he was confronted by throngs of pro-royalists, who forced their way into the hall singing *Rule Britannia* and the National Anthem. Their arrival precipitated a riot in which stones were pitched through windows, people punched one another, and Dilke barely escaped with his life. Slow to learn, he tried again six days later at Derby to speak to a crowd of 1,500 in the Temperance Hall. Immediately, fighting broke out between his supporters and his detractors. A month earlier he had been attracting vast, sympathetic audiences. Now it was popular to attack republican orators.[32]

The reaction against Edward's critics became too enthusiastic; and the nation was given the improbable experience of being lectured by the *Pall Mall Gazette* on the necessity of continuing respectful criticism of the Crown and the royal family whenever it was justified.[33] On the other hand, *John Bull* gleefully got some of its own back against the radicals, who had escaped its wrath during the height of their popularity. 'It is needless to say,' one of its writers stated, 'that the general sympathy, keen at all times, is intensified tenfold owing to the disloyalty and treasonable language employed by a few demagogues.'[34] The public poured gifts into Sandringham, most of which were returned to their senders; but a barrel of home-brewed beer was accepted with thanks and set in a dark cool cellar to await Edward's recovery. Quacks descended in force on King's Lynn with cures of every sort to propose; a few even managed to make their way into Sandringham House before being detected. Throughout England, public prayers were conducted for Edward, and the Archbishop of Canterbury sent out a special appeal to the churches for prayer services. In India the Parsees held a great prayer meeting at their Chief Fire Temple at Hormusjee Wadia; and in Jerusalem and the other holy cities, synagogues offered special prayers for Edward's recovery.[35]

The press and some of the medical journals violently attacked Lord Londesborough for allowing the drains under his house to fall into such neglect; and his position in the country became so menaced that he was obliged to print denials of the charges and to request an investigation by a committee from the staff of the *Lancet*. No definite conclusions were reached in the ensuing examination, and the inquiry was clouded by the discovery that one of the stable wells at Sandringham was infected. That revelation notwithstanding, Lord Londesborough's life was made very uncomfortable for a time.

When on December 18 the doctors announced Edward to be out of danger, there was general rejoicing throughout England. Dr Gull, who had brought Edward through his ordeal, was offered a baronetcy and plans were laid for a formal day of public thanksgiving, which was held on February 27 1872. The London service was held at St Paul's Cathedral and was attended by 13,000 people.[36] There was a tremendous, loyal response when Edward, Alix and the Queen, who had agreed to attend the service with the greatest reluctance, drove through the streets to St Paul's. All doubts about Edward's popularity were dispersed and republican sympathies vanished in the new sun of royal favour. Both for the Prince and for the Crown, the thanksgiving service was a great personal triumph.

Hundreds of sermons were preached in the United Kingdom in observance of the Prince's recovery. His old friend, Dean Stanley, preached one in Westminster Abbey on March 3 on the theme that Edward had been given that rare chance, the opportunity to begin his life a second time: 'Hardly ever, in the long course of our history, has so heart-stirring a prospect been opened, of beginning life afresh, of taking the lead in all that is true and holy, just and good, of finding in the hundred calls of duty a hundred openings for the best and purest enjoyment....'[37] The Dean found it impossible not to snatch the Prince Consort from the tomb and shake the dead man in his son's face: 'He [Edward] knows, as few in like position have known, the mighty power for good which has, within our own memory, been exercised in that lofty sphere by one who, from his early manhood to his sudden and untimely end, wore "the white flower of a blameless life", unscathed and unspotted even in that "fierce light which beats upon a throne...." ' There was more of this sort of language before Stanley concluded with a plea for the restoration work on St Paul's Cathedral, drawing a connection between the completion of the work and the Prince's recovery.

Dean Stanley struck the 'stern note' of duty in his sermon, and it was echoed by nearly every other divine who spoke on the Prince's recovery. In sermon after sermon Edward was warned to alter his way of life, to devote himself to the paths of righteousness. The often unstated premise for the assertion that Edward's life should be blameless found expression in the vicar of Chantry's sermon, in which he said, 'The throne is the pivot around which everything else works. . . . As the head of the family is the representative of all its members, so is the monarch the representative of the nation, the head which so often thinks for us; the mouth which speaks for us; the hand which acts; the person in whom we are everyone of us honoured or insulted.'[38]

The vicar was not alone in believing that a real connection existed between the monarch's moral life and the welfare of the state. A Rev. E. S. Ffoulkes insisted that England had escaped from the convulsions of revolution because of the 'spotless lives and surroundings of Queen Adelaide and Queen Victoria'.[39] He spoke, apparently, for a large number of Edward's subjects, who, whether or not they were prepared to assert the existence of such a direct connection, felt the power of Ffoulkes' statement. There have been tribal kings who were not allowed to lie down for fear the wind would stop blowing and the grass cease to grow. There seems to have been something of that primitive dread in the public demands for Edward's moral rectitude, and the press encouraged the general public to believe that the welfare of the country required Edward's compliance with the moral code of the middle classes.

It has been asserted that Edward learned from the Mordaunt divorce case to leave young, newly married women alone. But it is not easy to point to anything of an equally precise nature that his illness taught him. Indeed, why should it have taught him anything? Lady Macclesfield has left a record of Edward's sick-bed repentances, but they should be taken somewhat cautiously, especially since they, like his rather alarming revelations of names and occasions, whispered or shouted, were made in delirium and could hardly be thought binding and were probably not even remembered. Shortly after her husband's recovery, Alexandra wrote that they were enjoying a 'second honeymoon', and there is no reason to disbelieve her. Edward was in a weakened, possibly chastened, state and temporarily quite willing to recover in his wife's company. There are, however, no grounds for believing that his manner of living was permanently changed by his sickness. He recovered at Osborne, and then he and Alix left for a three-month Mediterranean holiday.

Had Edward's life been shaped by a single, unmistakable force, either for good or for evil, or had he been a man whose existence was moulded by some dominant interest, it would be easier to come to the core of his life and speak of its triumphs and its failures. But it was not shaped by any of these things. What lay at its centre was boredom, anticlimax and frustration. Gladstone's struggle in the years between 1871 and 1876 to provide Edward with a responsible position in government, utterly defeated by the Queen's relentless hostility, illustrates the pitiless folly which dogged Edward. It has been suggested that had the Prince been more determined, he would have overcome the resistance to his assuming his proper place in the direction of national affairs; but such a hope is scarcely sustained by the facts. Gladstone was prepared to negotiate directly with Edward over the Irish plan, and Edward expressed willingness to talk to the Prime Minister. The Queen, fearing that she was being circumvented, forbade Gladstone to conduct any part of the discussions with her son; and when Edward accepted his mother's command not to talk with Gladstone on the subject, the door swung shut. Gladstone eventually despaired of doing anything worthwhile for the Prince.[40]

By his training, by the agony of his father's death and by his guilt-ridden awe of his mother, Edward was rendered incapable of a sustained resistance to the Queen in any area where her authority as reigning monarch was involved. To have persevered and persisted until he had either won his place or provoked a government crisis or a permanent break between himself and the Crown, Edward would have had to be another man. His failure to act decisively on the Irish appointment issue is a demonstration of the disastrous effectiveness of his training. Edward was not a malingerer; he was a victim of long years of parental repression. Later, during the 1870s, when he began to make serious efforts to exert his influence as a diplomat, he was obliged to get most of his information from *Figaro* and from casual conversations, because neither his mother nor the Foreign Minister would tell him much.[41] In his position he could not be tragic; that dignity was denied him.

For a brief while following his recovery from the typhoid that nearly killed him, Edward was spared the jibes of those who saw in the Crown either an excuse for moralizing or a challenge to see whether or not it could be toppled. But in 1873 Samuel D. Beeton, Aglen A. Dowty and Evelyn D. Jerrold published *The Coming K---: A Set of Idyll Lays*, in which Edward is represented as Guelpho, a prince who succeeds to a throne. The book, written in comic imitation of Tennyson's *Idylls of the King*, which, it will be remembered, was dedicated to Albert, holds up to ridicule and scorn racing, whoring, drinking, going to music halls and most of the pastimes of the idle. The work is dedicated to Guelpho-Edward, and its attitude toward him is indicated in the following excerpt:

> Indeed, he seems to me
> Scarce other than my own ideal liege,
> Who did not muchly care to trouble take;
> But his concern was, comfortable ease;
> To dress in well-cut tweeds, in deerskin suits,
> In pants of patterns marvellous to see;
> To smoke good brands; to quaff rare vintages;
> To feed himself with dainty meats withall;
> To sport with Amaryllis in the shade;
> To toy with what Nerea calls *her* hair;
> And, in a general way, to happy be,
> If possible, and always debonair.[42]

The insult in the portrait lies not so much in the things that are said of Guelpho as in the easy familiarity with which the 'low' characters in the poems speak of him. An ex-prizefighter, The Nobbly One, in 'The Glass of Ale', reflecting on Guelpho's career, observes,

> If his papa had lived, quite likely then
> He might ha' got into a different set,

> Gone for preaching in the open air,
> Or p'raps ha' been a ritualistic cove,
> Or took delight in buildin' 'alls and shows,
> Or givin' lectures to good workin' men;
> But his Pa was nipped in the bud,
> It turned out otherwise.... [43]

He was not even to be taken seriously; and in the closing lines of the opening poem, 'Coming of Guelpho', the writers place him in his context:

> So came the turn of him, the Coming K---
> Whose brand is Henry Clay, brave brand to smoke,
> But not to smite – another one in store
> (Trade mark triangular, 'twould cost a crown
> To counterfeit) is Bass, X *calibre*. [44]

The light, if impertinent, tone maintained by *The Coming K---* gave way in 1874 to a harsher attitude representing a rapidly accelerating return to the hostility felt by large segments of the British population towards the royal family before Edward's illness. *The Siliad, or The Siege of the Seats,* published anonymously in January 1874, strikes a republican note and is less conciliatory than Beeton's piece. Introducing its theme, the dedicatory poem proclaims,

> The writing on the Wall, wayfarers see
> Is in a Roman hand, clear, fair and free;
> '*Thy days are numbered*', it proclaims aloud
> To rank and privilege, to Monarch proud...

The introduction goes on to attack the royal family for its handling of money, especially its alleged 'secret wills' and hoarding of cash, and demands that royalty spend what has been given to it or else, 'the sceptre from your hand departs'. [45]

Guelpho appears in the latter section of the work, and of all the individuals and groups dealt with (these include everyone from Haymarket whores to the brothers and sisters of the Prince) he comes off with the lightest treatment. In one episode the Queen upbraids Guelpho for his many vices as set forth in *The Coming K---*. He acknowledges that he is familiar with the book and that he and his friends have had some good laughs over it:

> What can it matter, even if 'tis true,
> I wouldn't be so glum if I were you.
> Suppose I am all that they say I am,
> I'm better so than live a priggish sham;
> I am not clever; why should I pretend
> To learning that I do not comprehend? [46]

The Queen is ruffled by that response and tries another attack, charging Guelpho with failing to love his German cousins enough and with spending too much money. She then urges him to be saving like his brother Alfred, who, in real life, had acquired a reputation for miserliness:

> Upon my honour, Ma (Guelpho broke in);
> That is not fair to talk about the tin;
> Remember, if you please, I have to do
> A heap of things that should be done by you.
> You choose to live an almost hermit life,
> Shut up from Royal state, and show and strife;
> Which means that I must, to a like degree,
> Come out and quite a proxy monarch be.[47]

The fact that the book came round to defending Edward against his mother was not particularly comforting, nor edifying, if for no other reasons than that he is made to appear a buffoon, with the conversation of a Guards officer and the morals of a croupier. The spate of such publications continued. Shortly after the appearance of *The Siliad*, *The Fijiad or English Nights Entertainments* sprang up – another offensive parody around the throne. An obvious imitation of its two forerunners, the *Fijiad* presents Fiji as a paradise inhabited by men who, aside from a little embarrassment caused by their being cannibals, are otherwise quite moral creatures. Englishmen arrive, bringing rum and so on, and turn the natives into slaves. Their prince, Fijitee, determines to visit England to become 'civilized'. Fijitee is surrounded by a group of scoundrels who pretend to be introducing him to English life by means of dinners and stories, told in the style of *The Arabian Nights' Entertainments*. There is a take-off on the press, a cutting attack on Victoria and John Brown, a lengthy verse on William of Prussia and Bismarck, and even a parody of Tennyson's 'Lady of Shalott', which begins,

> Bill Laine the fat, Bill Laine the troublesome,
> Bill Laine the silly man who lost his hat,[48]

followed by a lampoon directed at the Shah of Persia's visit to England.

Presented as an initially simple and naive individual who falls into the hands of men of low character who would corrupt him, Fijitee is, of course, Edward. He is handled less rigorously than his mother and other members of the royal clan, but one suspects that the gentleness stems from lack of respect more than from liking. Nonetheless, there is a definite drift in these attacks. In fact it may be inaccurate to characterize them as being simply attacks on the Crown. Culminating in a play, mentioned later, they increasingly single out Victoria for condemnation and adopt the Horatian tactic in regard to Edward of attempting to laugh him out of his follies.

1874 was more than simply a year in which Edward smarted under the sting of public ridicule. It was a year of remarkable activity, beginning dramatically in January, when he went to Russia to see his brother, the Duke of Edinburgh, married to the Grand Duchess Marie and to take part in a magnificent boar hunt. In July he and Alix held a fancy dress ball at Marlborough House, at which Edward appeared as Charles I and Alexandra as a Venetian lady. The ball was judged to be the most magnificent that the society of the day had ever seen, and for a generation it became the standard of elegance and brilliance against which all others were measured. The expense was enormous; but, then, if one is to appear as Charles I, one does well to fill the cup. Following the ball, Edward and the Princess left England for the continent. Alexandra went to visit her family while Edward went on to Baden.

At Baden he was to have spent his time quietly, taking the waters and playing a little roulette, but reports of gambling appeared in the English press, opening an old wound. This time, however, the issue was not moral but financial. He was reported to be in debt, presumably because of gambling and other extravagances. Until he became king, Edward was haunted by persistent reports that he was in the hands of loan sharks and usurers. On this occasion it was said that he was £600,000 in debt.[49] The report was denied by *The Times* and various of the Prince's spokesmen, but the denials did little to reduce the strength of the rumours among the public, which was predisposed to believe that Edward had been overextending himself financially. The general press was less than critical in its acceptance of the rumours.

Something new, however, began to appear in the press reports about his money troubles; and there is reason to believe, although no solid documentation is available to prove it, that this new element was being introduced from Marlborough House itself. In mid-October the *New York Times*, reporting on an article in *The Times* purporting to be in defence of Edward, insisted the piece was really an attack on the Queen and emanated from Marlborough House. The original article followed a stiff denial that Edward was seriously in debt with the following statement: 'There can be no doubt, however, that the Prince has in consequence of the Queen's persistent seclusion, been saddled with duties and obligations, which in the natural course of things would have fallen to his mother's share and were not taken into account in fixing his allowance.'[50]

This kind of comment had been made before; but now the article became more specific and admitted that Edward was eating into his capital at the rate of about ten to twenty thousand pounds a year, while the Queen, by her style of life, was piling up vast savings. Victoria had been given a life settlement of £385,000 a year, but only £60,000 of this sum was for the Privy Purse and under her direct control. The balance was to be allocated to Court expenses and where the sums were not spent, were, at the discretion of the lords of the Treasury, to be applied to meet an excess in another branch. It was never intended that the surplus be paid into the Queen's private bank account; but this is what was done; and as Victoria reduced her staff and went deeper and deeper into seclusion, more and more money went into her personal account. It was judged that by 1875 the Queen had amassed a private fortune of £5,000,000. The *New York Times* expressed the belief that Edward had been responsible for *The Times* article and that it was an attempt on his part to get some money out of the Queen.

The conjecture is an interesting one. Without question, Edward had been feeling the pressure of his expenses, and his capital was indeed shrinking. As *The Times* observed, he had been representing the 'Royal House of England for ten years in visits to the chief courts of Europe, and has been burdened with the expenditures required to discharge these duties'.[51] He had been, in that respect, more than an ordinary prince. But had he used this devious method to increase his income? It seems out of character, and there is nothing in his previous behaviour to prepare one for it. On the other hand, he was not on very good terms with his mother. Earlier in the year, she had refused, quite arbitrarily, to allow him to accept the honorary colonelcy in a Russian regiment which Alexander II had offered him, thus denying him the delight of wearing a new uniform. And later, during the press reports about his debts, he had been obliged to listen while his mother reminded him that the country would never tolerate another George IV.[52] He might have felt justified in allowing his private secretary, Francis Knollys, to take his case to the people. Knollys certainly had no reason to love the Queen. When, in June 1870, Edward appointed him to the position, he had done so over the Queen's remarkably strenuous objections. It is certain the Prince would never have risked his pride by taking his complaint in an open manner to either Parliament or the Queen, being right in his opinion that he would be rebuffed and probably given a lecture on domestic economy.

In November he was in the Midlands, visiting factories in Birmingham and Manchester, doing the things which the Queen ought to have been doing. In Birmingham he was received at the Town Hall by Joseph Chamberlain, the radical mayor of the city. As E. F. Benson has remarked, their principles should have led the two men to detest each other, but the result of their meeting was quite different.[53] During the hours they spent in one another's company that day, each developed a high regard for the other and laid the basis of an enduring friendship. Edward would later have the same effect on Charles Dilke, although not even Edward's friendship would save the politician from the ruin of a sexual scandal. Not enough credit has been given Edward for his efforts during the 1870s and after to bring into the warm circle of his recognition such leaders as Chamberlain and Dilke, who, by his influence, became the supporters rather than the enemies of monarchy. Edward rarely received public acknowledgement of his efforts to bring together the conflicting elements in English society.

There was, of course, another aspect of Edward's activities in 1874. This darker side was revealed in his frequent visits to Paris, visits usually taken incognito. It was during this period that he formed his close friendships with the great French beauties of the age (the period of which Proust was writing in *The Guermantes Way,* when Oriane de Guermantes captivates the Prince and wins him). After 1874 he established liaisons with the Comtesse Edmond de Portalès, the greatest of the French beauties who attracted him; the Baronne Alphose de Rothschild, whose receptions at her mansion in the Faubourg St Honoré became legendary; and the Princess de Sagan, wife of the great-nephew of Talleyrand.[54]

Edward's tastes were not, however, always so exalted. He frequently stayed at the Hotel Bristol and dined at the *Café des Anglais.* In this period Cora Pearl, the English woman who was currently reigning in Paris, was once served up on a huge silver platter as a naked Venus. Cora Pearl was a woman of considerable character. Throughout the siege of Paris, she had flown the Union Jack from her balcony on the Rue de Chaillot.[55] It was this Edward of the *Café des Anglais* and the Variétés Theatre whom Emile Zola caught and displayed in *Nana.*

But even as he played, the Prince watched the new French Government, and made up his mind that it would last. He had already made an official call on President Thiers, following his recovery from typhoid. He might visit Chantilly, home of the Duc d'Aumale, the very centre of ancient French lineage and culture and the heart of royalist France; but he could, at the same time, admire the efforts of the Republic to restore to its citizens a sense of personal and national pride and to recover the political and economic stability which had been destroyed in the military defeat of 1870. Edward was, in matters of politics, a pragmatist, functioning without bias, able in many ways to ignore the barriers of class or philosophical conviction. It is one of the ironies of his life and another example of the folly dominating it, that he was not encouraged to bring his great talents to bear on foreign affairs. What such talents he did use at last, he used effectively despite the Queen, her ministers, her government and his own brothers and sisters.

8

Elephants, Tigers and Republicans

Hunting was the labour of the savages of North America, but the amusement of the gentlemen of England.

Samuel Johnson

If Edward was ignored at home by the men shaping England's political
destinies, he was treated more seriously by European heads of state,
who would have welcomed the opportunity to deal seriously with him
on issues of diplomatic importance. But for the present he remained
largely without influence; and in almost a parody of his role as a man
of affairs, tailors from across Europe followed him on his trips to the
continent, taking extensive notes on his clothes and the manner of
wearing them.

There is a much-told story concerning Edward's waistcoat which
indicates the extent of his influence on men's clothing styles. One
morning, having dressed in a hurry, he emerged from his hotel with the
last button on his waistcoat undone and, in so doing, established a
permanent fashion.[1] It is a pleasant story; but he probably left the
button unfastened to mask the protruberance of his stomach, which
within a few months following his illness had exceeded its former
magnificence. Thanks to Edward, men's clothes took on a new importance during the 1870s. He owned over a hundred hats, had a room
filled with uniforms; and when he travelled took two valets with him
and left two at home caring for his vast wardrobe.[2] In London new
men's clothing stores opened in Savile Row, Clifford Street and Bond
Street to meet the heightened male consciousness in dress. When his
enemies sought to render Edward ridiculous, they often referred to him
as a tailor's dummy.

But Edward was never merely a fashion plate. He was aware that
clothes have a ceremonial as well as a practical function; and he was
equally conscious of the very great degree to which he was a ceremonial
figure, the more so because the Queen refused to assume her constitutional responsibilities in this area. In the early summer of 1873, a
typically onerous task came his way in the form of the forty-three-year-

old Shah of Persia, whom the Queen refused to entertain despite the fact that he was making a state visit. The Shah announced that he was travelling to improve his mind, but it was generally assumed that he was coming to England to learn how to industrialize his country. But his degree of sophistication is indicated by the fact that while he was crossing the Caspian Sea, he ordered all of his servants to lie prostrate on the deck around him to ward off seasickness.

The English greeted the Shah with great enthusiasm. Tickets of admission to the Admiralty Pier at Dover, where he was to land, simply evaporated. The *Mail* advised its readers to buy a good telescope and find a spot in the hills with an unobstructed view of the bay and from there view the Shah's arrival in comfort.[3] Fortunately, Edward found the Persian monarch diverting and was amused to learn that the silver charcoal burner which a servant kept lighted and close at hand was there in case His Highness wished to light a pipe or brew a cup of coffee. Edward also delighted in the stories of the Shah's barbaric conduct, particularly one involving a Russian noblewoman of the Tsar's Court who accepted an invitation to visit the Shah's rooms. When she entered his suite, he walked around her, examining her from head to heel, decided that he wasn't interested and strolled off without speaking to her.[4] Edward never tired of repeating the Shah's observation that the Duke of Sutherland, whose house they had visited, was 'too grand for a subject' and that 'you'll have to have his head off when you come to the throne'.[5]

The Shah's reception throughout England was astonishingly warm. For a few days even *Reynolds's* restrained itself from directly attacking him; but its patience soon gave out. When its assault came it was devastating. The people of Persia, it thundered, are 'a people clothed in rags, wallowing in filth, and devoured by vermin'. The paper accused the Shah of having plundered his subjects and squandered their substance. It then lashed out at the 'toadies' who had welcomed him to England.[6] It had certainly not been Edward's wish to bring the Shah into the country. The government, anxious to further its influence in Persia, was responsible; but it was Edward who became publicly associated with the visit. When at the end of three weeks the Shah left for home, Edward was relieved to be rid of him.

Perhaps sensing that he needed to do something that would give him prestige in the governing circles of his own country and add to his influence in Europe, Edward decided during the winter of 1874 to visit India and to do it in the grandest possible style as the representative of the Queen, the personal embodiment of the Raj. There was, of course, an immediate objection raised to his going. The Viceroy was the Queen's official representative in India, making it impossible for Edward to go in that capacity. It was equally clear that he could not go as a private citizen, because he was heir to the throne. But Edward put aside such objections as unimportant, forcing the Foreign Office to produce an elaborate scheme in which he would be the Viceroy's guest but would not spend much time in the Viceroy's company, thereby making it possible for the Prince to receive from the Indian rulers all the honour due the son of the Empress.

Another difficulty was money. Edward was in no position to finance a venture of the magnitude implied by the plans put forward; and Victoria, who did not want him to go at all, soon made it clear that she would not provide him with so much as a penny. Unhappily, the controversy spilled into the press. By July 1875, the newspapers were hotly arguing not only the funding of the venture but the trip itself. Not surprisingly, the division occurred along political lines, the Conservatives calling for a generous allowance and a national send-off and the Liberals and Radicals denouncing the trip as a pleasure jaunt and insisting that the poor were being robbed to provide Edward with a treat. Reluctantly, Disraeli assumed the task of persuading Parliament to provide the money; but he took a cynical view of the affair, writing to Lord Salisbury, Secretary for India, that Edward, whom he referred to as 'our young Hal', had tricked his mother into giving her consent to the trip by pretending that the government approved of it and had kept the entire matter completely secret from his wife.[7]

Edward's scheming, if that is what it was, can be attributed to the jealousy with which his movements were controlled by his mother and by the government of the day. He was kept on a very short rope; and, as a rule, could not even take his family to visit Alix's parents in Denmark without the Queen's permission. He had, however, set his heart on the Indian venture and was determined to plan it and carry it out on his own initiative. Just how profoundly he felt this need to exert his independence is revealed in an interview with Disraeli over the question of who should be included in his suite, Victoria having decided that she would draw up a list of those who were to accompany the Prince. Told by Disraeli of what the Queen's intentions were in the matter, Edward lost his temper and told Disraeli that not a single name on his original list would be altered and that the subject was closed. Disraeli scurried back to Victoria to advise her to drop the subject.[8] With customary bad grace she did so, grumbling that the list lacked 'eminent' men.

Edward's test for the members of his suite was congeniality. His personal guests were Lord Aylesford, 'Sporting Joe', one of the most renowned horsemen in England; Lord Charles Carrington, a close friend; and Lord Charles Beresford, another friend, who like so many of Edward's intimates in those years would later be a cause of trouble to him. These men were neither scholars nor statesmen, but they were good companions, knew and shared the Prince's tastes, and could stay on a horse and shoot. In India there would be a festival of pig sticking and shooting. As for statesmanship, none would be required of either him or his guests, beyond the fundamental acts of maintaining one's dignity in public and moving with grace and assurance through the various ceremonies to be attended. Edward's guests were eminently suited to perform these functions and indeed did perform them with the greatest credit to themselves. Not even Edward's sharpest critics found any fault with the deportment of his people. It must be admitted, however, that Aylesford's conduct in England could not have instilled in anyone confidence in his discretion. There was one persistent story – that when bored, 'Sporting Joe' would have his carriage driven through London at a gallop while he stood balanced on its roof, pitching bags of flour at pedestrians and roaring with laughter.

The suite Edward had arranged was entirely masculine and he was determined that it should remain so. Alexandra did her best to make him change his mind, for when she learned of the projected visit to India, she determined that she would go. Alix had thoroughly enjoyed her trip to Egypt and was enraptured with the idea of visiting the 'fairylike' subcontinent.[9] But Edward was adamant and so was the Queen, who, for once at least, sided with her son. Alexandra was defeated, but it was a costly victory for the Prince. For several weeks after leaving England, he was in a depressed state, his mood having been generated by what passed between husband and wife before his departure. Alexandra was never reconciled to having been left behind on that occasion, although she was not of a temperament to retain any mood for very long.

By the middle of July, Parliament finally acted to provide Edward with a travel fund. On the fifteenth a Conservative M.P. wrote an open letter to *The Times* urging that a sum of £100,000 be appropriated for the Prince's expenses. That same night, after a rancorous debate, the the Commons raised £60,000.[10] Disraeli further promised that the Indian Government would contribute another £30,000, a sum which was eventually raised to £100,000. Ridiculous though it sounds, one of the principal causes of the enormous expense of the journey were the fabulously expensive gifts to be showered on Edward by the Indian princes when he arrived in their country. When he began to gain some idea of the value of the presents, he was embarrassed to discover that his gifts to the princes would be far inferior to those he would be receiving. From the public relations standpoint, the gifts created another problem: Edward's presents to the princes were being bought by public funds, but the gifts being given to him were to become his private property.

Reynolds's Newspaper, along with a great many other liberal journals, was angry about the trip, the expense connected with it and the fact that Edward was going to be allowed to keep the estimated £200,000-worth of presents coming his way. The paper also aimed a shot at the Queen on the subject of money, observing that 'in all likelihood, a certain middle-aged lady, whose greed of gold is proverbial, chuckled over this ingenious way of getting rid of troublesome liabilities out of other pockets than her own'.[11] The reference is probably to those rumoured debts which the gifts were going to defray.

The *Mail,* on the other hand, expressed its conviction that the Prince of Wales, in going to India, would be discharging the most important public function which his position opened to him and that it was the country's responsibility to deal with the visit as a 'great public cere-monial'.[12] *The Times* also gave its sanction to the undertaking, and the Bishop of Oxford suggested that Edward's visit to India would help the missionary movement there. *Reynolds's* disagreed with the Bishop: 'The notion of Albert Edward, the hero of the Mordaunt divorce suit, the mighty hunter...being associated in even the most remote manner with the missionary or any other work where intellect and intelligence are required is supremely ridiculous.' Not satisfied with this attack, the writer went on to suggest that the only interests of Edward's 'crew' were 'pig-sticking and women'. In a fiery non sequitur the paper accused the Prince of maintaining a rural slum in Somersetshire, called 'Stap Street', first reported in the *English Labourer,* where people were crowded eight to a room in rows of hovels lacking all facilities for decent living and flouting the sanitary laws. It was a very nasty picture of royal landlordism.

Once the Commons had actually voted the grant of money, some of the passion went out of the press discussions on the subject of the pro-jected journey, but the public did not forget. When *Reynolds's* wrote that working men had been robbed in order that Edward might enjoy him-self, the paper spoke for a substantial section of the British people. In travelling through England in July and August, Edward encountered towns with hostile placards against him and his Indian trip. In Sheffield particularly there were uncomplimentary posters, and in Margate he made his appearance with the 6th Dragoon Guards and two hundred Metropolitan police controlling the streets.

In Hyde Park on July 18 a huge gathering, reminiscent of the mass meetings of the Chartists in the 1840s, assembled to hear Charles Bradlaugh's protest against Edward's Indian venture. Some sixty to seventy thousand gathered and welcomed Bradlaugh with round after round of cheers. Bradlaugh summarized Edward's wealth and de-scribed him as a 'Field Marshal'. That description produced roars of laughter. Then he referred to him as the brave, moral, intellectual, future King of England; and that sally evoked louder and more sustained laughter. 'The nation,' Bradlaugh continued, 'did not wish to prevent the Prince of Wales from going to India. Indeed, they would speed him on a longer journey than that.' There was more loud cheering followed by a proposal for a resolution opposing the expenditure of public money on the trip. The motion was carried unanimously. Similar meetings with similar motions were held that day in Edinburgh, Newcastle-on-Tyne, Manchester, Bradford, Leicester, Oldham, Derby, Crewe, Reading, Birmingham, Leeds, Hull and other cities.[13]

Bradlaugh's protest meeting and others like it were good-natured and produced no violence. Despite their serious intention, there was the air of a lark about them. But there was nothing at all good-natured about the way the nation received the news at the end of June that one of Edward's close friends, forty-five-year-old Colonel Valentine Baker, commander of the Prince's regiment, the 10th Hussars, was charged with attempted rape on the person of Miss Rebecca Kate Dickenson, a twenty-two-year-old governess, in a first-class railway carriage travelling between Petersfield and Clapham. A shock of horror and outrage swept the country. Not only was the case startling by the nature of the charges but also because it was heavily loaded with class hostility. Baker, an officer and a gentleman, had allegedly assaulted a young woman, his inferior in age, experience and social position, in a private railway carriage, where an English person's privacy is almost as sacred as in his home. The situation was ugly and inflamed class feeling in every section of the nation.

In the weeks between the close of June and the opening of the trial on August 2, there was continual ferment in the country; and a pamphlet was hawked in the London streets entitled *Alleged Disgusting and Indecent Outrage by Colonel Baker in a Railway Carriage; with a Narrative of the Courageous Conduct of Miss Dickenson*. The scurrilous sheet avoided being libellous, but it left no doubt in the reader's mind that Baker was guilty of every charge lodged against him. Citing this pamphlet, Baker's counsel attempted to get the trial postponed to allow public feelings to grow quieter and to change the venue of the trial because, as he told Justice Brett, presiding judge at the Croydon Assizes, it would be impossible in the Guildford area to secure his client a jury that would be impartial.[14]

That attempt by Sergeant Ballantine was denied by the judge, but it raised a storm of horror beyond the court. Edward's name was dragged into the mess, and he was accused of having attempted to subvert justice by using his influence to prevent the case from coming to trial and for interfering with the judge and the court in the outcome of the trial.[15] There is no evidence to suggest that Edward involved himself in any way with the case, beyond expressing his concern, as was characteristic of him when a friend was in difficulty. But the very fact that Baker was a close friend of the Prince only served to deepen public resentment against the unfortunate Colonel and to raise in many minds the baseless dread that royalty was interfering with the orderly process of justice. But it was a desire for revenge and not justice that had the mobs shouting in the streets.

The case opened on Monday August 2, at 10.30 am; and for hours before, the streets outside the court were crowded with people struggling to get inside, among them a large number of 'well-dressed women' who showed great endurance and courage in persisting in the crush. Two of the women were actually lifted up to windows and passed inside to friends while the mob jeered, groaned and cursed. The courtroom itself was, of course, packed. Among the spectators were the Earl of Lucan, General Sir Thomas Steele, General Airey, Sir W. Frazer, M.P., Viscount Halifax, the Marquis of Tavistock and several officers from Aldershot. Judge Brett called the court to order; and Baker, a man of middle size with close-cut black hair and moustache, was immediately placed in the dock and arraigned. He pleaded not guilty to all the charges.

The jury was then sworn in; but the noise of the crowd outside and the shouts of 'Turn out the women!' were so great that it was all but impossible for the opening remarks of the counsel to be heard in the courtroom. In desperation Judge Brett finally ordered the police to clear the streets in the vicinity of the courthouse, but before this was done a steady, deafening roar of angry voices obliterated all other sound. For Valentine Baker the sound must have been frightening, for it was the howl of a mob demanding his life.

The prosecution's case was simple. It alleged that on June 17 Rebecca Dickenson was travelling from Petersfield to join her brother, Dr Dickenson, and his wife for a trip to Switzerland. At Liphook Station, Baker entered the carriage and took a seat facing her. The train had no corridor, and passengers entered the carriages directly from the station platform. For some time Baker talked pleasantly with Miss Dickenson on general topics. Then, as the train left Woking for a twenty-mile run to Clapham, Baker began asking 'insulting questions'. Becoming more familiar, he sat down beside her and put his arm around her and kissed her 'forcibly against her will'.

Having appealed to him in vain to be left alone, she struggled to her feet and attempted to pull the communication cord, but there was none. Baker then forced her back into the seat and attempted to pull up her clothes. Breaking free a second time, she threw down the window and thrusting her head and shoulders through the opening, began to scream and was heard by several passengers. She then opened the carriage door and climbed out onto the footboard, 'determined to perish rather than re-enter the carriage'. Baker hung onto her and entreated her to step back inside. She refused and rode outside for the next five or six miles until the driver eventually saw her and stopped the train. He came back and took her down from the footboard, asking what was wrong. Pointing at Baker, she said, 'He has insulted me; he will not let me alone.'[16]

The next town was Esher, and there Baker was placed in another carriage with two men. They, along with the train guard, testified that Baker's clothes were 'disarranged'; and Henry Bailey, the guard, reported that 'his [Baker's] dress was all unbuttoned', but whether it was his waistcoat or his trousers was not established. Later in the trial, the word 'disarranged' would come to mean that his fly was unbuttoned, although that was never said in so many words; and when Baker's lawyer attempted to force Miss Dickenson to say whether or not Baker actually undid his fly, the judge compelled him to abandon that line of questioning and would not allow the point to be established one way or the other. The only answers that Miss Dickenson made to the initial enquiries in this direction were 'It had nothing to do with me' and 'I had an impression only'. Nothing more precise was ever said in the course of the testimony.

Miss Dickenson asserted that Baker had pressed himself against her and placed his hand on her leg above her boot. It was at that point that she struggled free and began screaming and eventually took refuge on the footboard. At Esher Miss Dickenson was put in charge of the Rev. Baldwin Brown, 'a Nonconformist Minister of the highest position', who accompanied her to Waterloo Station, where her and Baker's names were taken by a Constable Hatter. At Esher Baker was reported to have said to her, 'Do not tell what has happened; say you were frightened; if not, you do not know what trouble you will get me into.' Again at Waterloo he said to her, 'Let me write to your brother.' He said further that if he could speak with her brother for a few minutes, everything could be explained. Officer Hatter, who took the names and heard the complaint at Waterloo Station, testified that Baker had said to him, 'I do not know what possessed me to do it; me, a married man.' Under oath Baker vigorously denied having said any such thing.

The jury was out for just ten minutes before returning verdicts of guilty to the charges of assault and indecent assault but innocent of the charge of attempting to rape. The defence scarcely made any attempt to fight the first two charges and put all its efforts into clearing Baker of the rape charge. Brett called Baker to the bar for sentencing and spoke at length. He noted that a 'thrill of dishonour passed through the whole country when it was told that a young and innocent girl, travelling by the ordinary conveyances of the country, had been obliged to risk her life in order to save herself from a gross outrage;

10. Cartoons from *Ariel*, *Funny Folks*, the *Silhouette* and *Judge*, June and July 1891
By permission of the British Museum

A GREAT TRIAL.

"GLAD TO SEE YOUR ROYAL HIGHNESS. YOU MIGHT SPEND YOUR TIME A GREAT DEAL WORSE THAN BEING HERE, YOU KNOW."

11. 'A Great Trial': from *Moonshine*, June 1891
By permission of the British Museum

every household in England felt as though it had received a personal injury.' The judge made more remarks, mentioning 'vile passions', and then passed sentence: twelve months in jail and £500 fine. Baker heard the sentence without flinching; and when the jailer summoned him, 'he stooped, picked up his hat and umbrella and went'. There was a murmur of approval in the court as the sentence was read.[17]

Outside the court the crowds had broken the police lines and pressed forward again, struggling to get a glimpse of Baker. Worried that he might be harmed, the authorities sent an empty carriage to a side door of the jail to distract the mob and then spirited their prisoner out of the front door of the court building, giving him only a moment to say good-bye to his wife. Baker's departure for jail was not the end of the affair. Newspaper accounts of the trial continued to appear, and editors of the liberal journals lamented that he was not given hard labour and that he was to be allowed special privileges while in prison. One editorial writer called Baker 'as great a villain, ruffian, coward, and blackguard as ever faced a judge and jury'. The vituperation against Baker continued and was soon directed against his friends (who had stood outside the court and shouted, 'Bravo, Baker!' when he was driven away) and against upper-class society. Even at this distance the depth of the hostility expressed in the attacks is chilling.[18] Perhaps the nature of the unspoken emotions surging around this case is best indicated by the statement of Rebecca Dickenson's brothers, who, determined to see the case brought to trial, were reported to have issued the statement that 'the offence was committed by a person moving in what is called the highest circles of society and ought to be judged by a jury of our countrymen'.[19]

The case was a battle in the class war; and whether one saw Baker as a man sent to jail for having done nothing more serious than kiss a girl in a railway carriage or as a debauched monster, guilty of attempted rape and deserving death, who had escaped the full penalty of the law by the foul interference of the Prince of Wales and his vicious friends, depended largely on where one stood socially. But there is no doubt that the case further blackened Edward's image in the country and accounted, at least in part, for the unusual precautions for his safety taken during July and August while he was travelling in a public capacity. He embodied in his person an entire class; and when it pleased public opinion to hold that class to be savage exploiters and moral delinquents, Edward became the focus of that anger. That he had never assaulted a woman in a railway carriage was irrelevant. Apparently it was believed by one large group of Englishmen in the summer of 1875 that the Prince wanted to commit rape and would if he got the chance, that, in fact, he had already attempted it through the person of Valentine Baker.

G

Despite the Baker scandal, the India plans matured, and October 11 was set for Edward's departure. On schedule, he left Marlborough House at 7.45 pm, arriving at Charing Cross Station having driven with Alix through crowds of cheering Londoners, whose passionate response to Baker's trial seemed to have faded, at least temporarily, from their memories. A detachment of the Scots Fusilier Guards with band and pipers and regimental colour guard occupied the station and played continuously after Edward's arrival, while outside the station there was a constant roar of cheering. Scores of family and friends crowded the platform to shake hands with Edward and wish him a happy journey, making a scene that artists were to preserve for posterity, giving to the dark and smoky station a magnificence that had eluded it in its more mundane life. On the run to the coast, the festive air of the occasion was maintained by the illuminations gracing the stations between London and Dover and by the vast, enthusiastic crowds that greeted Edward and the Princess when they stepped out of the train.

Edward, Alix and the Duke of Edinburgh formed the centre of the suite sailing from Dover to Calais. Arrangements had been made for Edward to make an official visit to Paris before leaving for the East, and at Calais he parted from his wife. The actual separation or what had preceded it plunged Edward into a gloom that did not lift for several weeks. At Brindisi on October 16, he and his party went aboard the great, swift white troopship, the *Serapis*, which had been completely refitted to accommodate the Prince.[20]

From the beginning of the voyage, the Prince insisted on the strictest formality in matters of dress and deportment and received complete support in this from his party. However, one modification of dress that Edward approved and which became a permanent fashion was the substitution of a short, dark blue jacket to replace the swallow tail-coat at dinner. The dinner jacket was born.[21] Credit for inventing it is generally given to Lord Dupplin, although had Edward not adopted it, it would not have gained the swift acceptance accorded it by society. Aside from this minor adjustment in dress, however, the party adhered to a rigorous conventionality.

On November 8, the *Serapis* reached Bombay. At about 4.30 in the afternoon Edward and his party came ashore at the Mazagan Pier to the accompanying roar of naval and shore guns. Edward received a short speech of welcome from the Parsee, which had been written by William MacLean, editor of the *Bombay Gazette*, assuring Edward of the people's loyalty and expressing hope for the continuation of religious freedom. Edward thanked the Parsee for the speech, accepted it on behalf of his mother and assured his listeners that religious freedom was secure. Replying to some kind words which had been said about the

Princess of Wales, Edward remarked that she would have gladly visited India.[22] It was a moment for understatement.

The enormous crowds greeted Edward with loud cheering; and the city, decked out with bunting and lights, made a joyful setting for his reception into India. Along his route were tents and canopies dancing with streamers and lights, under which the wealthy Indians sat, waiting to greet him. One huge canopy, ablaze with lights and glittering from end to end with brilliant decorations, sheltered a group of richly robed and turbaned Mohammedan elders. They were immensely excited at the prospect of meeting Edward; and in anticipation of that honour, they had erected above the canopy huge square letters, lighted from behind, spelling out the message, *Tell Mama We're Happy*.[23]

If the note struck by that and similarly worded welcomes was naive, Edward gave no indication that he regarded them as amusing. Neither was he inclined to treat lightly the religious preferences of the people. As Sir Philip Magnus has demonstrated by quoting one of Edward's letters to Lord Salisbury, the Prince was deeply offended by the racial and religious prejudice he found among the military and political authorities in India. Having noted it, he took every opportunity afforded him in which to assert the need for equality of treatment for men of every colour and religious persuasion; but he had encountered a force too strong for him to control. Even as he made his way through the maze of public functions imposed on him, the practices of quiet exclusion and deliberate humiliation continued, often without his being aware of what had happened. Two instances, repeated over and over again in varying forms, will illustrate how Edward's attempts to bring Englishmen and Indians together was thwarted.

Shortly after reaching Bombay, he participated in the laying of the cornerstone of the Elphinstone Docks, which was to be carried out through the arrangement of the Masonic Order of Bombay. Everyone with social and political power in the city was invited, including the rajahs; but when Edward reached the seat prepared for him, the assembled Masons grouped themselves around him, giving everyone else, including the rajahs, only the view of their backs. Edward was completely hidden from sight. Resenting the slight, the rajahs promptly rose in a body and walked out of the ceremonies. Edward, unaware of their departure and unable to see past the circle of Masons facing him, began his speech: 'Right Worshipful, Worshipful and other Brethren, I thank you for your address. I have learnt with great pleasure the flourishing condition of the Craft in this part of India, and the efficiency with which lodges annually increasing in number fulfil the objects of their institution by uniting together men of various races and creeds in the bonds of fraternal brotherhood....'[24]

Before leaving Bombay on November 25, the Prince had already accumulated enough gifts to stock a museum. Aside from the gifts of precious stones and gold, he had been given daggers, Cutchee guns, tea services, necklaces, anklets, bracelets, shawls, carpets, ancient guns, suits of armour and a huge quantity of cups. He had also visited Elphanta, a small island in the Arabian Sea just to the east of Bombay, where the great temple caves are located. In the largest of these magnificent temples, carved out of the living rock, Edward held a banquet for 160 guests and lighted the cave with hundreds of lights. The banquet was certainly an improvement over the sixteenth-century Portuguese invaders' treatment of the shrine. These fanatical discoverers of the magnificent temples took one look at the great stone carvings of the Hindu deities, some as high as sixteen feet, and set about destroying them, considering it their religious duty to pull down pagan images.[25]

After leaving Bombay, Edward spent a month hunting elephants in Ceylon and visiting Portuguese Goa and Madras. He reached Calcutta on December 23 and came ashore to encounter certain ironies. Among the thousands waiting to greet him was the Maharajah of Patiala, who had bought the deposed Empress Eugénie's jewels and was wearing them for the occasion. The Maharajah of Rewa was also waiting, his face as red as fire; but it was leprosy, not excitement, that gave his face its glow. Instead of being driven away, he was placed in the first line of those to shake Edward's hands, the fact that he had £30,000 worth of diamonds on his turban alone outweighing the effects of his disease. Three young men dressed in black robes and sandals were there, the grandsons of Tippoo Sahib, who had put Sir David Baird in a water wheel and made him turn it for the amusement of his Court. Later he was killed by English and Indian soldiers. The boys were not greeted by the Prince, although by the terms of the treaty of 1793 they were unjustly being denied their birthright.[26]

Even in India Edward could not escape criticism, despite the heavy censorship imposed on Indian journals by the police. Mr Stuart Hogg, Chief of Police in Calcutta, read the official welcome to Edward, and the next day one of the local papers appeared in deep mourning in acknowledgement of the event. A leading Bengali poet, Hem Chandra Bandopadhgaya, wrote a satirical poem, 'Bajimat', making fun of Edward and the official visit; and a farce, *Gayadananda*, also mocking the Prince, appeared briefly in Indian theatres before being stopped by the police. Edward created another kind of stir among the local people by requesting to be allowed to penetrate the privacy of the women's living quarters in one of the Bengali homes. At first no one would come forward with an invitation; but finally Mr Jagadananda Mukherji, a member of the Calcutta High Court, asked Edward to his house, deeply offending his people's sense of propriety by the act. Nevertheless, as was usually the case, Edward had a delightful evening, having satisfied his curiosity about the domestic arrangements in Bengali homes.

The story of Edward's hunting exploits in India has been told many times. Participating in enormous drives, involving hundreds of men and elephants, he rode in a *howdah* from which he shot a great many tigers and other animals. On one occasion he shot an elephant and had cut off its tail when the tormented beast suddenly lunged to its feet and staggered off into the jungle before anyone could put another bullet into it.[27] He wrote letters home to his sons describing animal fights staged for him in which the animals escaped from serious harm, but those accounts were 'improved' versions of what actually happened. As Gay, the special correspondent in the Prince's party for the *London Daily Telegraph*, remarked, 'To be a sportsman in Kashmir, as in Spain, you must not be burdened with sensitive feelings.' At Jummoo Edward was obliged to watch a cheetah kill a black buck. The buck was released inside a circle of people standing in front of the Prince and his company. Then the cheetah was released. The cat attacked the buck and slowly clawed its way up the struggling animal's back until it reached its throat and finally killed it amid the appalling cries of the doomed buck. It was a bloody and disgusting spectacle, but it was only one of many similar 'entertainments' staged for Edward. However, his willingness to watch such abominations and to hunt aggressively won him a reputation for valour among the Indian ruling class, enabling him to carry away from India a degree of respect that was not based solely on fear of reprisal from the English power.

Once he reached India, Edward's spirits revived, and he threw himself into all of his activities with terrific energy and gusto. Whatever he did, he did in a spirit of lively and unfeigned interest, enjoying nothing better than the constant activity and changing scenes. The happiness of his stay, unfortunately, was sharply curtailed by a scandal in England which threatened to plunge him into the centre of a court proceeding even more lurid than the Mordaunt trial. In February he learned from Lord Aylesford, one of his party, that Lady Aylesford had written to say that she intended to elope with Lord Blandford, elder son of the Duke of Marlborough and brother to Lord Randolph Churchill, M.P. Aylesford left hurriedly for England and Edward denounced Blandford as 'the greatest blackguard alive'.[28] Since the scandal appeared to be on its way into the most public arena, his comment on Blandford was in keeping with his horror of scenes. He had recently emerged from the Mordaunt and Baker fires, and his reputation was still smoking. And there were letters.

As events revealed themselves, the worst of Edward's fears were allayed. Lady Aylesford did not elope with Blandford, because the latter was brought to see that to run away with Aylesford's wife would force both him and his mistress to leave England for ever. To prevent this from happening, everyone around these two excessively ardent lovers immediately set about trying to prevent a divorce. Lady Aylesford sent Blandford a packet of letters which Edward had written to her some years earlier, and Blandford gave them to Randolph to use in forcing Edward to prevent Aylesford from seeking a divorce. Randolph telegraphed Edward but did not receive a satisfactory reply. Losing his temper, he went at once to the Princess of Wales and told her that he had letters, written by her husband to Lady Aylesford, which, if they were ever to become public, would ensure that Edward would never occupy the throne of England. Alexandra was terribly upset by Churchill's visit and was thoroughly at a loss as to what she should do. When Edward learned that a man whom he thought to be one of his closest friends had descended to threatening his wife like a ruffian, he became so furious that he despatched a cable to Lord Randolph challenging him to a duel. Churchill sent back an insulting reply, saying that Edward knew perfectly well that a duel could not take place between a prince and his subject.

Eventually some order was restored. Disraeli, at the request of the Queen, interceded with Aylesford by way of Lord Hardwicke and managed to dissuade Aylesford from going to court. The Blandfords kept their differences quiet and a scandal was averted. Edward was not, however, satisfied. Yet again he had been obliged to write to his mother and ask her to stand by him, a request which she immediately granted. Despite his assurances to Alix that the letters were entirely innocent, he had been placed in a most difficult position with his wife. And one man, Randolph Churchill, had done this to him. However fascinated Edward was by Churchill's beautiful wife, Jennie Jerome Churchill, the attraction was not enough to save her husband. He made the Churchills social outcasts, refusing to enter a house where they were entertained. Randolph and his wife were driven out of England, and it was eight years before the breach between Edward and Lord Randolph was healed.

By the early summer of 1876 the trouble between the Prince and the Churchills had reached its climax and faded without creating a public convulsion. The letters remained private; no court convened to sit in judgement on the morals of the upper class. Edward could draw a comfortable breath, although there was fence mending to be done at home. Alexandra and Victoria had placed themselves squarely beside Edward during the trouble; and the Princess must have been pleased by the sincerity of Edward's anger over Randolph's treatment of her. But letters had been written. The Prime Minister had been obliged to intervene in a private matter, and no one could be said to have come out of the affair entirely unscathed.

Having been out of England for such an extended period of time and having won very favourable press coverage while in India, Edward would have been justified in thinking that he was coming home to a public situation in which he would be free from personal attacks. Such, however, was not the case. In 1876 Samuel Beeton, Aglen Dowty and Evelyn Jerrold brought out their second lampoon of Edward and his mother, *Edward the Seventh: A Play on Past and Present Times with A View to the Future.* The tone of their earlier *The Coming K---* had been light, but *Edward the Seventh* was often bitter. In the 'Prologue' the Queen is on a German ship sailing toward Scotland. The ship strikes and sinks a becalmed English yacht, the *Mistletoe,* drowning several of her company. The courts clear the Queen and the German prince of any blame. The episode is a very nasty piece of writing with the Queen coming under intense attack.

Edward is introduced as Prince Pagan and again as Guelpho. The Queen tells him that his duty is simply to remain at her side, but he responds,

> 'An't please your Majesty, I've other work
> To occupy my time; were I to spend
> My mornings with you at the Mausoleum,
> My evenings at the Chapel you've renamed,
> My nights in social converse with *his* bust,
> Who then would do the many acts of state
> I now perform...'[29]

The play itself begins with Victoria's coming to the throne and ends with Edward's assuming the Crown. Victoria is mercilessly depicted as selfish, dangerously pro-German, indifferent to England and a miser. It is the most unflattering of all the portrayals of her in print to that date.

Edward's treatment is more difficult to assess. In sections of the seven act play, he is represented as a buffoon, a roisterer, a deliberate wastrel.[30] In Act III a satirical review is presented in the form of a song about all the beauties of stage and social life. Sarah Bernhardt, with whom Edward had formed a liaison, is named. When the song ends, Prince Pagan says, 'I call that clever, and I know them all'. But in the last act, following the Queen's abdication, Pagan, preparing to ascend the throne, speaks in a paraphrase of Prince Hal's famous lines:

> 'God helping me, I will so reign o're England,
> She never shall repent the choice she made.
> Too long I've given my enemies the chance
> To point the scornful finger; given real friends
> Much cause for sorrow. Now those days are past,
> I now my loose behaviour throw right off,
> And pay the debt I never promised...'[31]

The strong appeal made in the play to Victoria to abdicate in favour of her son met with some support in the country; but most readers assumed that the work was designed to ridicule and condemn both Queen and Prince. A counter publication, *The Key To Edward the Seventh*, issued anonymously by one who claimed to be 'Behind the Scenes', made a vigorous defence of Edward against the lampooning attacks. The chief line of defence was that Edward served a very important function and served it well: 'The Prince is the sun round which revolve the stars in our social firmament. It is he, in fact, who gives warmth to the assemblages of high life, keeps gaiety pulsing and money circulating.... We candidly admit that the Prince has his faults, and we declare as candidly that we rather like him for that reason.... True, he is no Solon; but we do not want sages for our rulers, but prudent men who will permit the destinies of England to be guided by one or another of her statesmen, as the balance of power inclines.'[32]

While the unsettling airs of republicanism continued to blow around the royal residences, Edward made it his business to do what he could to woo the republican chiefs. In 1877 the three leaders of England's radical movement – Llewellyn Dillwyn, Joseph Chamberlain and Charles Dilke – had come together for the purpose of forming a new party. Shortly after that decision had been reached, Edward invited Joseph Chamberlain to dine with him at Marlborough House. The dinner was a success, and Dilke called the event an attempt at 'nobbling' his party. On July 4 of the same year, Dilke and Dillwyn attended the Duke of Devonshire's garden party at Chiswick. Edward was there, and Dilke was astonished to see the Prince bow to Dillwyn in a very friendly fashion. Enquiring rather hotly as to why Edward had shown 'his old friend' such attention, Dilke was further shaken to hear that Dillwyn had been pigeon shooting with the Prince. Dilke reproached Dillwyn for participating in the sport. But Dillwyn retorted with a flourish of his cane that not only had he enjoyed it but that the Prince had enquired who the old gentleman was 'who looked like a Methodist parson and shot like an angel'.[33]

Dilke had reason to believe that his party was being thoroughly infiltrated, but as yet he had no idea what an opponent he faced in the Prince, who in March 1880 invited him to dine at Lord Fife's and talked very seriously all evening with Dilke about French politics and the Greek question.[34] Edward made a friend that night. Later, when Dilke, with Edward's active support, became Under-Secretary of State for Foreign Affairs in Gladstone's second ministry, he gave Edward information the Queen would not supply concerning foreign affairs. There is a pleasant irony in the relationship of these two, very different, men: Dilke, the reconstituted radical, passing along secret information to the heir to the throne.

At the same time that he was making these domestic moves to head off a coalition of powerful political leaders who were avowed enemies of the constitutional monarchy, Edward was also keeping close watch on the growing Balkan tensions resulting from Russia's expansionist interests in that area and Turkey's crumbling power structure in Europe. When war between those two nations broke out in 1877, Edward, anxious to frustrate Russia's expansionist aims in the eastern Mediterranean, was determined that England should support Turkey and requested that he be allowed to go to the front in a command capacity. By the end of January 1878, Russia was at the walls of Constantinople. Disraeli now felt compelled to act in order to prevent the total collapse of Turkish power and forced a large war grant through Parliament. Edward clamoured to be attached to a regiment; but the Queen absolutely vetoed his demand, causing him great embarrassment because he knew this latest refusal would increase the number of jokes about his valour circulating at home and on the continent.

There were several days of tension during which it appeared that war with Russia was inevitable; but the Russians halted their advance, unwilling to commit themselves to another Crimean War. A few weeks later in March 1878, Russia and Turkey concluded their conflict with the Treaty of San Stefano. Thoroughly unsatisfied with the results of that treaty, which would have all but expelled Turkish power from Europe and replaced it with a Russian presence, Disraeli demanded that a complete reconsideration of Russian plans for reconstruction of the Balkans be undertaken. Bismarck, casting himself in the role of 'an honest broker', offered Berlin as the site of the proposed international conference of powers. That offer was accepted and the Congress of Berlin was convened. Because Disraeli was in poor health, Victoria was reluctant to send him to the conference; but Edward, fully aware of Disraeli's great powers, persuaded his mother to change her mind. Looking more than ever like a painted grasshopper, Disraeli dominated the Congress. Even Bismarck, who had hoped to advance German interests while playing the 'honest broker', admitted that 'the old Jew', as he called Disraeli, had exerted great influence. For one thing, England emerged from the negotiations having acquired Cyprus, a development which produced a shock of anger in France. He also subtracted a little Turkish territory and added it to Greece, telling Edward to regard it as a gift to Alexandra's brother, who was King of Greece.

This latest rift between England and France over the Cyprus matter provided Edward with yet another challenge. He was absolutely sincere in his determination to bring the two countries into a permanent alliance, and this new trouble over the island threatened that accord towards which he had been working with such patience. In the spring of 1878 Edward moved closer to the French Government by accepting the presidency of the British section of the Paris Exhibition, to which he loaned his recently acquired Indian collection. The event was a great success, giving Edward an opportunity for self-congratulation, not only for the smoothness with which the exhibition was conducted but also for the good feeling he had generated in French official circles.

By July, however, Lord Lyons, British Ambassador to France, warned Edward to stay out of Paris or run the risk of being publicly insulted. He told the Prince that so much ill will had been generated by England's acquisition of Cyprus that a serious split between the two countries was imminent. Ignoring Lyons's advice, Edward went at once to Paris and secretly invited Leon Gambetta, a shadow power in the Chamber of Deputies, to lunch. Reports of that meeting vary. The early, public, reports imply that the meeting was a success from start to finish, but other reports say that through the early stages of the meal both men were ill at ease. Gambetta was reportedly disturbed by the presence of the gigantic red- and gold-liveried servant posted behind Edward's chair; and, in turn, Edward was dumbfounded by the shocking state of Gambetta's bootlaces, frock-coat and tie. But all reports agree that coffee and cigars brought on a new mood and that the two men fell into a very serious and animated conversation lasting until after six o'clock. Edward had discovered a statesman, and Gambetta came to see that he was talking to one of the best informed men in Europe.[35]

Upon his return to England, Edward was able to tell Waddington, the Foreign Minister, that Gambetta would not attack the government over the results of the Conference, at which France had been fully represented. And Lord Lyons praised Edward's skill in successfully averting 'a disagreeable and even hazardous condition of estrangement between the two countries...'.[36] The praise from Lord Lyons, one of the most famous diplomats of his age, is significant and would never have been given without having been earned. In meeting Gambetta, Edward demonstrated once again that when he was free to act along those lines of personal initiative which he knew well, he was capable of being a powerful force for stability in the European community. Edward continued to meet with Gambetta and with other French political leaders; and when he and Gambetta disagreed and could not find an immediate compromise, they fell back on a formula. Edward would say, 'You are a true Republican, M. Gambetta.' The old war hero would respond with a touch of Gallic irony, 'Permit me to avow it, Sir. I find it logical that you, for your part, should be a royalist.'[37]

The 1870s had been a clouded decade for Edward, and yet there were some very good periods. His Indian trip, the success of his efforts to win the friendship of his powerful republican foes at home and his heading off a serious rift between France and England were notable achievements. The nation was finding it increasingly difficult to decide exactly what their prince respresented. Attempts to categorize him as an idle waster met with some success. In certain quarters he was held to be a mental lightweight and a paltry immoralist. But he continued to command affection from his subjects, who, if they were not yet sure which aspect of their national character he best exemplified, were certain that he was an embodiment of attributes which were distinctly English. For that, if for no other reason, they loved him.

9

Marking Time

One, who is not, we see; but one whom we see not, is...
Swinburne, 'The Higher Pantheism in a Nutshell'

Settled in his role of social representative of the Crown, Edward began the 1880s working harder than in any previous period; and, for the first time in his career, began to receive some recognition for that effort. Henry Burdett, a contemporary writer, published a record based on an intensive study of newspaper files of the Prince and Princess's support of a long list of public endeavours, among them being agricultural and commercial exhibitions, hospitals, homes, asylums, benevolent institutions of many types, museums, schools and art galleries, to name only a few. Burdett, writing at the end of the 1880s, estimated that over a period of twenty years Edward had made some 375 public appearances on behalf of charities, civic functions and benevolent institutions and given them additional support in the form of gifts of money, the association of his name, his appearance at openings or foundation-laying ceremonies. And these appearances did not include any of the other formal duties he fulfilled by visiting towns, greeting corporations, making and listening to speeches.[1]

It was one of the burdens of his position that Edward was obliged to give and to receive hosts of speeches. His were purely formal in character but never dull. A remarkably skilful occasional speaker when his interests were aroused, he could speak with force, as he did in his remarks to the meeting arranged by the Duke of Cambridge to consider ways of preserving the graves of those fallen in the Crimea. He could also be depended upon to speak with special enthusiasm when opening charities and commercial enterprises, such as the Mersey Tunnel which he dedicated on January 20 1886. Edward saw a clear relationship between the improvement of business and the betterment of the general living standard. The tunnel, he noted, 'cannot fail also before long to afford material benefit to the millions of hands in the neighbouring industrial centres by aiding the more rapid development of commercial intercourse'.[2]

Burdett expressed the opinion in his book, an opinion borne out by the collection of Edward's speeches published in the same decade, that the Prince was the hardest-working public figure in England.[3] And *Punch* in that same period referred to Edward as 'the most indefatigable creature in three kingdoms'. Whatever the slyness in *Punch*'s observation, since Edward gave his energies to race meetings as well as the opening of homes for the orphaned, he could and frequently did make do with little sleep, going to bed late and rising early. Occasionally his exertions wore him out to the point that his body rebelled. Sir Charles Dilke, attending the requiem mass for the murdered Emperor Alexander of Russia, watched Edward go to sleep standing and drop his candle.[4] But such slips were rare. The Prince knew his limits and generally worked within them as any true professional does.

His day began, as a rule, at 7 am with a glass of milk drunk in bed. At 10 am, following his correspondence, he ate a breakfast of boiled eggs, bacon, fish, potted meats and coffee. Lunch consisted of numerous dishes with chicken and lamb predominating. His tea, eaten at about five, was a large one including sandwiches, meats and confections. Dinner at Marlborough House and at Sandringham was served at 8.15 pm. There were usually five or six courses with joint, quail, lamb, turkey and chicken, all helped down with Rhine wine, champagne and brandy.[5] Reviewing this average day's eating, one is moved to astonishment that he had time to do anything else except eat. But even at Sandringham life was strenuous. Lady Paget, writing from Sandringham House to a friend shortly before her marriage, lamented that she had been out hunting all day from ten to four in the pouring rain, and that when she came in her body 'resembled a variegated rosebud with not one single white spot left...'. At the servants' ball the following night, they danced reels and jigs till five in the morning.[6] And this kind of activity was maintained while 'resting' in the country. In London the pace was more demanding, if less physically bruising to delicate bodies.

Was Edward's activity meaningful? Did it fulfil any function other than warding off boredom for the Prince and Princess? The answer is an unqualified yes. Edward strove to identify himself with Englishmen of all classes, at least to the extent that this was possible for a monarch, taking very seriously his responsibility to see and be seen. By participating in every major activity of the English people from steel production to horse racing, he mixed thoroughly in the life of the nation and won deserved credit by his actions. In this manner he went a very long way towards repairing the damage to the Crown done by his mother's retirement; and if he sometimes offended middle-class sensibilities by his escapades, they also made him more interesting and reminded his subjects that they had a Prince of Wales who was not simply an embodiment of his motto, 'I Serve.'

And yet it might still be argued that his appearances in the public world had little real effect on the life of the nation. Hospitals, to take a simple example, would have been opened without him quite as regularly. The response must be, however, that while the hospitals may have been opened, it is quite likely that they would have received much less support from that section of society most able to give it. There was considerable snob appeal in having one's name appear on the same list as that of the Prince of Wales, even if the list were a charity subscription; and his presence in 1884 on the Royal Commission on the Housing of the Working Classes contributed to making that Commission one of the most important of the decade.

His appearance in one of the small towns or cities of England for the purpose of opening a fair or a public building was taken by the people of the region as a major event in the life of their community, and elaborate records of the Prince's appearance were printed and sold with every evidence of sincere interest. One such book, which may be taken to stand for hundreds of others like it produced during Edward's lifetime, was published in 1889 as a memento of the Prince's visit to Middlesbrough, Yorkshire, in the Cleveland iron and steel district near the Tees estuary for the purpose of opening the new Town Hall and municipal buildings. For Edward it was a routine day; but for the people of Middlesbrough, it was a memorable occasion. The book is about eighty pages in length, bound in heavy red leather with gilt lettering. It contains a detailed account of the invitation to the Prince and Princess to attend the opening, their acceptance, the succession of events leading up to their arrival, including the furnishing and floral decorations at the royal reception rooms. The account continues with the reception, presentations, speeches, tour of inspection, concert, compliments, the fireworks (much loved by Edward), illuminations and architectural description of the Hall.

Anxious as he was to remain in touch with his subjects and to carry out his public duties in a spirit of enthusiasm, the constant round of appearances, during which he could never be bored or simply tired, was a great strain on him. His mishandling as a child had almost destroyed his ability to tolerate restraint or to exercise patience, but his public duties demanded both tolerance and patience in plenty. To another person of different psychological structure, the stress might have been no more than a routine part of the task to be done. For Edward the burden was of a greater magnitude and is reflected, at least in part, in his summary manner of dealing with those limitations which others, particularly his mother, sought to place on his behaviour. His irritability in these matters made him careless of other's feelings, careless, even, of what yet may be called the decencies. But at the same time, this directness was a sign of mental health and had its basis in Edward's clear understanding of his own needs and reflected a growing determination to live with and not apologize for those needs.

In 1881 Dean Arthur Stanley died. He had been a friend of the royal family for many years and had accompanied Edward on his first Egyptian trip. Victoria was mortified by Edward's refusal, after learning of the Dean's death, to cancel a ball he had planned; and she wrote in pain and anger to her son to condemn his having connived to move the Dean's funeral ahead a day so that it would not conflict with the Goodwood Races.[7] In March 1884, Edward's brother Leopold, the Duke of Albany, died. Edward had just been appointed to the Royal Commission on the Housing of the Working Classes; but he left England and neglected his committee responsibilities for nearly two months in order, in Sir Philip Magnus's opinion, to avoid the intolerable inactivity imposed by strict Court mourning in England. It is behaviour difficult to defend, but becomes more understandable when weighed against the fierce discipline under which for long periods he held himself while carrying out his official functions, and the tight reins on which he had been held in his behaviour by his mother and, when alive, his father.

During the '80s Edward was busy outside England as well as within its boundaries. His work with the French Government, on which he prided himself and which he regarded with the utmost seriousness, continued to hold his interest; and there were still unfinished items of business to intrigue him, left over from his interviews with Bismarck. In 1878 Bismarck decided to talk seriously with Edward, having recognized that, following his Indian trip, the Prince had become a force in England's foreign affairs. Of course, what Bismarck wanted was to drive a wedge between England and France, but he was also seriously interested in testing the Prince on the possibilities of establishing an agreement between Germany and England. As an initial step towards achieving both those ends, he suggested to Edward that if England were to occupy Egypt, Germany would undertake to keep France from becoming a nuisance; and he then asked what England's position would be if Germany found it necessary to check Russia's expansionism. Edward, intrigued by Bismarck's attention but still wary, replied that probably England would side with Germany.[8]

Bismarck, in characteristic fashion, did nothing further but allowed time to work its changes. He did not have long to wait. In 1881 a revolt broke out in Egypt and resulted, a year later, in England's singlehanded occupation of Egypt, when France refused to take part in putting down the revolt. Of course, French feelings were irritated, and this hostility tended to fix itself on the Prince. Bismarck smiled and watched. A deeper rift occurred between England and France when gambetta's government fell, carrying that friend of the English *entente* out of office and most of its French supporters as well. As a further embarrassment to the relationship Edward had struggled to establish between the two countries, they were competitors as colonial powers. In the spring of 1883, Edward, sensing his temporary helplessness, omitted taking his French holiday because the French press was working itself into a rage over the fact that he had been visiting Germany and while there had been made a colonel of the 5th Pomeranian Hussars. Informed French opinion certainly knew that Edward's chief interest in the appointment was in being able to wear another uniform; but the enemies of the Anglo-French Entente were in power and Gambetta was not. Although Edward's edifice of mutual understanding and common alliance seemed seriously shaken, he did not despair. He had faith in his ability to mend the damage once passions had cooled.

Despite his constant activity as an unofficial ambassador both at home and abroad, Edward may well have considered his private life to be more satisfactory than his public one. Unaffected by the hiatus of 1883, he still regarded Paris as his special playground. In 1882 he had created a sensation by appearing on stage in Sardou's *Fedora,* with which Sarah Bernhardt made her triumphant return to the stage. As a conclusion to one of the acts, Sarah wept beside the death-bed of a murdered prince; and on one evening Edward played the corpse.[9] His revels at the 'Chat Noir' kept tongues clicking busily on both sides of the Channel.[10] But he knew to within a fraction of a gesture how far he could safely allow liberties to go before he lost his special dignity as a prince. He continued to have a series of alliances with women, and the most important woman in his life in the '80s was Lillie Langtry, who was his first 'official' mistress. It was a mark of Edward's grip on his position in life and of his increased maturity that society could grant him such an indulgence without fearing he would let the affair become an embarrassment. Alexandra, who seems to have resigned herself to her husband's promiscuity, made Miss Langtry welcome at Marlborough house.[11] The relationship, however, quickly deteriorated when many doors previously open to Miss Langtry were closed by growing rumours of an approaching estrangement between Edward and Alix. In December 1881, with Edward's sponsorship, Lillie entered the theatre, making her stage debut at the Haymarket Theatre in Goldsmith's *She Stoops to Conquer.* Her future success was assured, and her new career gave Edward a graceful exit from a connection that was growing difficult to maintain.

The real relationship between Edward and his wife during this period of his life is difficult to assess. He invariably treated her and his family with the utmost consideration, while at the same time conducting a variety of affairs. As one observer of his life wrote, 'To touch upon the ladies of English society whom his Royal Highness distinguishes with exceptional attention would be a delicate task; suffice it to say that he recognizes impartially feminine merit of every degree.'[12] However catholic his taste in women, he managed, with the support of Alexandra, to keep before the general public the picture of a man firmly located at the centre of a happy and conventional English home. The truth was rather different. Georgina Battiscombe goes so far as to suggest that in this period Oliver Montague may have been Alix's lover.[13] The existence of such a relationship would account for the spate of rumours predicting a disruption of the Prince's family life. Speculation of this sort would not have been generated by Edward's infidelities. He was a man and they were to be expected. But even the breath of scandal touching Alexandra would have raised the possibility of separation. And yet, ironically, it was popularly believed Edward's affair with Lillie Langtry was the root of the problem.

On the whole, however, Edward's private life in the '80s was fairly free from scandal, a fact which led one contemporary writer to observe that the Prince of Wales was in 1885 very different from what he was in 1878, the *vie orageuse* being over and forgotten. The statement was more hopeful than future events would warrant – Edward had one more very large scandal in his future; but it was reasonably accurate about the decade. Up to and following the Jubilee year of 1887, the press was inclined to leave Edward alone. It is not likely that middle-class attitudes towards him had undergone any profound change, but the political ferment of the decade may have had the effect of taking pressure off the Prince and leaving him in relative peace. On the other hand, the press may have determined that in the face of radical agitation for social reform, it would be in the best interests of the propertied and monied classes to refrain from criticizing the heir apparent.

The year 1884 was an important one for Edward, and it began with his appointment to what was probably the most important committee on which he had ever sat and one which provided him with the potential for seriously influencing British society. On February 22, he was appointed to the Royal Commission on the Housing of the Working Classes. Charles Dilke was chairman and Cardinal Manning one of the members. The committee was not in full agreement in its attitude towards the poor and their problems. On the occasion of their first official meeting, held on March 11 1884, at No. 3 Richmond Terrace, Whitehall, Lord Salisbury expressed the view that the poor were attached to their slums, to which Charles Dilke replied, 'They are attached to them out of necessity.' Cardinal Manning's opinion was that there was something to be said on both sides.[14] Edward had made a serious effort to get the remarkable Octavia Hill appointed to the Commission, but Gladstone, who considered the appointing of a woman to such an august body too great a break with tradition, refused the request.

Octavia Hill had founded a society for buying and operating on financially profitable lines London slum property, while at the same time providing sanitary, reasonably priced accommodation for the tenants. She and her group worked with skill and success in the London area. In 1884 Romney Leigh, one of the biggest ground landlords in London, whose property held some 600 houses rented to the poor, appointed a woman trained by Octavia Hill to supervise all his slum property. Hill would have made an important addition to the Commission, but the idea of putting a woman in such a position of power was ahead of its time.

Edward had been stung by statements in the press in the latter part of the '70s accusing him of maintaining rural slum dwellings. In response to those charges, he instituted at Sandringham a programme of upgrading the workers' dwellings and drew from Lord Hampden a letter in the *News of the World* praising his improvements. The occasion of the letter was Edward's speech in the House of Lords proposing a Royal Commission to look into the living conditions of the poor.[15] He gave the speech following an exploratory trip, made in the disguise of a labourer, into the slums of Clerkenwell and St Pancras in the company of Lord Carrington, where the scenes of suffering, deprivation and human misery filled him with bitter indignation. Carrington had with great difficulty restrained Edward from pulling money from his pocket and giving it to the neediest of those they saw huddled in the cold and filth. Only Carrington's warning that Edward was risking their lives by making it known they had money in that quantity on their persons persuaded him to put away his sovereigns.

In his letter Lord Hampden outlined the principal problems governing the housing situation of the poor. The poor suffered from high rent, the dilapidated state of the houses in which they were obliged to find shelter and from overcrowding. Their difficulties were aggravated by the failure of local authorities to apply the laws governing sanitation and allied matters either through negligence, corruption or lack of power. In addition the ground landlords were neglecting their properties. Rackrenting was common practice and had produced a situation in which a single unfurnished room in Marylebone cost five shillings a week, making multiple occupancy of that room a certainty.

In its review of the housing problem in London, the *Pall Mall Gazette* remarked that 'Socialism *plus* the Ten Commandments has never had a nobler vista of work before it than that which is opened out by the appointment of the Royal Commission.'[16] *Reynolds's*, embracing with customary passion an opportunity to attack the rich and the privileged and defend the poor, was more direct: 'Dives was probably ill at ease when he lifted up his eyes and saw Lazarus in Abraham's bosom, but the great gulf between the rich sinner and the once a-hungered saint was a poor and feeble type of the gulf which exists between the English-men of today, if one lives in a palace-home on the bounty of the nation, and the other has to scrape along and keep himself and family in some artisan's hovel.'[17] Warming to the subject, the paper continued at a brisker pace, 'Ebony chattels are no longer merchandise, but instead we buy and sell disease, dole out death at three to four shillings a room-ful to the poor, and lay so heavy a blood tax on the indigent that it speaks more than much for the moral self restraint of the masses that revolution does not raise its frantic head in our midst.'[18] At this time, Charles Dilke was still travelling around the country preaching the socialist solution. The year before, in 1883, the Fabian Society had been founded; and the Webbs had begun their patient and profound labours which would, in the end, make people look anew at the politics of the nation.

Lord William Compton, son of the Marquess of Northampton, a ground landlord with extensive slum housing on his property, delivered a public lecture on housing for the poor in which he called on the ground landlords to take over the management of their properties, doing away with the middlemen, who, in his opinion, were responsible for half of the existing mischief. He observed that his father had been unable to do as much in the way of improvement as he wished to do because of leases held by these middlemen. Compton also expressed the belief that much harm was done by the wealthy living at one end of the city and the poor at the other.[19] Lord Compton's hope that the poor and the rich would mingle was as unrealistic as the aims of the Kyrle Society, founded in 1884 amidst general praise, 'to bring beauty home to the poor'.

In 1885 George Bernard Shaw took up the subject of the vicious in-ter-relationships of ground landlords and their middlemen in his first play *Widowers' Houses*. He dropped the play, because he thought it could not be produced, took it up again in 1892 and saw it produced in that same year by J. T. Grein at the Independent Theatre. In the Preface to *Plays Unpleasant*, which contains *Widowers' Houses*, Shaw said that the play shows 'middle-class respectability and younger son gentility fattening on the poverty of the slum as flies fatten on filth'.[20]

In *Widowers' Houses* Shaw's interpretation of the problem of slum housing is simple: the ground landlord, Lady Roxdale, leases her property to a middleman, Cokane, who employs a rent collector, Lickcheese, to 'screw' money out of the unfortunate tenants of the slum hell owned by Lady Roxdale, managed for a handsome profit by Co-kane, and ramrodded by Lickcheese. Lady Roxdale, being of the upper class, does not wish to concern herself with 'business' matters and settles for the lease fees. Cokane, as lease holder, does not wish to put any money into the properties but to extract from them as much profit as possible without going near them. Lickcheese, poverty-stricken with a family to support, and working on a commission, lives with the horrors of the houses and collects the rent, 'screwing' it out of the tenants.

Dr Trench, Lady Roxdale's nephew, has an income from his aunt which makes him financially independent. At the opening of the play he does not even know the source of Lady Roxdale's money. When faced with the choice between refusing to accept Lady Roxdale's 'tainted' money or having to live a life of penury, he comes to terms with his conscience and keeps the money. He also 'gets the girl', a Shavian irony in which winning the girl, whose love is not given but sold, becomes a moral defeat of the same order as keeping the money. Shaw's interpretation is incisive, if cynical: hypocrisy, greed and selfishness, embalmed in an economic system, account for slum housing; and until the system is changed, the slums will continue to grow.

At the outset of the Commission's deliberations, Edward was an interested member; but when in March his brother Leopold died, he was temporarily distracted, missed meetings and lost touch with the Commission's proceedings. Then, as has already been mentioned, he left England in order to avoid the tedium of enforced inactivity imposed by Court mourning, returning later in the summer to take up the Commission work once again. He remained in England through the autumn and attended the meetings until the conclusion of the Commission's work on December 5.[21] Despite his absences, he won good opinions from all levels of society for his work and proved himself capable of taking part in such endeavours with real effectiveness.

Unfortunately, he was never allowed to participate in another commission of equal importance while Prince of Wales, and it is only possible to guess at the reason for his exclusion. Gladstone's efforts had placed Edward on the Commission; and Gladstone's interest in providing Edward with a dignified role to play continued throughout his ministries; but there were many forces hostile to the Prince of Wales's assuming a substantive role in government. Among those jealous of his potential influence were, as before, the Queen and her advisers; the higher levels of the bureaucracy in both the foreign and domestic offices, who saw clearly the threat that a potent and influential prince would pose to their control of policy formation and implementation; and to the republican element who feared any increase in royal prestige. After all, Edward would be answerable to no Minister and would not have the welfare of any department in mind when arriving at decisions. Years later, one of Edward's Prime Ministers would do his best to play down the King's role in achieving the Entente Cordiale. No prime minister after Gladstone ever sincerely wished to see Edward's political effectiveness increased.

Politically, 1884 was a heady year. Reform was in the air, and the push towards it came not only in the form of the Royal Commission on the Housing of the Working Classes, but in a bill hammered through the Commons by Gladstone granting suffrage to agricultural labourers. The Third Reform Bill endowed England with virtual manhood suffrage, leaving unenfranchised young men living in their fathers' houses, servants who did not maintain separate households, and women. Gladstone had been forced to produce some legislation of this sort to counter the effects of Joseph Chamberlain's call for 'three acres and a cow' and the trumpetings of the radical Tories led by Lord Randolph Churchill, who were making a strenuous effort to win the working man's vote away from the Liberal Party by championing social legislation.

Although Dilke had characterized Edward as a 'very strong Conservative, and a still stronger Jingo', who only agreed with the Liberal Party in its detestation of Randolph Churchill, the Prince's mind was not closed on reform issues; and he strongly favoured the Third Reform Bill. Writing to congratulate Lord Rosebery on his speech in the Lords defending the Bill, Edward asked if he might vote with the government on the issue. Of course, constitutional considerations made it impossible for him to do so, and he was disappointed when the House of Lords defeated the bill.[22] The vote came in mid-July, touching off a powerful reaction in the country against the Lords and the system of hereditary legislators. Edward's opposition was a bold stance, taken in defiance of the tradition that England's royal family must be without political bias and reflecting Edward's independence in such matters.

All those who opposed the Lords' position on the Reform Bill joined together on July 21 to march in a protest procession through London. Edward, without seeking his mother's opinion, determined to be a witness to the procession and, in that fashion, indicate his support of the bill. It was a daring move with an element of risk. He chose as the point from which to make his witness the house of his friend Charles Carrington at number 8 Whitehall. Accompanying the Prince were Alix, their three daughters, the Countesses Spencer and Granville, the Duke of Roxburghe, the Earl and Countess of Dalhousie and the Earls of Clarendon and Cork.[23] As soon as Carrington was told that the Prince would appear, he notified the leaders of the procession and asked that as they passed number 8 they doff their caps and cheer the Prince.[24] Carrington never doubted that Edward would be well received by the marchers; but there was room for concern. The march was a protest against the Lords, and any organized expression of hostility to hereditary power was an attack on the throne.

London had not produced such an outpouring of people since the marriage of Edward and Alexandra. The crowd extended from the Blackfriars end of the Embankment to Apsley House Gate. The marchers passed through this crowd without a single injury. The procession started at about 3 pm in fine weather, the men marching seven abreast. One group was accompanied by a band playing the *Marseillaise* and drew loud cheering all along the route. Others carried red liberty caps on poles. About a thousand Kent and Sussex men came up from the farms to march together carrying brightly ribboned hop poles. There were, of course, forests of placards borne by the marchers; and some of them, edged in black, read, 'In Memory of the House of Lords'. This warning echoed a leader in *Reynolds's* which warned that if the peers did not cease from opposing the extension of the franchise, they would find themselves 'swept rudely away'.[25] Other signs read 'Stand on your rights, and sit on the peers', 'We respect law, not privilege', 'We demand the vote'.[26]

Waiting at Whitehall, and hearing the strains of the *Marseillaise* growing louder as the marchers advanced, Edward was fearful that the mood of the crowd might be truculent; but his fears proved groundless. To their immense satisfaction, the Prince and Alix were greeted with thunderous cheering. The only mild unpleasantness occurred when the Princess complained of a headache and withdrew from the marchers' view. The cheers instantly changed to catcalls and groans, making it necessary for her to rejoin her husband at the window and to remain there for the three hours that it took the procession to pass.[27] Three thousand police were on duty supervising the crowds, but no one was arrested. In Hyde Park, which was packed with people, seven platforms were raised for speakers. The *News of the World* had the highest praise for the demonstration, as did most of the other papers, with only the *Globe* accusing the Liberal leaders of sinking to the level of inciting a 'mob' to act in support of its policies. There was, of course, criticism levelled at Edward for participating in a political event; but he enjoyed the experience and had the satisfaction of knowing that his people were delighted that he had shared in their expression of support for the extension of the franchise. Without doubt, Edward had the ingredients for being a truly popular sovereign, but as Prince of Wales he was cramped and confined and denied his proper role.

During the '80s Edward's character began to appear increasingly brittle, more fixed, almost casehardened. At first glance, the man himself seems either to have drawn further behind the official mask or have come more and more to actually resemble that mask. Somerset Maugham wrote of men in Edward's exposed position that 'they play the part that is expected from them and with practice learn to play it very well, but you are stupid if you think that this public performance of theirs corresponds with the man within.'[28] Maugham also wrote that such individuals are too 'exceptional' to be satisfactory subjects for the writer of fiction because they cannot be made 'real'. It is possible that Edward had become so skilled in presenting himself to the public that he no longer revealed the 'real' person. But what is more likely is that those who wrote about him, even his friends, looked less closely than they had done a decade earlier and were content to present him in the stereotypic terms which had gradually come to be associated with him. That public image, however, was composed of many factors, and increasingly Edward was many things to many people.

Charles Bradlaugh's *The Impeachment of the House of Brunswick*, published in 1881, describes Edward entirely as his enemies had been characterizing him for the past ten years. He is mocked as a military officer, ridiculed as an investigator of social problems and praised, with malice aforethought, as a pigeon shooter and battueist of renown.[29] Bradlaugh trots out the Edward he has a use for and, once finished with him, stuffs him back into his bag of aristocratic straw men. It was Bradlaugh's intention to associate Edward in the public mind with the corrupt Hanoverian Georges in general and with George II's son, Frederick, Prince of Wales, who died before his father and of whom an anonymous poet wrote,

> Here lies Fred,
> Who was alive, and is dead.
> Had it been his father,
> I had much rather.
> Had it been his brother,
> Still better than another.
> Had it been his sister,
> No one would have missed her,
> Had it been the whole generation,
> Still better for the nation.
> But since 'tis only Fred,
> Who was alive and is dead,
> There's no more to be said.

While Bradlaugh's quarrel with Edward was of a political nature, making Edward's 'real' identity irrelevant, Mrs Gerard Cresswell's complaint against the Prince was altogether different and drove her to search for Edward the man in the jungles of London and Norfolk as white hunters once sedulously sought the okapi. She wrote a book about her search and gave the world one of the most fascinating accounts of Edward that have been put into print. The book was published in 1887, by which time Mrs Cresswell had left England and taken up farming in Texas. The change was less radical than it sounds since Mrs Cresswell had, for eighteen years, run Appleton, a large mixed farm on the Sandringham estate. She had taken over Appleton just prior to the estate's being purchased by the Prince Consort, and she met Edward shortly afterwards on one of his first tours of inspection. Cresswell liked him at once and commented very favourably on his 'extraordinary charm of manner'.

She and her husband had scarcely set the farm in order before Gerard Cresswell died; and Charles Kingsley, a close friend of the Cresswells as well as a friend of Edward's, came down from Sandringham House, where he was staying with the Prince, to beg her not think of continuing on the farm alone. The farm had 900 acres and 1,200 or 1,300 head of livestock. Mrs Cresswell, however, thought she could do the farming as well as her husband or another man could do it; and so she stayed on. But she was soon in difficulties, not with the farming but with the Prince. 'No one,' she wrote, 'can be more pleasant and agreeable than His Royal Highness, if you go with him in everything and do exactly what he likes; on the other hand, he can be very unpleasant indeed if you are compelled to do what he does not like....'[30]

What drove her into a quarrel with Edward was the ground game, swarms of which were introduced when Edward determined on the battue system of game management. Her husband had, early in their tenancy, made particular enquiries about the amount of game they would be required to support and was assured by Edward's lawyers that the rent would be fixed and there would not be any increase of game. That assurance proved hollow. 'A ruinous swarm' of ground game was introduced and had to be kept at her expense. The hares became such a plague that they ate everything growing. Driven to desperation, one of her farmer neighbours committed suicide and left a note which read 'Rabbits have killed me.' 'How much better it would have been,' Mrs Cresswell wrote, 'if he and his friends had killed the rabbits! I would have put down the hares quickly enough if anyone in this Prince-ridden country could have been found to help me.'[31]

Mrs Cresswell made repeated efforts to reach the Prince to tell him the state of affairs in Appleton, but she was never allowed to talk to him on the subject. Remarkably enough, all through this period she was a regular visitor at Sandringham House and, socially, was on good terms with Edward. On one occasion she was dancing a quadrille with him when another woman dropped a role of bank notes without noticing the loss. Mrs Cresswell scooped them up but Edward snatched the roll of £20 notes away from her and stuffed them into his pocket with the remark, 'Mine, Mrs Cresswell, mine; winnings at whist – delighted to get them back again.'[32] But social ease was not business communication, and Edward allowed his people to keep Mrs Cresswell at a distance over the question of game depredation.

The conditions under which she was working rapidly became intolerable and she was soon facing bankruptcy. During one particularly bad period, she lost her entire turnip crop because the Prince held a royal battue and ordered her workers off the fields three days in suc-

cession, with the result that frost killed the exposed roots and destroyed
the crop. A small army invaded her farm on hunting days. Boys with
royal colours in their caps and carrying blue and pink flags came, gamekeepers in green and gold, a horde of beaters in smocks and hats and a
'trailing off of loafers to see the fun'. The game was driven towards the
guns and the trampling and the slaughter was terrific. In one day's
shooting with 9 guns they killed 1,396 pheasants, 341 brace of partridge,
316 hares, 186 rabbits and 84 'various'.[33]

She tried again to see the Prince and failed. 'Kings may love those
who speak the truth,' she wrote, 'but I suspect they very seldom have
that felicity.' Disappointed but not defeated, she went to London and
confronted Edward's lawyers and his land-agent, presenting, at their
request, a bill of damages to the amount of £575.16 shillings. They
cheated her by paying half of the amount requested into her bank and
getting a receipt for it, leaving her to whistle for the rest. A Mr Reade,
M.P. for the area, was a friend of Mrs Cresswell's and without her permission he read out her complaint in the House. The London dailies
did not carry the item, but a rural agricultural weekly picked up the
story and printed it in full. Edward was told what had happened and
was furious. For the next three years she was treated to cold stares and
hostile frowns, 'in true Henry VIII style', whenever their paths crossed.

She continued to live with Edward's disapproval, his dislike being
fed throughout the period by gamekeepers and the land-agent, who
viewed her as a troublemaker. Then seventy-one pheasants were killed
in a single night and left dead in the woods. Urban poachers had been
coming in gangs during that period to raid the parks for pheasants;
but because they would not have abandoned the dead birds, the game-
keeper needed some explanations. He told Edward that Mrs Cresswell
had killed them or had them killed and recited the story in front of a
large party of the Prince's guests. Edward exploded, heaping epithets
on her head and giving way completely to his anger. Two or three
country people present later told Mrs Cresswell that they had never
heard such a row in their lives.

The upshot of that affair was that the Duke of Cambridge and Mr
Onslow, Rector of Sandringham and Domestic Chaplain to the Prince
and the Princess, and a friend of Mrs Cresswell, finally forced Edward
to be present at an enquiry with the Lord Lieutenant of the County as
cross-examiner and umpire. Mrs Cresswell was completely exonerated
of the charge, and Edward sent a message saying that the difficulty had
arisen from a 'misconception of facts'. 'Misconception of lies', was Mrs
Cresswell's correction. But although better feelings were brought into
being between her and the Prince for a few years, the truce was only
temporary. When Albert Victor came down with typhoid, she was
accused of having caused his illness by diverting farm drainage into the

Sandringham House water supply. She was also accused of blackening
Edward's name in a public railway carriage. The game was riddling
her farm again; and rather than go on facing the hostility of Edward's
people, she sold the farm and emigrated to Texas.

In her general remarks on the Prince she is consistently moderate and
reverts again and again to his affability and capacity for disarming
criticism. Speaking of the press, she noted that in the '80s it had been
more effectively gagged by Edward's 'condescensions' than their pre-
decessors had been by 'the pillories and penalties of olden times'.[34] Of
his private life, she was less tolerant; and remarked on the immorality
of the group surrounding Edward, expressing the wish that the Princess
would 'clean out' a few of the worst.[35] But there is very little bitterness
expressed towards the Prince, apart from her stated conviction that he
was too inclined to rely on the tales brought to him from all quarters
rather than on careful enquiry made by reliable agents in his behalf.
Oddly enough, she opposed Gladstone's bill granting sporting rights
with the argument that sport was a commodity like any other and
should be bid for. What she wanted was a guarantee of damages, not an
increase in democracy.

She had a number of observations to make on the reasons behind
Edward's popularity, and they come down, essentially, to the belief
that he won good opinions through his accessibility and affability to all
sorts and conditions of people. 'I believe,' she wrote, a little naively,
'all England would be invited to Sandringham, if they could be crammed in.' According to Mrs Cresswell, Edward took literally Disraeli's
advice that the way to be successful was to 'bustle about, get hold of the
press, and shake hands with everybody'. She added that the effect of
Sandringham on radicals was nothing short of wonderful, that it acted
as a 'patent conjuring machine – a Republican stuffed in at one end
and a Courtier squeezed out at the other'.[36] Mrs Cresswell's impressions
of Edward add to his complexity, to what she called his 'extraordinary
variety of character'. Buffoons and butts (Christopher Sykes was one),
as well as statesmen and politicians, tycoons, racing men and beautiful
women sat down at Edward's table; and all of them served the Prince's
needs. Swift to anger and quick to forgive, selfish and yet capable of
acts of generosity, sometimes harsh but more often kind, Edward
emerges from Mrs Cresswell's book a man rich in contradiction. It is
significant that while she had no reason to spare him, her portrait is
surprisingly sympathetic. He could inspire liking even in those who had
reason to despise him. It was one of his great strengths.

In April 1885 Edward made his third official visit to Ireland. In
every sense, it was a public function for which the private man had little
appetite. In a letter written by Knollys at the Prince's direction to the
Queen's private secretary, Knollys pointed out that 'neither the Queen

nor the Cabinet can suppose that he [Edward] expects to derive any personal pleasure from the visit...'.[37] The petulant tone of the note was a result of yet another embarrassing haggle over money between the Queen and the Prime Minister, the Queen insisting that the government should pay Edward's expenses and Gladstone responding that there was no reason why either the Queen or the Prince of Wales should not pay for it, as it was a function falling within their regular duties. Edward, as usual, was caught between the two (neither the government nor the Queen taking the trouble to communicate with him); and in anger, well justified, he informed Gladstone that unless the cabinet informed him in writing that they requested him to undertake the journey and were prepared to pay for it, he had no intention of making a trip to Ireland. Gladstone produced both the letter and the money.

If his manipulation by both his mother and whatever government happened to be in power was a source of pain to Edward, he managed to accept his lot without too much protest. But another problem about which he could not be philosophical was centred on his elder son, Albert Victor. Named after two paragons, Eddy, as he was called by his parents, was himself no paragon and increasingly a source of anguish to his mother and father. Just past his twenty-first birthday in 1885, Eddy had proved to be uneducable. Gentle and tractable, he was easy to love; but there was no question of teaching him anything. His lack of response to education was not of the sort his father's had been. It was simply that the fire of intelligence could not be lighted in his brain. A sweet vacuity, enlivened only by a taste for corrupt amusements, characterized the young man. His younger brother, George, had finally been released from his bondage to pursue a naval career after being held back in his training and kept in his brother's company in the vain hope that he would inspire Eddy. In despair over their older son, the Prince and Princess decided to take him with them on their trip to Ireland.

Edward was going to Ireland at a particularly unsettled period. A succession of crop failures with their attendant hardship on the peasants led, in 1880 and even earlier, to the eviction of many thousands of Irish tenant farmers living on English-owned estates. The Irish Land League, under the direction of Parnell and Michael Davitt, urged the Irish peasants to fight back by withholding rents, harassing estate agents and their employers and even maiming cattle. But they were to be even more ruthless toward anyone foolish enough to take over the farms of the dispossessed.

Gladstone's government was unable to deal with the disorders arising from Parnell and Davitt's work. Gladstone imprisoned Parnell and only succeeded in increasing the Irish politician's popularity. He outlawed the Land League, passed coercion bills, suspended civil liberties and imposed a kind of martial law on the country. Irish resistance to British rule only became more dogged. He appealed to the Pope to intercede and to the Irish people to co-operate with him in his efforts to solve the peasants' problems by supporting the new land acts passed by Parliament. Parnell, seeing that the land acts were likely to be effective in reducing or eliminating the injustices under which the Irish peasants struggled and not wishing to see the thrust towards independence slackened or his own influence diminished, worked to destroy the effectiveness of the land acts. He was successful.

Convinced that neither force nor appeal was going to quiet the Irish people, Gladstone suddenly reversed his policy and released Parnell from jail and repealed the coercion acts. Lord Frederick Cavendish was promptly despatched to Ireland as the new Chief Secretary; and on May 6 1882 he was murdered in Dublin's Phoenix Park, the victim of a political assassination. Everything had failed to stem the Irish march towards political independence; and, as has been so consistently the history of Irish political agitation, nothing stopped the pointless killings that marred the parade. A year later in 1886, at the beginning of his third ministry, Gladstone would declare himself in favour of Home Rule; but in the spring of 1885, with his Government being brought towards a crisis by Parnell and his Irish members, the Prime Minister was still trying to find some way out of his dilemma short of support for the Irish Nationalists. Edward had to go to Ireland to test the mood of the people.

Reception of the news that the Prince of Wales contemplated an Irish visit was not particularly encouraging. Healy, an Irish M.P., addressing the National League, said that Edward was being made the tool of a political faction in Ireland, headed by the Lord Lieutenant, Lord Spencer. Healy was certainly correct in believing that Spencer had an interest in Edward's coming to Ireland, because it was Spencer who submitted the initial request that Edward make the visit. Healy continued that the Prince, in agreeing to visit Lord Kenmore and the Duke of Kenmare on their Irish estates, was giving tacit support to 'thieves and plunderers'. 'It was to be regretted that the future king of the islands (shouts of No, No) should be so ignorant as to allow himself to be placed in such a position.'[38]

On April 7 Edward, Alexandra and Albert Victor left London for Holyhead. There was considerable anxiety concerning the safety of the train carrying the Prince; and on the Chester to Holyhead section of the route, extraordinary precautions were taken. The facing points were all double locked and watched. Men were stationed at half-mile intervals along the line; and near Flint, where there was a large Irish population, special police patrols were established and men with lamps

placed every twenty yards.[39] The Fenian violence, which had broken
out in the preceding year, and the truculent mood of the Irish Nationalists in general prompted the concern. But the only unpleasantness was
at Holyhead, where the citizens, angered by Edward's refusal to accept
an address from their local board, put out no flags or illuminations and
left the royal family to pass through their dark station without a
reception.

At Kingstown the following morning there were dense crowds and
warm cheering to greet the Prince and his family; but, nonetheless,
a heavy guard was kept around Edward. At Westland Row Station
galleries of spectators waited and there was again loud cheering, military
salutes and the continuous playing of bands. The Citizens' Committee
presented an address in which reference was made to a permanent
royal residence in Ireland. The suggestion prompted a fresh round of
cheers. Edward stepped forward to respond to the speech, but his remarks were lost in the combined noise of a ringing bell, the whistle of
escaping steam from a locomotive engine and the excited barking of a
collie dog that had decided to welcome the Prince and his family.[40]

In Dublin they travelled again in open carriages, escorted by a
squadron of the 16th Lancers, through a lovely bright day, their way
colourfully decorated and densely crowded with cheering people. They
entered the Castle by the Cork Hill entrance, and after a two-hour rest,
emerged again for a drive to Balls Bridge and the show of the Royal
Dublin Society. Edward had visited the show in 1868 and found it
much expanded. There was another speech of welcome, jumping to
watch and, finally, something which genuinely interested the Prince,
an exhibition of prize cattle. It is difficult to keep in one's mind the
almost contradictory fact that Edward the *Boulevardier* was also a
dedicated farmer who took the art of breed improvement very seriously.
Returning to the Castle through Dawson Street and the Mansion House
sections of the city, he again encountered dressed streets and heavy
crowds. There was still some sporadic cheering, but for the first time he
met with moments of stony silence, during which he waved and bowed
to unmoved throngs.

The Irish national press, except for the sycophantic sections of it,
deplored the reasons behind Edward's visit, or at least what they considered to be the reasons. The *Freeman's Journal* stated that 'the worst
British factions in this country are seeking and hoping to resuscitate
their power' and that 'the present system of government [in Ireland]
is only maintained by armed force and by the second force of police and
spies and informers'. Parnell issued his own statement on behalf of the
Irish National Party, which was widely printed both in England and
in Ireland: 'In view of the fact that the constitution has never been
administered in Ireland according to its custom and precedent; that the

powers of the Crown as wielded by Lord Spencer and other Viceroys is despotic and unlimited to the last degree, and that in the present instance the Royal personage is to be used by two English political parties in Ireland for the purpose of injuring and insulting the Irish National Party, and of impeding, if possible, their work, I fail to see upon what ground...the Prince is entitled to a reception from the independent and patriotic people of Ireland.'[41]

As a result of Parnell's campaign against the trip, Edward encountered more silences in the crowds through which he passed. But in Dublin the silences were not aggressive or even personally hostile. He was able to visit the Ship Street and Golden Lane section, a poverty-stricken area of Dublin, and to leave his carriage and inspect two of the slum dwellings without incurring the anger of the residents. When he emerged from the second building, his carriage was surrounded by a crowd of ragged women and children, who simply watched as he re-entered his carriage and drove to Coombe Area to look at artisans' houses. There he attracted a very large crowd, but there was no unpleasantness.

However, the strain under which the Irish were living expressed itself in a remarkable occurrence at the City Hall on July 13. A large crowd had gathered to see Edward off on his trip to the South and to cheer him on his way; and while they were waiting, Lord Mayor O'Connor drove up to enter the Hall and preside at a meeting of the municipal council. O'Connor was an outspoken nationalist; and as he ascended the stairs the crowd began to hiss him. O'Connor stopped at the top of the stairs and viewed the people below him with bewildered rage. Hissing began again, louder this time and accompanied by shouted remarks about O'Connor's trade, conduct and person.

Some friends attempted to induce him to go into the Hall, but he lost his temper completely and began to shout and wave his hat. At first, what he said was largely lost. Then he threatened to telegraph Cork and Mallow, two radical strongholds of nationalist sentiment, to tell them to harry the Prince. Following that, he bellowed, 'I will give three cheers for Parnell!' and did so without getting much support. Then he became wilder and said, 'I was determined to let the Prince go in peace; but you have hissed me today; and I was hissed by Orangemen, Freemasons, landlords and bailiffs. I will remember it all the days of my life and you will be sorry tomorrow.'[42] He was finally coaxed away from the steps by his friend T. D. Sullivan, and as he entered the Hall, the Prince drove past amid tumultuous cheering. The episode contained all the ingredients of a pathetic comedy perfectly embodying Ireland's sorry political state at that time: countryman pitted against country-man and all the folly and bitterness that such confrontation brewed.

Edward travelled from Dublin to Mallow and received a very

friendly reception at the station platform. In the station itself, however, a nationalist demonstration had formed, headed by O'Brien, John O'Connor, T. Harrington and Deasy M.P.s with four bands playing national airs and 'God Save Ireland'. The Royal Irish Constabulary cleared the station just before the Prince arrived, and the nationalists protested that undue force had been used. Driven out of the station, they took up positions on the embankment and groaned when the royal train pulled in. Edward and his family were immediately whisked away to Convamore, where they were the guests of the Earl of Listowel. Alix fished in the Blackwater River and caught a twelve-pound, fresh-run salmon.

His reception in the area of Mallow continued to be mixed. In his travels through the counties of Cork, Limerick, Kerry and Waterford, there were friendly groups formed to meet him at the stations where he stopped. But as often as not he was greeted outside the stations and along the train tracks by groups bearing black flags. One group displayed posters reading 'Lord Waterford's evicted tenants. Will the Prince reinstate them?' The same group cheered Parnell and Michael Davitt as Edward passed. However, his worst hours were yet before him.

On April 15, the Prince and his suite arrived in Cork. The Earl of Bandon and members of the city government received the Prince, and addresses were given. On his ride into the city, his carriage was surrounded by outriders, as it had been since he left Dublin. Escorted by the 11th Hussars, the group left the station and rode through streets crowded with people to the School of Art to declare it officially open, and from there to the Good Shepherd's Convent. But the reception was as bad as it could be without actually being violent. Wherever they went in the city, they were booed and pelted with onions. An equerry described the people who surrounded them as a crowd of 'hideous, dirty, cruel countenances, hissing and grimacing into one's very face, waving black flags and black kerchiefs – a nightmare'.[43] Later, Edward would refuse to talk about the experience. Given time, he might have won the favour of the people of Cork; but time was something he lacked, and he was obliged to carry away from Cork, along with the knowledge of a defeat, the memory of being heartily despised. It was particularly painful to fail at something he prided himself on doing so well, winning through presence and personal impact the liking of those who had previously disliked him. The wound festered.

To make the unpleasantness of the journey even more debilitating, Gladstone's second ministry was brought to an end by Parnell and his disciplined Irish colleagues in the House. After the results of the election following the dissolution were recorded, the Liberals once more had a plurality in the House but not a majority; and in order to govern,

Gladstone needed the votes of the Irish members. His response to that situation was to come out in support of Home Rule and a separate legislature for Ireland. In 1886 the first Irish Home Rule Bill was presented and defeated. Gladstone's ill-fated third ministry, which lasted only from February to July of 1886, went down in defeat, destroyed by the jingoist nationalism of such fire eaters as Lord Randolph Churchill, and religious bigotry, whose Northern Ireland exemplars warned that faced with rule under a Catholic Irish Parliament, Ulster would fight. Indeed, Ulster prepared to do just that, and held the gun of civil war to the head of the English Parliament. Gladstone's support melted away. Lord Salisbury led the Conservatives into power, setting the tone of the new ministry by comparing the Irish to Hottentots and treating them as one of 'the lesser breeds without the law'.[44]

Edward was not sorry to see Home Rule defeated; he was vehemently opposed to the breaking up of the empire; but he was still obliged to view the Irish visit as a personal failure in private diplomacy. Yet another personal failure for Edward in the '80s was his relationship with his nephew William, who succeeded his father to the Prussian throne on June 15 1888, to become Emperor William II. His uncle dubbed him William the Great.[45] But immediately following the death of Frederick III, towards whom Edward had felt a genuine fondness, the Prince attempted to encourage his sister Vicky to believe that William would grow steadier under the stress of responsibility and gradually learn wisdom. It was probably the last time Edward ever encouraged anyone to believe William capable of improvement. On his side, William had developed an intense, if unreasonable, hatred of his uncle because of Edward's efforts to arrange, despite William's strong objection to the match, the marriage of William's sister Victoria with Prince Alexander of Bulgaria, the handsome Sandro.

In 1885, determined to make mischief, William took himself to Vienna at precisely the time that Emperor Francis Joseph had invited Edward to be a guest of the Austrian Government and added that he did not wish to have his uncle in the capital at the same time he was there. Edward was obliged to leave. 'I will show him,' William is reported to have said, 'that I am now an Emperor and he only a Prince.'[46] The good effects of those years between 1884 and 1888, during which Edward had put himself out to find some way of bringing England and Germany together, were erased. Edward would never forgive William for the Vienna humiliation. Lady Warwick wrote later that although she could regularly count on Edward's willingness to talk seriously with her about foreign and international affairs and was willing to hear her out on a variety of issues, he would never make the slightest concession to her efforts to persuade him to put his relationship with William on a more amicable footing.

A VISIT TO GRANDMA.

Mrs. Happy and Glorious.—"NOW, ALBERT EDWARD, HERE IS WILLIAM COME TO SEE US;
BE A GOOD BOY, AND SHOW HIM ALL THE PRETTY THINGS."

[*See Cartoon Verses*, p. 7

'A Visit to Grandma': from *Fun*, July 1891
By permission of the British Museum

TRANBY CROFT, 1890 (AFTER BUNYAN).

"The Interpreter takes them apart again, and has them first into a room, where was a man that could look no way but downwards, with a muck rake in his hand. There stood also one over his head, with a celestial crown in her hand, and proffered him that crown for his muck rake; but the man did neither look up nor regard, but raked to himself the straws, the small sticks, and the dust of the floor."

* * * * * *

"Then said Christiana, O deliver me from this muck rake."

13. 'Tranby Croft, 1890 (After Bunyan)': 1891
By permission of the British Museum

The '80s were a decade of ferment and social change. In 1886 and 1887 those workmen whom *Reynolds's* had praised in 1884 for enduring poverty with patience threw aside that forbearance and marched with red flags flying into the West End, smashing the windows of the Carlton Club, looting shops in Piccadilly and turning people out of their carriages in Hyde Park. In 1887 on 'Bloody Sunday' unemployed work-men and police confronted one another in Trafalgar Square; and two squadrons of Life Guards had to be summoned from Whitehall to quell the disturbance. Then in 1889, fifty thousand London dockers, led by John Burns, closed down all shipping into London and won their wage increase of a penny an hour. The issue of Home Rule for Ireland was raised; and if the bill to grant it was defeated, Ireland's determination to be free was not.

Edward gave his support to the reform procession and to the housing commission, but it was not in him to be more active than this on behalf of social legislation. Aside from the constitutional restraints checking his movements, there were his deeply rooted conservative biases, which made him a defender of inherited privilege, the empire and social distinctions. He despised the socialists' approach to politics, saying in dismissal of it, 'Society is not made but grows.' In this period his activities as a mover of foreign affairs was not impressive, and the French Entente actually lost ground. Nevertheless, Sandringham House remained open to men of every political shade; and he cultivated the friendship of European leaders, thus laying the groundwork for good future work.

As far as social life went, upper class society had broken by the '80s into three major sets. The group surrounding the Queen and made up of the older members of the more socially conservative families was known as the Court Set, Edward's group was variously titled the Marl-borough House Set, the Smart Set, the Party Set or the Horsey Set. The third group consisted of the Souls.[47] According to one account it was Edward's friend Beresford who gave this name to that group surround-ing Arthur Balfour, Margot Asquith, Mary Elcho, Lord Curzon and others.[48] Edward was stuck firmly in his set and showed no inclination to go outside it. One writer of the day even went so far as to say that society was defined as 'the social area of which the Prince of Wales is personally cognizant, within the limits of which he visits, and every member of which is to some extent in touch with the ideas and wishes of His Royal Highness'.[49] The definition is unfortunate in its implications, but it is probably accurate in its description of Edward's personal view of society.

It is widely acknowledged that Edward had a strong and probably salutary effect on English society. He broke down old barriers, letting in Americans, shopkeepers, Jews, actors and actresses, journalists and

H

jockeys, regarding all as socially acceptable, and becoming close friends
with some. But despite his liking for Marie Corelli, he can scarcely be
said to have encouraged the arts or intellectual world of his time. It is
all the more puzzling since his very close friend, Charles Beresford,
was intimate with most of the members of that charmed circle. Sir
Leslie Stephen brought the *Dictionary of National Biography* into existence
in 1882; and on the eve of its publication, Sir Sidney Lee, Shakespearean scholar and future biographer of Edward, proposed to the
Prince that a dinner be given at Marlborough House to honour those
men who had worked to convert the dream of the *DNB* into a reality.
Edward was doubtful but asked to see the list of names. Discovering
that there were forty men on it, he was appalled and began to strike
names off the list. The first name he removed was Sir Leslie Stephen's.
With some difficulty Lee managed to restore Sir Leslie and keep the
remaining names on the list. The dinner was given. Looking around
the table, Edward's eye fell on Canon Ainger, who had written the
entries on Mary and Charles Lamb. 'Who is the little parson?' Edward
demanded of Lee. 'Vy is he here? He's not a wr-ri-ter!' 'He is a very
great authority,' Lee said apologetically, 'on Lamb.' Dumbfounded,
the Prince laid down his knife and fork and cried, 'on lamb!'[50]

Edward was happier with racing men and felt no need to apologize
for his preference. He had had all he wanted of learned men in his
youth. In 1885 he began a breeding stud at Sandringham, and with
the purchase of Perdita II made his move towards racing success. She
bore three great winning horses for Edward – Florizel II, Persimmon
and Diamond Jubilee. By the '80s racing had become his passion. He
occupied a suite of rooms in the house of the Jockey Club for the New-
market Meetings, and from 1885 onwards entertained annually all
members of the club at dinner at Marlborough House and later
Buckingham Palace. For the Grand National at Aintree he stayed with
Lord Sefton at Sefton Park, with the Duke of Richmond for Goodwood,
the Duke of Westminster at Eaton Hall for the Chester races; and, with
the exception of one fateful year, after Christopher Sykes lost Brantingham Thorpe, he stayed with Lord Savile at Rufford Abbey for the
St Leger at Doncaster.

Racing, shooting, yachting and hunting were the seasons of his social
year. Edward enjoyed them all. He had taken up tennis in the '80s, for
his weight, and baccarat, a card game that was rapidly replacing whist
as his favourite after-dinner game. There was simply no place in his life
for philosophical speculations of the sort that flew around the dinner
table of the Souls (and could become so absorbing that even a fire on the
first floor of the host's house could not drive the guests away from the
table, where they sat holding towels to wipe away the water descending
on them from the burning floor above and arguing hotly the question

of immortality!)[51] This was not Edward's world. It was a world he never penetrated, perhaps a loss both to himself and the arts. But his separation from this intellectual world was indicative of the swift falling away of the artist from the centres of power. Tennyson still visited Queen Victoria, but they were relics of another age; and Edward was not intimate with the old poet.

Edward closed the decade of the '80s with a quarrel with Parliament, which was resolved by the Prince of Wales's Children's Bill, passed on August 5 1889. The bill's passage brought to an end the haggling between the government and the royal family over the question of money allowances for the Queen's children and grandchildren. National allowances for any of the royal children and grandchildren, except for those directly in the line of succession, were vigorously opposed by the radical members of Gladstone's cabinet – John Morley, Mr Labouchere and Thomas Burt.[52] Gladstone finally managed to construct a bill that was acceptable to the radicals, but the contest had been sharp and revelatory. Once again, the Queen's parsimony had precipitated a crisis, for every member of the government knew how much money she had accumulated and how it had been done. Edward's money troubles pursued him into the 1890s and continued without abatement until his accession to the throne.

In 1887 the nation put aside its resentment of the Queen's failures as a constitutional monarch and entered enthusiastically into the Jubilee celebrations marking her fiftieth year on the throne of England. The festivities became an occasion for national self-congratulation for real and imagined achievements, and in them Victoria came to be regarded as the symbol of that greatness. The nation demonstrated its latent affection for the Queen in its outpouring of warmth during the celebrations. The public attitude towards Edward was less warm; and he was condemned in some circles of society as the leader of a fast set, whose morals were a scandal and whose example to the nation was pernicious in the extreme. It was not only the sexual morality of the Marlborough Set that had the puritans trembling with indignation. Betting was becoming so widespread that many considered it to be a national curse as deeply ingrained as drinking had been forty years earlier.[53] The Marlborough Set led the country in its dedication to betting on horse racing and gambling at cards. One reporter of the social scene estimated that in the first nine months of 1890 Edward attended twenty-eight race meetings.[54] Naturally he bet at all of them and not only on his own horses.

A few influential writers, such as W. T. Stead, had begun to take up the betting issue; but Edward was not pilloried in the press. However, a storm was approaching which had its inception in gambling and which was to drive Edward hard onto the reefs of public anger. By a bitter irony, the trouble can be traced to the financial collapse of another of Edward's friends. This time the victim was Christopher Sykes, one of Edward's 'tame cats' and a man who beggared himself entertaining the Prince. Sykes's great-nephew, in *Four Studies in Loyalties,* reports that his great-uncle has his name inscribed on a brass plate in one of the royal chapels, making the observation that 'Christopher Sykes would have been very touched and grateful.' He adds, 'I am glad that he did get something out of his long career of painful, of agonizing devotion.'

What was so terrible about Sykes's relationship with Edward was not only that he allowed Edward to pour, literally, wine and cognac down his neck and over his head year after year, and to submit himself to the most cruel practical jokes imaginable, but that he spent in dinners and parties, given at Edward's request, his entire fortune, finally losing his country house in Yorkshire, Brantingham Thorpe, to his creditors. In the autumn of 1890 Sykes was on the verge of bankruptcy, and Edward was unable to stay with him for the Doncaster races. Sykes's financial collapse led Edward into a scandal of such proportions that the very throne of England trembled.

10

'Ich Deal'

> I do not call a gambler a dishonest man, but I call him an unsocial man, an unprofitable man.
>
> Dr Johnson

The Sir William Gordon-Cumming trial or the Baccarat Scandal, as it was universally called, burst over England and produced shock waves of anguish, outrage, and mirth throughout the nation and across Europe and North America. Not since the Mordaunt trial had Englishmen been treated to such a spectacle. That the bomb was lighted in September of 1890 and smouldered until the following June only intensified public reaction to its eventual detonation.

For those with a taste for irony, the Baccarat Scandal provided a varied feast. Even the circumstances that brought the Prince to Tranby Croft, Arthur Wilson's country house, have an ironic twist. The Prince had been in the habit of staying with Christopher Sykes at Brantingham Thorpe while attending the Doncaster races, but by the autumn of 1890 Sykes was nearly bankrupt.[1] He had gradually beggared himself playing host to Edward and putting together expensive parties to amuse him. Denied Sykes's hospitality, the Prince was forced to accept the invitation offered him by Arthur Wilson, a merchant shipping magnate, to come to Tranby Croft. Had he been able to stay at Brantingham Thorpe, the scandal might well have been avoided. That Sykes was also present as a guest at the Wilson house gives a Wildean touch to the opening scene of this pathetic farce.

The uneasiness he felt at staying in a strange house for the St Leger race week deepened into gloom when the Prince learned that Lady Brooke was forced by the unexpected death of her uncle to cancel her plans to join the Prince at Tranby Croft.[2] The Prince's attention, however, was soon diverted from the loss of one of his favourite companions by events of a much more disturbing sort. These were to be the beginning of a series of events which grew in intensity during the months between September and June and released hostilities that, although never more than hinted at in the trial, were nonetheless at the heart of it. The events themselves, viewed from a distance of eighty years and separated from the social and political context within which they occurred, appear almost pathetically insignificant; but their culmination in Lord Coleridge's court in the early summer of 1891 produced something close to national hysteria.

The party at Tranby Croft was large, including many people from the Wilsons' circle of friends whom Edward, in the ordinary course of events, would not have met socially. Perhaps because of this, the small group of Edward's friends and the members of the Wilson family who were devoting themselves to the task of keeping the Prince entertained became the players in an astonishingly nasty drama. Directly involved in the events to follow were a young lieutenant in the Scots Guards, Berkeley Levitt; Arthur Wilson's son-in-law, Lycett Green; Mrs Green; Mrs Wilson and her son, Arthur Stanley Wilson.

Mr Wilson did not make up one of the group around the Prince, and there has been much speculation as to why this was so. One report says that he was ill, but an equally reasonable guess is that he was offended by the Prince's refusal to act on his hint that he would prefer not to have gambling in his house. The problem with the second suggestion is that he would have to have been deaf and blind not to have known of Edward's obsessive attachment to gambling at this point in his life. What is most probable is that he was occupied with the remainder of his guests, who formed a quite separate group in the house and may have been feeling their ostracism from the select circle around the Prince.

Also included in the Prince's group were several old friends: Mr Reuben Sassoon, the banker; Lord Edward Somerset; the Earl of Coventry; Lady Coventry; General Owen Williams and Sir William Gordon-Cumming, Bart, destined to stand in the very centre of the approaching storm. Gordon-Cumming was forty-two years old, a Lieutenant-Colonel and twenty-three-year career officer in the Scots Guards, a decorated veteran of the Zulu War and the Egyptian campaign of 1882, and a member of the Carlton, Turf, Marlborough, and Guards clubs. In addition to the family seat in Scotland, he owned a house in London and was in possession of an income, exclusive of his Guards' pay, of £80,000 a year. An occasional visitor at Sandringham and Marlborough House, he had known the Prince for twenty years and had been a close friend for the past ten. He was one of the small group who had accompanied the Prince on his journey from London to Tranby Croft.

On Monday Gordon-Cumming attended the races with the Wilsons, whom he knew casually, and was one of the group that, after its return to Tranby Croft at about 6 pm, watched the Prince fill a champagne bucket with whisky, champagne, crushed ice, two glasses of maraschino, a dash of angostura, declaring the concoction to be a cocktail made precisely according to a recipe sent to him by a friend in Louisiana. Dinner passed merrily; and when the men had finished their cigars in the smoking room, the Prince suggested a game of baccarat. It was generally known that Arthur Wilson objected to the game being played in his house – in fact his wife was to testify to that fact under cross-examination; but in deference to the wishes of the Prince, three tables were thrown together to create a playing surface. The counters were provided by the Prince.

The set, a gift from Reuben Sassoon, was made of Russian leather and was in denominations of from five shillings to ten pounds, and each piece was engraved with the Prince's insignia of three feathers, a detail a German cartoonist was to use with devastating effect when he drew these three feathers emerging from a crown and captioned the drawing 'Ich Deal', thus parodying the Prince's motto: 'Ich Dien' – 'I serve'. The Prince acted as banker; and when at about eleven o'clock play commenced, Sir William was one of the dozen or so gamblers who took seats at the converted whist tables.

Precisely what happened on that and the following nights will probably never be known with absolute certainty, despite the thousands of words of direct and indirect testimony that were addressed to the subject when the issue was finally placed before a jury. The allegations, however, are soon stated. Play had scarcely begun before Arthur Stanley Wilson, the host's twenty-year-old son, concluded that Gordon-Cumming was cheating.

At the close of the first coup, Wilson was later to assert, Sir William had a single £5 red counter wagered; but when he saw he had won, he dropped three additional £5 counters on the single already bet and collected £20. The baronet did this, according to Wilson, by keeping his hands cupped over the single counter and releasing the three additional counters from the palm of his hand when play ended and he was sure of being a winner. Wilson alleged that Gordon-Cumming repeated the deception on the next deal.

Staggered by what he had seen, Wilson whispered to Berkeley Levitt, a young subaltern in Sir William's regiment, who was seated beside him, 'My God, Berkeley, this is too hot.'

'What do you mean?' Levitt asked, probably only half listening, as the game was still in progress.

'The man next to me is cheating.'

Startled, Berkeley snapped, 'What utter folly. You must be mistaken. It is absolutely impossible.'

'Well, look at him.'

Levitt watched; and a few coups later he muttered to Wilson, 'It is too hot.'[3]

The final occasion that Wilson was later able to recall of Gordon-Cumming's cheating that night occurred when the baronet pushed a £2 counter on to the sheet of white paper on which he was staking his bets and keeping a record of his wins and losses. Play had in fact stopped, and the baronet was assumed by Wilson to be deliberately cheating the bank, which was being kept by the Prince of Wales.

The game lasted about an hour and a half. When it was over the guests drifted off to bed. The Prince had no idea that anything was wrong and was already looking forward to the next day's racing. No one but Wilson and Levitt had found the baronet's method of play suspicious. The two young men went to Levitt's room, bursting with anxiety, to talk about what they had seen. Levitt threw himself on his bed and expressed astonishment that an officer in the Scots Guards should be a cheat.

'What's to be done about it?' Wilson demanded.

'For God's sake, don't ask me,' Levitt replied. 'He is in my regiment, and was my captain for a year and a half. What can I do?'

'I know what I can do,' Wilson said. 'I can go straight to my brother-in-law.'

With that Wilson left Levitt's room, but he did not go to Lycett Green. Instead he went to his mother and told her what he and Levitt had seen. Upset by the news, she burst out: 'For goodness' sake, don't let us have a scandal here.'[4]

One of the many puzzling features of the Wilson family's behaviour in the crisis is that young Wilson did not go to his father with the information. It is not even certain that Mrs Wilson told her husband that night of her son's suspicions. Probably she did not. Throughout, Arthur Wilson remains a shadowy figure, standing on the outer edge of all that was to happen in the ensuing months.

Determined to take some action and undoubtedly highly agitated, young Wilson went to the butler and ordered that a proper table for the next night's play be set up in the smoking room. In his testimony Wilson said that he altered the arrangements in order to prevent any further cheating. Mrs Wilson testified that the table was produced at the Prince's request. The table selected had a green baize cover, providing a very satisfactory playing surface.

The following morning he took a walk with his brother-in-law and told him what he had seen and that he had ordered a new table for the evening's play. Returning from their walk, Lycett Green repeated Arthur's story to his wife before the party set out for the races. By now, five and possibly six people were in possession of the story that Sir William had cheated at cards. Unfortunately, everyone but young Wilson appears to have believed that the best course of action was to do nothing. At least the son, Arthur Stanley, had located a new table.

The day was, in general, a repetition of the day before. Everyone attended the races, enjoyed a leisurely luncheon, brightened with champagne; socialized; wagered on the horses and returned to Tranby Croft in anticipation of dinner and another pleasant evening. So far as is known, only those already named had the slightest idea that anything was amiss. Certainly the Prince, Lord Coventry, and General Owen Williams, the senior members of the party, were wholly ignorant of young Wilson's accusations.

In all probability Lycett Green, Levitt, Arthur Stanley Wilson, his mother and his sister spoke together some time on the ninth and discussed what they were to do. Later, conflicting, evidence obscured whether or not the five agreed to watch Sir William's play that evening. It is known through testimony that the young lieutenant, Berkeley Levitt, deliberately avoided watching Sir William's play on the second night and after the momentary excitement in his room following Monday night's game, remained an extremely reluctant witness to Gordon-Cumming's action. Lycett Green and the others hotly denied under oath that their intention in providing a new table was an attempt to trap Sir William or that they had acted in concert in observing his play on Tuesday night.

When the baccarat players assembled that evening, the new table was in place. At the Prince's suggestion, a white chalk line had been drawn five or six inches in from the outer edge of the table. Counters placed inside the line were wagers while those remaining between the line and the outer edge of the table were out of play. Whatever had or had not been agreed upon among themselves, all, with the exception of Berkeley Levitt, who had knowledge of Gordon-Cumming's alleged cheating, watched the lieutenant-colonel's game; and all asserted in their deposition, made the following day to the Prince, that they saw Gordon-Cumming cheat on the night of September 9, the second evening of play. He cheated, according to their charge, by on one occasion flicking an additional £10 counter across the line when he saw that he had won, and on another occasion by dropping extra counters on his wager from his cupped hand after the coup had ended.

When Lycett Green saw what he construed to be cheating by the baronet, he was horrified and temporarily withdrew from the game. Going into an adjoining room, he wrote his mother-in-law a note and directed one of the servants to pass it to her at once. Mrs Wilson was at the gaming table at the time. Having received and read the note, she went on playing without any obvious concern. Why did Lycett Green write to Mrs Wilson and not to her husband? Is it possible that the latter did not know what was going on under his own roof? The questions were skirted in the trial and never, on record, answered elsewhere. A few minutes after writing the note, having conquered his nervousness, Green returned to the table and began to play again. He had asked Mrs Wilson to stop the play, but she had chosen to do nothing. He shrank from taking more purposeful action on his own initiative.

Nothing further was done that night, but the following morning Green spoke to Lord Edward Somerset, one of the Prince's party, informing him that he and others had observed Gordon-Cumming cheating. Somerset listened to Green's charge and said that he wished to confer with Captain Somerset. The two men met again shortly afterwards with Green and told him to place the matter before Lord Coventry. George William Coventry, ninth Earl of Coventry and Viscount Deerhurst, was a close friend of the Prince and, after him, the ranking member of the party. The interview between the Somersets and Green was concluded; and the guests went to the races, as they had done on the two previous days. The party did not include Mr and Mrs Wilson, however, because Mrs Wilson learned before leaving that her brother had died. She now had grief to add to what must have been great anxiety.

The Prince continued to follow his programme completely unaware of the approaching calamity. Gordon-Cumming was equally oblivious. His winnings for the two nights had been £225; and when the Prince had remarked laughingly on the extent of his good luck, Sir William replied, 'How could one fail to win with such a tableau,' showing the Prince his record of the games, which he had kept on a slip of paper.[5] He was, undoubtedly, hoping to continue his run of luck that evening, when the game would be resumed, as he had every reason to assume it would be, given the Prince of Wales's passion for baccarat, a passion that had become an embarrassment even to his closest friends.

Following the races, however, the final steps in exposing Gordon-Cumming were taken; and the course of events became irreversible. Green waited until everyone was once again back at Tranby Croft and then, with young Wilson and Captain Arthur Somerset present, repeated to Lord Coventry what he had told Lord Somerset that morning. Lord Coventry sent for General Williams, and Green again repeated the charge, adding that he was ready to confront Sir William.[6]

Williams and Coventry went directly to the Prince and broke the news to him as he was preparing for dinner. He must have experienced an immediate shock of terror once the implications of the situation were fully grasped. He had been implicated more than once in scandal and had come to dread it. However, the Prince did not waste time agonizing over the situation. After a brief discussion with Williams and Coventry over the possibility of framing a document that would bind Gordon-Cumming to a pledge to refrain from cards for the rest of his life and the others to a pledge of secrecy, he sent the two men to tell Gordon-Cumming of the charge which had been levelled against him.

Entering the baronet's room, Lord Coventry said, without pre-
liminaries, 'Some of the people here have objected to your manner of
playing baccarat.'

'Good God, Coventry,' Sir William said in alarm, 'what do you
mean?'

'Certain people in the house have asserted that you resorted to foul
play at baccarat, and they have gone to the Prince of Wales.'

Having vehemently asserted his innocence, the Lieutenant-Colonel
asked what he was to do and requested an interview with the Prince.
Williams and Lord Coventry told him they would see about arranging
a meeting with the Prince after dinner, but suggested no course of
action to Sir William, perhaps because they knew what solution the
Prince favoured and chose not to reveal it to Sir William until they
were more in command of the facts. Having shaken hands with him in
a solemn fashion, they left his room and hurried to dress for dinner.

Innocent or guilty of the accusation made against him, it can easily
be imagined what agony of mind Sir William endured as he sat through
that incredible dinner, taking part in the general effort to pretend that
nothing was out of the ordinary. Following the meal, the group even
made a brief attempt at casual conversation. Then the Prince withdrew,
and a short time later summoned Gordon-Cumming. The baronet went
to the interview without any clear idea of how he should defend himself.

'I went to His Royal Highness,' Sir William testified at the trial,
'and said I wished an interview with him as some persons in the house
had brought a foul and abominable charge against me. They said I
cheated at cards, a charge that I utterly and emphatically deny.'

He added that he had tried to act as an officer and a gentleman for
twenty-five years.

'What can you do?' the Prince replied. 'There are five accusers
against you.'

The Prince was later to be attacked for that answer. Referring to it
during the trial, the Solicitor-General, Sir Edward Clarke, Gordon-
Cumming's counsel, asserted that the Prince had 'jumped recklessly
to a wrong conclusion on bad evidence'.[7]

The Prince of Wales had not, at that time, interviewed Lycett Green
or any of the others. That meeting was to occur a short time later. The
Prince was acting on the strength of the report which had been brought
to him by General Williams and Lord Coventry, who had it from Lord
and Captain Somerset and Lycett Green. No details of the cheating
seem to have been known at that time by any but the original five
accusers. Faced with the Prince's unsympathetic response to his denial,
Gordon-Cumming said that he was inclined, in these circumstances,
to grossly insult his accusers at the next public opportunity.

'What good would that do?' the Prince demanded, undoubtedly

anxious to prevent any such thing happening and giving credence to Clarke's later assertion in court that Gordon-Cumming had been sacrificed to protect the Prince.

'What am I to do?' Sir William asked, repeating the question he had asked of Coventry and Williams before dinner.

No one ventured an answer; and he withdrew, after waiting for General Williams to unlock the door, which had been fastened, the General said, in order that the servants would not hear.[8]

The Prince met next with Lycett Green, Arthur Stanley Wilson, and Berkeley Levitt with Lord Coventry, General Williams, and Edward and Arthur Somerset present. Green was principal spokesman for the group, but at one point the Prince turned to Levitt and asked him to clarify some point concerning the play. Levitt said that he did not like to speak because he was in Gordon-Cumming's regiment. He was probably also reflecting on the officers' code, which he had sworn to uphold and which laid on him the duty of reporting to his commanding officer any incident in which a fellow officer was guilty of behaviour unbecoming to an officer in Her Majesty's service. It must have been in Levitt's mind that neither the Prince nor General Williams could be unaware of that responsibility.

The Prince listened to Levitt's answer and replied, 'Of course, of course', excusing Levitt from making a response to the question.

The conference ended; and Green, Wilson, and Levitt withdrew, leaving the Prince, Coventry, Williams, and the Somersets to decide upon a course of action. The original plan for scotching the scandal was reviewed and accepted. In fact the undertaking, which was to be called the 'document' in the trial, may have been written before the conference with Green and the others took place. Conflicting testimony was given during the trial as to exactly when the paper was drawn up or who originally suggested it. By Lord Coventry's testimony it was written by himself and General Williams after the Prince's interview with Green. Green testified that the paper was already drawn up when he entered the Prince's apartment.

At about eleven o'clock Lord Coventry and General Williams brought Gordon-Cumming back to the Prince's rooms. Once there, Sir William found the pledge ready for his signature. It was presented to him – the Prince no longer being present – with the statement that his signing it was the only way of avoiding a horrible scandal.

Gordon-Cumming read the paper and, turning to his two friends, said, 'If I sign this, it is tantamount to a confession of guilt.'

His first response was to refuse to accept their solution and, instead, place himself in the hands of his commanding officer.

'You can do so if you like,' General Williams replied, 'but he will not be so lenient to you as we have been.'

Lord Coventry and General Williams were longtime and very intimate friends of Sir William; and he had, with reservation, placed himself in their hands. Depending on how the case is viewed, it could be
seen either as the wisest course he could have taken or else as an act
of the rankest folly. At that moment, however, he must have been overwhelmed by the fact that not only was his career in jeopardy but also
his standing as a gentleman. Should he lose that standing, every social
connection he had built up over a lifetime would be severed; and he
would be ostracized, totally, irrevocably.

It was a terrible moment for Sir William. It was obvious to him that
Coventry and Williams were prepared to act as though his guilt were
an established fact. If he went to his commanding officer, he would be
going with the knowledge that five people were prepared to label him a
cheat and that he could expect no support from the Prince, Williams,
or Coventry.

'Coventry,' he said, 'you are a friend of mine, and you recommend
me to sign this paper?'

'If I were in your place, I should sign it,' Lord Coventry responded,
'because I do not think your commanding officer would take so lenient
a view as we have done.'

Appealing to General Williams, he said, 'Owen, you are a very old
friend of mine. Do you advise me to sign it?'

The General's answer was in the affirmative; he added that if Gordon-Cumming did not sign it, he would have to leave the house at once
and that he would be warned off every racecourse in England.[9]

Without further hesitation but still asserting his innocence, Gordon-
Cumming picked up the pen that had been provided for him and
signed his name to the following pledge:

'In consideration of the promise made by the gentlemen whose
names are subscribed to preserve silence with reference to the accusation made as to my conduct at baccarat on September 8 and 9 at
Tranby Croft, I will on my part solemnly undertake never to play
cards again as long as I live.'[10]

In addition to Gordon-Cumming's signature, those of Albert Edward, Lord Coventry, General Williams, Edward Somerset, Arthur
Somerset, A. S. Wilson, J. Wilson, Lycett Green, Berkeley Levitt, and
R. Sassoon were later added. The Queen was furious with Lord
Coventry and General Williams for having permitted the Prince to
sign the document, insisting that they had unnecessarily allowed him
to compromise himself. It seems unlikely, however, that once having
appraised Edward of the charges, they could have prevented his taking
control of the situation. He may not have ruled much, but what he
ruled he ruled absolutely; and he would have considered a matter such
as this unequivocally within his sphere of discretion.

The moment was past. Before opening the door for Sir William to leave, Williams told him that Lycett Green had originated the idea for the document and that its purpose was to prevent Gordon-Cumming from, at a later date, 'insulting his accusers, denying the whole affair, or bringing an action'. Why Williams lied to Gordon-Cumming about the origin of the document is not at all clear. Later, under cross-examination, Sir William was asked why, if he was innocent, he had signed such a damning document and why he had left to others a decision on a question affecting his honour.

'When a man is in the position I was in,' Gordon-Cumming replied, 'he is not responsible for his actions. I had a pistol presented to me in the form of a most horrible charge, and I lost my head,' adding, 'I have never ceased to regret it.'[11]

The following morning the paper was given to Lycett Green to sign, but he protested that signing it would expose him to action by Sir William. General Williams assured him that there was no danger of such a thing happening because Gordon-Cumming's signature was a confession of guilt.[12] Green signed the statement, and the affair appeared to be closed. Gordon-Cumming, still responding to his friends' advice, left Tranby Croft early on the morning of September 11, followed shortly afterwards by the Prince, who watched the day's racing from the Cavalry Barracks at York.[13] The Prince did not return to the Wilsons' house. He had seen all he ever wished to see of Tranby Croft.

The unpleasantness of the events at the Wilsons' was only a preliminary scouting of the painful ground to be covered in the ensuing months. By November the secret was out, and the London clubs were alive with rumour of what had happened at Tranby Croft. Someone had failed to keep his part of the bargain.

But who? Gossip had it that the Prince had confided in Lady Brooke and that she had actually mentioned the matter to several people, including Gordon-Cumming, accusing him to his face of having cheated at cards. Of all the witnesses called at the trial only the Prince was not asked if he had given away the secret, a slip on the part of the solicitors, Russell's and Clarke's – if it was a slip – which led to speculation that it was the Prince who had 'blabbed'. Edward Legge, however, in his first biography of Edward, insisted that it was neither the 'popular English lady' nor the Prince but 'quite another person whose name was then only moderately known in English society'.[14] Stead, writing in the prestigious *Review of Reviews,* was also convinced, or pretended to be, that the Prince had not given away the secret.

Inevitably, William Gordon-Cumming discovered that he had been exposed. His career in jeopardy, he took steps, very belatedly, to defend himself and on February 6 1891, took out an action for slander against the five persons who had accused him of cheating at baccarat while a guest at Tranby Croft.

On March 3, in a tersely worded quarter column under the heading 'The Baccarat Scandal', *The Times* announced that William Gordon-Cumming's court action for slander against certain persons with whom he had played cards at Tranby Croft on the evenings of September 8 and 9 of the preceding year had been issued as a writ on February 6 and the statement of claim delivered on the twenty-seventh. Sir William claimed £5,000 in damages from Mr E. Lycett Green, Mr Arthur Stanley Wilson, Mrs Arthur Wilson, Mrs Ethel Lycett Green, and Mr Berkeley Levitt.

The day before, *The Times* had commented at length on the remarkable growth of Methodism and on the reasons for its rapid expansion. Nothing in those reasons could have led the Prince to believe that the Nonconformist element among his subjects would view the Tranby Croft episode with indulgence. There were other signs in the wind of the feeling of the country regarding breaches of moral decorum. Almost exactly two years before, *Littell's Living Age* had reprinted an article from the *Quarterly Review* entitled 'Gambling'. The essay made a strong case for the view that there was widespread lay and church opposition to gambling and that hostility towards it was increasing daily.

The *Quarterly Review's* position seems to be borne out by the zeal with which the clergy fell on the issue, swooping down from their pulpits like birds of prey: 'You all know,' the Reverend George Martin told his parishioners at the Lewisham High Road Congregational Church, 'you all know – it is no secret – that a very general impression has existed that the life of the Prince thus far has not been such as we could desire. This has led many to feel deep and painful anxiety about the state of his soul – a most solemn thing.'[15] The Reverend Martin went on to voice the hope, expressed without conviction, one feels, that the Prince would 'come forth from the furnace of affliction as gold purified and made to reflect the Refiner's image'.[16] It is probable that his listeners heard this in the same spirit in which it was uttered.

Mr Vincent, a popular dissenting minister in Plymouth, took the line that the Prince must reform, or he would cause the Church serious embarrassment. 'For how could they read prayers,' Vincent demanded, 'for their most *religious* and gracious King? What would they do – insult him by leaving out the word "religious" or insult God by retaining it and applying it to such a chief governor?'[17] A more subtle clergyman in Eastbourne did not refer directly to baccarat, but after the mention of the Prince of Wales's name in the Litany, he paused for a couple of minutes, in the manner which is customary when prayers are 'earnestly desired' for someone.[18]

From November, when all hopes for burying the scandal were dashed by club gossip, the Prince moved with increasing speed towards a confrontation with those elements in the nation who honoured the memory of John Wesley and all that he represented in terms of moral rectitude. It is another irony that the scandal occurred in the centenary year of the death of Wesley and that, at the time of the trial, religious convocations were being held in various places in England, Scotland, and Wales, providing the physical and the emotional settings from which attacks on the Prince could be launched with self-righteous vigour. The Prince of Wales was not blind to his position, and his efforts to prevent a public confrontation between himself and the mass of his subjects show how clearly he perceived his danger.

Gordon-Cumming came to a full understanding of his predicament rather more slowly but no less inevitably. He had certainly not held very high hopes that the affair could be permanently hushed up. Writing on September 12 to General Williams, with whom he continued to correspond throughout the winter, he acknowledged that he now saw 'little before him' to make his life worth living, but that he supposed 'in the meantime' he must try to live as of old.[19] The futility of that effort was soon brought home to the baronet. Club gossip became too general to be ignored. His exposure to insult was increasing daily.

By early January Sir William had resolved to press his cause in the courts before his clubs took up the issue and tried him in their informal but weighty congresses. There was also a growing danger of a court-martial; and he knew that if one were held and he were found guilty, he would have lost all hope of gaining redress in a public trial. To prevent this from happening, he submitted his papers to his commanding officer, Colonel H. D. D. Stracey of the Scots Guards, asking to be allowed to retire on half pay.

There were, however, already powerful forces being mustered against him. The Prince, through his informants, had learned that Gordon-Cumming was applying for retirement and he meant to carry his case into the courts. This publicity was precisely what the Prince wanted to prevent. Acting through his friends, his first effort was directed at stopping Gordon-Cumming's retirement, which would have put him safely out of reach of a court-martial.

On February 4, Lord Coventry and General Williams were despatched to place the Prince's wishes before the Adjutant-General, Sir Redvers Buller, V.C., who heard the account of events at Tranby Croft, an account which was formally submitted to him later in the day in written form. Buller's response was immediate. He denied Gordon-Cumming's request to retire and ordered a court of inquiry to look into the Lieutenant-Colonel's behaviour at Tranby Croft. The Prince appeared to have successfully defused the baronet's attempt to get his case into the public court and to have protected himself from exposure to public scrutiny. The proceedings of the military court would be private and could be counted on to protect the Prince from any embarrassing revelations.

Fortunately for Gordon-Cumming, however, he had retained solicitors who were experienced and worthy men, and his chief counsel was Sir Edward Clarke, Q.C., the Solicitor-General. It was to be argued later that Clarke's position in the government prevented him from prosecuting his case with the vigour it demanded, but his presence in the case must have impressed the Adjutant-General. Arguing for fair play, the baronet's solicitors, Messrs Gill, requested that General Buller reconsider his previous refusal, let the case come to trial and not grossly prejudice the outcome of the trial by conducting a prior hearing. General Buller hesitated, conferred with the Judge Advocate-General, and cancelled the military enquiry.[20]

The Prince was, of course, deeply disappointed in the action taken by General Buller and did not conceal his feelings about the Adjutant-General's decision, calling Buller's action 'to say the least of it, extraordinary'. Buller, however, remained unmoved. Although the Prince could see his chances for heading off a public confrontation with Gordon-Cumming lessening, his secretary, Sir Francis Knollys, attempted another flanking movement. This time the Prince sought to pressure the Guards Club into convening a committee to look into Gordon-Cumming's action at Tranby Croft, hoping by this move to discredit the baronet in advance of the trial; but the plan was defeated in a meeting of the membership, specially called on February 20, by twenty-nine votes.[21] The rebuff to the Prince was unmistakable.

In a letter to Ponsonby, he expressed his disappointment and also revealed his unwillingness to admit what the vote meant to his standing with the Guards: 'The decision of the Guards' Club is a terrible blow to the Scots Guards; and I feel most deeply for the officers who have the honour of their regiment so much at heart. Should Cumming, by any legal quibble, win his action, I think nearly every officer would leave the regiment.'[22]

Earlier Gordon-Cumming had written to General Williams, notifying the General that he had applied for retirement and had told Colonel Stracey of the undertaking he had signed. He added that Stracey had said that the fact of his having signed the document could not be overlooked. Replying to the letter and beginning, 'Dear Bill', Williams advised Gordon-Cumming to place himself 'unreservedly' in Colonel Stracey's hands as he had done in the case of himself and Lord Coventry. 'You are quite at liberty,' General Williams wrote, 'to tell Colonel Stracey that you signed the document under pressure, under promise of secrecy, and that you never for a moment ceased to deny the accusation.'[23]

Later, under oath, Lord Coventry was to insist that Gordon-Cumming had not been placed under any pressure to sign the document. What were General Williams's motives in giving the advice that he did to Sir William? Was he deliberately setting him up for a second fall; or had he, on both occasions, given advice that he thought to be in the best interests of his 'friend'? Throughout the affair, General Williams acted in such close concert with the Prince that doubt is cast on the purity of his motives in dealing with the baronet. It must be said in his defence, however, that he appears to have been convinced of Gordon-Cumming's guilt from the time of his first interview with Lycett Green. Whether or not he was too easily convinced of that guilt is another matter.

With the Guards Club's refusal to enquire into Sir William's conduct, the Prince appeared to be checked. There is, however, reason to think that he did not wholly abandon the idea of lessening the danger of his position that would result from a thorough exploration in court of the Tranby Croft episode. Indeed, it would have been astonishing had he done so, considering his vulnerability. While it is impossible to document exactly what moves were made by the Prince and his agents, the sudden breaking of a story in the *Daily News* and the *Echo* on March 17 killed what may have been a final behind-the-scenes attempt to limit the proceedings in the case and bring about a pre-arranged settlement.

On March 17 the *Daily News* and the *Echo* printed the following despatch from the Press Association: 'There is every reason to believe that the trial of the action instituted by Sir W. Gordon-Cumming in connection with the baccarat scandal will be a very short affair. The Plaintiff is determined to go into court, and will not hear of any retraction until his case is laid before a jury and he has, on oath, given an emphatic denial to the charges preferred against him. But, acting in consonance with the Royal personage who has been mentioned in connection with the matter, it is stated in well-informed circles that there will be no cross-examination and no attempt to prove the allegations; that an apology will be tendered, and the business of the jury will be to fix such damages as under the circumstances Sir William Gordon-Cumming may think fit to accept as compensation for the injury done to his character and reputation.'[24]

Messrs Lewis and Lewis, solicitors for Lycett Green and the other defendants, immediately took out an action against the Press Association and Mr Passmore Edwards, the proprietor of the *Echo*, charging them with contempt of court and with seriously damaging their clients' chances for a fair trial. Passmore Edwards immediately presented the court with an affidavit in which he assumed responsibility for what the *Echo* had printed; but Robbins, manager of the Press Association, denied his responsibility in the matter.

Both the *Daily News* and the *Echo* immediately printed retractions, acknowledging that they had been misinformed. The *Echo,* however, printed a leading article commenting on the press report, placed it directly under the release itself and followed both items with the printed retraction. Edwards stated in his affidavit that because of the way in which the type was set up, it was not practical to delete either the news release or the lead article.

The article expressed indignation over the fact that the case might not be actively prosecuted, insisting that justice demanded a vigorous examination of all aspects of the case and that the public had better know all the details of the scandal in order to prevent the assumption from growing that a greater evil had occurred at Tranby Croft than was actually the case. The writer also took the opportunity of pointing out the viciousness of gambling and the horrible example set by the Prince of Wales in having served as banker in an illegal game. 'The sense of justice is shocked,' the writer continued, 'when a couple of street urchins are sent to prison for playing pitch and toss, whose offence in its essence is in no wise distinguishable from that of peers and princes.'[25]

Edwards was also careful to point out in his affidavit that his newspaper used seventy or eighty articles a day from the Press Association and that he had 'hardly ever known instances where the information so supplied had been incorrect'. Edwards also, by reprinting the retraction in several subsequent issues of the paper, managed to repeat the essence of the original release and the original article, thereby guaranteeing the widest possible circulation of the release and the message contained in the *Echo*'s leader.

The Press Association reported to Lewis and Lewis that the information had been gathered in 'the usual way' from the Press Association's law correspondent and there had been no reason to doubt its authenticity. Lewis and Lewis retorted that it seemed odd to them that the Press Association or their correspondent had not taken the trouble to call either solicitors in the case in order to verify the truth of what had been alleged.

What had been the source of the story? No explanation was ever offered by the press correspondent, who was never identified but who sent his apologies by way of Robbins to Lewis and Lewis. He certainly did not invent the story. It is possible, of course, that the reporter had picked up irresponsible gossip in the courts and passed it along to his office; but such an answer seems inadequate. What is more likely, but still conjecture, is that the reporter had somehow got word of negotiations that were, in fact, going on between the Prince and the principals in the case.

It is an interesting coincidence that at almost the same time as the

'false' press release was published, another news report announced that
Arthur Wilson had been appointed High Sheriff of Yorkshire and that
he would soon be knighted. The *New York Times* took the cynical view
that Wilson's appointment and his anticipated knighthood were being
bestowed on him as a coat of whitewash to cover up the stains which he
had acquired as host at Tranby Croft when the cheating scandal
occurred.[26]

The *New York Times*'s explanation is not particularly convincing.
Neither the Prince nor the Queen had any reason to 'whitewash' Wilson,
particularly at that time. It was Wilson's family who had exposed
Gordon-Cumming and the royal family would not be anxious to draw
more attention to the affair by advancing Wilson unless some very real
advantage was to accrue to the Prince. The only such advantage would
have been a damping of the public outcry.

With the exception of Berkeley Levitt, the defendants in the case
were all members of the Wilson family. Levitt played throughout a very
reluctant role in the action taken against his superior officer. He
declined to report to the Prince specific instances of Gordon-Cumming's
cheating and refused to observe the baronet's play on the second night.
He also proved to be a very non-communicative witness at the trial.
In all probability he would have been happy not to press the issue,
although that is not to say that he would have been willing to be branded
a liar.

It is at least possible to suggest on the basis of the evidence that the
honours being bestowed on Arthur Wilson were an inducement to Mrs
Wilson and other members of the family to reach an agreement with
Gordon-Cumming in advance of the trial that would allow everyone
concerned to emerge from the case with his good name intact and at the
same time spare the Prince from public humiliation.

Whatever was, or was not, going on behind the scenes when the Press
Association release appeared, its publication ensured that the defendants would prepare themselves for a genuine fight. The news
release effectively destroyed the possibility that any of those involved
in the case would seek any solution other than the one offered by trial
before a jury. The power of the press, rightly or wrongly asserted in this
way, had been brought to bear on the case; and from March 17 onwards the Prince had no other course open to him but to prepare for his
ordeal and to hope that he could count on the Lord Chief Justice's
offering him the same degree of protection that he had enjoyed in the
Mordaunt trial. What he expected from the jury is suggested by comments in a letter to his sister, the Empress Frederick: 'The British Jury,'
he wrote, perhaps preparing himself for the worst, 'are composed of a
peculiar class of society, and do not shine in intelligence or refinement
of feeling.'[27]

It was not merely a desire for privacy or horror of being exposed as a gambler that had driven the Prince to such extreme efforts to prevent the Tranby Croft affair from becoming a *cause célèbre*. There was a powerful and expanding radical political movement, dating back at least to the '80s, making itself felt in England. The movement was hostile to the entire concept of monarchy, limited or otherwise; and the Queen and her son were right to fear that a scandal involving the Prince would strengthen the radicals. The evangelical section of the community would certainly be deeply offended by the Prince's behaviour, especially in view of the fact that in the recent past the Duke of Clarence's actions had been found reprehensible by a large segment of the public.

The note that was to be sounded by the Liberal and the Conservative as well as the radical press once the trial was launched was struck as early as February 8 by the *New York Times*. The harshness of the newspaper's comment is all the more striking when one recalls the enthusiastic reception the American press had given the Prince on his visit thirty years before. The lack of sympathy for the Prince and for his position is particularly marked.

The article takes as its point of departure the announcement in the London papers of Gordon-Cumming's suit against Green and the others. After describing the scandal as one of the 'vulgar and disreputable sort', the writer pauses briefly to attack the Queen for living the life of a recluse and hoarding the money she should be spending in the encouragement of trade, then focuses again on the Prince and asserts that the scandal would be likely to prove very injurious to the Prince because it would be 'fatal to his reputation for seriousness and solidity'. What he might have got away with as a young man, the writer concludes, was one thing, but he was now a man of fifty and had discredited himself by being found to be addicted to gambling in 'disreputable company'.[28]

'The English people have no wish for a repetition of the Court of George IV,' the *New York Times* continued, 'and such a story as this which has just been published, coming after the revelation of much darker scandals concerning the third generation of royalty, can hardly fail to have an important political effect. The Prince of Wales showed no appreciation of public opinion when he used his utmost exertions to prevent the exposure of the proceedings of a gambling party of which he was a member to the "comments of the Radical press".'[29]

With remarkable accuracy the paper had underlined precisely those aspects of the affair that the British press would take up in detail once the trial was under way. The Prince had cause enough for alarm when a foreign newspaper, addressing itself to a people that had on innumerable occasions expressed the warmest regard for the heir to the

British throne, could anticipate so exactly the republican sentiment which would be aroused by his exposure.

Perhaps generated by the gambling scandal, rumour to the effect that Edward was deeply in debt was general by the spring of 1891 and darkened the clouds gathering around the Prince. On May 10, *The Times* attacked him on the score of his indebtedness and was forced to print a retraction on the seventeenth. *St Stephen's Review, Vanity Fair, Truth* and *World* published similar accounts of his financial troubles and printed no retraction. People began to force themselves on the Prince in an attempt to loan him money. In Paris, when he was staying at the Hotel Bristol, he was so beset with money-lenders' agents that he was forced to complain to the English Ambassador, Lord Lyons. Lyons went to the Prefect of Police, who let it be known that anyone troubling the Prince in this fashion in the future would be arrested as a vagrant. The harassment ceased, but the conviction that the Prince was badly in need of money remained.

Conservative as well as radical opinion was against the Prince and made common cause in attacking him; criticism went far beyond simply blaming him for exposing himself to the humiliation of a public trial. One Conservative newspaper assailed him for his choice of friends: 'The Prince of Wales has been singularly unfortunate in his friends, and this the more strange as *his circle of intimate friendship is naturally exceptionally limited.* Two of these are in exile for cheating at cards, and a third is now charged with a similar offence. A fourth is in exile for a detestable charge [probably a reference to Valentine Baker] and it would be difficult to say how many have passed through the Bankruptcy Court. The annals of the Divorce Court, moreover, would furnish several accounts of misfortune having overtaken the male and female companions of His Royal Highness. . . .'[30]

The radical and dissenting press were more concerned with the Prince's attachment to gambling in general and the 'turf' in particular, with its attendant vices, than with his public embarrassment at being named in a lawsuit. 'Do you not know what goes on in Doncaster. . . during the great race-week in early September?' the Reverend W. Evans demanded, addressing himself directly to the Prince in the *General Baptist Magazine.* 'Importation of scores of prostitutes, immigration of scores of practical thieves, thimble-riggers, pick-pockets, gamblers, and cheats of every description, liquor shops open at night, houses of ill fame all open, drinking, cursing, swearing and fighting; in plain words, "Hell broke loose in the slums of Doncaster".'[31]

If such an outburst seems an exaggeration, even an absurdity, born in the over-heated imagination of one who has taken his moral line too seriously, it is only necessary to glance at Kellow Chesney's *The Victorian Underworld* to find that Evans's remarks probably paint the racing scene in something less than its true horror: 'It was just this mingling of the rich with the criminal classes that made racing so corrupt,' Chesney concludes. 'Race courses were often the scene of disorder, brutality and lewdness; yet, only a few feet away, ladies brought up to display on ordinary occasions an almost pathological delicacy sat in their carriages twirling their parasols and picnicking....'[32]

Later in his account of race meetings, Chesney describes the attack by a mob on a bookie who failed to meet his bets at Alexandra Park Court, Muswell Hill, in the late '6os. The unfortunate bet-maker was pulled down by the crowd, beaten, kicked, and had his clothes torn from his body; and although the police at last intervened and carried him under the grandstand, hid him in a hole, and took him home under the cover of darkness, he died within a few days from the mauling. No charges were brought against anyone, although the mounted policeman who rode between the fallen man and his attackers narrowly escaped being dragged down and beaten to death.

It was against this background of corruption and violence, well-known but seldom noted, that the Tranby Croft scandal must be placed in order to understand why it aroused such a storm of protest. That and the fact that the affair forced into public view other equally well-known but carefully veiled realities about life among certain elements of the upper class, particularly the Marlborough House set, which was, of course, made up of the Prince's special friends and acquaintances and was largely his own creation. These realities had to do with more than gambling and drinking; they involved as well the loose sexual life which characterized country house weekends.

Nothing sets the tone of how these parties were looked upon by the cognoscenti more accurately than a set of verses by Hilaire Belloc, written after Edward's coronation but capturing the spirit of the earlier period when he was still Prince of Wales. It should be noted that in the original both the house and Mrs X are named:

> Near XYZ in Sussex you may see
> A house of large dimensions on a slope,
> Diversified by many an ancient tree
> And spreading garden lawns of ample scope;
>
> And here it is that, when the Dryads ope
> Their first adventurous arms to catch the Spring,
> There comes a coronetted envelope;
> And Mrs X must entertain the King.
>
> The party will be large and very free
> And people will be given lots of rope.
> The Duke of Surrey, M.F.H., K.G.,
> Will bring a divorcee in heliotrope.

And Mr Hunt, who manufactures soap,
Will answer for Victoria, Lady Tring,
And Algernon will partner Mrs Scrope –
And Mrs X will entertain the King.

There will be bridge and booze till after three
And, after that, a lot of them will grope
Along the passages in *robes de nuit*
And dressing-gowns, in search of other dope.

And a trained nurse will be sent down to cope
With poor De Vere, who isn't quite the thing,
And give his wife the signal to elope –
And Mrs X will entertain the King.

  Envoi.
Prince! Father Vaughan will entertain the Pope
And you will entertain the Jews at Tring.
And I will entertain a pious hope,
And Mrs X will entertain the King.[33]

Such verses were the common fare of a London clubman's evening and provided him with much amusement. But this tolerant laughter was not shared by the great majority of the English citizenry, and what went on among the wealthy and worldly was, even if not known at first hand, generally deplored by all levels of society. The cartoons, for example, that appeared in such rich profusion at the time of the Tranby Croft scandal featured champagne bottles and women in exaggerated *décolletage*, as well as the Prince at cards. The gambling, the cheating, and the Prince's appearance in a court of law were only the tip of the iceberg. It was the way of life that lay below the surface and which had thrust the Tranby Croft affair into the gaze of the offended public that aroused the wrath of whole segments of English society.

There is solid evidence that what lay behind much of the anger expressed by the organs of middle-class opinion was a deeply felt resentment at having to take account of the Tranby Croft affair at all. The *National Observer*, touching on the baccarat case, first in March and then in June, ridiculed the evening papers for having set up such a 'hue and cry about baccarat' and referred to them as 'those geese which the British Public keeps for its delectation'.[34] It deplored the fuss made about gambling, calling it a fashion; and although the Prince was mildly chastised for his behaviour, hope was expressed that he would soon be in popular favour again because he was 'a person of remarkable discretion and ability throughout at least three hundred and sixty-four days per annum'.[35]

The tone of the piece changes significantly, however, when the

Wilsons come into the discussion. It was the Wilsons – mother, son and son-in-law – who initiated the actions that eventually led to the trial; and the hostility revealed towards them by the *National Observer* writer can best be accounted for by concluding that, like the unfortunate messenger who is executed for bringing bad news, they had sinned in exposing Gordon-Cumming: 'As to that singular collection of persons generally spoken of as the Wilsons, they have passed, we hope, from the pages of contemporary history as suddenly as they appeared upon it, and if they never re-emerge from their native obscurity no one will regret it. Themselves least of all, if their brief occupation of the thoughts and tongues of ladies and gentlemen has taught them anything of the feelings with which such persons as they, and such doings as theirs, are generally regarded.'[36]

Edward knew that whatever the outcome of the trial, he would emerge from it damaged in reputation and that the standing of the Crown might well be impaired. Throughout the spring his letters to and from the Queen reflect this concern. Writing to the Empress Frederick in early June, Victoria lamented, 'The Monarch almost is in danger if he is lowered and despised', and the Prince nearly worried himself into an illness, admitting to Prince George that the affair had caused him 'the most serious annoyance and vexation...'.[37]

The degree to which his nerves were being tested is revealed by his response to the Queen's expressed wish, in a letter written in the early spring, that he give up baccarat. In a sudden outburst of anger, he sent word to his mother that unless he had her promise that no mention of giving up baccarat would be made, he would cease to visit her at Windsor. She immediately capitulated, showing the good judgement that never fully deserted her; and the visits were resumed. It should be added that from the first moment the scandal became public, the Queen placed herself squarely in support of her son and worked quietly but vigorously to mute the bad effects of the exposure.

The Times reported regularly the pre-trial developments in the case; and on April 7 it noted that plans had been adopted to form a new courtroom in what had been previously used as an arbitration room in the Lord Chief Justice's court. Although the fact was never stated, the room was being put in readiness for the baccarat trial. It was to be equipped with a raised bench, a witness box, and chairs instead of the usual seats. The report closed with the observation that should the room prove 'suitable to the purpose' it would be retained as a permanent court.

Less than a week later *The Times* reported with carefully controlled excitement that the case was only 'nineteen down the list' and that a jury might be formed within a week; but hopes were dashed on April 20 when the paper reported flatly that the case would not be heard before the Trinity sittings, which were to begin on May 24. On May 13 it was announced that Lord Coleridge had set the date for the trial on June 1, and on the thirtieth readers were warned that spectators would be admitted only by ticket, that a number of visitors would be accommodated on the bench, that thirty seats had been reserved for the press, and that the remaining places would go to members of the bar, witnesses, and special guests.

It was the *Manchester Guardian,* however, that put the affair into its proper perspective: 'The hearing of Sir William Gordon-Cumming's action for libel against Mr Wilson and others will begin today in the Lord Chief Justice's Court. Everything is being done to make the affair a success. Special rows of seats for "distinguished visitors" have been provided; the Prince of Wales will be present; and "sensational disclosures" are confidently expected by society.'[38]

The disclosures appear, at this distance, to fall short of the sensational, but the very fact of the Prince of Wales being present in the court as a witness made the proceedings unique, even bizarre, and invested the trial with an atmosphere more appropriate to a race meeting than to a court of law. As Lord Coleridge was to point out in his summing up, the streets of London had throughout the period of the trial been thick with placards carrying the latest news releases of what was going on inside the courtroom. Interest in the case was intense and grew more pronounced as the hearings developed and one after another of the principals in the case took the stand.

Admission to the court was by ticket, and from the first day the room was crowded well in advance of the opening hour. Among those regularly present on the bench, in the galleries and in the well of the court were Lady Coleridge, Lady Clarke, Lady Esher, Lord Marcus Beresford, Colonel Hughes Hallett, and Lady Tenterden. The Prince attended the first six sessions but was not present for the Lord Chief Justice's summing up on June 9, the seventh and last day of the trial. His place was on the bench beside Lord Coleridge, where he was exposed to the curious stares of the thronging spectators, a large proportion of whom were women. His arrival each day was awaited with eager anticipation which reached a climax with the court's rising at the entrance of the Prince. It remained standing until he had taken his seat to the left of Lord Coleridge, whose wife, throughout the trial, occupied the seat to his right.

The attitude of the spectators in the opening hours of the trial was one of absorbed fascination. Gordon-Cumming was the first to be called to the stand, where he created a stir in the audience by deliberately turning his back on the Prince as he took his seat in the box and keeping that position throughout the delivery of his testimony. A buzz of hostile comment rose in the court when it became clear that the baronet was 'cutting' Edward, but the hostility towards Sir William quickly warmed into sympathy as he gave his testimony in a clear, steady voice that penetrated into every corner of the room, answering with calm assurance the questions put to him by Sir Charles Russell and repeating with absolute conviction that he was totally innocent of the charge of having cheated at baccarat.[39]

By Friday the sentiment of the spectators was not only solidly behind Sir William but had turned into open hostility towards the defendants. It would be difficult to understand on the basis of the testimony alone how such a climate of opinion could have been formed. One after another the witnesses took their place in the box and testified either to having seen Sir William cheat at the game played on the nights of September 8 and 9, or to having accepted without reservation the word of those who claimed to have seen him cheat.

The answer, in part, is that Sir Edward Clarke, with consummate skill, used every opportunity presented to him to make it appear that Gordon-Cumming was the victim firstly of a hasty and ill-founded accusation; secondly of a trap laid with malice aforethought; and thirdly, a devious plan constructed to preserve the Prince from exposure in a scandal. Clarke made his first move in response to Lord Coleridge's opening comments in the trial, which were directed to the Solicitor-General, calling his attention to the fact that the Prince of Wales was present and that 'it was desirable that His Highness should not be kept waiting any longer than necessary'.

Clarke recognized at once that the Chief Justice's remarks, which continued to reveal a judicial bias evident throughout the trial, were designed to place him at a disadvantage by making it appear that he was guilty of harassing the Prince and of seeking to cause him embarrassment. Clarke astutely turned the remarks to his advantage by saying that although he did not know at that time whether or not he would call the Prince, he certainly desired to serve the convenience of His Royal Highness and was anxious 'to make any arrangements with regard to his being called as would suit His Highness's convenience'. He simply carried Lord Coleridge's line of giving special consideration to the Prince so far that Coleridge was forced to say, somewhat testily, that the Prince was not there as a spectator but as a witness, summoned by both parties.[40] Clarke had made his point; or, rather, he had forced the Chief Justice into making it for him.

Gordon-Cumming's examination continued throughout Monday and into Tuesday. When he had stepped down from the witness box, Sir Edward called the Prince, who had been showing increasing signs of nervous stress throughout the morning. The examination lasted twenty minutes and neither Clarke nor Russell asked the Prince to testify to anything more than the facts of the case as they had been revealed. Despite the delicate treatment, Edward remained very tense, and not more than two or three of his answers were audible throughout the court.[41]

A curious thing occurred during his questioning, an occurrence which caused quiet amusement among the more sophisticated spectators but which was to have a powerful influence on the jury. One of the jury members rose during the Prince's testimony and asked, 'Did your Royal Highness observe anything in the plays of Sir William Gordon-Cumming on either of the nights that was suspicious?'

'No, I did not,' Edward replied. 'We were playing in a country house among friends. I was busy, acting as banker, and had no suspicion of such a thing.'

The man was still not satisfied, and he asked what the Prince's opinion was at the time as to the charge made against the plaintiff.

'The charges seemed so unanimous,' the Prince answered, 'that there was no course open but to believe them.'[42]

Whatever Edward's doubts about the intelligence of an English jury, he had, with that response, thrown his word behind the defendants and against Gordon-Cumming's sworn statement of his innocence. Added to Lord Coleridge's summing up, it was one of the most decisive pieces of testimony given in the trial; and however much the staunch juryman may have amused the spectators by presuming to question the Prince, he had asked the question and received the answer that all but assured the outcome of the trial. Sir Edward was never able to shake that testimony: 'The charges seemed so unanimous that there was no course open but to believe them.'

The court recessed for lunch at the conclusion of the Prince's examination, and Lord and Lady Coleridge entertained Edward and other distinguished guests at a lunch provided in one of the chambers. Edward lunched at least twice during that week with the Coleridges, making it difficult for the court to retain its spirit of disinterest, and increasing the holiday air of the proceedings. The *Manchester Guardian* opened its Friday account of the trial with the usual formula: 'The trial of the action brought by Sir William Gordon-Cumming was resumed yesterday in the Lord Chief Justice's Court...', though concluding the introduction with quiet malice 'in the presence of the usual carefully selected and fashionable audience. Many ladies were present, and some were busily engaged in sketching.'[43]

By the end of Friday, all the witnesses had been called. General Williams followed the Prince to the box; then Arthur Stanley Wilson, who reluctantly admitted under Clarke's probing that the counters used in the game belonged to the Prince; Berkeley Levitt; Lycett Green; Mrs Lycett Green; Mrs Wilson; and finally Lord Coventry. Sir Charles Russell began his closing statements for the defendants when Lord

Coventry stepped from the witness box, and he was followed by Sir
Edward Clarke on Monday.

Clarke created a sensation in the court by observing in the course of
his remarks that 'it would be impossible that anyone should be able to
remove the name of Sir William Gordon-Cumming from the army list,
and that the names of Field Marshal the Prince of Wales and General
Owen Williams should be allowed to remain'. When he spoke of
Williams's and Coventry's action as having stemmed from a desire to
spare the Prince from scandal, there was cheering in the court, quickly
suppressed.

When he came to deal with the Wilsons, he spoke with withering
scorn, observing that Mrs Wilson had so little understanding of what
was at stake in accusing Sir William of cheating that she was simply
prepared to 'forget it'. Arthur Wilson he dismissed as young, inexperienced and rash, prepared to see anything he wanted to see. He
described Lycett Green as a man of such little substance that he was, at
thirty years of age, content to be a Master of Hounds and to hunt four
times a week for his occupation, and to be so little in command of himself that when he supposed that he had seen Sir William cheating, he
could think of nothing better to do than to sit down and write his
mother-in-law a letter. As for Arthur Wilson, Senior, he 'seemed to
hold a sort of ornamental position in his own house, was carefully kept
in ignorance of the plot and plan that was going on to entrap one of his
own guests'.[44]

Recognizing the influence the Prince of Wales's answer to the member
of the jury was likely to have on the jury's thinking, Clarke attempted
to blunt the effect of that testimony. He said that he did not understand
how the Prince, Lord Coventry and General Williams could have believed the accusation on such flimsy evidence and that Williams and
Coventry had asked a comrade to sign such a paper as that document
could only be explained as a move on their part to save the Prince from
scandal.

Clarke had brought the court to a state of extreme tension with his
peroration, and when he closed with a plea that justice be done and
that the plaintiff be restored to rightful place among his comrades,
the court exploded in wild cheering. The ushers sought to quiet the
uproar and Lord Coleridge shouted, 'Silence! Silence! This is not a
theatre.'[45]

The Prince sat through the cheering, maintaining an appearance of
stoic calm; and when the court was adjourned for the day, he went out
of the room between the rows of now silent spectators without being
exposed to any expressions of hostility. But six days of sitting in court,
looking over or through the increasingly critical stares of the crowd
had been more than enough to endure. He did not attend the final

session on Tuesday, when Coleridge made his charge to the jury.

The summing up could be seen either as a masterpiece of juridical objectivity or as an equally masterful piece of jury tampering. In the course of the trial, Clarke had pointed out to the jury that there were many things beneath the surface in this trial, and he hoped that the jury would take note of those things. Against this, as a judge, Lord Coleridge warned the jury; they were there to determine whether or not Gordon-Cumming had cheated at cards. He most emphatically protested that 'they had nothing to do with things underneath the surface'. He then paused to attack the charge that General Williams and Lord Coventry had sought to shield the Prince at Sir William's expense. Constructing a counter charge, he told the jury that Williams and Coventry acted as they did in order to protect Gordon-Cumming fully as much as to protect the Prince.

'We must go and tell him [Sir William] this is a serious matter,' the Chief Justice said to the jury, presenting an imaginative re-creation of the scene between Williams and Coventry as they were making up their minds on a course of action after having talked to Green. 'We have come to the conclusion that he is guilty: we must judge of what defence he has to make, for we cannot – although we have a very strong impression against him – we cannot be certain what we have to do until we see him.'[46]

Of course, as the Chief Justice himself was to say later in his charge, they had already determined on a course of action, and this was to persuade him to sign the paper, by which action he would be confessing to having cheated. But the discrepancy between that decision and what Lord Coleridge told the jury was in the minds of Williams and Coventry escaped the Chief Justice, and he went on to cast the strongest doubt on Sir William's claim to innocence. He further dismissed as utterly unconvincing Clarke's suggestion that Gordon-Cumming had acted out of a willingness to spare the Prince from pain: 'Could they believe,' he asked, and the question was clearly rhetorical, 'a man perfectly innocent would allow himself to write down his name to a dishonouring document, to a document which said in effect that he had cheated and taken money out of the pocket of the Prince of Wales by a card sharping trick simply that the world might not know that the Prince of Wales had played baccarat at Tranby Croft for very modest stakes?'[47]

A remarkable feature of the case is that although much time was devoted to the question of why Sir William signed the document confirming his guilt, none was given to the question of why a man with an income of £80,000 a year and not in financial difficulty should set out to cheat his friends out of a few hundred pounds in a card game and thereby risk his honour and reputation. It was never then or later suggested that Gordon-Cumming was a habitual cheat. His name had never been attached to turf scandals or any other difficulties involving his honour. Apparently Lord Coleridge saw nothing puzzling about the lack of motive, however, and pressed the jury to decide for the Wilsons. He concluded his summation by saying that in passing their judgement on Sir William's honour he hoped 'they would not be unmindful of their own'.

The jury withdrew at 3.23 pm. and returned in twenty minutes with a verdict in favour of the defendants. The spectators had risen to their feet as the door behind the jury box opened and the twelve jurors filed into the court. At the announcement of the verdict there was a sudden outburst of such loud and sustained hissing that the ushers, calling for silence, could not put it down. Lord Coleridge looked up angrily, but concluding that he could do nothing to stop the outpouring of hostile feeling, bent his head over the formal document of judgement which he was engaged in writing.

Earlier that day, the Prince, who had abandoned the court for the opening day at Ascot, rode to the royal box through crowds which greeted his arrival with hisses and boos, but Lady Brooke was with him and she dined that night at Marlborough House, despite the fact that Alexandra had refused to meet her. The Prince appeared determined to defy someone. As for Gordon-Cumming, he walked out of the court-room a popular hero while the Wilsons had to be smuggled away from the court in secret for fear that they would be set on by the angry people who had gathered outside the court to await the verdict.

On the day after the trial, to the disgust of the Prince, who called it 'the crowning point of his infamy',[48] Gordon-Cumming married the American heiress Florence Garner of New York, at Holy Trinity Church, Chelsea, with Major Vesey Dawson of the Coldstream Guards as his best man. Miss Garner had an income of between 60,000 and 100,000 dollars a year. Added to Gordon-Cumming's £80,000 yearly income, this amount would be sufficient to ensure that the couple would not starve despite the fact that Sir William could no longer play baccarat. A small crowd gathered outside the church and greeted the couple with cheers when they emerged. A reporter in the crowd asked Sir William if he would comment on Sir Edward Clarke's remark that 'there were circumstances behind the case which had not come out'.

'My mouth is closed,' the baronet replied. 'I believe that most people hoped that I would win. Now that it is all over nothing I can say would do any good. I hope to visit America shortly.'[49]

Sir William and his bride left London for his country seat in Forres, Scotland, where he was received by the local population with enthusiastic warmth and good feeling. The town was dressed in bunting, and the Provost made a speech of welcome. But the damage to Gordon-Cumming's career was devastating. On the evening of June 12, under the date of June 10, the *Official Gazette* announced that the name of Sir William Gordon-Cumming had been removed from the list of officers in the army, 'as Her Majesty has no further occasion for his services'. Effectively cut off from society by the outcome of the trial and by the hostility of the Prince, Sir William and his wife lived at Altyre in an exile as profound as though they had been transported.

Edward, however, could not disappear, though there were times during and after the trial when he must have dearly wished to emulate Sir William and done so. The comments which he had been forced to listen to in court were probably less galling to his pride than the scolding note he had been sent by his nephew who told him his behaviour was unbecoming to a Prussian officer, and the criticism levelled at him from other quarters of Europe which he had always regarded as his special sanctuaries.

An article in *The Times* titled 'The Baccarat Case' and dated Vienna, July 10, is typical of the line taken in European capitals. Edward was a Colonel-Proprietor of an Austrian regiment, and Austrian and Hungarian officers had followed the trial with great interest, 'intensely curious to know,' the correspondent wrote, 'whether His Royal Highness's ideas of military duty tallied with those held in the Emperor of Austria's army'. It had become clear that they did not. Had he gambled with men of his own rank and age, there would have been no grounds for finding fault with his conduct; but that His Royal Highness should have sat down to gamble with young men, one of whom was a mere lieutenant in the army, was deplorable. 'It is simply unimaginable,' the writer continued, expressing the judgement of the Austrian military officers, 'that a German, Austrian or French Field-Marshal should sit down to win money from or lose money to a mere lieutenant, who, if he gambles, must be paying away his father's money or prematurely squandering his inheritance.'[50] The correspondent concluded his article with the observation that the opinions he had reported would soon be echoing over the whole Continent.

So profound was the effect of the disturbance that sober prediction on both sides of the Atlantic held that the English monarchy would not survive the death of the Queen. 'The scandal cannot fail to add,' a *New York Times* writer had stated as early as February, 'to the growing conviction that "royalty" is a burden to the British taxpayer for which he fails to receive any equivalent.' And a Wesleyan minister, preaching in Leeds at the time of the trial, warned that while 'we are glad to be loyal to the throne and to the Prince...we have a right to demand that the future King of England shall set an upright example, and obey those laws which he expects his subjects to respect.'[51] Even more direct were the comments recorded by the editor of the *Review of Reviews*, who, testing the opinions of country gentlemen of his acquaintance, found

THE GREAT CARD SCANDAL.
THE QUEEN OF HEARTS GIVES THE JACK OF CLUBS "WHAT FOR."

[See Cartoon Verses, p. 86.

4. 'The Great Card Scandal': from *Fun*, February 1891
By permission of the British Museum

From the Pall Mall Budget.] [June 11, 1891.
THE PRINCE: "Ah! well, I must give up baccarat and take to
cribbage with Mamma."

From the Pall Mall Budget.] [June 18, 1891.
KING HENRY IV. ACT II. SCENE IV.
PRINCE HENRY (P. of W.). POINS (Sir Francis Knollys).
" By heaven, Poins, I feel me much to blame,
So idly to profane the precious time;
Give me my sword and cloak: Falstaff, good night."

From the Australian Boomerang]

Says Her Gracious 'o her graceless Son and
He'r, " This is flat!
Just this once I'll help to make your banker
square ; Mind you that !
If you promise me as follers—
To provide for ' Cuffs and Collars,'
And to plank none of the dollars
On baccarat.'

Oh, Theosophy is looming
On its way,
And the Brotherhood is booming
Every day
With its wonders Oriental—
Psychic, hypnotic and mental,
Mystic things experimental—
So they say.

[May 16, 1891.
Holy Moses! says the Hebrew to the bear,
Have a care !
Your growling cheek's enough to make me
swear,
I declare !
Asking me to lend you roubles,
Or to blow you golden bubbles,
While you cause the Jews such troubles
And despair !

15. Cartoons from the *Pall Mall Budget* and the *Australian Boomerang*, May and June 1891
By permission of the British Museum

them unanimous in their certainty that the Prince would never rule over them, that he was a wastrel, a gambler, and a whoremonger. Having asked for proof, the editor was told that 'it was not merely bacarrat...but the kind of life of which this was an illustration that was the cause of their disgust'.[52]

The Queen, upset as she was by the criticism being directed against the Prince and the monarchy, cast about for some way of coming to her son's aid. Finding none, she appealed to E. W. Benson, the Archbishop of Canterbury, for advice; after reflection Benson suggested an open letter in which the Prince condemned gambling. Victoria despatched Lord Cadogan to Marlborough House to ask the Prince to write such a letter to the Archbishop with a view to its being published in *The Times*. Lord Cadogan must have told Edward that the Queen's plan had received the strong support of the leader of the opposition, William Gladstone.

The Prince listened to what Lord Cadogan had to say and then said that he would not write such a letter. Sir Philip Magnus attributes the Prince's refusal to an unwillingness to be cast in the role of hypocrite. There is undoubtedly much truth in what Magnus suggests; but since the Prince was to have a free hand in defining gambling before denouncing it, there was no necessity to appear as such. It seems more likely that the Prince felt that he had demonstrated sufficient humility in putting up with the embarrassment of the trial. He had already expressed his resentment to Lord Salisbury that the government had not prevented things injurious to himself from being brought out in the trial, and he was particularly angry that Clarke had not been muzzled.[53]

He disliked intensely interference in his private life. He had not been willing to give up baccarat when the scandal had become public, even though his mother had appealed to him to do so. Now he was not in any mood to write anything that could be construed as a public apology for his personal conduct. The government had already carried his apology to the Commons for failing, as an officer in the army, to report Gordon-Cumming's cheating to his superior officer. The Secretary for War, Edward Stanhope, speaking on behalf of the Prince, admitted that an error had been made and regretted that error. Great as Edward's appetite was, he had little stomach for humble pie; and he had eaten his fill of it and more during the past weeks.

Despite the support he received from Lord Salisbury, who felt that such a letter would be an expression of weakness and a poor precedent, the cumulative pressure to take some action to stem the flood of public criticism forced him to open a dialogue with the Archbishop on the subject of an open letter. Such a letter was finally composed. Addressing himself to the Archbishop, the Prince deplored the trial, criticized the press for having attacked him unjustly, 'knowing that I was defenceless', and expressed resentment that he had been subjected to public abuse by 'the Low Church and, especially, the Nonconformists...I have a horror of gambling,' he continued, 'and should always do my utmost to discourage others who have an inclination for it, as I consider gambling, like intemperance, one of the greatest curses that a country can be afflicted with.'[54]

He added that he saw nothing wrong with horse racing and that people who gambled would gamble on anything. The letter did nothing to reinstate the Prince in the eyes of his subjects and could scarcely have been taken as sincere by anyone who knew the least thing about the Prince. Philippe Jullian described it as being a first class example of the homage which vice renders unto virtue.[55] Perhaps he is right, but the hyprocrisy was not Edward's alone. It was shared by many of his countrymen, and not least by those of the middle class who had raised their hands in pious horror at what they so frequently practised in private and condemned in their Prince when it was made public.

Of all the attempts to reconcile the Prince's behaviour with God's will, none is more astonishing than the lead article, 'The Prince of Wales', which appeared in the July issue of the *Review of Reviews*. Written by the journal's editor, William Thomas Stead, the essay opens with the prayer from the Book of Common Prayer, asking for special blessing for the Prince and the rest of the royal family. By ingenious reckoning Stead calculated that the prayer had been repeated a thousand million times since the birth of the Prince. As a demonstration of the efficacy of prayer, Stead points out, it amounts to a 'dramatic fiasco', because in answer to all those prayers, which may not have been repeated with 'passionate fervour, but with a conscious desire, more or less tepid, that their humble beseechings on behalf of the Prince may be heard at the Throne of Grace', the nation had been presented with the Baccarat scandal.

Although, in Stead's words, 'all the prayers of the Church for fifty years had been but as the whirling of prayer wheels innumerable in pious Tibet', he placed the blame for the Prince's trouble on the nation: 'Even the most fervid Christian has come to recognize that if you allow a girlchild to be reared in a haunt of vice, and suckled on gin, you have no more right to expect a miracle to be wrought in response to your prayer that the girl might grow up a vestal virgin, than you have to expect Snowdon to be cast into St George's channel.'[56] It would have come as a surprise to the Prince Consort to learn that he had raised his eldest son in a 'haunt of vice', but what Stead meant was that the life the Prince had been forced to live encouraged him in his endless search for diversion.

'If the Prince of Wales had been saddled with his father's duties,' Stead speculates, 'he might have developed somewhat more of his father's virtues.'[57] Others were equally inclined to find excuse for Edward's behaviour. 'The English have no right to get indignant with their Heir-apparent,' *Figaro* insisted. 'If they want princes to be prepared to act as kings, they must not keep them entirely out of the domain of politics.... Prince! He is so little of a prince, the Prince of Wales.'[58] The *Independent* of New York took the same line, pointing out that while Frederick of Germany as Crown Prince was kept full of care and responsibility Edward had little to do: 'The Prince of Wales is past fifty, and has not yet had responsibility enough to have ceased to be frivolous. The whole system is bad.'[59]

Such tolerance, however, was rare among the comments. Much more characteristic of the collective response, in fact almost a précis of it, is the resolution passed by the Methodist New Connection Conference, which met in June at Leeds. It speaks for a far wider group of Englishmen than could be counted among its membership: 'The Conference feels bound to express its deep sorrow at the recent revelations in a court of law, of gambling and cheating in gambling, by those who occupy high positions in society, and from whom, therefore, a high example of virtue should proceed. But it is most concerned that His Royal Highness the Prince of Wales should have been so prominently and intimately involved in these disreputable proceedings. The Conference feels that such encouragement of vice and immorality by one from whom the nation has a right to expect impulse and encouragement to its higher life is fraught with great danger to its future well-being. It earnestly hopes that all such practices by one who aspires to be King of a Christian people will henceforth cease.'[60]

In its final issue of 1891, *Punch* ran a cartoon showing the Prince of Wales, Falstaff and Mr Punch meeting in 'A Room in the Boar's Head Tavern, Eastcheap'. The three speak of how times and the customs of princes have changed and of how serious and regular the life of Edward is in comparison with that led by Prince Hal. Falstaff agrees but soon slips into calling Edward Hal, and Mr Punch suggests that the Prince requires diversions. The Prince himself says that fifty years of laying foundation stones and attending 'ceremonials' has wearied him. Falstaff sympathizes, toasts the Prince, calling him 'most Royal imp of fame', as well as 'sweet boy' and 'my King'. Punch seconds; the scene closes. Friendly as it is, *Punch* ushers out 1891 with Edward in the company of Sir John Falstaff, a pairing with which few Englishmen at that time would have found serious fault.

A Brush with Death

Adversity is not without comfort and hopes.
Francis Bacon

While the Baccarat scandal was slowly and painfully unravelling before
a shocked public, another and potentially more dangerous scandal was
threatening to break over Edward and engulf him. At its centre was the
ludicrous, laughable and yet intensely acted drama of a letter and love
gone wrong. One of Edward's oldest and closest friends, Charles
Beresford, was a principal in the action, as were Beresford's wife and
his mistress, Lady Brooke. In its beginnings Edward had nothing to do
with the absurd affair; but before it was over, he had been pushed down
onto a sofa, challenged to a duel, forced to write a letter of apology, had
lost a friend and gained a mistress. It was an imbroglio more suited to
comic opera than real life; but its absurdities in no way mitigated the
danger it carried for Edward, whose character was already partially
blackened by the Tranby Croft scandal.

Charles Beresford and Lady Brooke had been lovers for several years;
they had been conducting their affair, if not quite secretly, then with as
much discretion as was needed under the circumstances, when quite
unexpectedly Mina Beresford, Sir Charles's wife, became pregnant.
There was no question as to who the father was; it was Sir Charles.
On hearing the news, Lady Brooke flew into a rage, denounced Beresford as an unfaithful wretch and threatened vengeance.[1] It was bad
enough that she made this display in a flood of tears at a party and in
front of her guests, but little real harm would have resulted had she left
matters there. Unfortunately, she sat down and wrote Charles an
hysterical letter in which she told him, among other things, that he
had no right to sleep with his wife.

Had she stopped to think, Lady Brooke would have remembered that
Beresford was away at sea; but she was in no condition to think, and the
letter was sent. In her husband's absence Mina opened the letter. Now
it was her turn to be enraged. After giving the letter to her solicitor,

George Lewis, to keep as evidence, she wrote to Lord Salisbury, the Prime Minister, telling him what Lady Brooke had written. In the meantime Lewis notified Lady Brooke that he had her letter in his possession and was waiting further instructions from Mina Beresford.

Sufficient time had now elapsed for Lady Brooke to have regained some of her common sense and to realize that she should get that letter back and destroy it. But how? She had almost despaired of recovering it when, as a last hope, she thought of Edward and went to ask him for help. He should have expressed his sympathy and his regrets and shown her the door. Instead he found himself looking at this beautiful woman and, finding her very desirable, he made up his mind, foolishly perhaps, to help her. Although it was after midnight, he immediately set out for Lewis's house and asked the solicitor to show him the letter.[2] Edward read it and departed. Then he went to Lady Beresford's and asked her to give the letter back to the Countess. She refused. He called a second time and once more she refused. Edward now made a serious mistake. He intimated to her that if she persisted, he would no longer make her welcome at Marlborough House. She did not surrender. Instead, she wrote again to Salisbury, describing Edward's visit and suggesting that Edward had fallen under Lady Brooke's spell. She was certainly right about that.

Lady Brooke began to appear everywhere with Edward; and whenever he was invited to a weekend party, Lord and Lady Brooke were also invited. Mina Beresford bore her child, a girl, but was not placated by the event and bombarded her husband with demands that he do something to vindicate her. Meanwhile, Edward had kept his promise. Lady Beresford was no longer being invited to the gatherings of the Marlborough group. Charles's sister, waging her own war, published anonymously a pamphlet titled *Lady River,* in which the offending letter was reproduced in full.[3] Society was enjoying a good laugh, but Charles Beresford, back on land, was not.

Thoroughly irritated by his wife's importuning and resentful of Edward's role throughout the affair, he threatened to go to the press with tales about Edward unless a letter of apology was written to his wife and she was reinstated in society. On one occasion he actually met Edward, apparently in Lady Brooke's rooms, where something close to a physical struggle occurred. Either Beresford doubled his fist preparatory to striking Edward and was stopped at the last moment by Edward's command, 'Do not strike me'; or he pushed Edward backward onto a sofa. At last, to protect himself against public exposure, Edward wrote Lady Beresford an apology, assuring her he never intended to cause her any inconvenience. On March 24 1892, the letter was returned to Lady Brooke; and Edward could give his undivided attention to the beautiful woman who had now taken Lillie Langtry's place in his affections. He had, however, lost the friendship of Charles Beresford; and they remained estranged until the end of their lives.

The strain on Edward and on the Princess throughout the summer of 1891 had been extreme, creating in the Prince's family what E. F. Benson described as 'domestic tension'. Alexandra had accepted her husband's liaison with Lillie Langtry, countenancing it to the extent of making Mrs Langtry a frequent guest at Marlborough House and Sandringham. Alix was not prepared to extend the same civilities to Lady Brooke, although when it looked as though the Beresford scandal would become public property and Mina Beresford was demanding Lady Brooke's expulsion from society, Alexandra made a point of being seen in the Countess's company. Nevertheless, with the end of the season, Alix took her two daughters and left for Denmark on an extended visit, going on from there to the Crimea with plans for spending the winter with her sister Dagmar, the Tzarina.[4]

Edward also left England, going to Hungary for a lengthy stay with Baron Maurice Hirsch, the Jewish millionaire who had recently become friends with the Prince. For several weeks Hirsch gave Edward some excellent shooting and proved to be a most amiable host. The superb shooting must have given Edward some much-needed release from tension. In one week he and the other guns killed 11,000 partridges.[5] Following the visit, Edward returned to Sandringham to prepare for his fiftieth birthday celebration on November 11, an event from which his wife was conspicuously absent. During the festivities, Prince George sickened; and the doctors were soon able to diagnose typhoid infection. By now the disease might well have been called the royal disease. Certainly most of Edward's family were infected by it at one time or another. The Queen had it at the age of sixteen; the Prince Consort died of it; Edward stood on the threshold of death struggling with it. The Duke of Edinburgh and Prince Albert Victor survived it; while another of the Queen's grandsons, Prince Christian Victor, perished from it. Fortunately, George quickly threw off the illness and was soon quite recovered.

At the first news of George's illness, Alexandra hurried home, putting aside, at least temporarily, whatever quarrels she still had with her husband. With George recovering and amity restored between them, the Prince and the Princess turned their attention to their other son, Albert Victor, whose behaviour in the company of his fellow officers was so debauched that he was in grave danger of being brought up on a criminal charge. He had, on a recent occasion, been discovered during a police raid in a house of prostitution catering to male homosexuals. As Philippe Jullian points out in his description of the affair, Lord Castlereagh, who, seventy years earlier, had been found in a similar establishment, committed suicide in order to escape the consequences of his discovery.[6] Eddy showed no inclination to kill himself, at least not at once and certainly not out of remorse. The young man's reputation had become so evil that it was whispered he was Jack the Ripper, a charge that has been made and remade over the last three-quarters of a century without having been proved or disproved. To this day it remains an ugly and persistent rumour.

Edward determined that some decisive action would have to be taken on his son's behalf, since Eddy was incapable of taking any but the most depraved himself. It was determined that he must marry; and because of constitutional bars he could not marry the girl he loved, the Catholic Princess Helene de Orléans, who, astonishingly, seems to have genuinely loved him. It was decided that he should marry Princess May of Teck. He proposed and was accepted on December 3 1891. 'I am quite proud,' Edward announced at the Civil Service dinner, at which he was an honoured guest shortly after the announcement of the engagement, 'to think that my son marries one who was born in this country, has been educated in this country, and has the feelings of an Englishwoman.' The match looked ideal. May was sensible, intelligent and steady. She was, in short, expected to provide her husband with all those qualities which he so conspicuously lacked. *Punch* published a half comic, half serious cartoon of the two young lovers with hands entwined, giving it the caption 'England, Home and Beauty!'

The Duke of Clarence was twenty-eight; his bride-to-be, four years younger. Whether the Princess May had a full understanding or knowledge of the character of the man she was to marry is not known. What does seem certain is that she was travelling along a tragic course, matched to a libertine who lacked intelligence and judgement. The *Punch* poet wrote,

> An English bridal it will be
> When March brings round the spring time,
> And English hearts will hail with glee
> The coming of the ring-time.[7]

Fortunately for May, she was never called upon to honour her agreement. The Duke of Clarence had returned from his most recent cruise looking ill and worn down in general health. His dissipations were undermining his constitution. On January 8 1892, he was attacked by a new virus infection called the Russian Flu, which made rapid and alarming inroads in the Prince's resistance. Pneumonia developed, and on January 14 he died. His death was a terrible personal loss to his immediate family, but for the nation it was a deliverance. Prince George became engaged to May in the spring of 1893 and they were married in the summer of the same year.

The Duke of Clarence's death was a severe blow to Edward, who, whatever his other failings, sincerely loved his children. Coming as it did on the heels of two long-drawn-out and debilitating imbroglios, the Bacarrat scandal and the Beresford affair, Albert Victor's dying temporarily diminished that great energy that had for so long characterized Edward's bearing. There were an increasing number of comments from those who saw the Prince regularly to the effect that he seemed to be losing his 'grip' and demonstrating a lack of interest in those formal ceremonies that had previously engaged his close attention. One writer saw this as one more example of the fin-de-siècle *ennui* and as evidence that Edward's extended apprenticeship was sapping his vitality.[8] But he seems in fact to have been partially stunned by events, and required only time to work his way back to his original vigorous response to life.

Following his accession, observers were often surprised by Edward's forcefulness. They should not have been. He ruled vigorously whatever domain was his to command. When he was limited to setting men's fashions and presiding over the social scene, he made it his business to be a master of style, an expert in the protocol of wearing orders and an accomplished host. In his role as diplomat he showed an astonishingly detailed knowledge of the ruling families of Europe, their interrelationships and their ambitions. After he became king, his obsession with detail proved a hindrance to the efficient handling of routine business; but it was also an important ingredient in his success in bringing about the Entente Cordiale and, later, reform of the armed services.

Following George's illness and Albert Victor's death, there were no further rumours of trouble between the Prince and the Princess. They made their peace with one another and abided by it. Lady Brooke was still in the ascendant, but her impetuosity was controlled by Edward's presence. There were to be no more stormy scenes in public of the sort that had launched the Beresford scandal. As a further check on her ebullience, Lady Brooke had in the early years of the '90s developed a deep and genuine interest in politics. She became a convert to socialism, an ideology intolerable to Edward. In addition, he thought it unsuitable that women should take part in the rough and tumble of politics. As a consequence of these feelings, he gradually found Lady Brooke less satisfactory as a companion, although he never lost interest in her. She was, despite all these complications for him, one of the most beautiful and fascinating women of her age.

Another less intimate but oddly interesting relationship that Edward enjoyed for several years in the '90s was that with Oscar Wilde, whose 'fall' in 1895 resounded all over the western world. Edward had frequently visited Wilde, was amused by him as a casual companion and thoroughly enjoyed his plays. When *An Ideal Husband* opened at the Haymarket on January 3 1895, Edward watched from a box and was delighted with the performance. He congratulated Wilde on his triumph and advised him not to change a word of the play.[9] Edward had met Wilde in 1892 in Hamburg, where Wilde was recovering from his unsuccessful struggle with the Lord Chamberlain over *Salomé*, in which Sarah Bernhardt was to have appeared in the Palace Theatre opening. The licence had been denied on the grounds that the play dealt with religious subjects.[10] In fact, the play was repressed for quite other reasons – its salaciousness and its thinly-veiled exploitation of sadism and perhaps even necrophilia. Wilde had threatened to leave England, and *Punch* caricatured Wilde in the dress of a French legionnaire.[11] Although Edward openly sympathized with Wilde, he completely escaped any taint from knowing the notorious green carnation.

Edward also knew Alfred Douglas, Wilde's beloved but vicious 'Bosie', who finally compassed his friend's destruction by persuading him to bring the legal action against Lord Queensberry which resulted in 1895 in Wilde's conviction and imprisonment. While Douglas was a child visiting his grandfather in Hamburg, the Prince had often come to dine informally with the family. Years later, when he had become king, Edward had occasion to express his great displeasure with Alfred Douglas's actions. Douglas had eloped with Olive Custance, following that young lady's official engagement to George Montagu, son of one of Edward's friends. The King had congratulated Olive's mother in writing on her daughter's engagement, and Douglas's intervention made Edward furious.[12] How much lingering dislike for Douglas may have remained with Edward from the Wilde affair is not known. As he grew older, he developed an increasing horror of public actions which breached the walls of convention. He may simply have been objecting to the impropriety of the elopement.

The Prince's inner circle of acquaintances became more narrow and more fixed during the '90s, while his tendency to gather around him men of wealth became more pronounced. He introduced into society such diamond and gold millionaires as W. W. Astor, Colonel John North and J. B. Robinson. Speaking of Edward as king, Philippe Jullian described him as 'the incarnation not only of monarchy but also of capitalism'.[13] The designation is accurate. Edward considered wealth to be an important gauge of social acceptability. However much his attitude scandalized the more conservative elements of the aristocracy, his decisions were binding. If he chose to introduce Baron Hirsch and Ernest Cassell, both rich men who had acquired wealth rapidly, as he did, into the circle of his intimates, they had to be accepted. In the '90s, no social barrier put up against his will could stand. He might allow a hostess to refuse to entertain one of his new millionaire friends on the grounds that she did not know him; but he would not tolerate her refusing an introduction. If she did, she suffered social death. And Edward had his way.

His favourites were now quieter men than those he had chosen in earlier years: Ernest Cassell, who looked so much like Edward that the resemblance excited comment; the Marquis de Soveral, Portuguese Ambassador; Alexandra's brother, the King of Greece; and his father-in-law, the King of Denmark.[14] In 1894 a debauched peer, the fourth Marquess of Ailesbury, died at the age of thirty, having burned out his life drinking, gambling and whoring. Lord Rosebery said of him that 'his mind was a dunghill, of which his tongue was the cock'.[15] In 1882 he would certainly have been in Edward's circle. In 1892 he was not connected with Edward or his set. Discretion was settling, like a mantle or a pall, over Edward's actions. He wanted no repetitions of Tranby Croft.

In any case he was being kept increasingly busy by matters of state. His brother-in-law, Alexander III, was taken fatally ill in October 1894, while in Livadia in the Crimea; and Lord Rosebery, sensing a marvellous opportunity to bring England and Russia together, asked Edward if he would undertake to represent the nation's interests in Russia by cultivating the new young Czar, Nicholas II. Edward accepted the challenge at once. Nicholas was engaged to Princess Alix of Hesse, Edward's niece; and the couple had recently been guests of the Queen and the Prince at Balmoral and at Sandringham. Edward liked the young man and his fiancée without seeing much strength in the Czarevitch. Nicholas's simplicity, which was genuine, had captivated the Queen; but Edward distrusted it, and time proved him right. The stupendous funeral observances at St Petersburg were long and involved, even barbaric by some standards. The corpse was decaying; and in the final ceremonies all the participants in the funeral had to pass by the coffin and kiss the dead man on the mouth, an ordeal through which Edward passed safely if uncomfortably.[16]

Edward remained a month in Russia, trying his best to win the confidence of his nephew Nicholas. The mourning for Alexander had to be interrupted for a week to celebrate the marriage of Nicholas and Alix – Russian Church law prohibited marriage in the period between Christmas and Easter. The mourning period was then re-imposed. Edward bore for a month the heavy burden of being his nephew's constant attendant, striving to make the young man see the advantages of a close and friendly relationship with England. The British Government considered Edward's efforts to have been of the greatest use, but the Prince was less certain. He did not feel that his nephew was made of solid stuff. He doubted especially Nicholas's rambling incoherencies about universal disarmament. 'It is the greatest rubbish and nonsense I ever heard of ...' he wrote to Lady Brooke. Although Nicholas initiated the first world disarmament conference, which met in 1899 under the title of the First Hague Peace Conference, and sought to establish world peace by advancing international law, neither Edward nor any other world leader took his efforts seriously. His vacillations and incompetence in foreign affairs led in 1905 to a disastrous war with Japan, which nearly toppled him from the throne. At home his inability to deal with political realities produced a resurgence of revolutionary activity.

Edward's other imperial nephew, William II, was furious with Edward over the Russian visit. His uncle's efforts to win favour with Nicholas only confirmed the already half-mad William in his conviction that Edward was the British agent of a master plan to isolate Germany in Europe and rob his nation of its proper place as master of that continent.[17] William had an unreasonable distrust of Edward not unlike the dislike he felt towards his own mother. Strangely enough, he revered his grandmother, Victoria; and it often fell to her to deal with her grandson when no one else could make him see sense. She knew his weaknesses, never lost her temper with him and never indulged him, as others did, in his wilfulness. In return he adored her.

One of the imponderables of history is the degree to which the mutual antipathy Edward and William felt for one another contributed to the outbreak of war between their countries in 1914. William was jealous of his uncle's ability to win the liking and respect of people; and he envied the Prince of Wales's skill as an ambassador. He also wanted a close link between Germany and England and thought, mistakenly, he could best achieve this by trying to undo all the work Edward had carried out with the French and Russian Governments. Following Edward's visit to Russia, William wrote letters to Nicholas containing the most ridiculously false charges about England's intentions to betray Russia. When the calumnies became too excessive, Victoria wrote him a scolding letter in which she expressed the conviction that William had *not* meant the things he seemed to have said and that he must be very careful not to create false impressions. Such corrections always left William full of contrition, which he invariably expressed in long, jumbled letters to his grandmother. Edward fumed, but left the problem of dealing with the difficult young man to his mother.

In the early '90s William began visiting Cowes each year for the Regatta. Edward had to entertain the young Emperor and found it a burdensome task. William was there for the purpose of creating goodwill between his country and England, and by and large the English press was willing to accept his presence in that spirit; but it was less easy for Edward and the government to see the visits in this light. William offended his hosts by insisting on his own and Germany's importance, taking too serious an interest in winning the races, which he finally did with his huge yacht *Meteor II,* whose performance so outstripped the smaller *Britannia*'s that Edward's joy in yachting was temporarily dissipated. William's determination not to be outdone had that effect on many of those who had to deal personally with him.

In the summer of 1895 William came to Cowes' Regatta in a more than ordinarily bellicose mood. Edward's Russian visit was still a fresh memory; and to compensate for his sense of having been somehow slighted, he arrived with two of his newest and fastest warships, the *Worth* and the *Weissenburg*, as escorts. In addition, on the afternoon of August 4, the day of his arrival, five German battleships and a cruiser steamed past Spithead and fired a salute of twenty-one guns, returned first by the garrison battery, then the port and, finally, by the flagship of the Naval Commander-in-Chief. The social occasion had been suddenly converted into a state occasion.[18] Edward was irritated by the grand manner his nephew was displaying, and worse was to come.

The *Worth* had been named in honour of a German victory in the Franco-Prussian war; and in a surprise visit to the battleship, William noted that it was the twenty-fifth anniversary of that proud occasion. In the speech he made to the assembled crew, he called their attention to the great military heritage that was in their keeping and expressed the hope that they would serve their land bravely and 'fight with heart and courage for God and Fatherland'.[19] The sabre-rattling speech, delivered aboard a German warship anchored in English waters, was a serious breach of diplomatic decorum, causing the British Government embarrassment because of the insult to French sensibilities. Edward was thoroughly disgusted, but the damage was done.

To add to the general unpleasantness, William invited Lord Salisbury to come aboard the *Hohenzollern* to talk about the Turkish question. Such an invitation was, of course, in the nature of a command. Salisbury, grown old in service and cynical almost to bitterness, arrived at the imperial yacht an hour late, making it clear that he was not very much disturbed by his failure in punctuality. William was coldly, smilingly furious; but he invited Salisbury to return the following day for more talks, having spent much of the time being icily jocular about tardiness. Reportedly, Lord Salisbury misunderstood what the Kaiser had said about the following day; as a consequence, he did not come at all. William was thrown into another rage.[20]

Throughout William's visit, the English press played down the political significance of the Kaiser's presence at Cowes. The *News of the World* wrote, 'There is no political meaning in the visit, as some would have us believe, and the Kaiser is just now probably far more interested in the pleasant social life of Cowes in the regatta week than in any great international questions.'[21] The German press, on the other hand, was in fighting mood throughout William's visit. It gave dramatic coverage to his *Worth* speech, stressing the personal rule of the Kaiser and warning England of the necessity of entering into a binding alliance with Germany.

Underlying the public discussion of the Anglo-German relationship was the issue of colonialism, particularly the two countries' expansionist aims in Africa. In a very long editorial, the *Standard* dealt frankly with the African problem, summing up the government's position by saying, 'English administrators have always held that Africa is large enough to give free scope to the civilizing energies of all comers.'[22] Everyone was being conciliatory towards William, but the effort was lost. Deeply offended by Salisbury's failure to appear for their proposed second meeting, the Kaiser returned to Germany with his ironclads to announce that his attempts to establish friendly relations between his country and England had failed because of English jealousy and suspicion.[23] Would the result have been different had Edward and William liked one another? Perhaps not; but Edward was unable to commit himself to establishing close, friendly ties with Germany chiefly because of his strong distaste for his nephew. How personal William's animosity was is difficult to measure. Following the 1895 regatta, he had the huge *Meteor II* built, returning with the yacht the following year to beat the *Britannia* and to crow over his victory. In 1897 Edward stopped racing.

If Edward failed to achieve a satisfactory understanding between the British and German Governments, he exerted a thoroughly beneficial influence on the bizarre events surrounding the Venezuelan boundary disputes, which in December of 1895 threatened to precipitate an armed confrontation between England and the United States. The source of the trouble was the discovery of gold in the vast jungles that formed a vague boundary between Venezuela and British Guiana. As a result of the discoveries, both countries had claimed the entire gold country, but in 1887 England had refused to submit the dispute to arbitration and Venezuela broke off diplomatic relations with England. There the matter rested for eight years until President Cleveland, with the support of American imperialists, saw a threat to the Monroe Doctrine in Britain's claims against Venezuela.

Richard Osley, the American Secretary of State, sent a strongly worded telegram to the British Prime Minister, informing Salisbury that 'the United States is practically sovereign on this continent' and that it would get what it wanted. Salisbury waited four months to reply, a reply which coldly corrected the Secretary of State's impression that the dispute involved the Monroe Doctrine in any way. Cleveland then sent a message to Congress, saying that the United States should locate the boundary and then enforce it. Such a message was tantamount to threatening war and was met with general support in the country. The farce was rapidly becoming dangerous.

Edward considered the United States to have a special relationship with England and refused to believe that a dispute over a boundary lost in the steaming Central American jungles could seriously mar the friendship of the two nations. Most of the English press began by sharing his view, dismissing the excitement by saying that the President's message to Congress was an election-year gimmick. By December 19, however, the *Pall Mall Gazette* reported that a genuine war fever was sweeping the United States and was astonished and dismayed by the support Cleveland was receiving. *The Times* warned that both political parties would support the President if the crisis deepened.

Although by the twentieth both countries were beginning to have second thoughts about the extreme positions they had taken, something was needed to restore a proper perspective and reaffirm the fundamental good feeling existing between the two nations. Edward recognized an opportunity and seized it. Joseph Pulitzer, owner of the *New York World,* asked Edward to state his views on the dispute. Without heeding Salisbury's warning that it was the Prince's constitutional duty to remain silent, Edward sent a short reply which captured exactly the required tone: 'I earnestly trust, and cannot but believe, the present crisis will be arranged in a manner satisfactory to both countries, and will be succeeded by the same warm feeling of friendship which has existed between them for so many years.'[24] The Prince's telegram was printed on Christmas Eve in the *World* and widely reprinted. The crisis abated. The dispute went to arbitration and all was settled amicably. Thanks to Edward's initiative in sending the telegram, England and the United States signed an agreement following the affair that they would never threaten one another again.[25] In the next period of years, England supported the U.S. in its war with Spain, encouraged its expansion into the Pacific and, at Manila Bay, put its fleet between a German naval force and the Americans, warning the Germans that it intended to support the Americans. Rudyard Kipling welcomed the States into the band of colonizing nations with 'The White Man's Burden', commemorating the U.S. entry into the Philippines.

Another crisis, over which Edward had no control, occurred immediately following the Venezuelan trouble. On December 30 the notorious Jameson raid occurred, which would lead to the Boer War and the almost complete isolation of England from her European neighbours. In matters concerning the empire, Edward was often inaccessible to reason. For example, he supported the sortie conceived by Cecil Rhodes and led by Leander Starr Jameson into the Transvaal designed to capture Johannesburg and coincide with the outbreak of armed revolt Rhodes was to generate in the Transvaal. Both efforts failed. Following Rhodes's resignation as Prime Minister of the Cape Colony and his return to England to face a parliamentary inquiry, Edward openly demonstrated his support for Rhodes by attending the hearing and taking Rhodes's arm when he entered Westminster Hall.[26] Beneath the play of imperial politics reflected in the public support for Rhodes was a deep personal feeling of resentment directed against William, who, in one of the most ill-considered acts ever committed by a reigning head of government, apparently without a goal of war, sent an open telegram to President Kruger, congratulating him for having repulsed the invaders.

English public opinion, already strongly supportive of Rhodes, swung against the German Kaiser, and William's telegram served to draw attention away from the illegality of Rhodes's action and to cast him in the false role of hero. It is not possible to prove that William behaved as he did because of his experience with Salisbury at Cowes a few months earlier, but the conjecture is a reasonable one. And it is not beyond the bounds of possibility that Edward's remarkably exaggerated association with Rhodes following the Kaiser's telegram can be traced to a personal determination on the Prince's part to snub his nephew. Whatever the true causes behind the actions of these disparate men, their two countries moved sickeningly towards war. Had Germany sent armed assistance to Kruger, as William at first said he was ready to do, hostilities would have occurred. The Queen finally restored William to his senses with a well-timed letter; but she could not live for ever. In dealing with his nephew, Edward could only give offence.

Throughout this period Edward was making serious efforts to be kept informed on matters concerning foreign affairs, and was having difficulty convincing Lord Salisbury to treat him with confidence in these matters. The Queen, of course, remained unchanged in her conviction that Edward should be given no access to the red dispatch boxes. But if he was not successful in overcoming Salisbury's indifference, he met with great success in another quarter. In June 1896 he won the Derby and achieved, as the *Mail* expressed it, 'a delight unsurpassable in its intensity'. Persimmon, ridden by J. Watts, delivered the blue ribbon of the Turf into Edward's hands, defeating the favourite, St Frusquin, by a neck. A month earlier his horse Thais ran away with The One Thousand Guineas. After nineteen years of persistent effort, the Prince's horses were beginning to pay; and his stables continued to be a profitable investment throughout the '90s, making Edward one of the very few men in England who made money racing.

Winning the Derby was a great achievement, but would have only passing interest were it not for the fact that his victory precipitated a national outpouring of loyalty and affection for Edward that was astonishing in its degree. Before Persimmon had reached the wire, the shout, 'Persimmon wins!' was raised; and the spectators gave themselves over to a fantastic display of emotion. For a very long time

Edward was kept busy bowing from his box while the jockey and track officials struggled to bring the Prince's horse back through the crowd of people. When Edward finally succeeded in reaching the course to lead in Persimmon, the men sent their hats soaring into the air amid a continuous roar of cheers. For half an hour following the race, there was an excited crowd in front of the royal box. Rumour immediately spread that Watts would be made a C.B.E.; but *Reynolds's Newspaper* reported that the story was false.[27]

The joy was not confined to the racecourse. Word reached London ahead of Edward, who, with Alexandra, left the Derby early. There was unusual excitement outside the Stock Exchange when news of Persimmon's victory reached the City, and the brokers trooped into the street to give three cheers for Edward and his horse. Throgmorton Street was nearly impassable for a long period of time as more and more people jammed into it to take part in the festivities. 'It was,' one reporter tartly observed, 'a very mixed crowd.' At the Middle Temple, where Edward was a 'Bencher', there was a victory celebration. That night at the India and Ceylon Exhibition at Earl's Court, the combined bands of the Grenadier and Coldstream Guards played 'God Bless the Prince of Wales', and thousands joined in the chorus. When the bands stopped playing, there was prolonged cheering and applause.

In referring to the Prince's victory, the *Mail* suggested that 'to win the Derby is much, but it is even more to know that a whole nation joins in congratulating him upon his success and in rejoicing because he is glad'. In what follows, there is some indication of why the Derby win released such a flood of feeling. Having listed among the Prince's good qualities such things as 'unfailing dignity, tact and circumspection', the writer notes that 'To a larger circle still he is a typical Englishman, and that is a character which cannot be fully attained except by one who shows himself to be in sympathy with that love of sport which is almost a passion with all ranks and classes in this country.'[28]

Edward received telegrams of congratulation from all over the world. He could enjoy his triumph, and his people could rejoice with him. They were more than ready to do so. There were, of course, some expressions of disapproval. Dr Fergus Ferguson, speaking on behalf of the Religious Tract and Book Society of Scotland, suggested that their colporteurs should be sent to the Derby in the hope that the Prince might be induced to try for a higher race. On an inside page *Reynolds's*, which had published one of the most enthusiastic accounts of the Prince's Derby victory, qualified its front-page approval with a brief editorial: 'Our only desire is to point out to the pious loyal people that their idol, the Prince of Wales, is a racing man, a player of illegal games (baccarat to wit) and has no respect for the conventional

English Sunday.' But the attack was self-conscious and half-hearted. It was Edward's triumph and no mistake. The popularity he won with the Derby victory remained his for the rest of his life.

Except for rare and isolated instances, such as the churlish comments on Edward's character appearing in some papers immediately following Victoria's death, the press abandoned its attacks on the Prince. In part the truce was a result of long familiarity, in part an increased circumspection in Edward's life which made scandal almost impossible, and, finally, the general acceptance that he would soon be king and that the nation had no intention of getting rid of the monarchy. Edward had become one of the best known and best liked public men in the world. Not only was he the representative English gentleman, he was the embodiment of a tradition that was in decline or under severe attack in every corner of the western world. Hereditary power had so waned that it was possible to view with sentimental attachment one of its last representatives. And, finally, credit must be given to Edward for having retained an identity that refused to be washed out and which imposed itself, at last, on the consciousness of the nation in spite of the long attack it had undergone in the press.

Many things begun in the '90s would endure through the reign. His habits were fixed, his interests formed – racing, stock breeding, shooting, playing cards and tennis, to which he would later add riding in automobiles as fast as they could be driven. But his great domestic work of the decade preceding his accession was in charities. He worked with Joseph Lister to found the Lister Institute and gave support to Father Damien's work with lepers. He also identified himself with the anti-tuberculosis campaign, taking as his theme, 'If preventable, why not prevented?'[29] When he was called upon to establish some memorial for his mother's Diamond Jubilee in 1897, he hit upon the idea of forming a fund to aid the perennially impoverished London hospitals.

The endeavour became known as the Prince of Wales's Hospital Fund and was established with the intention of collecting £100,000 annually. Planning to give the appeal as broad a base as possible and, thereby, encouraging every segment of society to take part in its formation, Edward invited to Marlborough House the Lords Lieutenant of London and Middlesex; the Bishop of London; Cardinal Vaughan, head of the Roman Catholic Church in England; the Chief Rabbi; a leading Nonconformist minister and the Governor of the Bank of England.[30] The committee was representative of a remarkably broad segment of the middle-class population and bore the stamp of Edward's preparedness to unite the disparate elements of his people into a common venture. The Fund became a very successful memorial to the Queen. £200,000 was raised the first year, and the sum increased every year thereafter, continuing for decades beyond the end of Edward's reign. During the Jubilee year, the Royal College of Physicians, in recognition of his efforts to further medical research and alleviate human suffering, made him an Honorary Fellow.

Meanwhile, as the decade wore to a close, Edward looked beyond the borders of England with increasing dismay. Where were Great Britain's friends? The answer was that aside from the United States they did not exist. England's hope for easing of tension with Russia, begun so well by Edward in the winter of 1894, failed under the stress of the conflicting expansionist aims of the two countries and the strong anti-British bias of the Russian Foreign Minister, whose hatred of England was readily fanned by the folly-laden letters being written by Kaiser William to undermine Nicholas's confidence in the English attachment. The situation in France was, if anything, worse and a source of great sorrow to the Prince of Wales, who saw the work of years being eroded by successive waves of French popular antagonism.

At the centre of the French trouble was the incident which had occurred at Fashoda in 1898. Following General Gordon's death at Khartoum, the Sudan had endured ten years of chaotic misrule under the original, and then a second, Mahdi. Still technically under the suzerainty of Turkey and a constant menace to the safety of Egypt, the Sudan remained a tempting prize to British power in Egypt, represented on the civilian side by the forceful Consul General, Sir Evelyn Baring, later Lord Cromer, and Herbert Horatio Kitchener, the forty-eight-year-old sirdar of the newly reconstituted Egyptian army. By 1898 Lord Kitchener's force had penetrated into the Sudan as far as Omdurman, some six hundred miles south of Wadi Halfa and the second cataract, at the junction of the Blue and White Niles. There Kitchener's army, a completely Egyptian force officered by a few Englishmen handpicked by Kitchener, met the dervishes at Omdurman and destroyed them, annihilating the wild desert horde and scattering to the winds the Mahdi's power. Gordon's death was revenged.

Free now to move along the rivers, Kitchener occupied Khartoum; and with a small force of a few hundred men and several gunboats sailed up the White Nile to Fashoda, where he encountered a French force under the command of Captain Marchand. The French, having reached Fashoda from the French Congo, were waiting for a second expedition making its way towards them from French Somaliland by way of Ethiopia. The second expedition did not arrive, and Kitchener, determined to claim the area for England, requested Marchand to pull down the tricolor and concede the position. This, through negotiations between the two countries, Marchand finally did; but anti-British feeling in France became very intense. In the spring of 1899 Edward was hissed in Paris, an event that greatly pained him and sent him hurrying out of the city to the Riviera. A year later he decided to abandon his French visit altogether, deeming it wiser to avoid aggravating the hostility towards the English which the outbreak of the war between England and the Boer Republic in the summer of 1899 had intensified. He was also hurt and angered by the fierce French press attack on him and his mother, continued even through the Queen's final illness two years later.

In place of the French visit, Edward decided to substitute a Danish holiday, accompanying Alexandra to her home, a decision which nearly cost him his life. On April 4, Edward and Alix left London by train for Copenhagen, arriving in Brussels in the afternoon. As soon as the royal train stopped and Edward had emerged with Sir Stanley Clarke to walk up and down on the platform, the station master invited the Prince to make use of the royal waiting rooms, but Edward declined, saying that he wanted to 'walk about a little'.[31] He and Clarke strolled undisturbed along the platform for a short time, waiting for the train to depart. It was generally known that he and the Princess were in the station, but he was left undisturbed to take his exercise and enjoy a cigar.

As soon as the train was ready to leave, he stepped back into his carriage, where Alix, Charlotte Knollys and an equerry were waiting and chatting, and the train began to move. Suddenly a boy rushed forward from the crowd, leaped onto the footboard of the royal car, drew a revolver, thrust his arm through an open window and fired two shots at Edward at point-blank range.[32] Both shots missed their target, one going out of a window and the second lodging in the woodwork above Edward's head. An instant later Edward's attacker was knocked down and disarmed. Charlotte Knollys wrote later that there was no time to be afraid, the only outcry being made by the Princess's tiny Chinese dog which was terrified by the sound of the shots.[33] There is disagreement among the various reports as to how many shots were actually fired at Edward, but none about the fact that the muzzle of the gun could not have been more than six feet from his head when the boy began shooting.

The youth who had attacked and nearly killed Edward was Jean Baptiste Sipido, a dark-haired, dark-eyed sixteen-year-old Belgian tin-smith apprentice, one of nine children. It is very difficult to determine the level of his intelligence or just how much he understood of what he had attempted. Following his capture, he testified that the plot to kill the Prince of Wales had been hatched in the preceding week between him and two other men at a drinking house, the Maison du Peuple, a favourite anarchist hang-out in the city. He gave sympathy with the Boers as his reason for the attempt. Expressing no remorse for what he had done, he told the police that he was only sorry to have missed, that the Prince had caused thousands to be slaughtered in South Africa and deserved to die. He also told the police that he was an anarchist.

Edward remained perfectly calm throughout the incident. As soon as he was informed that Sipido had been arrested, the Prince ordered the train out of the station and on to Copenhagen.[34] On April 8, Edward attended morning service in the English Church in Copenhagen and heard a service of thanksgiving for his escape. Crowds cheered him and Alix as they drove to and from the service.[35]

The British press was surprisingly tolerant in its treatment of the affair, choosing to regard Sipido as a deluded and mentally incompetent person. Sipido's parents wrote a remarkable petition and sent it to Queen Victoria and to Edward begging for clemency for their son, pointing out that they were poor but honest people and that their son had been made a dupe. Edward seems to have regarded the boy in the same light and even asked that the bullet dug out of the train's woodwork be preserved as a souvenir. The German *Maddeburg Zeitung* expressed thankfulness over Edward's escape, doing it in such a way, however, as to take away what it gave. Expressing horror at the action, the editor wrote, 'Little which could excite our sympathy is known of the Heir to the English Crown', adding as a kind of apology or explanation for their deploring the attack on his person that he was the son of the Kaiser's grandmother.[36]

European sympathy for Edward was far from excessive. The Belgian authorities tried Sipido in July and found him innocent of criminal intent and released him under parole. He immediately escaped to France, where the French police allowed him to 'disappear'. The Kaiser wrote to Edward that he thought the behaviour of the Belgians outrageous: 'Either their laws are ridiculous, or the jury are a set of d—d, bl—y scoundrels; which is the case I am unable to decide. With best love to Aunty and Cousins.'[37] One could never charge William with a lack of feeling; and there is something in his letter that tempts one to believe that he could have been approached and made to see reason, led to temper his arrogance and control his suspicion. That he was beyond such appeal, at least from anyone but his grandmother, was probably a mark of his madness. As for general European feeling towards the attack on Edward, it was formed around the political response to the Boer War, all of which was anti-British. In France especially – one is reminded of the wrath of a woman scorned – this hostility was turned into a personal attack against Edward, and he was ruthlessly caricatured in the French press.

The Sipido affair faded away without sequel, except for the possibility that it was one of the influences on Joseph Conrad who in 1907 produced *The Secret Agent*, a study of anarchists and their folly. In this book a simple-minded boy carries out an anarchist's plan to explode a bomb at the Greenwich Observatory, and dies in the attempt.

There was nothing for Edward to do but sit out the trouble and do his best not to make it worse. He returned to England in the third week of April and received a genuinely enthusiastic reception as he drove through the streets on his way from Charing Cross Station to Marlborough House. His personal popularity at home had never been higher, and it continued to rise through the spring with a remarkable series of wins at the race meetings. His domestic affairs were running smoothly; and, except for the sorrow occasioned by the death of his brother, the Duke of Edinburgh, and the knowledge that his sister Victoria was also dying of cancer, his personal life was tranquil.

A considerable portion of that tranquillity was due to the presence o two remarkable women who, by a notable coincidence, had both entered his life in February 1898. These women were as unlike as possible, except for their beauty, and filled different but equally important roles in his life. Edward met the twenty-nine-year-old Alice Keppel, the wife of Sir George Keppel, some time before the beginning of their special relationship, but they seem to have reached an understanding over dinner on February 27, the occasion of Edward's first being entertained at dinner at the Keppels' London house.[38] However swift the beginning of their love affair, it was to be permanent; and Mrs Keppel won the devotion and admiration of all who knew her, including Alexandra, who was not, at first, inclined to welcome a successor to Lady Warwick.

The second woman was Agnes Keyser, a trained nurse, forty-six years old, daughter of a wealthy Stock Exchange figure, Charles Keyser. Her passion in life was nursing, and by the time Edward knew her, she was entering middle age, devoted to her profession, thoroughly private and just the woman Edward needed when the stress and excitement of his life became unendurable. Anita Leslie says of her that she gave Edward the comfort given to English children by their nannies and that having been deprived of that pleasure in his childhood, he cherished it all the more when he found it.[39] Did he sleep with her? No definite answer can be given, but her appeal for the Prince may not have been sexual, although with Edward it would be rash to say, where a woman was involved, that there was no sexual attraction. He found Agnes Keyser comfortable, and she loved him in her own controlled way. His appeal for her may have been his need to be sheltered and comforted, because she had an almost obsessive compulsion to minister to men; and Edward went to her for quiet dinners and the solace of her concern. It was a relationship based (and perhaps such relationships are the most firmly based) on the strong, individual, thoroughly selfish and yet mutually gratifying needs of two highly complex people whose lives could not conceivably have mingled except under these unique circumstances.

1901 opened with widespread anxiety over the Queen's health. She seemed to be fading away. Edward continued his regular activities but with a distracted mind. Then, on January 18, he received word that he should go at once to Osborne, where his mother was staying. The nation was sunk in gloom. The Queen was dying, the wretched South African war dragged on, and England was isolated in a sea of ill will. A sense of the popular feeling comes through a diary entry for January 19 by the young Kathleen Isherwood, mother of the English novelist Christopher Isherwood, who wrote, 'Very bad report of the dear Queen...It would be such a terrible thing for the country if anything happened to her...'.[40] Another indication, coming one day later, was Canon Scott Holland's request which preceded his opening the service in St Paul's Cathedral: 'Today I again beseech your earnest prayers for her who for so many years has been a mother to the nation. So long as we can remember anything, her name and her presence have been felt in every beat of our hearts and pulse of our blood....'[41]

Edward had scarcely arrived at Osborne, however, when he was obliged to return to London to meet William, who arrived in England on the twentieth. On this occasion, at least, William was not a burden to Edward, although he caused the equerries, secretaries and attendants of the royal family much trouble. He genuinely loved Victoria, and under the stress of the situation, all the charm and tact and warmth of feeling of which he was capable was directed towards his uncle. The crowds remained constant outside Mansion House, waiting to read the telegrams concerning Victoria's health, although there was no real hope for a recovery. Edward was with his mother at noon on the twenty-second when she rallied sufficiently to recognize him. Putting out her arms, she said, 'Bertie!' Edward embraced her, but was unable to maintain his calm. William wept openly. The family continued to visit her throughout the afternoon, but she was now unconscious. At 6.15 she died.

The Times for Wednesday January 23 was printed with heavy black borders and the columns separated by black margins. Six full pages were devoted to a summary of her life. One of the most revealing items of praise given to her was that 'she lived all her life subject to the guidance of wise men'. The paper also quoted Elizabeth Barrett Browning's lines about 'child-Queen, who wept to wear the Crown'. We now know, of course, that Victoria gloried in that crown; and she did not weep to wear it.

Following the tribute to the dead Queen, The Times printed a second item, 'The King: A Loyal Appreciation', in which the writer encouraged his readers to take heart: 'If there is anything which can in some measure console the nation for the irreparable loss which it has just sustained, it is the well-founded conviction that the Queen has left behind her a worthy successor, who may be trusted to walk in her footsteps.'[42] In two full columns there was no single word of criticism. The editorial on the same page praises Edward while admitting that there were things in his past that 'those who respect and admire him could not but wish otherwise'. The following Sunday, *Reynolds's* printed a very cool résumé of the nation's hopes for a worthy successor to Victoria. The editor observed that 'it cannot be said that the life of the new Sovereign has been altogether edifying'; but he consoled his readers with the observation that 'in any case the new king's wild days are over'. The *Pall Mall Gazette* was more humane, more civilized in its appraisal. Commenting very sympathetically on Edward's past difficulties as a prince without power, the paper stated that 'there is no more popular figure in the world today than his Majesty King Edward VII'.[43] The *Gazette* had more truly captured the feeling of the country towards its new king.

On the twenty-third Edward left Osborne at 10.30 am for London to attend his first Council, held at St James's Palace. Leaving William in charge of affairs at Osborne, the King, accompanied by the Duke of Connaught, the Duke of York and Prince Christian, the Duke of Argyll, the Lord Chamberlain, Mr Balfour, Sir Francis Knollys, the Hon. Derek Keppel and Captain Holford, arrived at half-past twelve at Victoria Station. Throngs had gathered at the station and along Buckingham Palace Road and the Mall. As he drove to Marlborough House, he passed between tightly packed lines of Londoners, standing bareheaded and in silence. Edward repeatedly raised his hat in recognition to the crowds, but the streets, palely lit by the winter sunshine, held no sound but the rumble of the carriages.

At about 2 pm the Lord Mayor arrived at St James's Palace, followed shortly by Edward, escorted by a small detachment of the Royal Horse Guards (Blue), and driven by a coachman wearing a scarlet cloak and cape, with footmen similarly dressed. Deeply affected by the ceremony, Edward received the oath from Frederick Temple, Archbishop of Canterbury, and delivered a brief speech to the Council members and guests. His principal announcement was that he intended to assume the style of King Edward VII, 'so as not, in any way', as he put it, 'to challenge comparison with the unique position of his illustrious father, who will be known in history as Albert the Good'.[44] *The Times* thought it a wise decision, Albert being 'a foreign name' that had not quite become naturalized. *Reynolds's* reported the speech as follows: 'I have resolved to be known by the name of Edward, which has been borne by six of my ancestors. In doing so I do not undervalue the name of Albert, which I inherit from my ever to be lamented, great, and wise father, who by universal consent is I think deservedly known by the name of Albert the Good, and I desire that his name should stand alone.'[45]

The problem of what name Edward would take as king dated back at least to 1864, when, on the birth of his first son, he raised the question with Victoria. In her characteristic fashion, the Queen had written, 'It would be *impossible* for you to *drop* your Father's. It would be *monstrous*, and Albert *alone* would *not* do...as there can be only *one Albert*.'[46] Having pointed out that no English sovereign had ever ruled under a double name, he refused to commit himself to accepting his mother's decision that he should name himself Albert Edward. It is apparent that from as early as the 1860s, he had determined to take the name Edward. Yet how intriguing is that ghostly echo of his mother's voice, sounding through Edward's Accession speech to the Council, telling his listeners that Albert's name 'should stand alone'. Did he guess at the irony? Probably not.

No record was made of Edward's Accession Council speech because it was generally thought that the King spoke from a draft or at least notes. Such was not the case. His speech was impromptu; therefore an exact record of it does not exist. E. F. Benson has written that following the Queen's death, 'the body of average respectable opinion felt the gloomiest anticipations of the probable effects of his accession, and wondered whether the days of George IV would return'.[47] Benson has certainly overstated the case, at least as far as existing records of public sentiment show. But it was widely noted that in his accession speech Edward made no reference to God, but sought help in his task from Parliament and from the people.[48] Some gloomy sermons were preached over Edward in those early weeks of the new year. Once again it was a case of the man's myth appearing in men's minds with more clarity than the man himself. Those who wished to see him as antichrist, marching on Jerusalem under the banner of his racing colours, did so; but it would now appear that the vast majority of Englishmen welcomed the arrival of Edward at his proper place. He was sixty years old, worn, fat and short of breath; but he was king at last.

A Working King

Without the slightest self-constraint he was invariably himself and invariably equal to the occasion.
                                M. Poincaré, Prime Minister of France, of Edward VII

On its slow journey to London, Queen Victoria's body was transported from Osborne to Portsmouth on board a cruiser, with the royal yacht following. The ship and the trailing yacht were scarcely under way when Edward, standing on the bridge of the cruiser, noticed the yacht's standard flying at half mast. Asking why, he was told, sharply, 'The Queen is dead, Sir'. In his most decisive voice he retorted, 'The King of England lives', and the standard was immediately raised to the top of the mast.[1] Edward intended to be king, not merely an embarrassing reminder of what the nation had lost. Not everyone was prepared for the change. Some of that unreadiness was expressed by Kathleen Isherwood, who lamented in her diary, 'It seems to me so horrible, the way the moment the Queen is dead everyone talks of the King.'[2]

But getting used to the fact that England now had a king was just what the nation was obliged to do. If many thought that Edward would usher in a period of moral laxity in court life, and mourned Victoria's passing the more on that account, far more sensed the dispersing cloud and the lifting of a gloom that had been brooding over national life for nearly half a century. Victoria's necrophilia had effectively reduced court life to the dreariness of an endless contemplation of death. Hidden in Scottish mists or not, she could not be forgotten; and the image of her sable shrouded figure hung over the nation like a huge raven, perched on the bust of Albert, croaking 'Nevermore', to joy. It was not in the nature of the age for its people to be able to speak frankly of their deliverance. Even Edward could not openly rejoice in accession, despite the fact that Lord Esher, watching the new king busying himself with his tasks, was able to describe Edward as a man suddenly freed from restraint and 'unconsciously revelling in his liberty'.[3]

If revelling seems too excessive a word to describe Edward's response to his new role, it is only so because of the great tact which he brought to the moment of his apotheosis. In his first days as sovereign, he moved with deliberation, making no great changes in the existing court staff, except for purging his mother's Indian retainers from Windsor, where they had occupied King John's tower and from that stronghold spread the exotic odour of curries across the Berkshire countryside. For the most part Edward retained the private staff which had served him for so many years, Sir Francis Knollys and Sir Dighton Probyn becoming the chief administrators of the household. The senior staff member was Sir Maurice Holzmann, who served as Marlborough House librarian and in the office of the Duchy of Cornwall for thirty-eight years.[4] The Queen's private secretary, Sir Arthur Bigge, was kept on as an extra equerry, later raised to the dignity of Lord Stamfordham and named private secretary to Knollys. The remainder of the Queen's staff was gradually dispersed.[5]

While never allowing his suite to reach the huge size maintained by his mother when she travelled on the continent, Edward did not, as king, travel as lightly as he had done when Prince of Wales. He saw his new position as demanding a greater ostentation than had the old one. Some of the more colourful members of his attendant staff were the Swiss courier, Fehr; the footman, Hoepner, a former Prussian Grenadier of imposing height and size; and C. W. Stamper, Edward's chief chauffeur, who later wrote a very entertaining book about his years of service with the King. Another of his servants, the Superintendent of the Wardrobe, H. Chandler, was distinguished by being the lightning rod that drew the fire of Edward's wrath.[6] When frustration, irritation, weariness or boredom ignited the King's explosive temper and circumstances prevented him from giving vent to his feelings, the patient Chandler would be sure to suffer as soon as he came within the King's reach.

Edward's irritability increased with the years and was matched by a corresponding decline that was almost psychological in his capacity to be unemployed. Unoccupied for even the shortest time, he would begin to move about uneasily and to become angry, reducing everyone around him to a state of nervous anxiety as they waited for the moment when his rage would burst through his dwindling self-control and vent itself on his wife or whoever was at hand.

The coronation was postponed for eighteen months in order that no taint of mourning would mar its splendour. Edward also hoped that in that period the South African war might be brought to an end, removing at last a terrible blight on the nation and beginning the long process of restoring England to the European community of nations, from which she had been increasingly excluded by the widespread unpopularity of Britain's military excursion against the Boers and her increasingly brutal methods of securing a victory. The practice of herding the Boer women and children into concentration camps in the hopes of denying the guerrilla soldiers access to clothes and provisions was especially condemned. Campbell-Bannerman, one of the pro-Boer partisan leaders in England, had referred to Lord Kitchener's methods as barbarous. Edward, incensed by this characterization of the British strategy, issued a warning to Englishmen that they should say nothing that would appear to be giving aid to the enemy.

Edward was thoroughly dissatisfied with the management of the war, considering that a terrible series of tactical and administrative errors by the War Office had shamefully prolonged the conflict. He made it clear that he considered the army medical service to be incompetent to the point of corruption and staffed by men completely unequal to the tasks they faced. He also thought that the horses being sent to the army were inferior; and that too often Kitchener, instead of being given every assistance in carrying out his task of bringing the war to a speedy and successful conclusion, was thwarted and hindered by mediocre men who did not know enough about military matters to conduct themselves intelligently. Of course, there *was* incompetence in the conduct of the war, but Edward's irritation with the War Office was chiefly the product of his mounting frustration at not being given what he wanted, a swift and victorious end to the fighting. Unwilling to settle for less than a complete Boer defeat but genuinely desirous of bringing the war to a close, he found it impossible to face the fact that the English forces could not simply sweep away their opposition. Nevertheless, the army's performance in the war convinced Edward that modernization of that branch was essential. The Czar wrote asking that Edward find a way of negotiating a peace, adding that England was carrying out a war of annihilation against the Boers and that such conduct was unsuited to a nation of England's power and prestige in the world. Edward was excessively nettled and found it difficult to deal calmly with such annoyances as Nicholas's well-intentioned but insensitive advice or the unrelenting attack being made in the French press against England's continuation of the war.

His sense of humour, normally to be relied on even in difficult times, had begun to fail him under the stress of his newly assumed office. When he went sailing with Sir Thomas Lipton aboard the tea magnate's yacht, *Shamrock II*, and was nearly struck down by the collapse of her mast, he declared the boat unlucky. His displeasure extended to the owner as well, whom he accused of entering the American Cup race for the sole purpose of advertising his tea.[7] This failure of kindness, which had been one of Edward's most admirable characteristics, is attributable to the sense of urgency surrounding his early months as king. It was as though, coming late to his task, he felt a driving need to make up for lost time.

He was also deeply distressed by his sister Vicky's approaching death from cancer, the disease which had killed her husband, the Emperor Frederick, in 1888. She died on August 5 1901, following months of terrible suffering, which her German doctors declined to mitigate with drugs. Edward visited her shortly after the Queen's funeral, but he had been unable to prevail on anyone to insist that her dosage of morphine be increased sufficiently to end her pain. Both her suffering and her death were causes of great sorrow to him; and he was obliged to fight hard against the onset of depression, which, as the decade advanced, became one of his most besetting and troublesome afflictions.

In that first year following the Queen's death, the court was in heavy mourning, deepened by the death of the Empress Frederick; but Edward refused to remain idle. He found his administrative tasks increasing to the point that he could no longer even sign in his own hand every army commission, as his mother had done. Deeply regretting the necessity, he was finally driven to using a rubber stamp, signing personally only those commissions granted to individuals whose families were known to him. His principal occupation before the coronation, however, was sorting out the various royal residences and determining what should be done with them.

The task was immense. There was the initial problem of deciding which of the residences would become the primary centre of the court. Buckingham Palace had been neglected since the 1860s, and there were rooms there, originally occupied by the Prince Consort, which were as he had left them at the time of his death. His private correspondence was in his desk. The organ on which he played still stood in his bedroom, and his library remained untouched and smothered in the dust of years. The building was without electricity, proper heating or other improvements and was appropriately described by Edward as the Sepulchre.[8] A vast amount of work needed to be done to restore it to a comfortable state, and Edward was not very much interested in establishing the court there. Nevertheless, everything in the Palace had to be sorted out and dispersed, or cleaned and renovated if it was to be preserved. At the outset of the work, Edward insisted that everything be submitted to him for inspection before being assigned a fate.

One of the first actions taken was to dismantle the cobweb-hung rooms once occupied by Albert. They were stripped and purged of those relics of the dead past to which Victoria had clung with such tenacity. Even the books, with which the Prince Consort had surrounded himself and which were a natural extension of his mind, were dispersed. Few were set aside for inclusion in the Windsor library. It is futile to guess to what extent Edward was aware of the implication of his thorough exorcism of Albert's ghost, but his actions at Buckingham Palace were at one with his decision to style himself Edward instead of Albert Edward.

Edward was ridding himself of emotional encumbrances which he had borne with patience and humility for forty years.

Dissatisfied with both Buckingham Palace and Windsor, what Edward truly desired was to reclaim Hampton Court and make that beautiful house the centre of his court. Unfortunately for him, a survey of the changes required to make Hampton Court habitable proved that the costs of renovation were far too great to justify continuing the plan. Ruefully he abandoned his scheme, working off his frustration in a rather mean fashion by requiring all future visitors to Hampton Court to pay a fee for taking snapshots of the house. Baulked in his desire to live by the Thames, Edward turned his attention to Windsor Castle. There he found the confusion to be greater by far than at Buckingham Palace. Having removed Victoria's Indian servants and restored the solid English smells of roast mutton to the Castle, his next task was to gather together all the statues of John Brown which Victoria had strewn through the rooms, and destroy them, along with the fittings of the Prince Consort's rooms, which here as in Buckingham Palace had remained undisturbed. His father's rooms received Edward's personal attention, because it was his intention to have them laid bare, refurbished and made ready for his own occupancy. He was claiming his inheritance.

Clearing out old emotional encumbrances was only a part of the task posed by Windsor. The clutter in the Castle was almost beyond description. Edward's parents had not, apparently, ever thrown anything away. On the other hand, Victoria had not paid any particular attention to what she had been accumulating over the years. The value of her accretions was enormous, but their worth had been reduced by the shocking treatment they had received. Irreplaceable items such as the Sèvres and Dresden china, collected by George IV, had been subjected over the years to treatment and neglect which had left them cracked and chipped.[9] Since becoming Empress of India, gifts had poured in to Victoria – jade from China, ivory from Africa, gold, crystal, boxes of armour, plate and tapestries – a treasure of great worth piled in corners, stuffed into cupboards and drawers and left to moulder from neglect.[10] Everything was sorted and arranged and laid out for Edward's inspection. With great determination he looked through the entire collection, dispensing some of the best paintings to the National Gallery and keeping others, selecting the furniture and plate that would be retained and ordering the rest stored or sold. It was a herculean task; but he completed it. Windsor was purged.

The problem did not, of course, end with turning out the rooms. Windsor Castle had an appalling reputation as a health hazard. Its drains were inadequate, sluggish and redolent; its plumbing primitive. Modernization began immediately, and the old ghost of typhoid was routed. Sandringham House remained the King's personal residence, the one he considered home. Its popularity would continue through successive generations, endearing itself to royal children as a place of delightful memory and appealing to their parents as a sanctuary.

Balmoral was kept for the shooting season, but Osborne was marked down for abandonment. Edward had no intention of living there, and Prince George was even less enthusiastic about the house than was his father. It had been Victoria's wish that Osborne be kept permanently as a royal residence. Of the royal living places it was the one most closely connected with the memory of Albert, who designed the house and planned the grounds and the miles of drives. Ignoring the clear intention of his mother's will that the house be preserved as a memorial to the Prince Consort in the form of a joint family home, kept up at the King's expense, Edward enlarged the grounds surrounding the adjacent houses which Victoria had given to Edward's two sisters, the Princesses Louise and Beatrice, and presented the remainder of the estate to the country. The stables and adjoining ground were to become a naval college; the large wing, a military hospital for invalid officers; and the central portion, a memorial to the Queen.[11] The same sort of house cleaning that had been conducted at Windsor and Buckingham Palace was carried out expeditiously. As far as was possible without publicly repudiating his father, the King had freed himself from the physical reminders of his long and painful childhood, an experience lengthened by the Queen's unflagging watchfulness into Edward's late middle age, during all of which time he was never allowed to forget how superior his father had been to him in every respect.

Edward was bringing to his new role the personal style and method of dealing with his affairs which he had forged as Prince of Wales. Circumspect when more powerful authority than he possessed faced him, direct and decisive where his own authority was clearly established and impatient of delay or hesitation in those around him, Edward began to impose his personal stamp on the monarchy from the moment of his accession. Whereas Victoria had been retiring and remote, Edward was conspicuous and gregarious. He remained almost as active in associating himself personally with dedications, trade fairs, charities, agricultural shows, race meetings and other public events and functions as he had been while still Prince of Wales. He placed an indelible stamp of public service and visibility on the office that his death did not eradicate.

Edward chose June 26 1902 as the date for his coronation and established a new order, the Order of Merit, in honour of it. Plans were, of course, laid months in advance of the event. He decided that no crowned heads of state would be invited but that they would be represented by heirs to the throne, thus avoiding the enormously difficult

problems of deciding matters of precedence which a gathering of
monarchs would entail. As a further gesture of recognition of the
approaching ceremony, Edward broke with tradition and made
Alexandra the first Lady of the Garter, installing her banner in St
George's Chapel despite the opinion of the Garter-King-at-Arms that
such an act was contrary to the rules of the order. Perhaps he found
strength to carry out his wish regarding his wife in the statesmanlike
manner with which he dealt with the question of the Poet Laureate.

Following his mother's death, it became his responsibility to decide
whether or not to reconfirm Alfred Austin in the post. Of course,
Kipling should have been laureate, but he had disqualified himself with
the poem *The Widow at Windsor,* containing the lines.

> Walk wide o' the Widow at Windsor,
> for 'alf o' Creation she owns:
> We 'ave bought 'er the same with the sword an' the flame,
> An' we've salted it down with our bones.

and referred to the Union Jack as 'the bloomin' old rag over'ead'. Even
the refurbished Swinburne, whom Watts-Dunton had nursed back to
physical health in Putney and who was now writing 'proper' poetry
under Watts-Dunton's watchful eye in place of his earlier revolutionary
verse, could not sufficiently escape his past to qualify for the job.
Following the death of Lord Tennyson in 1892, Alfred Austin had been
the only poet to apply for the post of Laureate, and an embarrassed
Lord Salisbury had, with the greatest reluctance, appointed him to the
vacancy. Salisbury told the King that he was entitled to refuse to renew
the appointment if he wished and seek a new poet to become official
bard. Edward considered the matter very seriously, swinging first this
way and then that in his opinion. He did not like Austin's poetry, but he
did not wish to cause pain to the man himself. Finally, with a characteristic gesture, he decided to retain Austin. 'As long as he gets *no* pay,'
he wrote to Salisbury, 'it would be best to renew the appointment in
his favour.' Austin retained the post until his death in 1913, having
won the hearts of his countrymen, not through his poems, which remained consistently dreadful, but through his love of English gardens
and the books he wrote celebrating them.

As the time for his coronation approached, Edward cast about for
something he could do as a special favour to the poor. They could not
all be invited to the ceremonies. There were too many of them. Something else was needed; and Sir Thomas Lipton is generally credited
with having suggested to Edward the idea of giving a free meal to
London's needy. Edward seized on the suggestion at once. On March
11 1902, he summoned the Lord Mayor and announced plans to provide
dinner for 500,000 of his poorer subjects and told the Lord Mayor that

gifts in kind would be welcome, saying that his contribution would be £30,000. A survey was immediately conducted, and it was learned that the number to be fed would have to be raised to 600,000.

In deciding who would be eligible for the feast, Edward was determined that qualifications be kept at a minimum. Those charged with making up the lists of people to be entertained were told that so long as persons were not of known bad repute, they were not to be rejected, that 'no residential qualifications should be insisted upon, and no inquisitorial examination of character'. Indoor paupers, those confined to beds and wheelchairs in publicly supported institutions, and children under the age of ten were not invited, it having been decided that they would be fed separately at their lodgings. The Jewish poor were also to be dealt with separately in accordance with their own dietary law.[12]

A very elaborate invitation card was designed in colour and distributed. The King and Queen's pictures were on the card along with a variety of allegorical decorations and the words, 'King Edward Heartily Bids You Welcome To His Coronation Dinner on July 5th, 1902.' Fifteen hundred musicians, singers and entertainers volunteered their services for after-dinner entertaining. To ensure a merry mood at the feast, Messrs Bass & Co. agreed to provide 27,827 gallons of ale; and Messrs R. White and Sons made the Dinner Committee a gift of 72,000 gallons of assort soft drinks. In all the places where food was to be served, a special temperance table was set aside for those who would not sit down with Demon Drink. Feelings were beginning to run high in England against spirits and beer, feelings which in 1906 led to the Liberal Party's unsuccessful attempt to control the sale of beer and liquor.

Perhaps the most astonishing gift given to the poor on the occasion of their dinner was made by Rowntrees of York. Rowntrees had made 600,000 tin boxes with the King and Queen's pictures on the covers, done in fourteen colours. To fit into the boxes, 569,562 cakes of chocolate were prepared. The tins and the chocolate weighed forty-five tons, and twelve Great Northern Railway trucks were required to carry them from York to London. These tins were eventually distributed to every person connected with the dinner either as guest or helper. Every cake of chocolate was wrapped by hand in tinfoil and placed by hand in the boxes.

Photographs were taken of the diners seated at the tables, and reproductions of these pictures appear in an elaborate book, published in 1902, bound in white with gold lettering on the cover and sporting gold edged pages, and titled *The King's Dinner To The Poor: In Celebration of Their Majesties' Coronation, A.D. 1902*. There are enormous variations in the appearances of the guests pictured in the book. In some of the boroughs, Battersea for example, those sitting at the tables are obviously

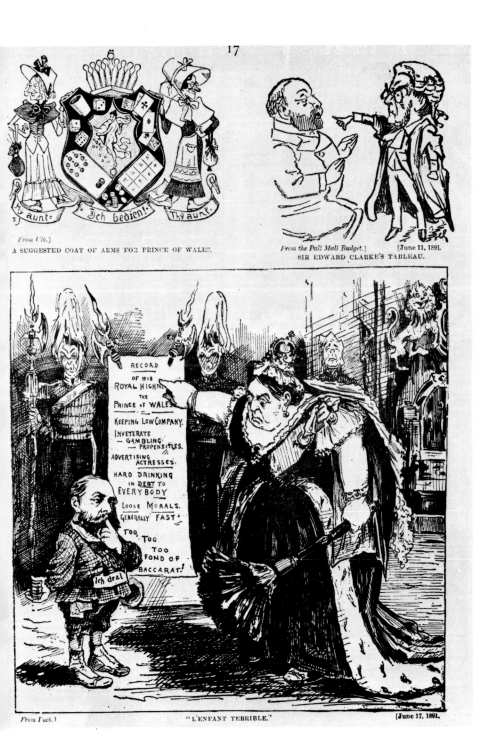

From Ulk.]

A SUGGESTED COAT OF ARMS FOR PRINCE OF WALES.

From the Pall Mall Budget.]　　[June 11, 1891.

SIR EDWARD CLARKE'S TABLEAU.

From Puck.]　　"L'ENFANT TERRIBLE."　　[June 17, 1891.

Cartoons from *Ulk*, the *Pall Mall Budget* and *Puck*, June 1891
By permission of the British Museum

EDWARD MAKES A VOW

"I've been aboard a host of ships, but never will one see
Me enter in a pardner-ship again with Germany!"

17. 'Edward Makes a Vow': from *Harper's Weekly*, March 1903
By permission of *Harper's Magazine*

poor. Inhabitants of other boroughs, such as Hammersmith, appear to
be comfortably middle class, facing the camera with self-confidence,
the enormous hats of the women sailing majestically over the scene like
feathered balloons. In none of the pictures are there to be seen ragged or
wretched people. Everyone looks spruce. Whatever Edward's instructions had been about who was to be entertained, in the pictures at least
the editors' hands are everywhere apparent.

Edward looked forward to the approaching celebration with increasing pleasure. Late to come into his inheritance, he intended that
the ceremony marking that entrance should be as impressive as possible; and because he loved ceremony and the appurtenances of royal
show so dearly, he strove to make every part of the forthcoming observances as rich in detail as possible. A slight cloud was the difficulty
which he was having with his throat, a condition calling for daily
spraying by one of the court physicians. No one appeared to be the
least bit concerned with the irritation, however, and no thought was
given to issuing a medical bulletin. Only *Reynolds's Newspaper* reported
in the spring that the King was not well; but the report went unremarked.

Buckingham Palace was made ready for occupancy barely in time to
receive the first of the royal visitors, who began to arrive for the
coronation early in June. At Westminster Abbey churchmen and other
participants were busily engaged in rehearsing the complicated ritual of
crowning the king, but Edward did not attend, one of his equerries
taking his place.[13] Throughout London the great houses were opening
their doors to the arriving guests; and the Ritz, the Savoy and Claridge's
were full. Everything was going ahead in the liveliest fashion. The
populace looked ahead to June 26 and 27 with the keenest anticipation.
The firework displays were prepared, flowers ordered, the streets and
bridges in London decorated. The city seemed to hold its breath in a
mood of delightful suspense.

On June 14 Edward and his family were at Aldershot for the annual
review, an event which always pleased Edward. On this occasion,
however, he appeared to take no interest in what was enacted in front
of the royal stand, but sat slumped in his chair. His daughter, Victoria,
told her mother to rouse Edward, that he was being 'too boring'.
Alexandra, however, paid no attention to Victoria's criticism, and
continued in her childlike way to be absorbed in the spectacle of
marching men. Later that night, Victoria went to say goodnight to her
father and found him in terrible pain, his stomach swollen to the extent
that she was unable to loosen his belt. The Queen was summoned, and
she cut the belt away, using the knife from Edward's bedside table,
which was always placed there with a cold fowl and a bottle of wine
in case the King became hungry in the night.[14]

K

A doctor was summoned at once. That Edward was seriously ill was known to the physician, Sir Francis Laking, at least as early as Edward's Aldershot visit; and he may have known from that date the true nature of the King's ailment. By the twenty-first Edward was so ill that he could not attend the great banquet given at Buckingham Palace in honour of all the royal guests. Still no true account of his condition had been allowed to leak out. One section of the press was so determined to keep Edward's illness concealed from the public that an enterprising reporter, having ferreted out the fact that Edward's life was probably in danger, sent a wire to his office saying 'The King is seriously ill', only to be immediately fired.

On June 23 Edward returned to London from Windsor, riding from Paddington Station to Buckingham Palace wrapped in a heavy coat. During the week since Aldershot he had rested and kept to a bland and light diet, neither treatment being of the least benefit. Edward was by this time in terrible pain, and on entering the Palace, he suddenly fell forward in a dead faint, remaining unconscious for seven minutes. Some time later, he was examined again, though merely as a formality because by this time Laking and the other doctors knew that Edward was suffering from a diseased appendix and that peritonitis was developing. Informed that he must have an operation, Edward refused, saying that he would not disappoint his people and that he would be crowned.[15] Laking persisted, forcing Edward to grasp the fact that if he did not allow Treves to operate, he would certainly die. The King gave in.

The decision to operate had not been arrived at easily. Six doctors, among them Lord Lister, the first medical man to be called to the House of Lords, the surgeon, Sir Frederick Treves, Sir Thomas Smith, and Edward's personal physician, Sir Francis Laking, consulted with one another immediately following Edward's collapse. A serious disagreement arose over whether or not an appendicectomy, a serious operation in 1902, should be performed. Laking was strongly in favour of it, but he was opposed by Lister, who finally gave way before the combined opinions of the remaining physicians. The evidence seemed almost overwhelmingly in favour of operating. Edward's temperature had risen to 102, he was vomiting violently and his strength was rapidly failing.[16] The operation was successfully done on June 24, and lasted forty minutes. Waking from the sedation, Edward asked, 'Where's George?'[17] Popular report had it that he asked if his people would ever forgive him for falling ill and postponing the coronation.

The announcement of his operation, made late in the afternoon of the twenty-fourth, created consternation throughout the country. The true extent, as well as the nature, of Edward's illness had been carefully kept from the nation. Of course, rumours that the King was seriously ill were circulating. On June 22, *Reynolds's Newspaper* warned its readers that they were being misled by the Court physicians, who were giving out the information that Edward was suffering from lumbago. The paper stated flatly that he had appendicitis, that his throat was giving trouble and that 'it may be taken as certain that no optimistic view is possible under the existing circumstances'.[18] On the following day *The Times* correspondent reported that he had asked Sir Francis Knollys if there were any truth in the *Reynolds's* story and Knollys replied, 'There is not a word of truth in the report.' On Tuesday, *The Times* was still calling the illness an 'indisposition' and speaking as though the coronation was still to be held.[19]

Later, there was much speculation as to why Edward's true condition was kept a secret. There is no doubt that Laking and others on the staff earned the hostility of the press as a result of their deception; but the members of the press themselves, as well as their employees, connived to deceive the public. Hindsight may allow one to praise the courageous reporting of the *Reynolds's* staff; but the paper was severely criticized then and earlier for alarming the public. On October 27 1901, *Reynolds's* printed a report on the King's health in which it insisted that Edward had been operated on for cancer of the larnyx. This report does not now appear to have been true, but the paper was right in saying that he had been having trouble with his throat. *Lancet,* however, among other publications, attacked *Reynolds's* and some went so far as to demand the imprisonment of *Reynolds's* editor.

Some of the reluctance to believe or to reveal that Edward was ill in June is understandable. The plans for the coronation were all but complete. The entire nation was in a holiday mood. Thousands of pounds had been spent by businessmen producing commemorative china and mementos of every description, all boldly proclaiming that on June 26 1902, Edward was crowned according to plan. Laking, on whose shoulders most of the responsibility rested for deciding the content of the health bulletins released, appears to have hoped against hope that the abdominal flare-up might subside. If this happened, it would be foolish, perhaps even irresponsible, to frighten people with reports of the King's serious illness. In any case, he decided to keep Edward's true condition quiet. Trading on what appears to be a universal tendency of all palace guards to be secretive, Laking had no difficulty in persuading Edward's staff to conspire with him in the matter.

The plan was certainly effective. Kathleen Isherwood recorded in her diary that she and her mother learned that the coronation was postponed from a busman on Tuesday as they were going to Harrods. The busman had just seen the notices posted in the City, where the Lord Mayor had made a solemn announcement that Edward was to undergo a serious operation.[20] Philippe Jullian describes another scene occurring that Tuesday at the Ritz dining-room, crowded with the rich and the royal from America and Europe, when César Ritz suddenly entered the room, his face drained of colour, called for silence and announced to his stunned listeners that the King was seriously ill and that the coronation would not be held.[21] *The Times* noted that the effect of the news on London could hardly be imagined by those who had not seen it. An instantaneous change in mood came over the city as news of the King's illness spread. The throngs of people, who had already caught the holiday spirit, grew quieter and an anxious silence settled over the streets.[22] The decorations continued to flutter from the shop fronts, public buildings and along the bridges, but the gladness was all gone, turned now into fear and a dumb waiting, characterized by the quiet watchfulness of the vast crowds gathered outside Buckingham Palace.

Fortunately, the suspense was brief. Almost from the moment the operation was concluded, the doctors were able to report that Edward was recovering satisfactorily. And Edward's recuperation progressed with remarkable swiftness. Within a few weeks people were even going so far as to say that it was a good thing the King had fallen ill, that it had increased his popularity. Unquestionably it did that. Even his old enemy *Reynolds's* admitted that 'there is something really tragic in this untoward event. The King had a very long wait for the throne. He has made himself exceedingly popular during the brief time he has been sovereign; and we have no hesitation in expressing our belief that it was his desire to do his best to please all ranks in the community.'[23] Heady praise indeed, from a paper which a short while before had insisted that if a book were written telling the true character of Edward, no publisher would dare touch it, so explosive would be its contents.

During the first week of the baulked coronation festivities, there was considerable confusion in the country as to what changes in community observances were demanded. A portion of the nation felt that the coronation should be held whether Edward could participate in the ceremony or not, a rather bizarre attitude that leads one to wonder if the significance of the ceremony was always understood. The greatest difficulty arose over the plans for the King's dinner to the poor. In some towns, officials announced that the dinner would have to be postponed; but that order was almost immediately rescinded. It was not done quickly enough in Watford, however, where a serious riot followed the Coronation Committee's announcement that the dinner and the distribution of sixpences would be delayed. Forty people were arrested and a great many injured before peace was restored. As soon as he was sufficiently recovered from his operation to issue statements, Edward ordered that the dinner be given; and it was, very successfully, on July 5.

The King rested briefly at Buckingham Palace and then continued his recovery cruising on the *Victoria and Albert*. His recovery was swift, and his general health improved by the enforced dieting and rest. In gratitude for their services, Edward conferred baronetcies on Laking and Treves. They had saved his life, and all England was in their debt.

The coronation took place on August 9 1902. Edward went through the ceremonies without showing undue fatigue and emerged from the Abbey glowing with happiness not only because of the ceremony but also because he knew that he had been taken into his people's hearts. That high priestess in the cult of Victoria worshippers, Kathleen Isherwood, wrote that he was more popular now, following his illness, than he had ever been before. She added that although she 'could never feel the least spark of loyalty like one did to Victoria, one admires his courage'. It was a beginning, at least, even in that hostile quarter. Elsewhere in the nation he was almost adored.

Some unusual productions connected with the coronation included A. B. Grimaldi's genealogical table 'proving' Edward's descent from King David, which among other things provided 'a necessary link in proving the Identity of the British Nation with the Ten Lost Tribes of Israel'.[24] Raja Sir Saurindra Mohun Tagore issued a compilation of the proceedings laid down in classical Hindu works for the coronation ceremony, including a warning that if Edward did not cherish his subjects, he would be guilty 'of having committed that sin which attaches to one kicking a sleeping cow'.[25] On June 22 1902 *Reynolds's* printed a cartoon showing a tipsy John Bull with a cigar in his mouth, carrying flags and a bottle in his hands, dancing while other countries watch and singing,

> Come to the Coronation, boys, and watch me do it right,
> Feasts and follies all the day and fireworks at night.
> I'm a champion at grovelling and like to do it well,
> So I'll shout and scream and act the goat and get as drunk as —.

Most of the material published concerning the coronation, however, was more conventional. Perhaps typical of much of the verse written on the occasion was the poem by a Scottish minister, L. MacLean Watt, who won the *Good Words* contest for the best coronation ode to be submitted to them. It has the sound of Kipling in its rhythms and diction and is jingoist enough to satisfy the most demanding patriot. It is titled 'Ode on the Coronation of King Edward VII', but it should have been called 'The Dead of England'. Like many other poems composed for the coronation, there is a strong minor note asserting itself amidst the general affirmation. Part of the poem is narrated by those who have died for England. Their tone is truculent and aggressive. The narrator follows them with assurances that Edward will prove equal to his task, despite the doubts that assailed the nation when the Queen died:

> Great shall that monarch be,
> Great on the shore, and the sea,
> And the nations near and far
> Shall see his star.

But the tone of triumph does not hold. In the concluding stanza, the death note comes again:

> With thunder, and cries of war, and battle drums,
> And, through the distant hills,
> Rumbling, shall growl the voice of coming ills...[26]

Most towns and cities produced their own programme celebrations of the coronation to accompany their own observances, complete with songs, hymns and commemorative verse. The verses and hymns were printed and sold on single sheets for 2s. 6d. per hundred. The variety of verse is remarkable and most of it better than one has any right to expect. There was much written and sung that was boastful and aggressive. Much was plainly silly. But in the serious pieces, over and over again, one hears the doubt coming through, as it does in William Watson's very fine 'Ode On the Day of the Coronation of King Edward VII':

> And yonder march the nations full of eyes.
> Already is doom a-spinning, if unstirred...

The Edwardian age, with all its half-realized anxieties so dramatically reflected in its literature, was being ushered in with the troubling sounds of doubt disturbing a moment of great national affirmation.

That Barnum and Bailey character, Horatio Bottomley, who rose to national attention during the First World War through the pages of *John Bull* and whose name, along with those of two other great journalists of the war period, Arnold Bennett and H. G. Wells, was blazoned on the sides of London buses, once remarked that with King Edward on the throne of England, Parliament was a redundancy. The exaggeration is typical, not only of Bottomley, but of one segment of opinion concerning Edward's influence on England's foreign affairs after he had become king. The excessive claims made for the King's role in that area led writers such as Sir Sidney Lee to attempt a balancing of the record following the King's death. The unfortunate result of this attempt was to make general the equally distorted view that Edward had no influence on the nation's foreign affairs at all and that he had never contributed a single idea of substance to his governments in the nine years of his reign. Jealous politicians, who were eager to claim as much credit as possible for the achievements of their ministries and equally anxious to check any growth of royal power, were quick to agree that Edward's contribution to the governing of the country had been miniscule.

Disagreement over Edward's influence became particularly sharp regarding the Anglo-French Entente Cordiale, signed on April 8 1904, on which Edward had set his heart for more than a decade. But from this distance it seems apparent that Edward played an active and important, perhaps even decisive, role in bringing the agreement into being. His contribution was essentially personal and persuasive, but it was founded on historical and political realities which set off those contributions most effectively and enhanced their importance. Edward alone could not have brought about the Anglo-French alliance. Neither, on the other hand, despite the favourable political climate which had come into being after the close of the Boer War, could Lord Lansdowne's Tory government ever have achieved the Entente without the King's help.

Anti-British feeling in France following the Fashoda incident had been extremely high and was exacerbated by the Boer War. The French press was so inflamed that even Victoria's death failed to stem the flow of vicious caricature, lampoon and savage personal attack, aimed principally against Edward, now that Victoria was dead. As noted earlier, Edward had decided to give up his much-loved spring holidays on the Riviera, and Paris was entirely out of the question – he was now so unpopular with the French. Throughout these troubles, however, the French government had behaved with absolute correctness. It saw, if its people did not, that some accommodation with England would have to be reached once that nation's attention could be diverted from South Africa. France had territorial ambitions in various parts of the world, but in order to realize those ambitions, she would have to have the support of Great Britain, whose power abroad was too mighty to challenge in any overtly aggressive way.

France was fortunate in its leadership at this time; President Loubet was sympathetic towards a rapprochement with England, and his brilliant Foreign Minister, Paul Delcassé, who had been furious over Kitchener's behaviour at Fashoda, put that anger behind him and determined to find a basis of agreement between England and France. England was also fortunate in its government. Lord Salisbury had stepped down in favour of Lansdowne, who was open to the idea of forming European alliances, thus bringing to an end the policy of isolation which had characterized British foreign policy from Canning, through Palmerston, to Salisbury. The stage was set for great events.

In the spring of 1901 Edward had been interested by Lansdowne's efforts to discover some means of arriving at a diplomatic agreement with Germany, and the King made arrangements to meet with the Kaiser in late August. The death of the Empress Frederick on August 5 hastened his departure time. Describing the event, Sir Philip Magnus has written that Edward 'impulsively' thrust into the Kaiser's hands notes prepared by Lansdowne, intended for the King's eyes only, on the areas of possible discussion open to Edward. Magnus accounts for the King's remarkable behaviour by calling attention to Edward's distraught emotional state and his anxiety to avoid any unpleasant discussion of Anglo-German differences.[27] The argument is persuasive, but not entirely convincing. It is equally possible that Edward, repelled, as usual, by his nephew's overbearing manner, felt little inclination to exert himself in the matter of an Anglo-German alliance. Never incompetent, but intensely personal, there is certainly a strong likelihood that he declined to persevere with William in the matter of a diplomatic breakthrough because he so strongly disliked his nephew.

Whatever the exact reason for the collapse of the Anglo-German rapprochement and Edward's failure to press for an agreement, its collapse made it more likely that England and France would attempt to reach a common understanding. Counter-indications to such an agreement, however, were the lingering traditions of mutual distrust and ancient hostility which had marked the relations of the two countries for centuries. Edward pitted himself against these difficulties, determined that he would bring the two nations together. France was Edward's oldest love, and to the claims of the heart he could respond with vigour and enthusiasm. Gallantry he also understood. During the Boer War, for example, he had to be almost forcibly restrained from sending President Kruger a letter of condolence when his wife died. In his negotiations with France, there would be nothing as crude as his action of thrusting government notes into the Kaiser's hands, for his heart and not simply his head was involved.

In the spring of 1903, Edward set out on a Mediterranean tour without Alexandra, having sent his wife and daughters off to Copenhagen. He stopped at Gibraltar, Portugal and Italy, where he had an interview with the aged Pope Leo XIII. On April 30, Edward left Rome for Paris. His reception by President Loubet was cordial; but the French populace gave him an icy welcome, letting him pass along the boulevards in his carriage without applause or else breaking their silence to shout, 'Vivent les Boers!' or 'Vive Fashoda!'[28] His speech, responding to an address by the British Chamber of Commerce, had already been printed in the French papers; and although it was very warm in its tone, it had failed to win French hearts. Nevertheless, Edward was not discouraged. He sat beside Loubet in the President's carriage, dressed in a scarlet uniform, bowing and smiling to the grim Parisians, ignoring the shouted insults. By the time he reached the Place de la Concorde, the crowds were doffing their hats and cheering occasionally. But the arrival was in no way a triumph.

His decision to visit France had been his own and was, originally, strongly opposed by Lansdowne, who insisted there would be danger to Edward if he were to appear in public in France. This opposition by his Foreign Minister was simply another indication of the lack of warmth between Edward and Lansdowne, who, along with Balfour, had been shocked when Edward refused to take a ranking minister with him. Instead, he invited a young Under-Secretary, Charles Hardinge, to make the historic journey. The King was determined to have his tour on his own terms, and he was absolutely set on visiting France. He would bring an end to England's isolation, and he would restore good relations between the two countries, alone if necessary. Certainly, Edward did not want some heavy-footed politician muddying the water when he got to France.

After dining at the British Embassy, Edward and Loubet went to the Thèâtre Français to see a performance of *L'Autre Danger* by Maurice Donnay. The audience was very cold in its reception, and the evening appeared ruined. Still, Edward did not lose confidence. During the first interval he walked in the foyer and saw Mlle Jeanne Granier, a French actress. Edward approached her and having kissed her hand, said, 'Mademoiselle, I remember applauding you in London where you represented all the grace and spirit of France.'[29] This small speech was the necessary magic. In a matter of minutes, his words to Mlle Granier had spread through the theatre. When he returned to his box the whole audience rose and cheered him.[30] The following day he was cheered on his way to a review in his honour at Vincennes and a reception at the Hôtel de Ville.

That evening, following an afternoon at the races at Longchamps, he dined with Loubet at the Elysée and responded to M. Loubet's toast with the words, 'I am glad of this occasion, which will strengthen the bonds of friendship and contribute to the rapprochement of our two countries in their common interest. Our great desire is that we may march together in the path of civilization and peace.'[31] On his way to the Opéra after the dinner, his carriage was surrounded by cheering throngs, whose earlier cries of 'Vivent les Boers!' had changed to 'Good old Teddy!'[32] The English Ambassador, Sir Edmund Monson, wrote to Lansdowne that the visit had been 'a success more complete than the most sanguine optimist could have foreseen'.[33] Edward had done what neither English nor French politicians could have done, which was to put the French people in a frame of mind receptive to closer ties with England. Edward had won. The Entente for which he had struggled all of his adult life was now a possibility.

A year later that possibility became a reality. Some of Edward's biographers have suggested that English public opinion was hostile to the rapprochement, but certainly the press coverage of the signing in April of 1904 gives no indication that there was any widespread dissatisfaction in Great Britain or, for that matter, in Europe with the Entente Cordiale. The *Neue Frei Presse* of Vienna told its readers that no uneasiness need be felt over the signing: the Germans might be expected to complain that their colonial ambitions would be curbed; but on the whole the peace of the world would be served. The Russo-Japanese war would be contained, for example; and the threat of conflict between England and Russia would be substantially reduced. In summary, the *Presse* commended the 'far-seeing wisdom of King Edward', who had worked to bring the agreement into being.[34]

The English press was almost universally happy over the signing. The *Pall Mall Gazette* thanked Lansdowne, Delcassé, Loubet and King Edward for their work in formulating the treaty. *The Times* said, 'We in this country have always recognized how great a part has been played in the furtherance of Anglo-French cordiality by the King, nor have our neighbours across the Channel been slow to acknowledge the fact. King Edward's visit to Paris last year, followed as it was later in the summer by the arrival of President Loubet as a warmly welcomed guest in England, furnished the most favourable of opportunities for an expression of good will. . . .'[35] *Reynolds's* reported, 'To the King, undoubtedly, must be given the credit of having engineered the movement which has led to the good understanding between England and France.'[36]

Edward was in Copenhagen when the treaty was signed. He and his wife were celebrating King Christian's eighty-sixth birthday, an event which brought Edward much pleasure, not only for his wife's sake, but for his own as well. He had a special affection for Alexandra's father, which had increased with the years. He had the further satisfaction of knowing that even as the foreign ministers of England and France were putting their names to the instrument of accord, the official Russian papers were abandoning their anti-British tone and expressing appreciation for Edward's efforts to limit the area of conflict between Russia and Japan. The Viennese *Politische Corres-pondez*, a semi-official organ of the government, had already written that 'the only goal of King Edward's policy was the maintenance of peace', praising his initiative and his method. The contribution Edward made to the signing of the Entente was one of his greatest achievements. He had the double satisfaction of seeing the work brought to a successful conclusion and having his efforts praised both at home and abroad.

In one sense the French alliance came as a result of another, broader policy which Edward pursued from the outset of his reign – one of personal politics conducted through foreign visits to the heads of European states in a calculated design to consolidate England's political position on the continent and to ensure peace among the nations by maintaining a close personal connection with all the ruling groups. Legge has pointed out that Edward's peripatetic method revived a custom of the sixteenth century, when Charles V, Henry VIII, Philippe II and Henry IV all travelled for these purposes.[37] One French writer observed of Edward's influence and that of sovereigns in general that 'they negotiate from within as well as from without . . . abroad they serve as standard-bearers and ambassadors. They can exercise influence over events in proportions as they possess that art of dealing with men and discussing questions which constitutes diplomacy.'[38]

Successful personal diplomacy of the sort represented by the Entente is rare in any age and, unfortunately, cannot be imitated at will. Edward's achievement was based on years of intense study of the French political scene and the psychology of its leadership. What Edward accomplished was not a public relations stunt but a piece of solid work, and in doing it he demonstrated what might still be achieved by a determined and knowledgeable monarch, despite constitutiona restrictions. That his successors did not follow him in this and other areas is due more to their failure to grasp possibilities or to a lack of interest than to the political weakness of the Crown.

Edward did not rest long on his achievement. Just over two months after the signing of the Entente, he accepted the onerous task of making a state visit to Ireland, which he had postponed in March 1902, in a fit of temper because the Irish Nationalist Members of Parliament had stood and cheered in the House when news of fresh Boer victories were read out.[39] But these disturbances were now part of the past; and, in any case, Edward forgave quickly. The visit was designed to create popular support in Ireland for yet another Conservative proposal before Parliament to help the Irish peasants purchase land. The ten-year period from 1895 to 1905 was one of Conservative political ascendancy, during which a succession of bills – the Irish County Council Act of 1898 being an outstanding example – were passed by Parliament and designed, as Arthur Balfour put it, to 'kill Home Rule with kindness'. The Act returned control of local government to Irish citizens, taking it out of the hands of the grand juries, appointed by sheriffs, who were appointed by Dublin Castle. This reform was followed by massive Conservative efforts to bring about peasant ownership of land. By offering the land at a price below market value and providing very low-rate interest loans, the land acts were a great economic success. Emigration began to decline sharply, and Ireland's population actually showed an increase. There was a general upturn in the prosperity of the nation that had not been equalled for 150 years.[40]

However successful from an economic point of view the land purchase scheme was, it did nothing to mollify the nationalists of Southern Ireland, who wanted political independence, their own parliament and control of their foreign policy. This segment of the Irish populace saw the King's visit, quite understandably, as a political manoeuvre by the Conservative Party to win support for a partisan scheme by introducing the King into the action, in the hope of masking its essentially political nature. The nationalists were also uncomfortable about the special favour Edward had won with the Irish populace by his sympathetic treatment of Catholics. He had, for example, objected to the rigorous anti-Catholic language of the coronation oath. The nationalists' concern with Edward's pro-Catholic stance was a double one. First, following the Church's repudiation of Parnell, the nationalists were deeply divided on the issue of the Catholic Church's proper role in Irish politics; and, second, the nationalists did not wish the Irish public to weaken its commitment to Home Rule by strengthening its allegiance to the British Crown. Following his accession, Edward was occasionally accused of having Roman Catholic leanings. Shortly before his Irish visit, H. Martyn Gooch, Secretary of the Evangelical Alliance, in an address to the annual convention of the Protestant Missionary Society, quoted one of their representatives on Malta as saying that Malta's Catholics believed Edward to be a secret communicant of their faith. Such rumours persisted even beyond his lifetime, and it was hinted that at his death he had secretly received the last rites of the Roman Church.

On July 20, Edward and Alexandra left London by train from Euston Station for Holyhead in Wales. As was the case on his previous visit, men were stationed along the track in sight of one another to signal the approach of the royal train. All level crossings were heavily guarded and special precautions were taken to be sure no other trains were on the track. Along the route people were out waving handkerchiefs and cheering. The stations were also packed with cheering crowds. Unlike the dark emptiness that had greeted him on his previous arrival at Holyhead, on this occasion the town and harbour were brightly decorated, with the Channel Fleet turned out in full dress to receive them. Arriving in brilliant sunshine, they went aboard the *Victoria and Albert* and received a twenty-one-gun salute from the Fleet. That night the ships were illuminated in honour of the occasion, turning the waters of the harbour into dancing fires and encompassing the royal yacht in a blazing ring of light. Fireworks and illuminations delighted Edward and filled Alexandra with childlike joy. Robbed of the pleasures of hearing, she delighted in spectacle.

The following day they arrived in Dublin, receiving a courteous welcome; but the crowds were smaller than those which turned out to greet Queen Victoria. Shortly after his arrival, Edward made a reference to the death of Pope Leo XIII, who had died on the twenty-first, and sent a letter of condolence to Cardinal Logue, thereby winning popular support among the Catholic majority of the country. Nevertheless, the local governing body, the Corporation of Dublin, voted against presenting him with an address of welcome, although other Irish groups came forward with addresses. He made the conventional visits to colleges, libraries and exhibitions and suffered none of the coldness that had greeted him in 1885. Even his visit to Cork was a success. On August 1 he issued a statement of thanks to the Irish people for the kindness of their reception and praised the beauty of the country and the quality of its people.[41]

James Joyce presents Edward as a nightmare figure in *Ulysses*; but earlier, in *Dubliners*, he makes the King's 1903 visit the subject of one of the stories in the collection, 'Ivy Day in the Committee Room', set in a Dublin ward office in 1902. What the story does, among other things, is to show how, even within the Nationalist Party, attitudes towards Edward varied enormously. It is also an illustration of one of the facts of Edward's life – that he was a particular object of fascination to writers, although cartoonists and caricaturists, especially Max Beerbohm, also found him irresistible. George Moore, John Galsworthy, D. H. Lawrence, Ford Madox Ford, Henry James, James Joyce, to list a few of the better known writers of the age, all found occasion to include reference to him in their work. When he appears, it is not merely as a representative of royalty or wealth and privilege, but as a distinctive personality embodying pronounced values, around which conflicting points of view swiftly emerge. He is a presence in his world. The cigar, the hat worn at a slightly rakish angle, the beard, the aura of the racecourse were his unmistakable hallmarks; and they attracted or repelled according to individual tastes. He was not a man about whom one could be indifferent. His colour was too high, his style too pronounced. On the whole those qualities in him were an asset, lending excitement and glamour to national life, bringing vitality and imbuing the routine of politics with drama.

His reign was distinctly different in character from his mother's. He restored the monarchy to the people and, at the same time, began to reassert the Crown's role in the decision-making processes of government. That Edward's efforts to revitalize the monarchy were resented by many leading politicians is made clear by their efforts, even after his death, to rob him of any credit in bringing about the French alliance. But nine years were not enough to fully reverse the erosion of the preceding sixty years. Nevertheless, even a causal look at the record of those nine years is enough to justify the tentative conclusion that a significant role existed in national political life for the monarch who would stir himself. Edward made a respectable beginning before ill health and then death cut off the effort.

Edward was solidly conservative in politics and in his social views, but he also possessed a keen awareness that his authority depended on the tolerance of his subjects. That political understanding taught him the value of compromise and gave him the ability to identify on the horizon those clouds, often no bigger than a hand, that had in them the potential for growing into tornadoes. Such a cloud in the form of the Liberal Party's Temperance Bill put in its appearance in 1908. The Bill polarized the two Houses of Parliament and created a confrontation between the Lords and Commons that presaged the later and vastly more destructive battle over Lloyd George's People's Budget, submitted in 1909. Edward watched the developing battle with alarm.

There is little doubt that temperance legislation was widely popular with a large portion of the British population, and the decisive victory of the Liberal Party in 1906, which returned 513 Liberal members and their supporters, ensured that agitation for government control of drinking would be proposed. Profoundly opposed to the egalitarianism of the Liberals, the Lords set itself the task of defeating or reducing to ineffectiveness most of the major pieces of legislation which the new government brought before it. Looking for some way in which to break the Lords' opposition, Asquith hit upon the idea of introducing a temperance bill, something that would have immensely wide popular appeal and which, as a consequence, the Lords would be forced to pass. The result was the Temperance Bill of 1908.

The bill contained something for every element in the British temperance movement; and despite the intervention of a by-election in Peckham, which was lost to the Liberal candidate on the temperance issue, the bill went through the House with an overwhelming majority of 237.[42] The Lords saw the bill as a menace to private property because of a clause in the proposed legislation providing local boroughs with the authority to close down existing drinking houses and to forbid new ones to be opened. A great many fortunes rested on the free sale and distribution of beer and spirits; thus the opposition to these being curtailed was formidable. Nevertheless, Edward, able to see beyond the immediate issue, warned Lord Lansdowne that if the Lords opposed such popular legislation, the upper House would be placing inherited privilege in jeopardy.

Lansdowne did not listen. He would have been wise to do so if for no other reason than that no man in England was more jealous of retaining the principle of inherited privilege than the King. Instead, the Conservative leader summoned to Lansdowne House in Berkeley

Square 250 Tory noblemen, who were determined to crush the bill when it came before the Lords. Edward, still anxious to prevent such a confrontation, urged compromise but without success. Others warned that the Lords were digging their own graves with such behaviour, but the warnings were wasted effort. Determined to crush any hint of socialism before it could gain a footing, the Conservative majority in the House of Lords swept the legislation away by a vote of 272 to 96.[43]

Edward could scarcely hope to prevent this sort of injudicious use of power from eventually wounding its source, but he could and did worry about it, as his mother had done before him, although for different reasons. Knowledge is sometimes inadequate to stave off disaster, and so it proved in this case. The last years of King Edward's life were to be darkened by that struggle between the two Houses of Parliament which Gladstone had anticipated in his later ministries. It has often been said that if Parliament passed a bill calling for the execution of the sovereign, constitutionally, that sovereign would be obliged to sign his own death warrant. As will be made clear later, something similar to that situation actually emerged in the final year of Edward's life, when he was confronted with the possibility of having to appoint to the House of Lords enough Liberal peers to defeat the Conservative majority in that House and thus ensure the passage of a Parliament Bill. It was a situation guaranteed to fill Edward with horror, for it amounted to the final destruction of the political power of the House of Lords, while ensuring the passage of tax legislation that would strike at the landowner and the holder of unearned wealth, thus helping to create a world which was growing steadily more incomprehensible to him.

Had Edward remained in good health, he might have been able to deal more effectively than he did with the crisis. Unfortunately, his energy reserves were low, his strength unequal to the task of carrying on the intense personal effort needed to bring about a compromise between the upper and lower Houses. And while it is possible that no compromise could have been made to work, Edward did not really attack the problem with his customary force, as will be seen later. Further, had he lived in good health, he might have increased the discretionary powers of the Crown as the power of the Lords declined. But he did not survive, and, while he lived, proved unequal to the task of dealing forcefully with both the parliamentary issue and reform of the armed services. England is, perhaps, fortunate that he chose to deal with the question of the navy; but his strength was certainly in decline. Following his father's death, King George seemed willing to continue the monarchy at the reduced level of force at which Edward, out of physical weakness, had been finally obliged to conduct it.

By 1908 other troubles had come upon him, the worst of which was his failing health. This weakened condition, centred primarily in his lungs and manifested through recurring bouts of bronchitis, increased his irritability and made his regular March excursion to Biarritz a necessity rather than a pleasant stage in the year's calendar of activities. To complicate matters, Sir Henry Campbell-Bannerman, the Prime Minister, was himself seriously ill. Before leaving for Biarritz, Edward had arranged with Herbert Asquith, Chancellor of the Exchequer, that in the event of Campbell-Bannerman's inability to continue his duties, Asquith should come at once to Biarritz to be appointed Prime Minister. Such a development did, in fact, occur. Rendered incapable of directing the government, the Prime Minister insisted on resigning immediately, over the protests of the King, who asked that he retain his post until the royal party could return to England. Edward's doctors had, however, insisted that he himself needed more time in Biarritz. The country, therefore, found itself without a functioning government.

With great haste Asquith travelled to the south of France, there to be asked to form a new government. The crisis was past, but Edward temporarily lost favour with his subjects, many of whom mistakenly thought that he was simply too self-indulgent to interrupt his pleasant holiday and attend to his duties. When it was announced that the King's health demanded he have an extended rest at Biarritz, criticism was not reduced, merely given a new object. Recalling how the nation had been misled in 1902 on the matter of Edward's appendicitis, which had been reported as lumbago, the press pointed out that if the King was indeed ill, a full account of his illness should be made public. It was a very minor skirmish, but one which ought not to have occurred at all. Edward was back in England within a week of Asquith's return; and a week later was off again, this time on a Scandinavian tour.[44] Edward's behaviour in the Biarritz affair was very uncharacteristic. Throughout his adult life, he had been punctilious to a fault in the performance of his duties. In addition, he hated any change in established forms. His decision to appoint a new head of a British Government while on foreign soil was to break completely with tradition. Only failing health and diminishing reserves of energy can account for his conduct, that and a growing detachment, brought about, perhaps, by flagging interest in a world grown strange and vaguely threatening.

There were however still solid spots of pleasure and achievement for him in the final years. Working against the personal animosity of Charles Beresford and the accumulated intransigence of an entrenched bureaucracy, he provided Sir John Fisher, the First Sea Lord, with enough support to see England's first Dreadnought into being and to reform the navy at a critical time in the nation's history. Fisher, in turn, was warm in his praise of the King even following his enforced retirement from the Admiralty, which was brought about by Charles Beresford's constant intriguing, Fisher's contempt for the War Office and Asquith's unwillingness to come to his First Sea Lord's defence. 'He wasn't clever,' Fisher wrote of Edward, 'but he always did the right thing, which is better than brains.'[45]

In that same period Edward had the satisfaction of seeing army reforms, in which he took a personal interest, carried out under Richard Haldane, and the establishment of the Territorial Army by the Territorial and Reserve Forces Act of 1907. Edward was determined to increase the size of England's land forces to the point at which they might be despatched to the continent in time of need. Of course the concept was controversial, it being a widely held belief that England's chief defence lay in her navy and that a large land army, on European models, was unnecessary. Edward would have gone farther than simply establishing a large land force; he would have manned it through conscription. That idea was, however, ahead of its time; and the fierce battle over conscription was not fought until the opening years of World War I. It was, nevertheless, adumbrated in Edward's frequently expressed fears that, at a time of crisis, volunteers would not respond in sufficient numbers to make the army effective.

These struggles to reform the military, to bring it into line with what Germany was doing, wearied Edward. Still, he had the pleasure of knowing that he was popular with his people. Wherever his claret-coloured cars stopped, crowds soon gathered, even when the King and Queen were not in them. When they were parked, people would ask permission of the chauffeur to touch them. They held their children up to look in the windows, and they asked such questions as, 'Where does the King sit?', 'Does he ever drive?' Then, their questions exhausted, they would form queues to walk around and around the cars, just for the pleasure of looking at them because they were Edward's cars.[46]

In addition to the warm affection of his subjects at large, he enjoyed the special care and attention of Mrs George Keppel and Mrs Willy James, heroine of Hilaire Belloc's poem. His relationship with his son George was remarkably close; and the two were seldom long out of one another's company. And there were his horses. Persimmon, which had won the Derby for him in 1897, was still kept at stud; and Edward never tired of looking at the animal. No visitor to Sandringham escaped a walk through the stables, being lectured all the way by a delighted Edward. But if Persimmon were being exercised, Edward would stop and gaze in wrapt wonder, saying over and over again, 'Isn't he beautiful? Isn't he beautiful?'

His love of Persimmon was justified when on May 26 1909, one of

L

his favourite's offspring, a horse named Minoru, just succeeded in winning the Derby by a head against 4–1 odds. The scene on the race-course was one of delirious joy as the gigantic and ecstatic crowds burst into 'God Save the King' and surrounded the beaming Edward as he brought in Minoru to cheers and shouts of 'Good Old Teddy!'[47] The English press indulged itself in a holiday of celebration. On May 27, full page coverage marked the event and headlines that read THE KING'S DERBY – MINORU'S BRILLIANT VICTORY were splashed across front pages. Although the Prince Regent had once won it, Edward was the first king to have had the honour of carrying away the Derby Stakes; and in recognition of his achievement he was solemnly referred to in the press as 'The First Figure on the British Turf'. His annual dinner following the race for the members of the Jockey Club had a special quality that night. He had known how to enjoy his victory as Prince of Wales, and age had not dimmed that talent. Following the dinner, he attended Lady Farquhar's ball and played bridge until dawn, a thoroughly delighted man.

It was as well he had the joy of that victory. A month later Lloyd George threw his 'People's Budget' down like a gauntlet before the House of Lords; and the battle over who would rule England was finally joined in earnest. From the passage of the First Reform Bill of 1832, the armies of change and enfranchisement had been massing against the strongholds of privilege. In 1831 the Duke of Wellington, seeking to check the rising political aspirations of the middle class, had declared the British parliamentary system was, as constituted, the best the world had ever seen and that it answered 'all the good purposes of legislation, and this to a greater degree than any legislature had ever answered, in any country whatever'. The speech destroyed the Duke's support in the Commons and he was soon forced to resign. So it was to be eighty years later. The might of the Commons would prevail over the entrenched resistance of the peers.

Late in April 1909, Lloyd George's budget, containing proposals to tax land not in agricultural production and to tax unearned income, went before the Commons. There immediately followed a bitter and acrimonious debate lasting all summer between the members of the two Houses and their supporters over the virtue of the bill itself and the proper response of the Lords to it. Not for two hundred years had the Lords rejected a budget; but this time they were determined to do it, despite Edward's agitated warnings that their stance would precipi-tate great trouble and Lord Rosebery's warning that they were risking self-destruction. Lloyd George travelled about the country, loosing a storm of abuse on the 'Dukes', whom he singled out for castigation. In a speech in the London slums of Limehouse, he observed that 'a fully-equipped Duke cost as much to keep as two Dreadnoughts' and couldn't be melted down. Edward was distressed by such language from one of his ministers and sent a note to Asquith protesting at the tone, complaining that such a speech was 'an insult to the Sovereign when delivered by one of his confidential servants'.

In early November, the Liberal-Labour-Irish Nationalist pro-Budget majority in the Commons passed the money bill without difficulty. The Lords retaliated by throwing it out, thereby precipitating a political crisis and making a general election necessary. As soon as the Lords, by a four-fifths majority, had rejected the Budget, Asquith called on the King and requested that he dissolve Parliament. Edward was extremely upset by the direction events were taking, because there was the distinct possibility that a major constitutional crisis was in the making, the end of which might be the government's calling on him to create a sufficient number of Liberal peers to assure the passage of the government's money bill. The old talk of 'mending or ending' the House of Lords, begun in 1885, was once more in the air.[48]

Following the general election, in which the Liberals were returned with a severely reduced majority, the House once again passed the Lloyd George Budget, and the Lords passed it the following day, April 28. On the twenty-seventh Edward returned from Biarritz, hopeful that the crisis would be eased. It was not. Things had gone too far. Feelings of profound resentment had been awakened in the Commons against the upper chamber. The Commons was determined to settle, once and for all, the issue of that troublesome second branch, 'one-sided, hereditary, unpurged, unrepresentative, irresponsible, absentee . . .'.[49] Above all, Edward wished to avoid taking sides in the controversy and especially, since he found his government's social policies repugnant, to avoid any appearance of favouring the Liberal cause. Immediately after the election, Edward hoped, without sufficient reason, that Asquith, with his reduced majority, would shelve the case against the Lords; but knowing that he could count on the Irish Nationalist and Socialist votes in the struggle against the upper House, the Liberals pressed for a restriction of the Lords' power to impede legislation.

The King and his Prime Minister were now boxed in. Every effort at compromise had failed, and Asquith felt compelled to ask that Edward be prepared to assert the Royal Prerogative and create enough Liberal Peers to force a Parliament Bill through the Lords. The situation was critical, but Edward was spared the necessity of resolving the impasse, which was settled in 1911, when the Commons once again passed the Parliament Bill and King George agreed to create as many new peers as should be needed to pass the bill in the Lords. The upper House capitulated, passed the bill and placed the legislative power of the nation in the hands of the Commons.

Edward was done with governing; his life was rapidly drawing to a close. During his nine years of rule, he had refused to allow the Crown to diminish in prestige, despite the rapid growth of democracy and the steady shift of political power away from the upper, and, to some extent, middle classes. In fact he strengthened the monarchy and made his will felt with every government which served him. Given the historical allegiance of king and commoner, there is reason to suppose that, had he lived, Edward might have found his natural allies among that great mass of people newly emerging from political obscurity. He was certainly popular, and his conservatism no lasting barrier to such an alliance. Much as he sympathized with the hereditary principle, he was not in the least sympathetic with those Tories who sought to check the growth of political democracy. In his attitude toward the physical and economic welfare of his countrymen, Edward was more inclined to support liberal legislation than to oppose it. It is true that he sought to preserve the empire, but he strongly opposed both religious bigotry and racist policies. His great personal tragedy, and perhaps the nation's as well, was that he came to the throne so late in life. But had his successors chosen to build on the foundations he had laid down, the English monarchy, without breaking its constitutional restraints, might have re-established itself as an active participant in the political life of the nation.

On April 30, in need of rest and quiet, he went to Sandringham. Pottering around in the gardens, which he called Persimmon's Gardens, since the money he had made from that horse had paid for them, he caught a chill and activated his bronchitis once again. On Monday he was back in London at Buckingham Palace, feeling far from well. Alexandra, yachting on the Mediterranean, was warned of her husband's condition. She reached London on May 5, but by that time Edward was too ill to meet her at the station, although he still refused to remain in bed and insisted on spending the day fully dressed and carrying out some of his lighter tasks.

The day following his wife's return, he was worse; but with characteristic spirit Edward refused to give in to his illness and insisted on rising and dressing and receiving visitors. The morning passed with nothing more dangerous than the usual coughing fits, intensified by the smoke from a large cigar, which he lighted after receiving Sir Ernest Cassel shortly before noon. Having eaten a light lunch, he felt well enough to move about the room and was playing with a pair of caged canaries when he suddenly collapsed, his strength no longer sufficient to support him. Almost immediately following his fall, he was seized with the first of a series of heart attacks, which came in rapid succession over the next few hours, making recovery impossible. Dauntless to the end, Edward refused to be put in bed and insisted on sitting up, clothed, in his chair. Warned by the doctors that the King was past hope, Alexandra, demonstrating great generosity of heart, summoned Mrs George Keppel and allowed her to say goodbye to Edward.

She went into his room alone and found him sitting in his chair, fighting for breath but still in command of his mind. What they said to one another is not known and does not matter. They had been lovers for twelve years. His mistress, his confidante, his adviser and his friend, Alice Keppel was more than all these things; she was the embodiment of Edward's insatiable desire for a passionate life. For fifty years that drive had dominated his existence and hammered out his character in its fires. The cigars, the dinners, the dancing, the horses, the clothes, the gambling, the beautiful women had their culmination in his love for Alice Keppel. Her beauty, her grace, her wit summarized the qualities with which Edward had sought to surround himself from those distant days when he learned from the French Court in the company of the Empress Eugénie and her ladies the symphony that passion plays. Its music haunted him for the rest of his life. In Mrs Keppel it had its final movement and its coda. Women loved Edward, no doubt, because he was a prince and then a king; but it is equally certain that they loved him because he loved them.

When Alice Keppel emerged from the sickroom, Prince George rejoined his father and was able to tell him that one of the Sandringham fillies, Witch of the Air, had unexpectedly won at the Kempton Park meeting. Edward replied, 'I am very glad.'[50] Others entered to speak briefly with him, but shortly thereafter, he slipped into a deepening coma. At 11.45 pm he died quietly, having ceased to struggle. Outside his window, beyond the Palace gates, a vast and silent crowd mourned his passing.

Notes

1 A Royal Roaring Boy

[1] *John Bull*, November 13 1841, p. 546.
[2] *Punch*, November 13 1841, p. 205.
[3] *The Times*, November 10 1841, p. 5.
[4] *The Times*, November 10 1841, p. 5.
[5] *The Times*, November 10 1841, p. 4.
[6] *John Bull*, November 13 1841, p. 550.
[7] *Evening Mail*, November 10 1841, p. 8, and *The Times*, p. 4.
[8] *Globe and Traveller*, November 9 1841, p. 2.
[9] *Globe and Traveller*, November 10 1841, p. 2.
[10] *Evening Mail*, November 10 1841, p. 8.
[11] Thomas Dikes, *Illustrations of Some of the Blessings and Benefits of the English Constitution: A Sermon* (Hull: John Davidson, 1841).
[12] n.a., *King Edward the Seventh* (London: Thomas Nelson and Sons, n.d.), p. 5.
[13] *Evening Mail*, November 10 1841, p. 4.
[14] *Punch*, November 11 1841, p. 222.
[15] *Punch*, November 11 1841, p. 222.
[16] *Punch*, November 11 1841, p. 222.
[17] *Punch*, November 18 1841, p. 258.
[18] *The Times*, January 26 1842, p. 3.
[19] Cecil Woodham-Smith, *Queen Victoria from Her Birth to the Death of the Prince Consort* (New York: Alfred A. Knopf, 1972), p. 289.
[20] *The Times*, November 10 1841, p. 4.
[21] *The Times*, January 26 1842, p. 3.
[22] *The Times*, January 26 1842, p. 3.
[23] *Punch*, January 1 1842, p. 36.
[24] *Punch*, January 1 1842, p. 53.
[25] *The Times*, January 26 1842, p. 4.
[26] *The Times*, January 26 1842, p. 4.
[27] *The Times*, January 26 1842, p. 3.
[28] *The Times*, January 26 1842, p. 3.

2 The Long Martyrdom

[1] n.a., *Who Should Educate the Prince of Wales?* (London: Effingham Wilson, 1843), p. 10.
[2] *Who Should Educate the Prince of Wales?*, p. 50.
[3] *Who Should Educate the Prince of Wales?*, p. 19.
[4] *Who Should Educate the Prince of Wales?*, p. 23.

[5] Lytton Strachey, *Queen Victoria* (New York: Harcourt Brace Inc., 1921), p. 77.

[6] Sir Sidney Lee, *D.N.B*, Supplement, January, 1901–December 1911, 1 (London: Oxford University Press, 1927), p. 547.

[7] George Dangerfield, *Victoria's Heir: The Education of A Prince* (London: Constable & Co., 1941), p. 41.

[8] Virginia Cowles, *Edward VII and His Circle* (London: Hamish Hamilton, 1956), p. 29.

[9] Lee, p. 548.

[10] Strachey, p. 125.

[11] Cowles, p. 44.

[12] Philip Magnus, *King Edward the Seventh* (New York: E. P. Dutton, 1964), p. 6.

[13] Dangerfield, p. 68.

[14] Magnus, p. 6.

[15] Magnus, p. 6.

[16] Dangerfield, p. 69.

[17] Frederick Waymouth Gibbs, 'The Education of A Prince', *The Cornhill Magazine*, no. 986 (Spring, 1951), p. 110.

[18] Lee, p. 548.

[19] Queen Victoria, *Queen Victoria's Early Letters*, ed. John Raymond (London: B. T. Batsford, Ltd., 1963), p. 74.

[20] Gibbs, p. 107.

[21] Gibbs, p. 116.

[22] Gibbs, p. 111.

[23] Sir Charles Petrie, *The Victorians* (London: Eyre and Spottiswoode, 1962), p. 59.

[24] Woodham-Smith, p. 403.

[25] Lee, p. 550.

[26] Lee, p. 549.

[27] Magnus, p. 15.

[28] Magnus, p. 101.

[29] Gibbs, p. 117.

[30] Magnus, p. 15.

[31] Lee, p. 549.

[32] Woodham-Smith, p. 361.

[33] Magnus, p. 19.

[34] Edward Legge, *King Edward in His True Colours* (London: Evelyn Nash, 1912), pp. 10–13.

[35] Magnus, p. 21.

[36] Lee, p. 550.

[37] Philippe Jullian, *Edward and the Edwardians*, trans. Peter Downay (New York: Viking Press, 1962), p. 140.

[38] Magnus, p. 22.

[39] Magnus, p. 23.

[40] André Maurois, *King Edward and His Times*, trans. Hamish Miles (London: Cassell and Co., Ltd., 1933), p. 32.

[41] H. Edwards, *The Tragedy of King Edward VII: A Psychological Study*, trans. n.g. (London: Victor Gollancz, 1928), p. 38.

[42] Magnus, p. 24.

[43] Magnus, p. 24.

[44] Cowles, p. 41.

[45] Dangerfield, p. 98.

[46] Magnus, p. 26.

[47] Magnus, p. 25.

[48] Magnus, p. 26.

[49] Edwards, p. 41.

[50] Roger Fulford, ed. *Dearest Child: Letters Between Queen Victoria and the Princess Royal 1858–1861* (London: Evans Brothers, 1964), p. 84.

[51] Fulford, p. 82.

[52] Fulford, p. 94.

[53] Fulford, p. 73.

[54] Fulford, p. 54.

[55] Woodham-Smith, pp. 403–404.

[56] Fulford, p. 144.

[57] Dangerfield, p. 99.

[58] Fulford, p. 142.

[59] Dangerfield, pp. 98–99.

[60] Fulford, p. 144.

[61] Fulford, p. 147.

[62] Fulford, pp. 148–149.

[63] Fulford, p. 152.

[64] Magnus, p. 28.

[65] Lee, p. 552.

[66] Magnus, p. 28.

[67] Dangerfield, p. 101.

[68] Legge, *King Edward in His True Colours*, p. 281.

[69] Jullian, p. 17.

[70] Magnus, p. 30.

[71] *Daily Telegraph*, Tuesday, September 20 1859, p. 4.

[72] n.a., 'A Prince At High Pressure,' *Punch*, no. 219 (September 24 1859), p. 126.

[73] Sir George Arthur, *Concerning Queen Victoria and Her Son* (London: Robert Hale, 1943), p. 95.

[74] Magnus, p. 31.

[75] Cowles, p. 49.

[76] *Daily News*, Thursday, October 27 1859, p. 4.

[77] Dangerfield, p. 107.

[78] Fulford, p. 243.

[79] Fulford, p. 173.

[80] Fulford, p. 198.

[81] Fulford, p. 208.

[82] Fulford, p. 245.

[83] Fulford, p. 173.

[84] *The Times*, Friday, November 11 1859, p. 6.

[85] *The Times*, Friday, November 11 1859, p. 6.

3 A Glimpse of Empire

[1] *Illustrated London News*, 38 (July 14 1860), 25. Hereafter *ILN*.

[2] Quoted in the *New York Times*, July 24 1860, p. [1]. Hereafter *NYT*.

[3] Quoted in *NYT*, August 1 1860, p. [1].

[4] Sir Sidney Lee, *King Edward VII: A Biography* (London: Macmillan and Company, 1925), p. 83.

[5] Lee, p. 83.

[6] H. E. Wortham, *Edward VII Man and King* (Boston: Little Brown & Company, 1931), p. 51.

[7] Lee, p. 84.

[8] *NYT*, July 12 1860, p. [1].

[9] Lee, p. 86.

[10] *NYT*, July 12 1860, p. [1].

[11] Lee, p. 86.

[12] *NYT*, March 28 1860, p. 4.

[13] Thomas Bunbury Gough, *Boyish Reminiscences of His Majesty the King's Visit to Canada in 1860* (London: John Murray, 1910), p. 48.

[14] *New York Daily Tribune*, July 24 1860, p. 6. Hereafter *NYDT*.

[15] Gough, p. 45.

[16] *TILN*, 37 (July 21 1860), 50.

[17] Gough, p. 90.

[18] Wortham, pp. 51–52.

[19] Lee, p. 88.

[20] *NYDT*, July 26 1860, p. 5.

[21] Lee, p. 89.

[22] Lee, p. 90.

[23] n.a., *H.R.H. The Prince of Wales, An Account of His Career, Including His Birth, Education, Travels, Marriage and Home Life; and Philanthropic Social and Political Work* (New York: D. Appleton & Co., 1898), p. 23.

[24] *ILN*, 37 (August 10 1860), p. 125.

[25] *The Prince of Wales*, p. 24.

[26] *The Prince of Wales*, p. 25.

[27] *ILN*, 37 (August 11 1860), 125.

[28] Wortham, p. 53.

[29] *NYDT*, July 24 1860, p. 7.

[30] n.a., *The American Tour of the Prince of Wales* (Boston: A. Williams and Co., 1860), p. 14.

[31] Nicholas Augustus Woods, *The Prince of Wales in Canada and the United States* (London: Bradbury and Evans, 1861), p. 182.

[32] *NYT*, August 31 1860, p. 4.

[33] Lee, p. 92.

[34] Kinahan Cornwallis, *Royalty in the New World Or The Prince of Wales in America* (New York: M. Doolady, 1860), p. 98.

[35] *The Prince of Wales*, p. 26.

[36] *ILN*, 37 (August 25 1860), 168.

[37] *ILN*, 37 (August 25 1860), 168.

[38] *NYT*, August 1 1860, p. 4.

[39] Lee, p. 39.

[40] *ILN*, 37 (September 22 1860), 272.

[41] *The American Tour*, pp. 15–17.

[42] Lee, p. 93.

[43] Woods, p. 183.

[44] Woods, p. 194.

[45] *NYDT*, September 19 1860, p. 6.

[46] *The Prince of Wales*, p. 26.

[47] *The Prince of Wales*, p. 26.

[48] *The Prince of Wales*, p. 27.

[49] *NYDT*, September 24 1860, p. 8.

[50] *NYDT*, July 28 1860, p. 4.

[51] *NYDT*, September 26 1860, p. 6.

[52] *NYDT*, September 24, p. 8.

[53] *NYDT*, October 2 1860, p. 6.

[54] *The Prince of Wales*, p. 27.

[55] *The St Louis Republican*, July 26, 1860, Quoted in *NYDT*, July 30 1860, p. 5.

[56] *NYDT*, October 2 1860, p. 6.

[57] Wortham, p. 56.

[58] Wortham, p. 56.

[59] Wortham, p. 60.

[60] Lee, p. 19.

[61] Lee, pp. 99–100.

[62] Lee, p. 100.

[63] Frederick W. H. Myers, *Collected Poems with Autobiographical and Critical Fragments*, ed. Eveleen Myers (London: Macmillan & Co., 1921), p. 85.

[64] *NYDT*, October 10 1860, p. 5.

[65] *The Prince of Wales*, p. 28.

[66] *The Prince of Wales*, p. 29.

[67] Wortham, p. 59.

[68] *NYDT*, October 15 1860, p. 4.

[69] *The Prince of Wales*, p. 29.

[70] Wortham, p. 62.

[71] *The Prince of Wales*, p. 30.

[72] *NYDT*, October 15 1860, p. 4.

[73] *The Prince of Wales*, p. 30.

[74] *BDET*, October 20 1860, p. 1.

[75] *BDET*, October 22 1860, p. 1.

[76] Gough, p. 67.

[77] *BDET*, October 22 1860, p. 2.

[78] Wortham, p. 64.

[79] Lee, p. 109.

[80] Lee, p. 108.

[81] Lee, p. 108.

[82] Fulford, p. 279.

4 Fallen from Grace

[1] *ILN* (November 24 1860), p. 37.

[2] Fulford, p. 282.

[3] Magnus, p. 43.

[4] Magnus, p. 43.

[5] *Dictionary of National Biography*, Supplement: January 1901–December 1911, ed. Sir Sidney Lee (London: Oxford University Press, 1912), vol. I, p. 5. Hereafter *DNB*.

[6] Edwards, p. 6.

[7] Cowles, p. 49.

[8] *The Times*, July 5 1858, p. 9.

[9] Fulford, p. 292.

[10] Fulford, p. 292.

[11] Fulford, p. 313.

[12] *DNB*, p. 556.

[13] Magnus, p. 43.

[14] Woodham-Smith, p. 411.

[15] Fulford, p. 318.

[16] Fulford, p. 356.

[17] Fulford, p. 320.

[18] Fulford, p. 320.

[19] Magnus, p. 47.

[20] *DNB*, p. 556.

[21] Fulford, p. 312.

[22] Fulford, p. 310.
[23] Fulford, p. 347.
[24] Fulford, p. 252.
[25] Magnus, p. 50.
[26] Fulford, p. 356.
[27] Fulford, p. 357.
[28] *DNB*, p. 557.
[29] Magnus, p. 51.
[30] Magnus, p. 51.
[31] Magnus, p. 51.
[32] Woodham-Smith, p. 418.
[33] Woodham-Smith, p. 423.
[34] Woodham-Smith, p. 427.
[35] E. F. Benson, *King Edward VII An Appreciation* (New York: Longmans, Green & Co., 1933), p. 47.
[36] n.a., *The Golden Book of Edward VII: Wise and Kindly Words of His Majesty* (London, Hodder and Stoughton, n.d.), p. 12.
[37] *Daily Telegraph*, December 19 1861, p. 6.
[38] *DNB*, p. 557.
[39] *Daily Telegraph*, December 16 1861, p. 4.
[40] *Evening Mail*, December 16–Wednesday, December 18, p. 8.
[41] *Daily Express*, December 21 1861, p. 3.
[42] *Evening Mail*, December 16 1862, p. 4.
[43] *Evening Mail*, December 18 1861, p. 8.
[44] Mrs Ellis, *The Women of England, Their Social Duties and Domestic Habits* (London: Fisher, Son & Co., n.d.), pp. 72–73.
[45] Alton Towers, *A Child's Life of the King from His Birth to His Coronation* (London: Wm. Heinemann, 1902), p. 70.
[46] Magnus, p. 52.
[47] Edwards, p. 46.
[48] Magnus, p. 53.
[49] Magnus, p. 54.
[50] *DNB*, p. 558.
[51] *Evening Mail*, February 7 1862, p. 8.
[52] *Reynolds's Newspaper*, March 2 1862, p. 4.
[53] Magnus, p. 53.
[54] Benson, p. 48.
[55] *DNB*, p. 558.
[56] *News of the World*, March 23 1862, p. 3.
[57] Magnus, p. 54.
[58] *Reynolds's Newspaper*, March 23 1862.
[59] *Reynolds's Newspaper*, February 16 1862, p. 1.
[60] *Reynolds's Newspaper*, April 13, p. 2.
[61] *TILN*, May 10 1862, p. 488.
[62] Dangerfield, p. 119.
[63] Dangerfield, p. 119.
[64] *DNB*, p. 558.
[65] Dangerfield, p. 120.
[66] *DNB*, p. 558.
[67] Magnus, p. 55.
[68] Benson, p. 49.
[69] Benson, p. 49.
[70] Magnus, p. 57.

5 The Danish Connection

[1] Hector Bolitho, *Victoria, The Widow and Her Son* (London: Cobden-Sanderson, 1934), p. 14.

[2] Magnus, p. 58.

[3] Benson, p. 55.

[4] Georgina Battiscombe, *Queen Alexandra* (Boston: Houghton Mifflin, 1969), p. 36.

[5] Bolitho, p. 16.

[6] Sir Sidney Lee, *King Edward VII A Biography* (New York: Macmillan & Co., 1925), p. 146.

[7] Lee. p. 147,

[8] Virginia Cowles, *Gay Monarch The Life and Pleasures of Edward VII* (New York: Harper and Bros., 1956), p. 59.

[9] Bolitho, p. 15.

[10] Lee, p. 148.

[11] Cowles, *Gay Monarch*, p. 63.

[12] Hope Dyson and Charles Tennyson, eds., *Dear And Honoured Lady: The Correspondence Between Queen Victoria and Alfred Tennyson* (London: Macmillan, 1969), p. 79.

[13] n.a., *Epithalamium in Honour of the Marriage of Their Royal Highnesses The Prince and Princess of Wales* (London: Charles Westerton, 1863), n.p.

[14] Tom Taylor, *A Marriage Memorial, Verse and Prose* (London: Bradbury and Evans, 1863), n.p.

[15] A. C. Rathbone, *The Dying Poet and Other Poems* (London: Simpkin, Marshall and Co., 1873), pp. 5–8.

[16] W. Edmondstoune Aytoun, *Nuptial Ode On the Marriage of His Royal Highness The Prince of Wales* (London: William Blackwood and Sons, 1863), p. 7.

[17] Rev. John Hunt, *The Marriage in Heaven*: A Sermon (London: George Ryneer, 1863), p. 3.

[18] Battiscombe, p. 45.

[19] Magnus, p. 67.

[20] *Lloyd's Weekly London Newspaper*, March 1 1863, p. 5.

[21] Magnus, p. 66.

[22] *Reynolds's Newspaper*, March 15 1863, p. 1.

[23] Cowles, *Gay Monarch*, p. 67.

[24] Battiscombe, p. 46.

[25] Cowles, *Gay Monarch*, p. 64.

[26] *Evening Mail*, March 6, 1863, p. 1.

[27] Battiscombe, p. 47.

[28] Battiscombe, p. 49.

[29] *Daily Telegraph*, March 11 1863, p. 2.

[30] Sir George Arthur, *Concerning Queen Victoria and Her Son* (London, Robert Hale, 1943), p. 115.

[31] Battiscombe, p. 50.

[32] Magnus, p. 67.

[33] Cowles, p. 67.

[34] Wortham, pp. 77–78.

[35] *Daily Telegraph*, March 10 1963, p. 4.

[36] *Evening Mail*, March 11 1963, p. 8.

[37] *Globe and Traveller*, March 2 1863, p. 4.

[38] *Globe and Traveller*, March 9 1863, p. 2.

[39] *Lloyd's Weekly London Newspaper*, March 8 1863, p. 1.

[40] *Reynolds's Newspaper*, March 15 1863, p. 1.

6 Birth of a Gentleman

[1] Magnus, p. 63.

[2] George Arthur, pp. 123–124.

[3] George Arthur, p. 124.

[4] Battiscombe, p. 58.

[5] F. M. L. Thompson, *English Landed Society in the Nineteenth Century* (London: Routledge and Kegan Paul, 1963), p. 291.

[6] Thompson, p. 21.

[7] Walter Bagehot, *The English Constitution* (Boston: Little, Brown and Company, 1873), pp. 266–269, and Introduction to the 2nd edition (1872), pp. xxvi–xxx.

[8] Moore, p. 325.

[9] D. H. Lawrence, *Lady Chatterley's Lover* (London: Penguin Books, 1969), p. 120.

[10] Battiscombe, p. 59.

[11] *Lloyd's Weekly London Newspaper*, January 17 1864, p. 6.

[12] *Daily News*, January 9, 1864, p. 4.

[13] Battiscombe, p. 62.

[14] Battiscombe, p. 65.

[15] *Evening Mail*, January 11 1864, p. 2.

[16] *John Bull*, January 16 1864, p. 40.

[17] *Lloyd's Weekly London Newspaper*, January 17 1864, p. 6.

[18] Magnus, p. 83.

[19] Fulford, p. 286.

[20] *Lloyd's Weekly London Newspaper*, April 17, 1864, p. 2.

[21] *Standard*, April 20, 1866, p. 4.

[22] Magnus, p. 84.

[23] Arthur, p. 121.

[24] *News of the World*, September 18 1864, p. 3.

[25] Battiscombe, p. 69.

[26] Magnus, pp. 86–87.

[27] Legge, p. 249.

[28] J. P. C. Sewell, ed., *Personal Letters of King Edward VII* (London: Hutchinson & Co., 1931), p. 43.

[29] *Daily Telegraph*, February 18 1867, p. 5.

[30] *The Globe and Traveller*, February 22 1867, p. 3.

[31] *Evening Mail*, March 1 1867, p. 3.

[32] *News of the World*, September 1 1867, p. 3.

[33] *Reynolds's Newspaper*, October 6 1867, p. 4.

[34] Maurois, p. 34.

[35] *Tomahawk*, July 20 1867, p. 130.

[36] *Tomahawk*, July 27 1867, p. 133.

[37] *Tomahawk*, August 17 1867, p. 134.

[38] Bagehot, p. 119.

[39] *John Bull*, March 7 1868, p. 173.

[40] *The Times*, March 5 1868, p. 7.

[41] Augusta Stanley, *Later Letters of Augusta Stanley 1864–1876*, ed. Dean Stanley and Hector Bolitho (London: Jonathan Cape, 1929), p. 111.

[42] *Nation*, April 18 1868, p. 552.

[43] *Evening Mail*, April 20 1868, p. 2.

[44] *Daily Express* (Dublin), quoted in *Evening Mail*, April 22 1868, p. 2.

[45] *Nation*, April 18 1868, p. 552.

[46] Petrie, p. 103.

[47] Jullian, p. 48.

[48] Magnus, p. 99.

[49] *Personal Letters*, p. 42.

[50] *New York Times*, June 11 1868, p. 2.

[51] Magnus, p. 100.

[52] Mrs Gerald Cresswell, 'The Lady Farmer', *Eighteen Years on The Sandringham Estate* (London: The Temple Company, 1887), p. 156.

[53] Mrs William Grey, *Journal of A Visit to Egypt, Constantinople, The Crimea, Greece, etc. in The Suite of The Prince And Princess of Wales* (London: Smith, Elder and Co., 1869), p. 50.

[54] Grey, p. 69.

7 Letters and Lampoons

[1] Wortham, p. 96.

[2] *The Times*, February 17 1870, p. 10.

[3] Magnus, p. 107.

[4] Battiscombe, p. 107.

[5] *John Bull*, February 19 1870, pp. 152–153.

[6] *Reynolds's Newspaper*, February 20 1870, p. 5.

[7] *Reynolds's Newspaper*, February 20 1870, p. 5.

[8] *The Times*, February 17 1870, p. 10.

[9] *Reynolds's Newspaper*, February 20 1870, p. 5.

[10] *Reynolds's Newspaper*, February 20 1870, p. 1.

[11] *Mail*, February 22 1870, p. 7.

[12] *News of the World*, February 27 1870, p. 5.

[13] *Nonconformist*, March 2 1870, p. 202.

[14] *Standard*, February 28 1870, p. 4.

[15] *Pall Mall Gazette*, March 2 1870, p. 6.

[16] *Tomahawk*, March 5 1870, p. 86.

[17] Battiscombe, p. 110.

[18] Wortham, p. 102.

[19] Wortham, p. 103.

[20] Wortham, p. 104.

[21] Wortham, p. 107.

[22] Charles Bradlaugh, *George, The Prince of Wales, With Recent Contrasts and Coincidences* (London: n.p., 1870), p. 2.

[23] Captain Pipeclay (pseud.), *The Battle of Foxhill, The Prince of Wales in a Mess, Or, The Mill, The Muff and the Muddle* (London: Frederick Farrah, 1871), p. 7.

[24] Magnus, p. 113.

[25] *Reynolds's Newspaper*, September 24 1871, p. 5.

[26] *Reynold's Newspaper*, September 24 1871, p. 5.

[27] Wortham, p. 93.

[28] n.a., *Newspaper Warfare the Great Pen and Ink Battle Between the Figaro and Reynolds's Newspaper* (London: H. Kerbey, 1872), n.p.

[29] Battiscombe, p. 113.

[30] *Daily News*, December 1, 1871, p. 3.

[31] *Pall Mall Gazette*, December 1 1871, p. 7.

[32] *Daily News*, December 5 1871, p. 3.

[33] *Pall Mall Gazette*, December 2 1871, p. 2.

[34] *John Bull*, November 25 1871, p. 817.

[35] *Lloyd's Weekly London Newspaper*, October 17 1871, p. 3.

[36] Magnus, p. 117.

[37] Arthur Penrhyn Stanley, *The National Thanksgiving Sermons Preached in West-minster Abbey* (London: Macmillan and Company, 1872), p. 52.

[38] Rev. W. Mitchell, M.A., Vicar of Chantry, *Our Prince's Sickness and Recovery: A Sermon* (London: John Hodges, 1872), pp. 7–8.

[39] Rev. E. S. Ffoulkes, B.D., *England's Crisis and England's Calling* (London: J. T. Hayes, 1872), p. 27.

[40] Magnus, p. 119.

[41] Wortham, p. 115.

[42] Samuel O. Beeton, Aglen A. Dowty, Evelyn D. Jerrold, *The Coming K——: A Set of Idyll Lays* (London: n.p., 1873), p. 3.

[43] Beeton, p. 142.

[44] Beeton, p. 16.

[45] n.a., *The Siliad or, The Siege of the Seats* (London: Ward, Lock, and Tyler, 1874), p. xv.

[46] *Siliad*, p. 233.

[47] *Siliad*, p. 233.

[48] n.a., *The Fijiad or English Nights' Entertainments* (London: Ward, Lock, and Tyler, 1874), p. 10.

[49] *The Times*, October 1 1874, p. 7.

[50] *New York Times*, October 16 1874, p. 1.

[51] *The Times*, October 1 1874, p. 7.

[52] Magnus, p. 128.

[53] Benson, p. 104.

[54] Jullian, pp. 99–100.

[55] Wortham, p. 116.

8 Elephants, Tigers and Republicans

[1] Cowles, *Edward VII and His Circle*, p. 130.

[2] Cowles, *Gay Monarch*, pp. 130–131.

[3] *Mail*, June 4 1873, p. 1.

[4] *Reynolds's Newspaper*, June 22 1873, p. 1.

[5] Magnus, p. 127.

[6] *Reynolds's Newspaper*, June 29 1873, p. 3.

[7] Magnus, p. 132.

[8] Magnus, p. 133.

[9] Battiscombe, pp. 129–130.

[10] *The Times*, July 16 1875, p. 5.

[11] *Reynolds's Newspaper*, August 8 1875, p. 5.

[12] *The Mail*, July 9 1875, p. 8.

[13] *Reynolds's Newspaper*, July 25 1875, p. 2.

[14] *Standard*, July 31 1875, p. 6.

[15] *Reynolds's Newspaper*, August 8 1875, p. 5.

[16] *Standard*, August 3 1875, p. 6.

[17] *Standard*, July 3 1875, p. 6.

[18] *Reynolds's Newspaper*, August 8 1875, p. 4.

[19] *Standard*, July 3 1875, p. 6.

[20] n.a., *Bourne and Shepherd's Royal Photographic Album of Scenes and Personages Connected with the Progress of H.R.H. The Prince of Wales Through Bengal, the Northwest Provinces, the Punjab and Nepal With Some Descriptive Letterpress* (Calcutta: Bourne and Shepherd, 1876), p. 1.

[21] Magnus, p. 135.

[22] J. Drew Gay, *The Prince of Wales in India or, From Pall Mall to the Punjab* (Toronto: Belford Bros., 1877), p. 53.

[23] Gay, p. 56.

[24] Gay, p. 552.

[25] 'Elephanta', *Collier's Encyclopedia*, vol. 7 (New York: Crowell-Collier, 1958), p. 225.

[26] Gay, pp. 173–175.

[27] Magnus, p. 137.

[28] Magnus, p. 141.

[29] Samuel O. Beeton, Aglen A. Dowty, Evelyn D. Jerrold, *Edward The Seventh: A Play On Past and Present Times With a View To The Future* (London: n.p., printed at 40 Bedford Street, Covent Garden, 1876), p. 10.

[30] *Edward the Seventh*, p. 23.

[31] *Edward the Seventh*, p. 83.

[32] n.a., *The Key to Edward the Seventh Being an Elucidation of the Dark Allusions in That Libelous Lampoon . . . By One Behind the Scenes* (London: Will Williams, 1876), pp. 8–9.

[33] Gertrude M. Tuckwell, ed., *A Short Life of Sir Charles W. Dilke* (London: Students' Bookshop, 1925), pp. 103–104.

[34] Tuckwell, pp. 129–130.

[35] Wortham, pp. 120–122.

[36] Magnus, p. 155.

[37] Wortham, p. 123.

9 Marking Time

[1] Henry C. Burdett, *Prince, Princess, and People An Account of the Social Progress and Development of Our Own Times, As Illustrated by the Public Life and Work of Their Royal Highnesses the Prince and Princess of Wales 1863–1869* (London: Longmans, Green and Co., 1889), p. 380.

[2] James Macauley, ed., *Speeches and Addresses of H.R.H. The Prince of Wales 1863-1888* (London: John Murray, 1889), p. 287.

[3] Burdett, p. 13.

[4] Magnus, p. 168.

[5] J. P. C. Sewell, ed., *Personal Letters of Edward VII* (London: Hutchinson & Co., 1931), pp. 38–39.

[6] Sewell, p. 31.

[7] Magnus, p. 172.

[8] Benson, p. 119.

[9] André Maurois, *King Edward and His Times*, trans. Hamish Miles (London: Cassell and Co., Ltd., 1933), p. 49.

[10] Legge, *King Edward In His True Colours*, p. 162.

[11] Battiscombe, p. 137.

[12] A Foreign Resident, *Society in London* (London: Chatto and Windus, 1885), p. 40.

[13] Battiscombe, p. 138.

[14] Dangerfield, p. 228.

[15] *News of the World*, March 2 1884, p. 2.

[16] *Pall Mall Gazette*, February 23 1884, p. 1.

[17] *Reynolds's Newspaper*, March 9 1884, p. 3.

[18] *Reynolds's Newspaper*, March 9 1884, p. 3.

[19] *Standard*, February 19 1884, p. 4.

[20] George Bernard Shaw, *Plays Unpleasant* (London: Penguin Books, 1970), p. 26.

[21] Magnus, p. 180.

[22] Magnus, p. 182.
[23] *Standard*, July 22 1884, p. 5.
[24] Magnus, p. 182.
[25] *Reynolds's Newspaper*, July 27 1884, p. 1.
[26] *Standard*, July 22 1884, p. 5.
[27] Magnus, p. 183.
[28] W. Somerset Maugham, *The Summing Up* (London: Penguin Books, 1970), p. 7.
[29] Charles Bradlaugh, *The Impeachment of the House of Brunswick* (London: Freethought Publishing Company, 1881), p. 97.
[30] Cresswell, p. 58.
[31] Cresswell, p. 95.
[32] Cresswell, p. 175.
[33] Sewell, p. 36.
[34] Cresswell, p. 168.
[35] Cresswell, p. 177.
[36] Cresswell, p. 168.
[37] Magnus, p. 188.
[38] *Reynolds's Newspaper*, April 12 1885, p. 3.
[39] *Lloyd's Weekly London Newspaper*, April 12 1885, p. 3.
[40] *Reynolds's Newspaper*, April 12 1885, p. 3.
[41] *Standard*, April 7 1885, pp 4–5.
[42] *Lloyd's Weekly London Newspaper*, April 12 1885, p. 7.
[43] Magnus, p. 189.
[44] Hall and Albion, p. 760.
[45] Magnus, p. 202.
[46] Maurois, p. 67.
[47] Ralph G. Martin, *Jennie The Life of Lady Randolph Churchill: The Romantic Years 1854–1895* (New York: New American Library, 1970), p. 239.
[48] Leslie, p. 229.
[49] A Foreign Resident, p. 31.
[50] W. H. Auden, *A Certain World: A Commonplace Book* (New York: Viking, 1970), p. 329.
[51] Martin, p. 242.
[52] Lee, p. 598.
[53] Benson, p. 149.
[54] Benson, p. 153.

10 'Ich Deal'

[1] Magnus, p. 223.
[2] Magnus, p. 223.
[3] *Manchester Guardian*, June 4 1891, p. 6.
[4] *Manchester Guardian*, June 4 1891, p. 6.
[5] *Manchester Guardian*, June 2 1891, p. 12.
[6] *The Times*, June 5 1891, p. 12.
[7] Magnus, p. 227.
[8] *Manchester Guardian*, June 2 1891, p. 12.
[9] *Boston Daily Globe*, June 2 1891, p. 5.
[10] *The Times*, June 6 1891, p. 17.
[11] *Manchester Guardian*, June 2 1891, p. 12.
[12] *Manchester Guardian*, June 5 1891, p. 8.
[13] Magnus, p. 224.

[14] Edward Legge, *King Edward in His True Colours* (London: Evelyn Nash, 1912), p. 138.

[15] George Martin, *Our Afflicted Prince* (London: Eliot Stack, n.d.) p. 15.

[16] Martin, p. 23.

[17] Quoted by Legge in *King Edward in His True Colours*, pp. 140–141.

[18] Quoted by Legge in *King Edward in His True Colours*, p. 140.

[19] *Boston Daily Globe*, June 1 1891, p. 1.

[20] Magnus, p. 225.

[21] Magnus, p. 226.

[22] Magnus, p. 226.

[23] *Boston Daily Globe*, June 1 1891, p. 5.

[24] *The Times*, March 25 1891, p. 3.

[25] Quoted in *The Times*, March 25 1891, p. 3.

[26] *New York Times*, March 26 1891, p. 4.

[27] Magnus, p. 227.

[28] *New York Times*, February 8 1891, p. 4.

[29] *New York Times*, February 8, 1891, p. 4.

[30] Legge, *King Edward in His True Colours*, p. 142.

[31] W. Evans, 'Gambling', *The General Baptist Magazine* (July 1891), p. 250.

[32] Kellow Chesney, *The Victorian Underworld* (London: Temple Smith, 1970), p. 282.

[33] Sir Francis Meynell, *My Lives* (London: Bodley Head, 1971), p. 5.

[34] n.a., 'Baccarat', *National Observer*, 4 (March 7 1891), p. 404.

[35] n.a., 'Exit Baccarat', *National Observer*, 8 (June 20 1891), n.p.

[36] 'Exit Baccarat', n.p.

[37] Magnus, 226–227.

[38] *Manchester Guardian*, June 1 1891, p. 4.

[39] *Boston Daily Globe*, June 1 1891, p. 1.

[40] *Manchester Guardian*, June 2 1891, p. 12.

[41] *Boston Herald*, June 3 1891, p. 3.

[42] *Manchester Guardian*, June 3 1891, p. 5.

[43] *Manchester Guardian*, June 5 1891, p. 8.

[44] *Manchester Guardian*, June 9 1891, p. 12.

[45] *Manchester Guardian*, June 9 1891, p. 12.

[46] *Manchester Guardian*, June 10 1891, p. 12.

[47] *Manchester Guardian*, June 10 1891, p. 12.

[48] Magnus, p. 228.

[49] *Boston Daily Globe*, June 11 1891, p. 5.

[50] *The Times*, June 11, 1891, p. 5.

[51] Quoted by W. T. Stead in 'The Prince of Wales', *Review of Reviews*, 4 (July, 1891), p. 26.

[52] Stead, 'The Prince of Wales', p. 27.

[53] Magnus, p. 229.

[54] Magnus, pp. 230–231.

[55] Philippe Jullian, *Edward and the Edwardians*, trans. Peter Downay (New York: Viking Press, 1962), p. 140.

[56] Stead, 'The Prince of Wales', p. 23.

[57] Stead, 'The Prince of Wales', p. 23.

[58] Quoted by Stead in 'The Prince of Wales', p. 31.

[59] Quoted by Stead in 'The Prince of Wales', p. 32.

[60] Quoted by Stead in 'The Prince of Wales', p. 28.

11 A Brush with Death

[1] Leslie, p. 132.
[2] Leslie, p. 132.
[3] Leslie, p. 134.
[4] Benson, p. 161.
[5] Cowles, *Gay Monarch*, p. 212
[6] Jullian, p. 144.
[7] *Punch*, December 19 1891, p. 294.
[8] Wortham, p. 197.
[9] Rupert Croft-Cooke, *Bosie: Lord Alfred Douglas, His Friends And Enemies* (New York: Bobbs-Merrill, 1963), p. 109.
[10] Croft-Cooke, p. 61.
[11] Croft-Cooke, p. 61.
[12] Croft-Cooke, p. 203.
[13] Jullian, p. 141.
[14] Wortham, p. 204.
[15] Sir Charles Petrie, *The Victorians* (London: Eyre & Spottiswoode, 1962), p. 24.
[16] Magnus, p. 248.
[17] Benson, p. 170.
[18] *Standard*, August 5 1895, p. 5.
[19] *Standard*, August 7 1895, p. 3.
[20] Wortham, p. 205.
[21] *News of the World*, August 11, 1895, p. 6.
[22] *Standard*, August 10 1895, p. 5.
[23] Benson, p. 167.
[24] Magnus, p. 255.
[25] Wortham, p. 210.
[26] Magnus, p. 253.
[27] *Reynolds's Newspaper*, June 7 1896, pp. 1–3.
[28] *Mail*, June 5 1896, p. 4.
[29] Wortham, p. 200.
[30] Benson, p. 186.
[31] *Standard*, April 5 1900, p. 3.
[32] *Pall Mall Gazette*, April 5 1900, p. 7.
[33] Battiscombe, p. 213.
[34] *Lloyd's Weekly London Newspaper*, April 8 1900, p. 1.
[35] *Standard*, April 5 1900, p. 3.
[36] *Standard*, April 10 1900, p. 3.
[37] Magnus, p. 265.
[38] Magnus, p. 260.
[39] Leslie, p. 207.
[40] Christopher Isherwood, *Kathleen and Frank* (New York: Simon and Schuster, 1971), p. 153.
[41] *The Times*, January 21 1901, p. 10.
[42] *The Times*, January 23 1901, p. 10.
[43] *Pall Mall Gazette*, January 24 1901, p. 1.
[44] *The Times*, January 24 1901, p. 7.
[45] *Reynolds's Newspaper*, January 27 1901, p. 4.
[46] Benson, p. 215.
[47] Benson, p. 214.
[48] Magnus, p. 271.

12 A Working King

[1] Wortham, p. 215.
[2] Isherwood, p. 157.
[3] Wortham, p. 217.
[4] Wortham, p. 218.
[5] Benson, p. 216.
[6] Magnus, p. 287.
[7] Benson, p. 223.
[8] Benson, p. 216.
[9] Benson, p. 217.
[10] Benson, pp. 216–217.
[11] Benson, p. 219.
[12] n.a., *The King's Dinner to the Poor: In Celebration of Their Majesties' Coronation, A.D. 1902* (London: Blades, East & Blades, 1902), n.p.
[13] Jullian, p. 187.
[14] Jullian, p. 187.
[15] Magnus, p. 297.
[16] *Reynolds's Newspaper*, June 22 1902, p. 5.
[17] Magnus, p. 297.
[18] *Reynolds's Newspaper*, June 22 1902, p. 1.
[19] *The Times*, June 23 1902, p. 10.
[20] Isherwood, p. 212.
[21] Jullian, p. 188.
[22] *The Times*, June 25 1902, p. 9.
[23] *Reynold's Newspaper*, June 29, 1902, p. 1.
[24] A. B. Grimaldi, *The King's Royal Descent from King David the Psalmist* (London: Robert Banks [1902]).
[25] Tagore, p. 25.
[26] L. MacLean Watt, 'Ode on the Coronation of King Edward VII', the *Critic* (July 1902), pp. 19–26.
[27] Magnus, p. 300.
[28] Magnus, p. 311.
[29] Magnus, p. 312.
[30] Legge, *King Edward in His True Colours*, pp. 167–168.
[31] Legge, p. 168.
[32] Magnus, p. 313.
[33] Magnus, p. 313.
[34] *Standard*, March 30 1904, p. 4.
[35] *The Times*, April 9 1904, p. 9.
[36] *Reynolds's Newspaper*, April 17 1904, p. 1.
[37] Legge, p. 30.
[38] Legge, p. 29.
[39] Magnus, p. 306.
[40] Hall and Albion, p. 764.
[41] Magnus, p. 318.
[42] Norman Longmate, 'Waging War Against Demon Drink', *Observer*, June 24 1973, p. 16.
[43] Longmate, p. 16.
[44] Benson, p. 270.
[45] Magnus, p. 376.
[46] C. W. Stamper, *What I Know: Reminiscences of Five Years Personal Attendance*

Upon His Late Majesty King Edward the Seventh (London: Mills and Boon, Ltd., 1913), p. 166.

[47] Magnus, p. 429.
[48] Hall and Albion, p. 813.
[49] Hall and Albion, p. 816.
[50] Magnus, p. 456.

Index